"It isn't often that I see a resource as thorough, spot-on, and hopeful as Integrative Mc
a doubt, this is what my family and I needed when I was struggling at a young age. I
continue to do so for years to come!"

    —**Jenni Schaefer**, author of *Life Without Ed*; *Goodbye Ed, Hello Me*; and *Almost Anorexic*

"Eating disorder recovery is a long and challenging process, and we've had far too few treatment tools that are accessible to patients and families. The IMT program changes this, integrating our leading evidence-based therapies into
easy-to-understand language and resources for patients, families, and providers in the trenches. IMT should be a go-to
resource for those looking to recover, or to help others recover, from an eating disorder."

    —**Kristina Saffran**, CEO of ProjectHEAL

"I am impressed at the lengths the authors went to in soliciting input from parents who successfully helped their child
with an eating disorder to recover. They have synthesized components from several evidence-based treatment models
into a manualized approach, presenting information in an accessible manner that prioritizes practical solutions to
improve the clinical-caregiver feedback and direction loop and provide the best chance for full recovery to patients/
clients. IMT is a promising and accessible format enabling a wide variety of clinicians to deliver state-of-the-art understanding and resources to families impacted by the devastation of an eating disorder diagnosis."

    —**J.D. Ouellette**, parent expert and activist/advocate in the field of eating disorders, and
        board member of Families Empowered and Supporting Treatment of Eating Disorders (F.E.A.S.T.)

"A truly comprehensive guide in the treatment of eating disorders during adolescence—their most common period of
onset. Deliberto and Hirsch seamlessly integrate the core components from several treatment modalities into one
extensive manual, with their own pearls of clinical wisdom interspersed throughout. This is a must-read for anyone
involved in the treatment of eating disorders."

    —**Stuart B. Murray, PhD**, assistant professor at the University of California, San Francisco;
        NIMH-funded researcher; and coeditor of *Clinical Handbook of Complex and Atypical Eating Disorders*
        and *Innovations in Family Therapy for Eating Disorders*

"This book is a godsend for clinicians working in the trenches with people who have eating disorders. This work offers
a clear, comprehensive, step-by-step guide to help clients and caregivers effectively fight back against eating disorders.
The main modality used by the authors is IMT, which offers a welcomed integration of evidence-based individual,
group, and family therapies into the treatment of eating disorders."

    —**L. James Climenhage, PhD**, adjunct professor at the University of Northern British Columbia, and
        mental health clinician at Child and Youth Mental Health

"This book is an invaluable resource for clinicians treating adolescent eating disorders. Not only have two expert clinicians described their experience with interventions, they have pulled together materials and resources that will help engage patients in the therapy process. Adolescent eating disorders can be difficult to treat—this book is like having an expert clinical supervisor always available to answer the inevitable, 'what do I do next?'"

— **Janet A. Lydecker, PhD**, assistant professor in the department of psychiatry at
Yale University School of Medicine

"A superb treatment manual. Tara Deliberto and Dina Hirsch are remarkable for their concise analysis of treatment for eating disorders in adolescents. IMT is an exciting and compelling tool for the patient, carer, and clinician. I congratulate the authors on their groundbreaking understanding of these very complex and deadly mental illnesses."

— **Donna M. Friedman, MS, LPC**, founder of the MUSC Friedman Center for Eating Disorders
at the Medical University of South Carolina

"At last! A practical, systematic, and evidence-based approach that breaks down the complexities of treating a complex mental illness, and turns confusion into confidence for clinicians, parents, and patients. By systematically engaging carers, this method also educates and incites the adolescent to fight against their own eating disorder."

— **Grace Ray Schumacher, RD, CEDRD**, behavioral health dietitian in Alaska, working primarily
in eating disorders treatment through a private practice: Nutrition Partnership, LLC

Treating Eating Disorders in Adolescents

Evidence-Based Interventions for Anorexia, Bulimia, and Binge Eating

. . . . .

TARA L. DELIBERTO, PhD
DINA HIRSCH, PhD

CONTEXT PRESS
An Imprint of New Harbinger Publications, Inc.

Publisher's Note

This publication is designed to provide accurate and authoritative information in regard to the subject matter covered. It is sold with the understanding that the publisher is not engaged in rendering psychological, financial, legal, or other professional services. If expert assistance or counseling is needed, the services of a competent professional should be sought.

Distributed in Canada by Raincoast Books

Copyright © 2019 by Tara Deliberto and Dina Hirsch
      Context Press
      An imprint of New Harbinger Publications, Inc.
      5674 Shattuck Avenue
      Oakland, CA 94609
      www.newharbinger.com

Cover design by Amy Shoup

Interior illustrations by various artists. Licenses for all illustrations acquired by Integrated Treatment LLC.

Acquired by Elizabeth Hollis Hansen

Indexed by James Minkin

Library of Congress Cataloging-in-Publication Data on file

Printed in the United States of America

21   20   19

10   9   8   7   6   5   4   3   2   1   First Printing

Contents

Appendixes

Note: Essential Online Components of This Program

The Integrated Modalities Therapy program outlined in this volume, *Treating Eating Disorders in Adolescents: Evidence-Based Interventions for Anorexia, Bulimia, and Binge Eating*, uses a wealth of client handouts for individual, group, and family interventions. These integral client resources, plus essential clinician resources, are available for free for clinician users of this manual:

1. Client Resources Part 1 Section 1: Individual Therapy Modality, Regular Eating (RE) and Regular and Appetitive Eating (RAE) Handouts (19 handouts)

2. Client Resources Part 1 Section 2: Individual Therapy Modality, Body Acceptance and Exposure (BAE) Handouts (25 handouts)

3. Client Resources Part 2 Section 1: Group Therapy Modality, Mindfulness and Acceptance (MAC) Handouts (19 handouts)

4. Client Resources Part 2 Section 2: Group Therapy Modality, Cognitive Behavioral Therapy (CBT) Handouts (13 handouts)

5. Client Resources Part 3 Section 1: Family Therapy Modality, Stage 1 Family (FAM), Family/Patient (FAM/PT), and Patient (PT) Handouts (39 handouts)

6. Client Resources Part 3 Section 2: Family Therapy Modality, Stage 2 Family (FAM), Family/Patient (FAM/PT), and Patient (PT) Handouts (30 handouts)

7. Clinician Resources

   • Case Conceptualization form

   • IMT Measures forms

   • Clinician's Checklists for TABLE Skills and ED Wins Habits

   • Clinician-Provided IMT Family Handouts (this is the same content as Appendix B of this volume, in printable PDF format)

Download these printable PDFs at www.newharbinger.com/42235. For download instructions, see page 304 of this book.

Acknowledgments

Thank you to our fantastic "volunteer squad" of readers: Kristina Saffran; Jenni Schaefer; Leslie Anderson, PhD; JD Ouellette; Stephanie Jacobs, PhD; Rebecca Skolnick, PhD; Joya Ahmed; Regina Monaco, PhD; Diana Jesse, PhD; Elaina Zendegui, PhD; Samantha Kimmel; Romi Ran, DClin Psy; Donna Peri, PsyD; Dr. Kassandra Gratwick-Sarll; Suzanne Straebler, NP, PhD; Rachel Luckman, MA; Jonathan Reinharth, PhD; Lauren Todd; Kathryn Huryk; Azeemah Kola; Bridget Whitlow, LMFT; Dean Haycock, PhD; Leslie Anderson, PhD; Erika Rooney, PsyD; Alison Tebbett, PhD; Althea Bardin, PhD; Chad Davis; and Rischa Gottlieb, PhD. Your feedback, input, and guidance have been invaluable. A very sincere thank you to all who wrote endorsements for this book. Your vote of confidence means the world. A special thank you goes to Millie Plotkin, the informationist of the eating disorder community, for helping to point us in the right direction; your resourcefulness is unmatched. Additionally, thank you to Camilla Mager, PsyD, and Melainie Rogers, MS, RD, who supported earlier versions of this work. Thank you so much to all our clients and their carers who provided such valuable feedback to us about the Integrated Modalities Therapy (IMT) material over the years.

—Tara Deliberto and Dina Hirsch

I am so grateful for the opportunity to thank the many people who contributed to this work both directly and indirectly. From the bottom of my heart, thank you to New Harbinger for taking a chance on IMT. Without your concerted effort, this work would never have been disseminated and would be unable to help those who need it most. I will always be grateful for this. A special thanks to Elizabeth Hollis Hansen, Clancy Drake, and Xavier Callahan.

Of course, thank you to Dina Hirsch, the co-creator of IMT. I have never been more encouraged by anyone to follow through with the materialization of ideas. Dina, without your encouragement and guidance, this project might have remained just a few scribbled-down notes. And thank you to my literary agent, Carrie Pestritto, who believed in me and this work.

A heartfelt thank you goes to the incomparable Evelyn Attia, MD, for inviting me to join the esteemed faculty at Cornell University's medical college, Weill Cornell Medicine, and to create an eating disorders partial hospitalization program at NewYork–Presbyterian Hospital. These experiences have been immeasurably valuable to me. I would also like to thank my brilliant colleagues Matthew Shear, MD, MPH; Sean Kerrigan, MD; Suzanne Straebler, NP, PhD; Melissa Klein, PhD; and C. Joy Somberg, MD, for their openness to IMT when it was in its early stages. This made the evolution of this project possible. And I would like to thank Dominique White, LMSW; Melissa Wright, LMSW; Brittney Lauro, LMSW, LSW; Katharine Blodget, LCSW; Theresa Artuso D'Onofrio, LCSW; and Betty Morin, LCSW, for their support of this project. A heartfelt thank you goes to all the patients I have had the pleasure of working with over the years. This would not be possible without you.

A very warm thank you goes to two people I have been lucky enough to call mentors over the years: Matthew Nock, PhD, and Dennis Tirch, PhD. Reflecting on that last sentence: it has been an absolute privilege. Thank you to Laura Silberstein, PhD, who advised on the self-compassion aspects of this work. These interventions are among my pet favorites. Thank you also to the wonderful team at Mt. Sinai's Eating and Weight Disorders Program for providing the best education about the treatment of eating disorders that anyone could hope for. Thank you as well to Peter D'Amico, PhD, my internship mentor at North Shore–LIJ, for his conviction regarding the utility of this treatment. I am very grateful to William Sanderson, PhD, for his guidance throughout the process of my dissertation, as well as to Sarah Novak, PhD, and Merry McVey-Noble, PhD. Your encouragement fostered the development of key aspects of this work. I would like to acknowledge the late Richard O'Brien, PhD, who taught me both the fundamentals of behaviorism and how to not take myself so seriously. His humor and guidance will never be forgotten.

From the bottom of my heart, thank you to my dear friend and fellow eating disorder advocate Romi Ran, DClin Psy. Your feedback on this work has been invaluable. I would also like to thank my friends, who have heard about, discussed, and read about the ideas in this work ad nauseam for the last seven years. In particular, enormous thanks goes to Anya, Regina, Andrea, Kristin, Priya, Sofia, Vanessa, Merri, Dana, Elyse, Stephanie, and Michelle. Behind every success for a woman is a team of friends cheering her on. It's been such a pleasure rooting for you. Thank you for rooting for me. A huge thank you also goes to Junior and Andy for their unparalleled hospitality during the writing of this work.

Thank you to my grandparents and parents. Your love and support mean the world to me. And, lastly, thank you to my loving husband, Cameron, to whom this work is dedicated. Your support during the writing, editing, and launching of this work for the many years prior to its publication made this work possible. For this, I will always be grateful.

—Tara Deliberto

First and foremost, I want to thank my coauthor, Tara Deliberto. It was immediately apparent at the start of Tara's tenure as a trainee that she would have a tremendous impact on the eating disorders field. Her boundless energy, passion, and creativity have been the foundation of this project, which started as something very small and has evolved into filling a void in our field. The collaborative spirit in which we worked has been both fulfilling and productive, resulting in something that we can take pride in—helping both colleagues and patients in treatment. It has been a great pleasure to work with Tara on this book, and I look forward to continuing our professional and personal relationship for years to come.

I'd like to express appreciation to Katie Taylor, PhD, whose abilities as a clinician are second to none. Katie was involved in an earlier version of this book and helped inspire what it has become.

My colleagues in the child psychology department at Zucker Hillside Hospital—Peter D'Amico, PhD; Stephanie Solow, PsyD; Meredith Owens, PhD; Barbara Libov, PhD; Madeline McGee, PhD; and Alison Tebbett, PhD (who deserves to be mentioned twice)—are the most amazing group of psychologists I know. Because of their incredible support and encouragement, my being a member of that department was instrumental in the creation of this book

I would also like to mention and thank several colleagues and previous supervisors. Jon Samuels, PsyD, has single-handedly had the strongest impact on my development as a family therapist. It's his influence that helped shape some of the concepts in the family therapy section of this work. Terri Bacow, PhD, and Kimberlie Glaser, PhD, eating disorder therapists extraordinaire, are colleagues and friends I have had the fortune to consult with over the years, sharing ideas that have helped make me the clinician I am today.

Of course, I'd like to extend my warmest thanks to my amazing colleagues at the Connecticut Children's Medical Center (CCMC) Eating Disorders Center, including Lindsay Moskowitz, MD, for her willingness to pilot IMT materials in the program, her influence on my thinking about treating people with eating disorders, and her tireless dedication to patients and families. I would also like to express gratitude to Gail Sumler, CSW, for her enthusiasm about IMT, for her support, and for cheering me on; and to Nicole Criscuola, Lynette Ramdeen, and Kathy McCoy for their friendship and support. Marty Fisher, MD; Linda Carmine, MD; Eric Weiselberg, MD; Ron Feinstein, MD; Nadia Saldhana, MD; Khalida Itreyeva, MD; Marigold Castillo, MD, and the other physicians and clinicians at CCMC Adolescent Medicine have been instrumental in educating me about the medical consequences of eating disorders. Their commitment to providing top-quality care to literally thousands of teens struggling with eating disorders is truly inspiring. And thanks to all my trainees who helped with this book: Erika Rooney, Alison Tebbett, Althea Bardin, Rischa Gottlieb, and Donna Peri, whose infectious passion for our discipline keeps me excited about helping others every day.

I would be remiss if I did not thank the many patients I've worked with since 2000, who have inspired me to learn and develop treatments that work. You are the reason we do what we do, and there's nothing more important than helping you get better.

Finally, thanks to my husband, Michael, for believing in me and encouraging me. And to my two amazing, beautiful children: you inspire me every day to be the best I can be, and I thank you for your unconditional love; you make me incredibly proud.

—Dina Hirsch

Abbreviations

AAN: atypical anorexia nervosa

AN: anorexia nervosa

ARFID: avoidant and restrictive food intake disorder

BAE: body acceptance and exposure

BED: binge eating disorder

BIB: body investigating behavior

BMI: body mass index

BN: bulimia nervosa

BOB: bulimia nervosa, other specified eating or feeding disorder (generally without AAN), and binge eating disorder

BPD: borderline personality disorder

CBT: cognitive behavioral therapy

EBBQ: Eating Beliefs and Behaviors Questionnaire

EDEB: eating dosorder–exacerbating behavior

EDNOS: eating disorder not otherwise specified

IMT: Integrated Modalities Therapy

IOP: intensive outpatient program

MAC: mindfulness and acceptance

OSFED: other specified feeding or eating disorder

OSFEDx: OSFED without, generally speaking, atypical anorexia nervosa

PHP: partial hospitalization program

PTSD: post-traumatic stress disorder

RAB: reinforcement-allowing behavior

RAE: regular and appetitive eating

RAN: health- or weight-restored anorexia nervosa

RE: regular eating

Rec-SPA: recovery-specific positive attention

RIB: reinforcement-interfering behavior

SAED: self-acknowledged eating disorder

SEED: self-eclipsing eating disorder

SUD: subjective units of distress

Key Terms

alexythymia–inability to distinguish the emotions one is feeling

anorexia nervosa (AN)–diagnosis (with restricting and binge/purge subtypes) in which weight loss is secondary to food restriction and one's body mass index (BMI) is in the underweight range; and fear of fatness is present

anosognosia–lack of self-awareness, including severe lack of insight into one's eating disorder and rejection of objective data regarding the negative consequences of its impact

apparent competence–seeming ability to cope or recover, masking actual difficulty in adaptively regulating negative emotions without engaging in maladaptive behaviors

asceticism–self-denial regarding perceived indulgences

atypical anorexia nervosa (AAN)–diagnosis in which weight loss is secondary to food restriction and one's BMI is not in the underweight range, although one's body may be underweight relative to what is healthy for one; and fear of fatness is present

avoidant and restrictive food intake disorder (ARFID)–feeding disorder characterized by low body weight and restrictive food intake, secondary to fear of something other than "fatness" (such as choking) and/or sensory aversion (to soft foods, for example)

behavioral experiment–in treatment, the testing of an adaptive behavior in order to experience potential benefits

behavioral family therapy–family therapy for eating disorders that incorporates behavioral principles

binge eating–eating while feeling loss of control over eating

binge eating disorder (BED)–disorder characterized by loss of control over eating

body acceptance–process of abandoning attempts to change one's body and learning to tolerate negative internal experiences (such as emotions) concerning one's body, work on appreciating one's body, and perhaps coming to like one's body the way it is

body avoidance–behaviors that hide the body and help one avoid negative internal experiences (fear of "fatness," thoughts like *I'm fat*, and so forth)

body gratitude–practice of honoring one's body parts for performing their functions and thanking one's body for allowing one to carry out one's hopes, dreams, and intentions in life

body image–from this perspective, the interplay among emotions, beliefs, and perceptions that results in the way one views one's body

body investigating–repetitive checking of one's body to examine potential weight fluctuations

body-related behaviors–behaviors that are part of an eating disorder and that are related to the body, including body avoidance, body investigating, comparing one's body to others' bodies, and exercising

bulimia nervosa (BN)–disorder characterized by fear of "fatness," food restriction, binge eating, and intolerance behaviors (purging, use of laxatives, and so forth) intended to decrease aversive internal experiences

carer–any primary caregiver (parent, stepparent, legal guardian, and so forth) who is actively involved in treatment

circular questioning–practice of asking each family member questions about interactions among other family members

committed action–action in line with one's values

compensatory behavior–in the eating disorder mind-set, the idea that one must make up for having eaten by engaging in behaviors to burn or otherwise get rid of calories

comprehensive IMT–administration of all three IMT modalities in a particular order for the treatment of anorexia nervosa or atypical anorexia nervosa

defusion–skill of noticing thoughts without automatically believing their content

defusion with the body–skill of decoupling one's body image from one's self and recognizing that one's body is separate from one's self

eating disorders–group of disorders (including the diagnoses of anorexia nervosa, atypical anorexia nervosa, bulimia nervosa, binge eating disorder, and other specified feeding or eating disorder) characterized by fear of "fatness" and fear of weight gain as well as by the overvaluing of a particular body shape and weight

ego-dystonic–describes a disorder that is incongruent with one's current self-image, and that one can recognize the desire to recover from (for example, a person with depression is able to report the desire to be less sad and to recover from depression)

ego-syntonic–describes a disorder that is congruent with one's current self-image, and that one is unable to recognize the desire to recover from

evidence-based practice approach–an approach that draws on evidence-based treatments and research in clinical practice and that uses available resources to best meet the needs of patients

externalizing the eating disorder–separating the eating disorder from the person who has the eating disorder

food avoidance–practice of keeping oneself from eating certain types of foods (such "fatty" foods, carbohydrates, and so forth) that are feared to cause "fatness" and weight gain

food obsession–repetitively thinking and ruminating about food, a cognitive process that can be fueled by behaviors that perpetuate such thinking (watching TV shows about food, for example) and, paradoxically, by the effort not to think about food (that is, thought suppression)

food-related behaviors–behaviors that are part of the eating disorder and are centered on food restriction, food avoidance, binge eating, purging food that has been eaten, taking laxatives, and so forth

food-related thought suppression–attempt to avoid thinking about food

fragilizing–underestimating the emotional strength and fortitude of someone (in this context, the patient with an eating disorder)

fusion with the body–identification of one's self with the appearance of one's body

imaginal exposure–confrontation with a feared stimulus that does not have concrete existence and must be imagined (for example, an apocalypse)

inevitability acceptance–realization that the destructive eating disorder is incompatible with a full and healthy life and that one must recover or face severely negative consequences

internal reinforcement–reinforcement that comes from the self (such as a feeling of accomplishment) after engaging in behavior rather than from an external or social source (such as a soccer coach)

intolerance behavior–any behavior (purging, exercising, taking laxatives, vowing to fast, and so forth) that follows the consumption of food if the function of the behavior is to help one avoid negative internal experiences (such as emotions)

in vivo **exposure**–confrontation with a feared stimulus that has concrete existence (for example, heights)

ironic processing–cognitive process by which thoughts one is attempting to avoid increasingly come to mind

learned association–relationship between two stimuli that is acquired through conditioning (as in classical or operant conditioning)

linked emotion–emotion (such as fear of abandonment) or emotional state (such as dysphoria) that, through learned associations, is connected to fear of "fatness" (for example, one fears abandonment if one gains weight)

mindfulness–process of bringing one's awareness to such internal experiences as thoughts, emotions, physical sensations, and urges to engage in behaviors

negative reinforcement–process (not to be confused with punishment) by which the removal of an aversive stimulus increases the likelihood of a future behavior

objective binge–episode of binge eating in which more calories are consumed than would typically be consumed in a day

positive reinforcement–process by which the likelihood of a future behavior is increased by the addition of a reinforcer, which may be pleasant or aversive

recovery behavior–behavior inconsistent with the eating disorder and in line with recovery

recovery-delaying behavior–any action or inaction—whether intentional, unintentional, or part of a diagnosable illness (as in purging after taking medication)—that gets in the way of success in therapy and has several natural consequences, including extension of the length of treatment, decreased trust, physical harm, and empowerment of the dangerous eating disorder

recovery-specific positive attention (Rec-SPA)–verbal attention (such as praise) and/or nonverbal attention (such as a smile) given for engagement in recovery-oriented behavior

refeeding syndrome–potentially deadly medical condition that can result when a person who has not been receiving adequate nutrition begins feeding again

regular and appetitive eating (RAE)–practice of eating appropriate amounts of food at regular intervals and in accordance with cues of hunger and fullness

reinforcement–something that increases the frequency of a behavior

reinforcement-allowing behavior (RAB)–any action taken by anyone who is responsible for implementing treatment rules (a parent, a hospital staff member, and so forth) that results in reinforcement of the eating disorder

reinforcement-interfering behavior (RIB)–any action taken by anyone who is responsible for implementing treatment rules (a parent, a hospital staff member, and so forth) that results in reinforcement of the blocking of an eating disorder behavior

restricting–act of limiting the overall amount of food eaten

role drift–result of the tendency of loved ones other than carers (siblings, for example) to take on the carers' role of implementing treatment rules by preparing food, supervising meals, supervising the hour after meals, and so forth

safety behavior–in the context of exposure therapy exercises, a behavior engaged in for the purpose of reducing negative emotions or other aversive internal experiences

self-acknowledged eating disorder (SAED)–disorder in which the self can be accessed and the desire to be free of the disorder can be verbalized (akin to an ego-dystonic disorder)

self-eclipsing eating disorder (SEED)–disorder in which the self cannot be fully accessed and expressed because of the disorder's presence (akin to an ego-syntonic disorder)

social reinforcement–reinforcement (in the form of rewards and punishments, for example) that comes from an external source (such as a coach)

stimulus control–limitation of triggers in the environment

subjective binge–episode of binge eating in which one experiences loss of control over eating but without consuming more calories than would typically be consumed in a day

subjective units of distress (SUD)–a determination of the degree of distress experienced during an exposure exercise on a scale of 0 to 10

thinness as a value–in the context of eating disorders, fusion with an ideal of thinness, often accompanied by the elevation of thinness above the self's other values, including spirituality, family, friends, and learning

thought suppression–active attempt to avoid thinking certain thoughts (about food, for example)

values–what is most important to one's self, as opposed to what is most important to the eating disorder

General Introduction, Implementation, and Core Concepts

General Introduction

Our Mission

Eating disorders are deadly illnesses that *must* be addressed and comprehensively treated. We cannot waste time divided by deference to our pet philosophies when research has shown multiple modalities of treatment to have merit. It is imperative that we pool currently available resources to treat and eradicate these illnesses. Many of us, knowing this intuitively, have scraped together our own personal compilations of interventions from materials published in the academic literature, presented at conferences, and scattered among unpublished manuals. But there is tremendous value in curating this knowledge and assembling it into one thorough, integrated collection of evidence-based interventions for the treatment of eating disorders.

As coauthors of this work, we share that stance, and so we set out to explore how we could use different evidence-based interventions to help our patients recover from eating disorders. We began by distilling core concepts from a wide range of treatment approaches and then designed handouts that clearly explained this important information to patients and families. Over time, three of our integrated collections of interventions developed into individual, group, and family treatment modalities. In this way, we conceived the treatment package that we call Integrative Modalities Therapy, or IMT (pronounced "eye-em-tee," not "imt"). Wisdom from a variety of evidence-based treatments is incorporated into each of the three IMT modalities, which are intended to be used on the basis of the individual patient's needs. We like to think of IMT as offering practical options for those times in clinical practice when you just need something adaptable to address a patient's presenting problems. IMT is a treatment package that was compiled, styled, and written *by* clinicians in the trenches *for* clinicians in the trenches. As such, this work reflects an approach to the treatment of eating disorders that is founded on evidence-based practice.

Language Referring to Adults Involved in Treatment Throughout the IMT material, we make broad use of the term *carer*. This term is intended to be inclusive of any adults (parents, stepparents, legal guardians, and so forth) who are primary caregivers and who are actively involved in therapy.

We quickly realized that an entire package of individual, group, and family interventions could seem a bit overwhelming, not just for clinicians in the trenches but also for patients struggling with eating disorders as well as for their distressed family members. And yet we knew that *all* the IMT material had to be experienced as simple. Therefore, our first and most important implementation-oriented goal became to present clinical information in a crystal-clear, approachable way. We used techniques from information design (the art of displaying information in an efficient and effective manner) and went to great lengths to make the IMT content easy to understand for patients, carers, and clinicians alike. When it comes to closing the treatment gap and standardizing care, we believe in the far-reaching potential of treatment material that can efficiently and effectively communicate important clinical concepts.

We began by designing the IMT handouts with patients' needs in mind. Broadly speaking, IMT handouts are easy to read and are written in a developmentally appropriate manner for adolescents with such eating disorders as anorexia nervosa (AN), bulimia nervosa (BN), binge eating disorder (BED), and other specified feeding or eating disorder (OSFED). Because of the way malnutrition can interfere with normal brain functioning, it can be particularly difficult for adolescents who have AN to process information, but similar cognitive impairments have also been shown to exist in patients with other eating disorders, such as BN (see Zakzanis, Campell, & Polsinelli, 2010). Consequentially, adolescents with eating disorders can be overlooked in treatment because it is all too easy for clinicians to communicate only with the parents. The participation of family members in treatment is often necessary, but why wait until remission to work directly with the patient? Instead of seeing decreased cognitive functioning as an insurmountable obstacle, we should seek to overcome it. In IMT, we attempted to do this in part by creating handouts for patients with fun graphics and clearly displayed information. Further, we found ways to make mindfulness exercises more concrete, making it easier for an adolescent with any type of diagnosed eating disorder to focus. For example, patients record their internal experiences on organized handouts during mindfulness practice. As another example, during the classic "leaves on a stream" exercise, the therapist plays recorded nature sounds to help refocus the patient's attention. In short, rather than bypassing the patient as a participant in treatment, the IMT material is specifically designed to meet adolescents with eating disorders where they are, both emotionally and cognitively.

Carers of patients with eating disorders are also in need of concrete information during treatment. When a child has severe eating disorder symptoms that require family-based therapy, many carers unexpectedly find themselves in the position of having to implement a lifesaving treatment for their child at home, without much support. In addition, and unsurprisingly, carers are often very distressed and have difficulty retaining information from sessions. Therefore, it seems inefficient to rely on verbal communication alone to convey crucial treatment rules and concepts. To solve this problem, carers are given clear IMT handouts, often with numbered lists, to guide them through treatment. Instead of being advised to read a whole book, carers, across multiple sessions, are given smaller amounts of relevant information that is presented in handout format and can be referenced and reviewed as necessary. Over time in treatment, as carers effectively contribute to the decrease in eating disorder symptoms—with the help of clear handouts describing how to execute behavioral interventions—they build a sense of experiential mastery. In this way, interventions explained by clear IMT family handouts can aid carers in executing the tasks that their role requires.

In the interest of better serving the eating disorder population, we also designed the IMT material to anticipate the needs of clinicians. People with eating disorders and their impacted families exist everywhere, but few clinicians are willing and able to treat eating disorders. By making the intimidating treatment of eating disorders more approachable, IMT aims to attract clinicians who might otherwise shy away from treating eating disorders. You can think of IMT as evidence-based treatment in a box—a way to make it easier for clinicians to administer evidence-based interventions for a category of disorders that is difficult to treat. We hope that if we can help clinicians become more able to treat eating disorders, they may also become more willing to do so. In this way, we hope to contribute to the efforts of our friends and colleagues in the field to close the treatment gap.

We also hope to contribute to the efforts of our community by offering a set of interventions that is not only scalable and flexible but also relatively easy to implement for therapists who have a foundation in evidence-based treatments across the spectrum of clinical experience. We have found that the IMT handouts allow for a treatment to be both standardized and individualized. Because patients receive core conceptual information in a streamlined fashion, space is made in session for the patient's individual needs. The eating disorder therapist who can draw on a comprehensive set of interventions is spared the effort of having to verbally reinvent the wheel by explaining each core concept to each new patient who begins treatment. In short, by decreasing the time that clinicians need to spend delivering core information, IMT saves time for care to be individualized. In addition, the IMT handouts a patient receives at one level of care can travel with that patient to a different level of care and be viewed by the new treatment team, and so the handouts can help, in a minor way, with continuity of care across treatment settings.

Our mission, in short, is to present this curated collection of evidence-based interventions for individuals, groups, and families in treatment for eating disorders as a way to help patients develop skills, support families, and provide a way for clinicians in the trenches to efficiently and effectively communicate core treatment concepts. And, given that we were already expending considerable effort to create this collection, it seemed to us that we could aim a bit higher, while we were at it, without too much additional effort. Therefore, our mission also includes closing the treatment gap with standardized, scalable, evidence-based treatments that can attract new clinicians who are willing to treat eating disorders and help standardize care in the field.

About This Book

- This book is a clinician's manual that describes how to implement individual, group, and family interventions for adolescents with eating disorders.

- All the IMT handouts referenced in this book can be downloaded at www.newharbinger.com/42235; see page 304 for download instructions. The reader without a general grasp of the IMT handouts will have little context for the material presented here. Therefore, we recommend that clinician readers download all Client Resources and Clinician Resources files before delving fully into this manual. The client handouts for individual, group, and family therapy settings will give you a feel for the range of interventions administered in IMT.

- This manual specifically describes interventions for treating *eating disorders*, such as anorexia nervosa, bulimia nervosa, binge eating disorder, and eating disorder not otherwise specified (EDNOS). Therefore, *feeding disorders*, such as avoidant and restrictive food intake disorder (ARFID), are beyond the scope of this manual. For ARFID and other disorders beyond the scope of this manual, we highly recommend the *Clinical Handbook of Complex and Atypical Eating Disorders* (Anderson, Murray, & Kaye, 2017).

- We also recommend reading the rest of this general introduction before administering any IMT interventions in clinical practice. It will explain how to use the IMT interventions with different diagnoses, with illnesses marked by varying degrees of severity, and at different levels of care. It will also emphasize that it is important, in determining the appropriate level of care for people with eating disorders, to integrate consultation with a medical provider, and it provides guidelines for doing so. In addition, the general introduction explains how to conceptualize eating disorders from a behavioral framework, in the specific style of IMT.

- Parts 1, 2, and 3 of this manual explain, respectively, how to deliver specific individual, group, and family IMT interventions. Therefore, these portions of the manual can be used as a reference book.

- The IMT measures found in the Clinician Resources for this manual (available online at http://www.new harbinger.com/42235) are used for tracking progress with respect to treatment targets.

How IMT Was Developed

If you, as a clinician, are not already practicing the range of evidence-based treatments for eating disorders, it will be particularly important for you to read the material that follows. An understanding of evidence-based treatments for eating disorders will help you use IMT in selecting appropriate interventions for each eating disorder diagnosis.

We initially created IMT as a collection of evidence-based interventions for AN, but we found very soon that the material was being put to use in the treatment of other eating disorders. As more clinicians began practicing with IMT, its use with other eating disorders quickly outpaced its use with AN. In part, this was because AN is simply not as prevalent as other eating disorders. But this is not the entire reason, of course. Another reason is that many clinicians who are formally trained in the treatment of other eating disorders reported not having received any training in the treatment of AN, and so they did not treat patients with this diagnosis, although they did need materials for treating other eating disorders. In addition, because IMT takes the form of a series of interventions, the individual and group materials in particular were being used flexibly to treat a constellation of eating disorder symptoms. We noted the need for a comprehensive set of interventions for adolescents with eating disorders, and so we decided to further meet the community's apparent needs by officially adapting this work to the treatment of eating disorders more broadly.

Because there are so few clinicians trained in evidence-based treatment for AN, by contrast with the number of clinicians who treat other eating disorders, we see the need to explain IMT's rather different approach to family treatment for the specific illness of AN. The current gold standard for treating AN in adolescents is family-based treatment (Lock, LeGrange, Agras, & Dare, 2001; Lock, LeGrange, & Russell, 2013), formerly referred to as Maudsley treatment, after the name of the London hospital where it was developed. Those who are unfamiliar with family-based treatment may be surprised to learn that, in essence, it involves carers (such as parents) completely taking control of food by preparing and serving it while monitoring the patient at all meals. This is done until the patient has regained a healthy amount of weight. This approach may sound forceful, but carers' intervention is both warranted and justified for this particular illness—eating disorders have the highest mortality rate among all mental illnesses (Arcelus, Mitchell, Wales, & Nielsen, 2011), AN is *ego-syntonic* (or *self-eclipsing*; see "Self-Eclipsing Versus Self-Acknowledged Disorders," later in this general introduction), and in AN the patient's cognitive ability is impaired. Anorexia nervosa *must* be stopped. Outside intervention by carers is certainly preferable to allowing adolescents who are physically at risk and cognitively impaired to be in charge of their own treatment. Setting firm limits and boundaries to save a child's life *is an act of love.*

A study by Lock et al. (2010) showed that 49.3 percent of patients were fully recovered twelve months after this gold-standard treatment ended. This is certainly a very meaningful portion of the population for which family-based treatment is helpful, and it is significantly higher than the 23.2 percent remission rate for patients who received adolescent-focused therapy without carers' control of food. Especially in view of the challenges that AN presents, we view 49.3 percent as a rather impressive remission rate. At the same time, there is an opportunity for us, as a field, to creatively devise solutions for the remaining 50.7 percent of patients with AN. It is our foundational belief that family-based treatment is exactly the right approach for the treatment of AN. Again, AN is a deadly disorder that is too dangerous to be left completely in the hands of an adolescent who has the cognitive impairment that is inherent in the illness. A team approach with carers must be taken whenever that approach is available, as should all possible measures to fortify this treatment and increase its chances of success.

When we were thinking of where to start in the work of fortifying this quite ingenious, evidence-based treatment for AN, we first thought that we should "behaviorify" it, so to speak. Of note, family-based treatment is actually *atheoretical*, and so it is not a behavior therapy. As such, family-based treatment is not an approach that uses universally effective behavioral principles, and so carers are not taught to use reinforcement techniques in their efforts to decrease eating disorder behaviors. Further, family-based treatment provides no behavioral guidelines for managing the oppositional behaviors that almost always emerge when treatment commences. At the same time, the two of us were finding that carers in our clinical practices reported wanting more concrete direction in fighting the formidable illness of AN. Therefore, providing concrete *information* to carers is not contraindicated in the IMT style of administering treatment. We believe that what builds mastery for carers is not in-session generation of strategies for combating the eating disorder but rather carers' *experiential success* in decreasing eating disorder behaviors. Moreover, family-based treatment currently includes neither evidence-based skills training nor exposure therapy for patients that is aimed at managing negative thoughts, behaviors, and poor body image.

Apart from the use of handouts to describe core treatment concepts, we developed four sets of interventions that comprise IMT-style treatment of AN:

1. We started by taking the foundation of family-based treatment and simply adding tried-and-true behavioral principles. In the context of treatment, we defined a list of eating disorder behaviors (such as negotiating about the type of food served, having an emotional outburst to avoid eating, and so forth) as well as recovery behaviors (such as eating the type of food served, eating the food while having negative emotions, and so forth). We then listed behavior therapy techniques that can be used by clinicians as well as carers to decrease these eating disorder behaviors and increase recovery behaviors.

2. Using acceptance-based, mindfulness-based, compassion-focused, and cognitive behavioral therapy interventions for patients, we compiled materials for imparting skills in group treatment.

3. For use after weight restoration, we aggregated a collection of evidence-based interventions that we call *regular and appetitive eating* (RAE), in which the patient is taught to eat three square meals per day while learning to attend to hunger and fullness cues. According to research by Tylka (Tylka & Wilcox, 2006; see also Smith & Hawks, 2006), this type of appetitive eating goes beyond the mere absence of disordered eating behaviors and represents the institution of psychologically and physically healthy replacement behavior.

4. We put together a collection of evidenced-based interventions that we call *body acceptance and exposure* (BAE) to address body-related behaviors, experiential avoidance, and body image.

These four interventions target such behaviors as excessive exercise, body avoidance, body checking, and body comparisons. To address body-related experiential avoidance, these interventions also introduce tried-and-true exposure therapy techniques, such as having patients imagine themselves gaining weight (to address their fear of "fatness") and incorporating mirror exposure therapy; both techniques have empirical support. The RAE and BAE interventions comprise the individual collection of interventions. In the treatment of AN, the family and group interventions are to be used *during* weight restoration, whereas the individual interventions are to be used *after* weight restoration.

This material as a whole became our arsenal for treating not only AN but also other eating disorders:

- It quickly became apparent at higher levels of care that the AN group material is useful across eating disorder diagnoses.

- Outpatient IMT AN groups were attracting patients who had eating disorders other than AN.

- In individual sessions, the RAE material was useful from the very start in the treatment of bulimia nervosa and binge eating disorder. Some patients who were more resistant to recovery were hesitant to engage in the BAE exposures, but this work is also clearly a good fit for these disorders, and it has been possible to weave it into later individual sessions.

- Clinicians who had reported no interest in treating AN began to show interest in IMT. In fact, during a nine-hour IMT workshop for anorexia nervosa that one of the coauthors conducted, only two of thirty eating disorder specialists reported that they were there to learn about using the materials in treating AN—and that was the turning point for IMT.

Given the circumstances, we were determined to contribute to the community with our compilation of interventions. There was a clear need to develop the material to suit all eating disorders. But why was this the case?

- Enhanced cognitive behavioral therapy (Fairburn, 2008) had been clearly established as the leading evidence-based individual therapy for adults, but it offered no treatments of this kind *specifically* for bulimia nervosa in adolescents until 2007, when family-based treatment was adapted to this population (see LeGrange & Lock, 2007).

- Family-based treatment for anorexia nervosa is necessarily forceful, given the life-threatening and ego-syntonic nature of the disorder, but family-based treatment for adolescents with bulimia nervosa is more collaborative. Bulimia nervosa, a much more ego-dystonic disorder than AN, often does not require the same level of intervention by others. As noted earlier, family-based treatment for bulimia nervosa is not appropriate in all cases, and so individual therapy must be employed (Nadeau, 2009).

- Family-based treatment for anorexia nervosa does not incorporate skills training for the patient, nor does it offer guidance on how to eat according to appetitive cues or body exposure work. Similarly, family-based treatment for bulimia nervosa also does not incorporate these aspects of treatment. Naturally, the same need also exists to expand into these areas with evidence-based interventions for bulimia nervosa. Therefore, we have organized a collection of available family, individual, and group interventions from which clinicians can choose in treating adolescents with bulimia nervosa.

- The treatment landscape for binge eating disorder and other specified feeding or eating disorder in adolescents is currently similar to the treatment landscape for bulimia nervosa before 2007. Cognitive behavioral therapy interventions are widely implemented by skilled clinicians, of course, but there is nothing standardized, flexible, or scalable in this area.

The Components of IMT

In its entirety, IMT includes the following components:

- This manual, to help clinicians select and implement interventions from the individual, group, and family therapy modalities

- *Client Resources for Treating Eating Disorders in Adolescents,* which comprises six groups of handouts for the individual, group, and family modalities; and *Clinician Resources for Treating Eating Disorders in Adolescents* (download client and clinician resources at www.newharbinger.com/42235; see page 304 for download instructions).

The handouts for the *individual therapy* modality include the following elements:

- Descriptions of how to establish regular eating (that is, how to eat appropriate amounts of food at regular intervals throughout the day)

- Exposure exercises for feared foods (such as carbohydrates)

- Descriptions of appetitive eating (that is, of eating in accord with hunger and fullness cues)

- A focus on fostering self-compassion and nourishment of the body

- Descriptions of the concept of body acceptance

- Exposure exercises regarding the body

- Psychoeducation and skills for decreasing compulsive exercise

- Psychoeducation and skills for decreasing body checking and avoidance

- Imaginal exercises for fear of "fatness" and for linked emotions (fear of failure, abandonment, rejection, and so forth)

- Exposure exercises aimed at increasing acceptance of recovery

- Exercises fostering gratitude for the body and improved body image

- Measures that assess individual therapy treatment targets week by week

The handouts for the *group therapy* modality include the following elements:

- Adolescent-friendly mindfulness group exercises with an emphasis on meeting patients where they are cognitively

- Adolescent-friendly exercises aimed at acceptance of support from others

- Descriptions of coping skills for decreasing restriction, binge eating, and purging

- A focus on fostering acceptance, self-compassion, and gratitude

- Descriptions of coping skills for disputing eating disorder thoughts

- A template for a relapse-prevention plan

- Measures that clearly display and assess group therapy treatment targets week by week

The handouts for the *family therapy* modality include the following elements:

- Information for carers about eating disorders

- Information for carers about implementing interventions at home

- Descriptions of behavioral skills for carers

- Templates for individualized treatment plans that can be completed with families

- Lists of treatment rules for families (the rules can be individualized)

- Psychoeducation for decreasing eating disorder behaviors with reinforcement

- Psychoeducation for increasing recovery behaviors with reinforcement

- Suggestions for managing oppositional behavior

- Descriptions of earned freedoms (that is, food-related responsibilities that a patient may regain over time) and a systematized protocol for allowing an adolescent the opportunity to earn freedoms back after physical and mental health has been stabilized

- Measures that clearly display and assess family therapy treatment targets week by week for the patient and carers

What Does "Integrative Modalities Therapy" Mean?

This treatment approach is called Integrative Modalities Therapy because each of the three therapy modalities—individual, group, and family—that comprise IMT is composed of interventions that integrate concepts from a wide variety of evidence-based approaches. IMT is also meant to be easily integrated into your current clinical practice, at any level of care, and to be used modularly on the basis of the individual patient's needs. For instance, if you work in an outpatient setting and have a patient with moderate binge eating disorder, you can use IMT modularly by administering mainly individual interventions while using select family interventions to provide psychoeducation to carers. If you work in a partial hospitalization program, however, you may primarily be administering the group interventions throughout the day, with all the patients enrolled in the program, while using select individual and family interventions with cases assigned to you. In this way, the clinician can modularly use a wide variety of evidence-based interventions, depending on what is best suited to each patient in a given setting.

The Individual Therapy Modality

The interventions that comprise the individual therapy modality are meant to be implemented in one-on-one therapy with the patient. As mentioned earlier, the individual material is separated into two distinct sections: *regular and appetitive eating* (RAE), and *body acceptance and exposure* (BAE).

Regular and Appetitive Eating

The general RAE objectives are as follows:

- Increase in autonomous but age-appropriate regular eating (eating three appropriately sized meals and two snacks per day)

- Increase in tolerance of the physical sensation of fullness

- Increase in the variety of feared foods eaten

- Increase in knowledge regarding the causal relationship between food restriction and binge eating

- Increase in tolerance of negative internal experiences (such as fear of "fatness," fullness, and so forth)

- Decrease in thought suppression (for example, trying not to think about eating)

- Increase in awareness of appetitive cues (hunger and fullness) via mindfulness and monitoring

- Behavioral increase, slowly and over time, in the use of appetitive cues (hunger and fullness) to guide eating while monitoring eating disorder thoughts and behavior

- Increase in self-care

The RAE material has a focus on teaching patients both to eat regularly (three square meals and two snacks per day) and to notice the appetitive cues of hunger and fullness. First and foremost in RAE, there is an emphasis on developing *regular eating* in treatment. According to the foundational work of Fairburn (2008, 2013), regular eating involves eating appropriate amounts of food at breakfast, lunch, and dinner as well as at snack times. A plan for regular eating is devised in session with the therapist. During the regular eating portion of treatment, challenges are also presented to eat specific feared foods. These food exposure exercises are influenced by the work of Steinglass and her colleagues (see Steinglass et al., 2012).

As regular eating goals are met with increasing success, appetitive eating interventions (for example, starting to identify hunger and fullness cues, eating when hungry, stopping when full, and so forth) are incorporated into treatment. These appetitive eating interventions are influenced by the Health at Every Size movement (Bacon, 2008), the intuitive eating literature (Tribole & Resch, 2012), Appetite Awareness Training (Allen & Craighead, 1999; Craighead, 2006), and Koenig's cognitive behavioral approach to appetite awareness (Koenig, 2005, 2007). This work is also informed by research showing that teaching patients with eating disorders (anorexia nervosa, bulimia nervosa, and eating disorder not otherwise specified) to eat according to appetitive cues is clinically indicated across diagnoses (Richards, Crowton, Berrett, Smith, & Passmore, 2017), although the implementation of appetitive eating interventions does vary on the basis of diagnosis.

Once a patient is more comfortable identifying hunger and fullness cues, the therapist guides the patient in eating regularly, both within a time frame (such as between 8:00 a.m. and 9:30 a.m.) and according to the patient's physical feelings of hunger and fullness. When patients are eating both regularly and appetitively, RAE interventions focusing on fostering gratitude are implemented. Aspects of this work have been influenced by the compassion-focused therapy work of Goss (2010). The RAE interventions have also been influenced by Polivy (Polivy & Herman, 1985; Polivy, 1998; Polivy & Herman, 2002; Polivy, Coleman, & Herman, 2005), the Academy for Eating Disorders' medical standards guide (Bermudez et al., 2016), novel psychoeducational interventions (Belak, Deliberto, Shear, Kerrigan, & Attia, 2017), acceptance and commitment therapy (Sandoz, Wilson, & Dufrene, 2011), dialectical behavior therapy (Linehan 1993, 2014a, 2014b), work on food-related thought suppression (Lavender, Jardin, & Andersen, 2009; Deliberto, Jacobs, Sanderson, & Hildebrandt, 2013), the Minnesota Starvation Experiment (Franklin, Schiele, Brozek, & Keys, 1948), and by the unpublished work of Romi Ran (www.villageforparents.com).

Body Acceptance and Exposure (BAE)

The general BAE objectives are as follows:

- Decrease in experiential avoidance of negative internal experiences (such as emotions) regarding the body

- Decrease in body-related eating disorder behaviors (such as body avoidance)

- Increase in tolerance of negative internal experiences (such as thoughts or emotions) regarding the body via exposure exercises

- Increase in acceptance of the body

- Increase in gratitude for one's body

- Increase in self-compassion

The BAE material, rather than having a focus on eating, is focused on body acceptance. These interventions are influenced by the work of Levinson and her colleagues (Levinson, Rapp, & Riley, 2014; Levinson & Byrne, 2015; Levinson et al., 2015) on fear of "fatness" and on exposure for people with eating disorders. It is also influenced by the work on mirror exposure conducted by Hildebrandt and his colleagues (Hildebrandt, Loeb, Troupe, & Delinsky, 2012) and by the compuLsive Exercise Activity theraPy (LEAP) program (Hay et al., 2018). The interventions are rooted as well in the classic exposure therapy used to effectively treat phobias (Bourne & McKay, 1998), obsessive-compulsive disorder (Foa, Yadin, & Lichner, 2012), and trauma (Foa, Hembree, & Rothbaum, 2007). The BAE material guides therapists in conducting both *in vivo* and imaginal exposure exercises aimed at increasing tolerance both of fear of "fatness" and of fears involving the consequences of "fatness" (such as abandonment). For instance, a therapist working from BAE handouts may help a patient work up to looking in the mirror for increasingly long periods, or a therapist may help a patient tolerate an imagined worst-case scenario of gaining weight and being dumped by a romantic partner. In addition, the BAE handouts are aimed at fostering gratitude and self-compassion and at improving body image. These interventions are influenced by acceptance and commitment therapy (Sandoz et al., 2011), compassion-focused therapy (Gilbert, 2009; Neff, 2011; Tirch, Silberstein, & Kolts, 2016), dialectical behavior therapy (Linehan, 1993, 2014a, 2014b), cognitive behavioral therapy (Beck, 2011), and Cash (2008).

The Group Therapy Modality

The interventions that comprise the IMT group therapy modality are separated into two parts: *mindfulness and acceptance*, and *cognitive behavioral therapy*. The collective objectives of the IMT group therapy modality are as follows:

- Increase in use of adaptive coping skills

- Identification of thinness as an invalid value, and fostering the healthful reprioritization of current values

- Increase in self-compassion

- Increase in mindfulness skills

- Decrease in cognitive distortions

- Decrease in eating disorder behavior

- Increase in use of adaptive coping skills to manage environmental triggers

- Increase in relapse-prevention skills

- Increase in the patient's self-sufficiency through the practice of coping skills

- Increase in acceptance of appropriate support from others

Mindfulness and Acceptance Group

The mindfulness and acceptance (MAC) group material integrates interventions influenced by acceptance and commitment therapy (Hayes, 2005; Luoma, Hayes, & Walser, 2007; Bach & Moran, 2008; Sandoz et al., 2011), compassion-focused therapy (Gilbert, 2009; Neff, 2011; Tirch et al., 2016), dialectical behavior therapy (Linehan, 1993, 2014a, 2014b), and components of family-based treatment (Lock et al., 2001; Lock & LeGrange, 2005; LeGrange & Lock, 2007; Lock et al., 2013). It also includes information about the function of eating disorder behaviors (Polivy & Herman, 1985) In addition, this material provides guidance for managing group behavior according to principles from behavior therapy, such as parent–child interaction therapy (Bodiford-McNeil & Hembree-Kigin, 2010).

Cognitive Behavioral Therapy (CBT) Group

According to Fairburn (2008), it was possible to adapt the 2008 transdiagnostic manual to extended cognitive behavioral therapy for use with adolescents—and, indeed, the interventions used in the CBT group material were adapted to adolescents in a group setting and are strongly influenced by enhanced cognitive behavioral therapy (Fairburn, 2008). These interventions are also influenced by work on cognitive behavioral therapy for anorexia nervosa (Garner, Vitousek, & Pike, 1997; Pike, Walsh, Vitousek, Wilson, & Bauer, 2003; Pike, Devlin, & Loeb, 2004), by an eating disorders prevention program to promote healthier body image (Stice & Presnell, 2007), and by Beck (2011), Leahy (2017), Burns (2008), Antony and Swinson (1998), and Costin (Costin & Schubert Grabb, 2012).

The Family Therapy Modality

The general objectives of the IMT family therapy modality are as follows:

- Increase in awareness of the medical dangers of the eating disorder and this treatment

- Increase in carers' skillfulness at decreasing eating disorder behaviors and increasing recovery behaviors at home

- Increase in carers' mastery in the implementation of treatment rules at home

- Increase in carers' skillfulness at providing reinforcement

- Increase in carers' skillfulness at managing oppositional behavior

- Increase in family's general knowledge of eating disorders (symptoms, etiology, and so forth)

- Increase, over time, in patient's sense of responsibility in treatment

- Increase in patient's tolerance of negative internal experiences when eating feared foods

- Increase in patient's self-sufficiency

The foundation for the IMT family interventions is unquestionably family-based treatment (Lock & LeGrange, 2005; Lock et al., 2001; Lock et al., 2013; LeGrange & Lock, 2007). This work is also very greatly influenced by standard behavior therapy principles as well as by parent–child interaction therapy (Bodiford-McNeil & Hembree-Kigin, 2010), a behavioral treatment for decreasing oppositional behavior. Given the degree of oppositional behavior that can result when carers begin to take control over food, adapting the principles of parent–child interaction therapy to the treatment of eating disorders was a natural choice. The IMT family interventions focus on teaching carers concrete techniques for shaping behaviors at home. Specifically, IMT family interventions are aimed at teaching carers to help decrease eating disorder behaviors and help increase recovery-oriented behaviors. In addition, this work references studies conducted by a number of esteemed researchers and colleagues in the areas of genetics, epigenetics, neurobiology, and temperament (Bulik, Sullivan, Weltzin, & Kaye, 1995; Klump, Kaye, & Strober, 2001; Mazzeo, & Bulik, 2009; Frieling et al., 2010; Hill & Dagg, 2012) as well as research showing that even a moderate degree of thin-ideal internalization predicts eating disorder pathology at the clinically significant level (Schaefer, Burke, & Thompson, 2018). The IMT family interventions emphasize that the onset of an eating disorder results from a combination of factors, and that no one person is responsible for the disorder's emergence.

Two Important Notes on Eating Disorders

Eating Disorders Do Not Discriminate on the Basis of Race

Eating disorders impact people of all ethnicities, socioeconomic backgrounds, genders, and ages (see Crago, Shisslak, & Estes, 1996; Sala, Reyes-Rodriguez, Bulik, & Bardone-Cone, 2013). In popular culture, the prevalent stereotype of eating disorders is that they primarily affect wealthy white girls. But this stereotype is detrimental to people with eating disorders. In fact, rates of eating disorders across racial groups are very similar, but people of color are much less likely to seek and receive help (Becker, Franko, Speck, & Herzog, 2003; Gordon, Brattole, Wingate, & Joiner, 2006). As a result, people of color who have eating disorders often fall through the cracks and do not receive treatment (Cachelin, Rebeck, Veisel, & Streigel-Moore, 2001). Never assume, on the basis of gender, ethnicity, sexual orientation, location, socioeconomic status, or age, that your patients do not have eating disorders. It is our belief that *everyone* should be screened for eating disorders in *every* type of mental health setting, and that such screening should be a required government standard.

Eating Disorders Do Not Discriminate on the Basis of Gender

Because eating disorders impact people of all genders, we have chosen not to use categorical gender-specific pronouns such as "he" or "she." Instead, in this manual we use gender-neutral language, such as "they," "their," "them," "themselves," "one," and "the patient."

TIPS

Tips (denoted by an icon representing a teacher) are included throughout parts 1, 2, and 3 of this manual. A tip is a piece of information likely to be helpful to the therapist. A tip may provide information about what a therapist can expect in a given scenario (such as the patient's possible anger in response to an intervention) and includes one or more suggestions for managing the situation (by using specific reinforcement techniques, for example).

IMT Measures

IMT measures are used in a clinical capacity to track the progress of specific treatment targets. There are IMT measures for RAE and BAE, for IMT groups, and for stage of family treatment. There are also patient and carer versions for both stages of family therapy. Together, they total seven treatment-specific IMT measures. In addition, given the functionally important role that bullying can play in the experience of patients enrolled in any portion of IMT treatment, there is an IMT bullying measure available at www.imt-ed.com.

It is important to note that the IMT measures were designed to make treatment goals clear not only to the therapist but also to the patient and carers. In a broader capacity, the IMT measures also serve as clinical tools for keeping treatment focused on achieving specific behavioral goals.

In practice, the treatment-specific IMT measures offer the following benefits:

- They allow the patient to read, in concrete form, very specific treatment goals (for example, "tolerate negative emotion," "eat full-fat and full-calorie foods," and so forth) and in this way to develop an understanding of expectations.

- They give the therapist information about carers' use of techniques at home, information that comes from carers' self-reports as well as from patients' reports.

- They enable the therapist to collect information that may not have been disclosed verbally.

- They allow the therapist to track progress toward treatment goals.

- They give the therapist objective evidence of treatment success or failure.

- They help the therapist craft appropriate *in vivo* and imaginal exposure exercises.

Please note that the treatment-specific IMT measures are intended to serve as clinical tools *only* and are not intended to be used for research purposes. Each individual answer to an item on an IMT measure is intended to provide the therapist with information about progress in treatment and about how to tailor future treatment. Scales and subscales are intentionally omitted from these clinical measures. Each item is individually helpful in a clinical sense. For readers interested in conducting research or augmenting clinical assessment, we recommend administering the Eating Attitudes Test-26 (EAT-26; Garfinkel & Newman, 2001) and the Eating Disorder Examination Questionnaire (EDE-Q; Fairburn & Beglin, 1994). For further suggestions, we suggest consulting the second edition of the *Handbook of Assessment Methods for Eating Behaviors and Weight-Related Problems* (Allison & Baskin, 2009).

Diagnosis and Mortality Rates

Before you use this manual, we strongly suggest that you review the current diagnostic criteria for binge eating disorder, bulimia nervosa, and anorexia nervosa as well as the diagnosis that still applies to the *majority* of people with eating disorders—other specified feeding or eating disorder (Keel, Brown, Holm-Denoma, & Bodell, 2011). We also suggest that you review the additional relevant information included about each of the disorders discussed in this section only after you have familiarized yourself with current diagnostic criteria and the various subtypes of the disorder, so that you will be able to provide the ever-important accurate diagnosis. In addition, we highly recommend that you read the Medical Care Standards Guide of the Academy for Eating Disorders; the guide is available for free, in ten languages, at www.aedweb.org (Bermudez et al., 2016). Even experienced clinicians are often surprised by the extensive medical risk that patients with eating disorders present. You must be informed, and it is beyond the scope of this manual to provide detailed descriptions of all the subtypes of eating disorders.

Binge Eating Disorder

Binge eating disorder (BED) is characterized by losing control of food and eating food rapidly. During objective binge episodes, a person feels a loss of control while eating a large amount of food. Subjective binge episodes are also characterized by loss of control, but involve eating a small amount of food. Over time in treatment, binge episodes can be shaped from objective binges to subjective binges (and, ultimately, to regular eating patterns). In terms of body mass index (BMI), people diagnosed with BED do not have bodies in the underweight range, but they absolutely can have bodies in the normal weight range. Having BED is not an indication, by any means, of having a body in the overweight range.

Notably, people with BED have overvaluation of shape and weight (Grilo, White, Gueorguieva, Wilson, & Masheb, 2013) as well as fear of "fatness" (Deliberto, Jacobs, Novak, Grabicki, et al., 2013). Therefore, after a binge, many negative emotions and aversive internal experiences (such as physically feeling full, or the thought *I'm fat*) can be experienced. Diagnostically, however, none of the behaviors that we call *intolerance behaviors* (such as purging, use of laxatives, and so forth) are then engaged in to maladaptively regulate the experience of those internal stimuli. Nevertheless, in our clinical experience, people with BED may engage in behaviors like vowing or planning to fast in the future, thereby decreasing negative internal experiences (such as emotions) after a binge in the moment. If these vowing or planning behaviors are occurring, they must be addressed in treatment.

Compensatory Behaviors or Intolerance Behaviors?   What are often called *compensatory behaviors* are referred to in this manual as *intolerance behaviors* so as to reflect their nature from within a behavioral framework. When engaging in these behaviors, the person is displaying intolerance of aversive internal experiences (such as negative emotions, physically feeling full, and so forth) rather than what we are aiming for in treatment—tolerance. Conversely, from within the mind-set of the eating disorder, the patient experiences the binge as "bad" behavior and is attempting to compensate for the perceived wrongdoing. Therefore, in this manual, we choose to reflect recovery-oriented language rather than eating disorder–oriented language.

Bulimia Nervosa

Bulimia nervosa (BN) is characterized by episodes of binge eating followed by efforts to regulate the negative emotions and aversive internal experiences (such as physically feeling full) that emerge after the binge. Similar to people with BED, people with BN can have bodies that are not in the underweight range where BMI is concerned. Their bodies can, however, be in the overweight or normal weight ranges. Never assume that a person cannot have BN simply because of the weight of their body. *Purging is not a weight-loss strategy but rather a dangerous and maladaptive means of regulating emotions.* Further, many clinicians are surprised to find that BN has a high mortality rate. In fact, whereas AN has a mortality rate of 4 percent, the BN rate is 3.9 percent (Crow et al., 2009). These mortality rates are more similar than previously thought. Therefore, it is certainly meaningful that the *number* of people who have perished from AN is higher; concurrently, the *rates* at which people are dying of AN and BN can be thought of as the same. It is very important not to underestimate the peril a person with this disorder is in. Close monitoring by a physician is essential (because of electrolyte disturbances, for example). This is particularly true if the patient is using alcohol and other substances. A person with BN may not always look as ill as someone with AN, but they are at the same level of risk.

Other Specified Feeding or Eating Disorder

Other specified feeding or eating disorder (OSFED) is the most commonly diagnosed eating disorder and continues to be the one that is least clearly defined. There were changes in the eating disorder classification system from the fourth edition (DSM-IV) to the fifth edition (DSM-5) of the *Diagnostic and Statistical Manual of Mental Disorders* (American Psychiatric Association, 2000, 2013), and these resulted in changes in the prevalence rate of disorders in the catchall OSFED category. One study (Keel et al., 2011) showed that 67.9 percent of people with eating disorders received this diagnosis under the DSM-IV system, whereas 53.5 percent now receive a diagnosis of OSFED under the DSM-5 system. In either case, the majority of people with eating disorders continue to be diagnosed with OSFED. Further, this disorder is no less dangerous than eating disorder not otherwise specified (EDNOS), as the DSM-IV names the other disorder in this category. Crow et al. (2009), in a study of the DSM-IV diagnosis of EDNOS, showed its mortality rate to be 5.2 percent. It is certainly very meaningful that this study demonstrated that more people died from this loosely defined disorder than both AN and BN, with mortality rates of 4 and 3.9 percent, respectively (Crow et al., 2009).

Atypical Anorexia Nervosa

Technically speaking, atypical anorexia nervosa (AAN) falls under the OSFED classification in the DSM-5. Nevertheless, the AAN designation deserves special mention. Similar to AN, AAN is a condition in which significant weight loss has occurred over a short period of time, in the context of fear of "fatness" and in the presence of eating disorder behaviors. AAN differs from AN in that people with AAN do not technically have bodies that fall in the underweight BMI range. A short synopsis of a case of AAN might be that of a fourteen-year-old male who formerly had a body in the obese range, was bullied regarding his weight, began engaging in extreme food restricting, lost one hundred pounds in a matter of six months, now has a body in the normal weight range, has stopped growing taller (that is, has stunted growth and has fallen off the growth chart, or curve), and is experiencing electrolyte imbalances. *People with AAN may not be in the underweight BMI range, but this does not mean that they do not have to gain weight, or that they are medically stable.* People with AAN often need to regain weight in treatment and are often at medical risk. It is our best guess that the 5.2 percent mortality rate of what was EDNOS in the DSM-IV (called OSFED in the DSM-5) is influenced by the people with AAN who are now subsumed under this category.

Anorexia Nervosa

As noted earlier, AN has a mortality rate of 4 percent, which is eleven to twelve times greater than the mortality rate for the general population (Miller, 2013). A person must have a body in the underweight BMI range to have a diagnosis of AN. Because treatment of AN necessarily involves weight gain—which is actually quite difficult to achieve in the context of intense fear of "fatness"—it is particularly important to accurately diagnose AN.

Eating Disorders or Feeding Disorders?   IMT is a treatment for the previously outlined eating disorders and is not intended for use with feeding disorders like avoidant and restrictive food intake disorder (ARFID), which is characterized by low body weight as well as by restrictive food intake secondary to a fear (such as fear of choking) and/or a sensory aversion (such as to soft foods). In clinical practice, we have seen this medically compromising disorder simply overlooked as picky eating before it became quite exacerbated. There is little current documentation on ARFID. Much of the IMT material is centered on fear of "fatness" and on body image, and so it does not apply to feeding disorders. In the past, however, IMT family handouts (covering treatment rules, recovery-specific positive attention, and so forth) have been used clinically to support the treatment of adolescents with ARFID in outpatient settings, partial hospitalization programs or day treatment, and inpatient settings. In the future, we hope to adapt IMT for ARFID because this is a major physical and psychological health concern for adolescents as well as adults we have seen in clinical practice.

TIP: Use an Imaginal Exposure Technique to Tell the Difference Between Anorexia Nervosa and Avoidant and Restrictive Food Intake Disorder

Sometimes in clinical practice it is difficult to make a differential diagnosis between AN and ARFID. In both disorders, the patient must have a body in the underweight range, secondary to a psychological condition. In AN, however, but not in ARFID, the psychological condition is fear of "fatness." People with ARFID have a fear of food (as in fear of choking) and/or an aversion related to food (such as an aversion to the texture of food). Therefore, if you are having difficulty making a diagnosis, conducting a mini-imaginal exposure of weight gain for diagnostic purposes can be helpful. Ask the patient to imagine that you have snapped your fingers, and that all the weight they lost has been instantly restored. If they express relief and gratitude, you are most likely dealing with a case of ARFID. People with ARFID are more than happy to gain all the weight necessary. This way, they can be done with treatment, without having to eat any of the food they fear. If the patient is visibly uncomfortable and anxious, it is likely AN. It is not the food that people with AN are afraid of, but rather the weight. Clinically, this has been a more helpful diagnostic tool than asking for a patient's self-report of whether they want to gain weight.

Rationale for IMT-Specific Terms

In clinical practice, the decision to implement interventions can often be made on the basis of specific symptoms or according to the person's individual presentation rather than on the basis of diagnosis. Therefore, for practical purposes, rationales are provided here for the following IMT-specific terminology that is used throughout this manual:

- *BOB disorders:* This term refers to the grouping of the disorders of BN, OSFEDx (meaning OSFED without, generally speaking, AAN), and BED. Several IMT family interventions are just for BOB disorders, typically with the exclusion of AAN.

- *OSFEDx:* AAN is technically subsumed under OSFED, but in clinical practice AAN is most often treated as AN, and so OSFEDx is used to refer to OSFED with the exclusion of most AAN cases.

- *AN and AAN/AN:* AAN is often treated as AN, and so the two disorders are often referred to jointly in this manual, but in part 3 (the family interventions), certain handouts simply and collectively refer to these two disorders as AN.

- *RAN:* This term refers to weight- and health-restored AN and AAN. RAN is a distinction used for a patient who has gained all the required weight and whose health is stabilized. Once a person has the RAN distinction, they may receive individual interventions, but not before. It is useful to have a term that denotes readiness for the individual therapy modality.

Diagnosis Over Time   The categories for eating disorder diagnoses are not static. People can move from one diagnosis to another over time. That said, providing an accurate current diagnosis is paramount in the implementation of appropriate care.

Implementation

Although the IMT interventions can be used transdiagnostically, implementation varies on the basis of both diagnosis and level of care. This section describes how IMT interventions are intended to be implemented.

IMT Implementation When Diagnosis Is Made in an Outpatient Setting

This section provides an overview of how to use IMT interventions from the three different modalities—individual, group, and family—for different diagnoses in outpatient settings. Because the vast majority of the clinicians we've spoken with have expressed the desire to use IMT for the treatment of what we refer to here as BOB disorders (BN, OSFEDx, and BED), this manual is organized so that the material relevant to most clinicians comes first. Later sections of the manual discuss criteria for referring patients to higher levels of care and the use of specific IMT interventions with different disorders.

Bulimia Nervosa

In the treatment of BN, it is recommended to have one session per week that incorporates the family alongside a weekly group. The degree of parental involvement depends on many factors. Medical issues, the level of severity of the disorder, availability of carers, and the ambivalence the patient has about recovery must be taken into account. If a full-scale family intervention is not warranted, it is recommended that there be a portion of the session devoted to individually discussing the material on regular and appetitive eating (RAE). Further, it is recommended that patients who engage in intolerance behaviors (such as patients with BN) be enrolled in a skills group. Alongside either a full-scale family intervention or a session that is a hybrid of family and individual work, group interventions can help foster skills to regulate emotions.

Regarding individual interventions specifically, the RAE material will be the initial focus of the individual portion of the session, and the material on body acceptance and exposure (BAE) will be introduced over time. Particularly for patients who display ambivalence toward recovery—and who therefore are not willing to take on intensive *in vivo* and imaginal exposure work—developing skills in group may help lay the foundation for future BAE work. After the patient has both mastered RAE and developed a sufficient set of skills from the group, the BAE material can be introduced into the individual weekly session.

Binge Eating Disorder

If the binge eating disorder is manageable with a session once per week, then sessions usually start out with a focus on RAE and move toward BAE over time, since a focus on establishing healthy behavioral patterns of eating takes precedence. For BED, however, we recommend starting with sessions twice per week, if that frequency is clinically indicated and if resources permit. Patients often need whole sessions to plan meals, shape eating behavior, and confront eating challenge foods in session. Without a second weekly session, the patient can be in treatment for many months before important BAE material is reached and related exposures are conducted. Therefore, we recommend having two sessions per week, one devoted to RAE and the other devoted to BAE, if possible. Over time, material from both RAE and BAE can eventually be presented in the same hour. How quickly this happens depends on a variety of factors, but mainly on how quickly symptoms remit in treatment.

We do not recommend the IMT group material for treating BED in an outpatient setting. The primary reason for this is that at the outpatient level of care, BED can be treated in individual sessions and does not require a group. Further, particularly if an adolescent who has BED has never had what we call *intolerance behaviors* (such as purging, laxative use, exercising, and so forth) as part of their presentation, introducing this patient into a group milieu may prove iatrogenic. It is more important to prioritize confrontation of negative emotions, if resources permit and if the interventions are indicated.

Please note, however, that there are some exceptions to the general rule that people with BED need only individual therapy. If severe functional impairment exists because of the disorder, and/or if there is a medical issue unique to this person that makes binge eating a particularly dangerous behavior—if the behavior is so impulsive that allergens are consumed, for example, or if the person has a preexisting disease that is made worse by binge eating—group and/or family interventions should be employed.

Other Specified Feeding or Eating Disorder

All IMT interventions can be used in à la carte fashion to address the needs of people with a diagnosis of OSFED. We recommend attempting to match the patient's OSFED diagnosis most closely to one of three diagnoses—BN, BED, or AN—and attempting to follow the treatment format from there. For instance, if a patient has a body in the normal weight range, fears "fatness," avoids foods, and is purging two times per month, then the diagnosis most closely resembles BN, and so the treatment would most closely follow the treatment for BN. If possible, perhaps involving carers to some extent would be necessary. Then proceeding with treatment largely focused on individual and group interventions would be recommended. If you are seeking consultation regarding the specifics of an individual case, the network of professionals at the Academy for Eating Disorders (www.aedweb.org) is recommended.

Atypical Anorexia Nervosa

Given the medical complexity of AAN, it is highly recommended that, whenever possible, patients with atypical anorexia see medical professionals who have experience treating eating disorders. It is crucial in these cases that the *appropriate* weight to which a person should be restored is targeted, and that health is monitored. *The fact that a person's body is not in the underweight BMI range does not mean that they do not have to gain weight or that they are not at medical risk.* On the basis of recommendations from a knowledgeable medical professional, a therapist must choose a treatment protocol to follow. Because it is often advisable to administer the protocol for AN, in IMT the protocol for AAN is coupled with the AN protocol. Occasionally, however, a less intensive version of comprehensive IMT is suitable in the treatment of AAN, depending on such factors as medical complications and the patient's current ability to engage in recovery behaviors without support. In cases where the patient is truly not at medical risk, does not need to gain weight, and is motivated to recover, the BOB version of family treatment may be more suitable. For more on treating atypical eating disorders, see Anderson et al. (2017). Again, if you are seeking consultation regarding the specifics of an individual case, the network of professionals at the Academy for Eating Disorders (www.aedweb.org) is recommended.

Anorexia Nervosa

The recommended implementation of IMT interventions for AN in an outpatient setting is very specific. If, as described earlier, carers are able to be involved, then the IMT family interventions must be administered first. If resources allow, it is recommended that group treatment be administered alongside family interventions, given that this provides the patient an opportunity to develop skills. This structure of twice weekly family and group sessions is maintained until the patient reaches weight restoration and has regained responsibility for food. At this point, two weekly sessions, one for RAE and the other for BAE, are recommended.

If a patient with AN does not have family members who are able and willing to implement interventions, then every effort should be made to ensure that the patient has support during weight restoration, either at a higher level of care (for example, in a residential treatment setting) or with licensed meal coaches (such as those provided by the Eating Disorder Recovery Specialists service). We do not recommend treating AN in an outpatient setting without family interventions.

Table I.1 depicts recommended uses of IMT interventions for different eating disorders at the outpatient level of care.

TABLE I.I. RECOMMENDED USE OF IMT IN OUTPATIENT SETTINGS BY DISORDER

	First Weekly Session	Second Weekly Session
Bulimia nervosa	Individual/family session	Group
Bulimia nervosa (recovering)	Individual RAE and BAE	Group
Binge eating disorder and bulimia nervosa (recovering)	Individual RAE	Individual BAE
Binge eating disorder and bulimia nervosa (recovering)	Individual RAE and BAE	
Anorexia nervosa (stage 1 treatment)		1. Mindfulness and acceptance (MAC)
Anorexia nervosa (stage 2 treatment)	Family	Group 2. Cognitive behavioral therapy (CBT)
Anorexia nervosa (stage 3 treatment)	Individual RAE	Individual BAE

IMT Implementation When Diagnosis Is Made at a Higher Level of Care

Bulimia Nervosa, Otherwise Specified Feeding and Eating Disorder, and Binge Eating Disorder

For people with all eating disorders, including BOB disorders, all IMT group material can be administered at a higher level of care. IMT family material for stage 1 of treatment may also be administered. For patients at levels of care (inpatient and residential) where staff currently supervise all meals and snacks, stage 1 family interventions can still be implemented in preparation for discharge. As described in more detail in part 1 of this manual, which covers the IMT individual therapy modality, RAE material may also be used in individual sessions for treating BOB disorders so as to establish regular eating patterns at higher levels of care. Select BAE material may be used as well.

Anorexia Nervosa and Atypical Anorexia Nervosa

As is true with respect to BOB disorders, all patients with AN and AAN may receive group interventions as well as stage 1 family interventions at a higher level of care. Nevertheless, patients with AN are not yet ready for IMT individual interventions. Most patients with AAN are also not ready. Readiness must be determined on an individual basis, as explained in greater detail in part 1 of this manual.

Table I.2 depicts IMT modalities that can be appropriately implemented on the basis of diagnosis at higher levels of care.

TABLE I.2. IMT Interventions at Higher Levels of Care

Binge eating disorder and bulimia nervosa	Individual	Group	Family
Anorexia nervosa		Group	Family

Using IMT Flexibly

The interventions across the three IMT modalities (individual, group, and family treatment) are largely intended to be used flexibly, on an as-needed basis. There is no strict protocol to be followed. Rather, interventions are provided with guidelines for use in various cases. This section provides information on how to use the IMT interventions flexibly.

In Outpatient Settings

Not all IMT interventions are appropriate for all outpatients. IMT interventions target behaviors or symptoms (such as compulsive exercising) that a given patient may not express. Therefore, if a given patient does not express a certain behavior or symptom that an intervention targets, simply do not administer it. The IMT material represents a comprehensive set of interventions for use at your disposal. It is by no means something that you must administer in full to everyone. Therefore, we recommend that you first read through the IMT interventions, familiarize yourself with the material, and then, after conceptualizing a case, decide which material to use. Regarding outpatient treatment, however, a small number of IMT interventions are core and must be administered under certain conditions, as described later in the manual.

At Higher Levels of Care

IMT is used even more flexibly at higher levels of care than in outpatient settings, with no requirements to deliver any one IMT handout. The treatment of eating disorders presents unique challenges, and the flexible implementation of evidence-based interventions across different levels of care is crucial to recovery. Because eating disorders have such an extreme impact on the body, patients are often required to attend treatment at higher levels of care (medical inpatient care, psychiatric inpatient care, and so forth) for varied periods of time while the focus is appropriately on *medical* (more than psychiatric) stabilization. This is unlike the situation in any other psychiatric illness. Therefore, material for eating disorders must be designed to meet this challenge.

Regarding the treatment of eating disorders, one consistent complaint that patients, families, and clinicians alike have about treatment at higher levels of cares is that it seems to be all about food. A focus on eating food is absolutely critical. At the same time, this complaint is a valid one. At higher levels of care, family meetings and groups are already taking place within an existing programmatic structure. Nevertheless, very rarely is standardized, high-quality, evidence-based material is being administered at those times. During whatever time a patient has in treatment at a higher level of care, if these types of interventions can be administered to carers in family meetings or to patients in groups, treatment can be moved even farther forward. Treatment at a higher level of care can move away from being just about food and toward preparing the family for eventual family-based treatment and equipping the patient with skills. Giving carers time to prepare for supporting the patient through thirty-five meals and snacks per week, every week, for months, is not an opportunity to squander, nor is maximizing the benefit of group time with patients. For example, if IMT group material is administered to people with eating disorders in an inpatient setting, then they are able to get evidence-based *psychological* interventions (rather than exclusively medical intervention) along with supportive group conversation.

Using IMT to Treat Anorexia Nervosa and Atypical Anorexia Nervosa

Given the fact that the treatment of AN and AAN requires specific implementation, this section provides a detailed description of how to administer IMT interventions in outpatient settings.

Are Family Interventions Essential to Treating Anorexia Nervosa and Atypical Anorexia Nervosa?

In the course of treatment for anorexia nervosa, patients with intense fears of gaining weight, and who believe they are "fat," are in a constant state of exposure for as many months as it takes them to gain the required number of pounds. Simply put, this process is brutal. It is extremely difficult to do this alone, and patients require as much support as is available. Therefore, in the treatment of anorexia nervosa and many cases of atypical anorexia nervosa, the priority should be to administer IMT family interventions whenever possible. The family work ultimately helps ensure that the patient gains the appropriate weight in treatment and that their health is restored—ultimately, the most crucial components of recovery for a host of medical and psychological reasons. In short, the family plays an especially crucial role in the recovery from AN and AAN. In our clinical opinion, every effort must be made to include carers in treatment, unless carers are unable to be involved. Unfortunately, however, it is not always feasible to include the family. (Table I.3 lists acceptable and unacceptable reasons for not employing any IMT family interventions with adolescents who have AN and AAN.) As clinicians, we must rise to the challenge and come up with creative and flexible ways to incorporate carers because the recovery of our patients may depend on it. Again, if you are new to this, join the Academy for Eating Disorders for support and guidance (www.aedweb.org).

TABLE I.3. Acceptable and Unacceptable Reasons for Not Employing IMT Family Interventions with Adolescents Who Have Anorexia Nervosa and Atypical Anorexia Nervosa

Acceptable Reasons	Unacceptable Reasons
Patient has no family or supports.	Family interventions are difficult.
Patient lives in a group home without supportive staff.	Family interventions are uncomfortable and easier to skip.
Carers are truly unavailable to eat with the patient on any day of the week.	There is mild to moderate discord in the home.
Carers have active eating disorders.	Carers cannot eat every single meal and snack with the patient.
Carers refuse to participate in treatment.	Carers are engaged in some form and degree of dieting behavior at the start of treatment.
Carers actively engage in abusive or neglectful behavior toward the patient.	Adolescent appears resistant to family therapy (when eating disorder is in control).
Carers are unable to put the patient's needs above their own.	
Carers, for any reason, do not have the patient's best interests in mind.	
Clinician currently lacks training (but will actively seek training instead of simply employing group and individual interventions for an adolescent who is underweight relative to what is healthy).	

Comprehensive IMT for Anorexia Nervosa in Outpatient Settings

Comprehensive IMT—that is, the implementation of all three IMT modalities in the outpatient treatment of AN and AAN—is depicted in table I.4.

TABLE I.4. Comprehensive IMT for AN and AAN

	Eating	Skills and Body Image
Stage 1	Family	1. Mindulness and acceptance (MAC) Group 2. Cognitive behavioral therapy (CBT)
Stage 2		
Stage 3	Individual RAE	Individual BAE

When IMT interventions are administered comprehensively, IMT family therapy and IMT group therapy can complement each other. During stage 1 IMT family therapy, the therapist teaches carers to take control of food responsibilities. Carers also learn to coach the patient in eating meals and snacks and to help them through difficult eating disorder urges. Stage 1 IMT family therapy terminates when the patient has reached weight restoration and stabilization. Although this is likely to improve the patient's cognitive and emotional functioning, the addition of a mindfulness and acceptance (MAC) group (in this case, called a *stage 1 group*) is intended to expedite this process. A MAC group has pathology-specific interventions to facilitate acceptance of carer control over food, provide skills training, and increase recovery behaviors (as defined in the IMT handouts) early in treatment.

With improved physical and psychological health at the completion of stage 1 of IMT family therapy, the time is ripe for the introduction of CBT coping skills to support the patient's process of reclaiming independence. Stage 2 IMT family therapy is focused on gradually and systematically handing food responsibilities back to the patient. Especially for patients who are afraid that the eating disorder will return, this process can be very anxiety-provoking. Therefore, the CBT group (or *stage 2 group*) is administered alongside stage 2 IMT family therapy to impart coping skills. While the MAC group (stage 1 group) focuses primarily on what are traditionally third-wave acceptance and mindfulness strategies, the CBT group focuses mostly on the development of CBT skills (such as thought disputation). Skill building in the CBT group also lays the necessary groundwork for exposure exercises in individual therapy.

After the patient's weight and health are stable, after the patient's eating disorder behaviors have significantly decreased, and after both third-wave and CBT coping skills are in place, a transition to individual therapy can be made in this suggested administration of IMT interventions. It is recommended that the patient receive individual therapy twice per week. One type of session fosters self-directed eating, while the other aims to improve body image. In RAE, patients are guided to eat regularly (three meals and two snacks) and, eventually, according to their own appetitive cues of hunger and fullness. Alongside RAE, the patient receives BAE, which includes a series of exposure and acceptance exercises for body size, body shape, and weight (such as imaginal exposure to seeing a modest weight increase on the scale) that facilitate tolerance of aversive internal experiences. This type of body-focused work is saved until stage 3 because the patient's weight has been restored and stabilized at this point in treatment. Finally, throughout both RAE and BAE in stage 3, self-sufficiency and relapse prevention are underscored.

Candidates for Comprehensive IMT in Outpatient Settings

Comprehensive IMT is intended for use with children and adolescents between the ages of nine and eighteen. In some circumstances, however, it may also be helpful for patients younger than nine or older than eighteen (such as college students who are residing at home). Largely, however, the term *patient*, as used in this section, refers to children and adolescents between the ages of nine and eighteen who have been diagnosed with AN or AAN.

Because the family interventions are the most important component of comprehensive IMT for AN and AAN, progress toward meeting goals in this portion of the treatment dictates which stage of treatment a patient enters. Table I.5 lists and describes patients with AN and AAN who may appropriately enter comprehensive outpatient IMT treatment at various stages. At the same time, however, it may be inappropriate for patients in the following populations to enter comprehensive outpatient IMT treatment:

- Patients who have intellectual or developmental disabilities, depending on the severity of these conditions (the IMT group interventions and many of the IMT individual interventions may not be appropriate for these patients)

- Patients who have feeding disorders, such as ARFID (a consideration here is the emphasis on body image and fear of "fatness" in the IMT group and individual interventions)

- Patients who have anorexia nervosa and traits of borderline personality disorder (we will have more to say about this topic in our discussion of comorbid personality disorders)

Criteria for Graduating Between Stages in Comprehensive IMT

The three stages of comprehensive IMT for AN in outpatient settings are meant to be distinct. As outlined in the previous section, depending on the severity of the disorder and the stage of illness, a person may enter at any of the three stages. This section, by contrast, explains the criteria for graduating a patient from one stage to another once the patient is enrolled in comprehensive IMT.

Criteria for Graduating Patients from Stage 1 to Stage 2 in Comprehensive IMT for Anorexia Nervosa

Patients may be graduated to comprehensive IMT, stage 2, when their weight has been restored and has been stable for about one to two months (this timing will vary). Nevertheless, although weight and health restoration and stabilization are necessary for this transition, they are not sufficient. Patients must also have displayed the following attributes for one to two months (again, this timing will vary):

- Minimal carer-supervised eating disorder behaviors

- No patient-directed eating disorder behaviors

- No engagement in any major intolerance behaviors (such as purging or use of laxatives or diet pills) during the preceding month

Criteria for Graduating Patients from Stage 2 to Stage 3 in Comprehensive IMT for Anorexia Nervosa

Patients may be graduated to comprehensive IMT, stage 3, when they have taken back from their families almost full control over food. They must also have coping skills (such as the ability to dispute negative thoughts, to self-soothe, and so forth), and they must not be engaging in self-injurious behaviors and must be engaging in only minimal intolerance (compensatory) behaviors (such as purging).

TABLE I.5. Candidates for Comprehensive Outpatient IMT Treatment of Anorexia Nervosa and Atypical Anorexia Nervosa at Various Stages

Stage 1[a]	Stage 2[a]	Stage 3[b]
Children and adolescents (ages nine to eighteen) who have been diagnosed with AN or AAN and have been determined to be sufficiently medically stable (in terms of lab work, EKG results, and a healthy, individual-specific BMI) for outpatient treatment by a medical professional	Patients who weight-restored during stage 1 of IMT family therapy and have carers in control of food	Patients who have completed both stages of the IMT family interventions
Patients who are being discharged from a higher level of care where they did not receive IMT family and/or group interventions	Patients who have carers in control of food (as when, for example, they have completed stage 1 of family-based therapy without the use of IMT family interventions)	Patients who have resumed control over food after completing treatment without IMT interventions (as when, for example, they have received treatment in a residential program, a partial hospitalization program, an intensive outpatient program, or family-based therapy)
Patients who are being discharged from a higher level of care where they received IMT family and/or group interventions		Patients who do not require support from others in control over food (as when, for example, relapse into severe restrictive behavior is currently unlikely, or when binge eating and purging are minimal)
Patients who recently weight-restored without guided help from an eating disorder specialist (as when, for example, they weight-restored on their own, or their carers instinctively took control of food) but who require support from others in stabilizing their eating behavior (as when relapse into severe restrictive behavior is likely, or when binge eating and purging have started, and so forth)		

[a] Patients with AN and AAN.

[b] Patients with the RAN designation (weight- and health-restored form of AN or AAN).

Criteria for Graduating Patients from Stage 3 and Terminating Treatment

Patients may be graduated from stage 3, and treatment may be terminated, when all their eating disorder–related medical symptoms that can be stable are indeed stable. A patient must also display the following attributes:

- No engagement in binge eating, purging, or other intolerance behaviors for the past several months

- Very minimal to nonexistent restriction and food avoidance

- Consistent reporting of only low-level guilt and disgust regarding the consumption of food, only low-level fear of "fatness," only low levels of other fears (such as fear of abandonment) that prompt fear of "fatness," and only low-level disgust with their body

- No engagement in compulsive body checking behavior

- No engagement in body avoidance behavior

- Reporting of a stably neutral to positive body image

TIP: TAKING THE PLUNGE INTO INDIVIDUAL THERAPY

Family members often burn out before a patient is fully ready to make the transition to stage 3. There can be a feeling of "ready or not, here it comes." Strategies for preventing this kind of burnout are discussed in part 3 of the manual, which deals with IMT family therapy. But if carers are simply drained, emotionally and financially, there is little the therapist can say or do to prevent the slightly premature handing off of responsibilities to the patient. Sometimes the plunge into individual therapy just needs to be taken. In these instances, it is best to work on accepting the circumstances and planning for relapse prevention.

Rules for Progressing Through Comprehensive IMT

Patients with AN and AAN move at different rates through six different components of outpatient comprehensive IMT:

1. Stage 1 family therapy

2. Stage 2 family therapy

3. Mindfulness and acceptance (MAC) group

4. Cognitive behavioral therapy (CBT) group

5. Regular and appetitive eating (RAE)

6. Body exposure and acceptance (BAE)

For instance, a patient may complete all the MAC group material before achieving weight restoration in the family component of the treatment. Therefore, we provide the following rules for moving through comprehensive IMT:

- In comprehensive IMT for anorexia nervosa and atypical anorexia nervosa, completion of the family therapy stages dictates the rest of the treatment. If a patient completes the MAC group before stage 1 of the family therapy modality is complete, it is suggested that the patient not progress to a CBT group but instead remain in a MAC group and then progress to a CBT group after stage 1 of the family therapy modality is complete.

- If a patient completes the CBT group before stage 2 of the family therapy modality is complete, it is suggested that the patient not progress to stage 3 (individual therapy) until stage 2 of the family therapy modality is complete, and that the patient remain in the CBT group.

- A patient may not start IMT individual interventions, whether RAE or BAE, until the stages of the IMT family therapy modality are complete.

- Until a patient is ready to progress in treatment, the patient may remain enrolled in a given IMT group even after having received all of that group's interventions. The decision to remain enrolled in a group at the same time that a given stage of the family therapy modality is being completed is based on multiple factors, including financial resources, clinical judgment, the patient's interest in repeating sessions, and the patient's willingness to do so. If the decision is made not to keep the patient in a given group, the patient will receive family therapy once a week until the given stage of this treatment is over. When the patient is ready to progress to the next stage, twice weekly therapy will resume. If a patient finishes the MAC group before stage 1 of the family therapy modality, the patient may discontinue MAC group attendance until stage 1 of the family therapy modality is over. At that point, the patient will enroll in a CBT group alongside stage 2 of the family therapy modality. If a patient finishes the CBT group before stage 2 of the family therapy modality is complete, the patient may discontinue CBT group attendance until stage 2 of the family therapy modality is over. The patient can then enroll in individual therapy (stage 3).

- Optimally, RAE and BAE will be conducted in separate sessions each week (that is, during two separate weekly sessions). Toward the end of treatment, RAE and BAE material can be reviewed in one weekly session.

Comorbid Personality Disorders

Overcoming Barriers to Diagnosing Personality Disorders in Youth

According to the DSM-5 (American Psychiatric Association, 2013), personality disorders can be diagnosed in people under the age of eighteen. Included in this provision is the possibility of diagnosing borderline personality disorder (BPD) in people under the age of thirteen. In the United Kingdom, official practice guidelines published in 2009 recommend that clinicians diagnose personality disorders in adolescents as appropriate (see the NICE guidelines on treatment and management, available at www.nice.org.uk). Nevertheless, only a very small minority of practitioners diagnose personality disorders in adolescents. One study (Martina Petronella Laurenssen, Hutsebaut, Jerta Feenstra, Van Busschbach, & Luyten, 2013) found that only 8.7 percent of clinicians do this; the reasons cited for not diagnosing personality disorders in adolescents were not knowing that personality disorders could be diagnosed in this population, the sense that adolescence is too transient a period for such a diagnosis, and the sense that these diagnoses are stigmatizing.

This section addresses these barriers to the proper diagnosis of personality disorders in youth. First, as just mentioned, personality disorders can be diagnosed in adolescents and, in rare cases, children. Because of the complex interplay between eating disorder and personality symptoms, it is particularly important to accurately diagnose both pathologies. Second, evidence suggests that personality pathology actually peaks *before* age twenty (Gutiérrez et al., 2012), and that it is certainly important to diagnose this pathology in adolescents. Third, the diagnosis of a personality disorder may indeed be stigmatizing, but a therapist still has the duty to diagnose and treat an illness. The illness should not be ignored because it is stigmatized by others. We have a duty as a profession not to feed into the stigmatization of these illnesses by treating them as if they are something to be ignored. We may not be diagnosing these illness, but that doesn't mean they aren't there. We must properly and professionally address these illnesses, and it is particularly important to diagnose and treat BPD in the context of an eating disorder.

Eating disorder treatment requires a series of food-related exposures that can trigger self-injurious thoughts and behaviors in patients with BPD, and so properly assessing and diagnosing adolescents with BPD is particularly essential to proper care. Because the IMT material offers additional body-related exposures, understanding a patient's current emotion-regulation skill level is an important component of knowing when the patient is ready for these interventions. Therefore, it is particularly important for therapists treating eating disorder behaviors to overcome barriers to diagnosing borderline personality disorder in adolescents.

Difficulties in Treating Comorbid Eating Disorders and Borderline Personality Disorder

A dilemma often exists for therapists treating people with eating disorders who also have a diagnosis of BPD or display traits of that disorder. Traditional clinical wisdom dictates that one must not conduct exposure exercises (such as reading a trauma narrative) with a patient who engages in self-injurious behaviors until the patient has learned at least some emotion-regulation skills. If these skills are not in place, then negative emotions may trigger self-injurious thoughts and behavior rather than arising and then subsiding after the exposure. In this way, exposure could reinforce maladaptive self-injurious behaviors rather than the adaptive behaviors of tolerating aversive internal experiences. Therefore, clinicians in practice, before introducing exposure therapy exercises, often choose to ensure that the patient is able to use some skills to prevent self-injurious behaviors. In addition, recent research (Harned, Korslund, & Linehan, 2014; Krüger et al., 2014) shows that enrolling patients concurrently in dialectical behavior therapy and prolonged exposure is also feasible and produces positive outcomes.

There is a bit of a snag, however, when the patient with BPD specifically has a fear of "fatness"—and by association food—in the context of an eating disorder. In the trauma literature, prolonged exposure typically means one ninety-minute session per week of therapy (Foa & Rothbaum, 1998; Foa et al., 2007), but eating disorder treatment requires what can be conceptualized as a *very* rigorous exposure regime of eating three meals and two snacks per day as well as feeling full five times per day. Because food—a necessary part of life—is feared, there is little to no time to wait for a patient to build emotion-regulation skills. It is essential to the person's health and wellness that food be eaten regularly throughout the day, every day, starting today. This process is, of course, extremely difficult for anyone with an eating disorder. If that person also has BPD, tolerating negative emotions and skillfully managing self-destructive urges will be added challenges. For basic reasons of health, regardless of whether a patient has BPD, establishing regular eating must be an early treatment goal for each patient with a health-compromising eating disorder.

If there is a risk of self-injurious thoughts and behaviors after an exposure exercise, then how can a person with BPD possibly undergo treatment for an eating disorder? The answer is that both disorders must be accurately *diagnosed* and *treated* at about the same time. Generally, it may be best to enroll the patient in dialectical behavior therapy and treatment for the eating disorder concurrently, when possible. If self-injurious thoughts and behaviors are triggered in response to eating regularly (for example, if the patient reports making a suicide plan in the context of eating disorder treatment), then a higher level of care is required (such as inpatient treatment, residential treatment, or partial hospitalization). Except in rare cases, for short periods of time, it is *not* acceptable to set aside the treatment of an eating disorder that has destabilized a patient's health just because regular eating triggers self-injurious thoughts and behaviors. For the patient's health, regular eating must be established *and* the patient must learn to cope with triggers, but this approach should be taken with much added support. Remember, the mortality rate for eating disorders is higher than the mortality rates for all other mental health disorders. It is important to establish an accurate hierarchy of potential threats to the patient. Therefore, treatment at a higher level of care may be indicated when patients with BPD have self-injurious thoughts and behaviors triggered by eating. If a higher level of care is required, then it is recommended that specialized eating disorder treatment and dialectical behavior therapy be undertaken simultaneously.

If it is impossible to treat both BPD and the eating disorder at the same time, then whichever disorder is more acute must be prioritized, whether that means BPD because of the patient's suicidal behavior or the eating disorder because of the patient's physical health. Once the prioritized course of treatment has concluded, treatment of the other disorder may need to begin. For instance, if a patient with BPD and BN is physically very unwell and has a suicide plan, then hospitalization on a specialized eating disorders unit may be best because the team there can work on the patient's suicidality in addition to stabilizing the patient's health, decreasing the patient's purging, and establishing a regular eating pattern. Subsequently, a discharge to an intensive program of dialectical behavior therapy may be recommended, to stabilize self-injurious thoughts and behaviors, before a continued course of eating disorder treatment is started. A treatment plan like this one may need to be implemented when concurrent eating disorder treatment and dialectical behavior therapy are not available or not appropriate.

Borderline Personality Disorder and Additional Eating Disorder Exposure Exercises

Because each patient already undergoes an arduous battery of necessary food-related exposures, patients with active borderline personality disorder may not yet be ready or willing to undergo additional body-related exposures, such as the ones offered in the BAE material. Therefore, it is suggested that such patients be enrolled in dialectical behavior therapy before exposure to the demarcated BAE handouts. Once a patient no longer struggles with self-injurious thoughts and behaviors, there is considerably less potential for the additional exposure exercises to backfire and produce the "safety" behaviors of nonsuicidal or suicidal thinking.

The Importance of Medical Clearance for All Eating Disorders

With people who do not have eating disorders, a licensed therapist can use a thorough verbal and/or self-report assessment to make a judgment call regarding the required level of care. This is not the case with eating disorders. Eating disorder behaviors impact the physical health of a patient, and so just talking to or looking at a patient who has an eating disorder is not enough for you to be able to determine the level of care, whether it turns out to be medical hospitalization, psychiatric inpatient care, residential treatment, a partial hospitalization program, day treatment, an intensive outpatient program, or regular outpatient treatment. Self-report measures don't cut it, either. We therapists need to collaborate with colleagues in other disciplines, and specifically with our colleagues in medicine. As a therapist, think of yourself as a project manager—your job is to help keep patients and carers accountable for health, but it is not your job either to determine how often a patient needs medical examination or to interpret the results. A physician needs to collect information through lab work, an EKG, and a physical exam before a determination regarding level of care is made. Often, before treatment at any level of care can commence, the therapist needs to have a brief chat with the physician to interpret the results of medical examinations and lab tests.

Although it is not a therapist's responsibility to determine whether a person is medically at risk, it is also true that physicians offering outpatient care rarely make referrals to appropriate levels of psychiatric care (such as a partial hospitalization program). Therefore, the therapist must also communicate with the physician to determine whether a given patient is appropriate for the therapist's practice. If a given patient's physician is not familiar with the treatment of eating disorders, quickly send the physician practice guidelines. It may also be helpful to provide the patient's physician with a copy of the Medical Care Standards Guide of the Academy for Eating Disorders (Bermudez et al., 2016). Appropriate decisions can be made when it is possible to communicate about the specifics of the practice guidelines as they relate to the results of the patient's tests. Thus, the patient with an eating disorder requires a multidisciplinary team consisting of at least a therapist and a physician who are in communication.

TIP: FACILITATE RATHER THAN AVOID THE INVESTIGATION OF POTENTIAL MEDICAL SYMPTOMS
There is an easy way to know whether a patient is at medical risk—send the patient to a physician. Fearful therapists with blanket concerns about medical illness turn patients away, and that's a tragedy for patients with eating disorders. Instead of turning away from treating people who *may* be medically ill, encourage investigation of potential medical illness. If a patient needs specialized medical care, it is within the discipline of physicians to call the shots. We need to develop a certain level of trust in our colleagues. They will know whether a patient needs inpatient medical care or a referral to a specialist, for instance. Only when a patient is healthy enough to be seen by you will the patient be seen by you. In this way, the risk to the therapist is mitigated.

Ongoing Medical Management in Treatment

Once the appropriate level of care has been ascertained, the frequency of ongoing medical assessment will need to be determined by the physician on a given patient's treatment team. If the patient is cleared for outpatient treatment, then the patient's pediatrician is part of the treatment team along with you. The same goes for any psychiatrists or dietitians with whom the patient may be working. Therefore, each individual patient may have a unique treatment team.

Deferring to the physician with respect to the frequency of medical visits is always recommended, but it is often necessary to introduce the idea of ongoing medical management throughout the course of eating disorder therapy to the patient and/or the family. If the physician is not familiar with the treatment of eating disorders, then this type of treatment and its underlying concepts may need to be introduced to the physician before the frequency of medical visits can be determined. Again, we must develop a level of trust in physicians and in their ability to contribute to the team.

Because it is the physician's job to make recommendations regarding the frequency of medical visits for each individual patient, we'll offer only examples of the types of medical management that may be recommended for various eating disorders:

- *BED:* On intake, a medical examination with lab work is often necessary to rule out purging (on the basis of amylase levels, for example). In the treatment of BED, by contrast with other eating disorders, ongoing medical management may be required relatively infrequently unless physical symptoms (such as acid reflux or diabetes) are present.

- *BN and OSFEDx:* The frequency of medical examinations and lab work varies according to the severity of symptoms. A general rule of thumb, to offer one example, is that there should be a medical exam and lab work every several weeks. Patients with BN or OSFEDx may also be required to see specialists, such as a gastroenterologist.

- *AN and AAN:* In the treatment of AN and many cases of AAN, patients are often required to have medical examinations and lab work at a higher frequency of about once per week or biweekly. Patients with AN or AAN may also be required to see specialists (cardiologists, endocrinologists, and so forth).

Dangerous Behaviors to Note

In addition to common eating disorder behaviors that are quite dangerous (such as purging, compulsive exercise while dehydrated, and so forth), there are some that may be particularly perilous and are worth mentioning here, although this is by no means a comprehensive list:

- If a patient is purging right after taking psychiatric medication, the medication may be coming up and not getting absorbed in consistent doses.

- Patients can be drinking alcohol and/or using drugs in addition to purging, and this behavior can result in electrolyte imbalances.

- Patients at *any* weight can be restricting water and fluid intake, and this can be particularly dangerous.

- Patients may be at particular risk for dehydration if they are restricting fluid intake, purging, abusing laxatives, compulsively exercising, and abusing alcohol or engaging in various combinations of these behaviors.

- Patients who are underweight can have any number of electrolyte imbalances at any time.

- Patients who are not underweight but who are engaging in eating disorder behaviors are also at risk for electrolyte imbalances.

- For patients who have severely restricted, especially those who have not eaten for many days in a row, there is a risk of refeeding syndrome. A nonmedical way of describing this syndrome is to say that the body goes into shock after the patient undergoes a period of starvation and then eats for the first time.

- Refeeding syndrome can lead to a heart attack, a stroke, a coma, or death. Therefore, a patient must be medically cleared before starting treatment and must continue to be monitored.

Why Lab Work Is Helpful in Therapy If a patient is purging, getting lab work can be very useful. It is always best to consult with a medical professional regarding the interpretation of lab results. At the same time, a nonmedical therapist can learn the basics. For instance, amylase levels can be elevated when the patient is purging. Sometimes, however, the patient can be purging and the level is not elevated, or the patient is not purging and it is elevated. This is why it is best to consult with a licensed medical professional. Regardless of occasional ambiguity, results can still be clinically helpful. For instance, if your patient denies ever having intentionally purged, but lab results are starting to come back week after week with increased amylase levels, then you might suspect purging. Confronting the patient on this issue may bring about disclosure of the behaviors. On occasion, we have had patients at higher levels of care with comorbid BPD who reported purging, but amylase levels were not elevated. It has also been clinically useful to have lab reports objectively backing up the team's assessments that eating disorder behaviors were not being engaged in.

Core Concepts

Is Training Required Prior to Administration?

We believe that the treatment of eating disorders is something all therapists can learn. There is nothing mystical about it. In our experience, navigating the medical piece can be a bit intimidating at first, if you have never done this before. However, after a couple of times making appropriate referrals, in collaboration with physicians who make the real determinations, the process becomes rather straightforward. Because the management of the various aspects of eating disorder treatment is simply different from the management of treatment for other disorders, it can be helpful to have a point person to guide you through your first cases. If you have never had supervision by a specialist in the treatment of eating disorders, it is highly recommended that you seek either formal supervision or consultation through the network of specialists at the Academy for Eating Disorders (www.aedweb.org).

Regarding the implementation of IMT interventions specifically, training may or may not be needed; that depends on the therapist's prior levels of experience. For instance, if a therapist has prior training in family-based treatment, enhanced cognitive behavioral therapy, and mindfulness, it is unlikely that specific IMT training will be required, although it may still be preferable. Therapists with less specific training may be able to readily implement IMT interventions as long as they have a solid foundation in evidence-based treatments and behavioral learning theory. Without these two prerequisites, however, it is highly recommended that training be sought out. Those interested in receiving IMT-specific training can visit our website (www.imt-ed.com) or email us (IMTtherapy@gmail.com).

A SOLID FOUNDATION IN BEHAVIOR THEORY

It is important to be clear about exactly what we are referring to as a solid foundation in behavior theory. There are some terms and principles with which it is important to be familiar before proceeding to administer IMT. Here are some behavioral terms that are often misused or misunderstood:

- *Negative reinforcement:* This term does not mean "punishment." It refers to the *removal* of an *aversive* stimulus (such as when one is no longer bullied for eating what is commonly called *junk food* after dieting) so that a behavior is increased in the future (as when the behavior of dieting increases because it has been *negatively* reinforced by the *removal* of bullying for postdieting consumption of junk food).

- *Positive reinforcement:* This term does not necessarily mean "reward." It refers to the *addition* of either a *pleasant* or a *motivating* stimulus that increases a future behavior. Therefore, positive reinforcement can be either a reward or a punishment (for example, if a child has to wash dishes as punishment for not doing homework, then the behavior of doing homework will be *positively* reinforced by the *addition* of the motivating stimulus of dishwashing).

- *Internal (automatic) reinforcement:* This term refers to reinforcement that does not come from an external source (such as a teacher) but from within the self (as when one feels a sense of pride for completing a task).

- *External reinforcement:* This term refers to reinforcement that comes from an external source (for example, a reward that is offered within an app) as well as from other people.

- *Social reinforcement:* This term refers to reinforcement from others—instructors, teachers, classmates, and so forth.

- The *function* of a behavior has to do with the type of reinforcement it elicits (for example, the function of purging may be to *decrease* negative emotions, which makes purging a negatively reinforcing behavior).

If the formal uses of the preceding terms are unfamiliar to you, we suggest that you become familiar with the basic concepts of behavioral learning theory (reinforcement schedules, extinction bursts, and so forth). The specific framework for the creation and implementation of IMT will be much clearer to you once you have an understanding of behavioral learning theory.

Eating Disorders: A Functional Conceptualization

Diagnosis unquestionably plays an important role in guiding the treatment of eating disorders. At the same time, the *functions* of all behaviors in eating disorders can be conceptualized transdiagnostically. We can think of a diagnosis as an indication of how the underlying mechanics of the eating disorder are expressing themselves *at a given point in time*. The current expression of behaviors in the form of diagnosis is actually quite important to understand, since different eating disorder diagnoses require specialized approaches (for example, anorexia nervosa necessitates the involvement of others such as carers). On a core functional level, however, similar behaviors are displayed and reinforcement systems are in place in all eating disorders, regardless of diagnosis.

For instance, anorexia nervosa, restricting type, is defined by a general lack of serious intolerance behaviors, such as purging, but this is not to say that the patient never engages in intolerance behaviors of any kind (for more information, see American Psychiatric Association, 2013). A person with this diagnosis certainly may engage in occasional compulsive exercise following a meal. Further, when enrolled in treatment, people with anorexia nervosa, restricting type, may begin engaging in intolerance behaviors when suddenly faced with the challenge of having to eat large volumes of food. Although these behaviors are clinically significant, their frequency may not warrant a new diagnosis (such as anorexia nervosa, binge-purge type).

It is also true, however, that people can morph from one diagnosis to another over time. For instance, a patient may start out having anorexia nervosa, restricting type; begin binge eating and purging at the end of the weight-restoration process, warranting a diagnosis of bulimia nervosa; and then eventually stop purging altogether while continuing binge eating, warranting a diagnosis of binge eating disorder. Regardless of whether a diagnosis reflecting binge eating is ever given, about 33 percent of people with anorexia nervosa engage in subjective binge eating (Fairburn, 2013), and more than 90 percent of people with anorexia nervosa will eventually engage in binge eating behavior at some point (Fairburn, 2008).

Taking a functional perspective on eating disorder behaviors fosters a transdiagnostic understanding—all eating disorder behaviors foster experiential avoidance of fear of "fatness" and weight gain. For instance, although a diagnosis of anorexia nervosa, binge-purge type, may no longer apply to a given weight-restored patient, an underlying fear of "fatness" and a proclivity for avoiding this fear with eating disorder behaviors remains. A patient may be eating adequate amounts of food after weight restoration, but perhaps they are still engaging in behavioral avoidance of specific foods (such as sugars), which in turn could paradoxically contribute to binge eating. Therefore, the diagnosis may morph into binge eating disorder.

Further support for this idea is the fact that the most common eating disorder diagnosis still remains other specified feeding or eating disorder (recall the study by Keel et al., 2011). This further emphasizes the importance of a *functional* understanding of eating disorder behaviors and the development of appropriate treatments that address the shared components of eating disorders.

Although there appear to be uniform and transdiagnostic elements to the function of eating disorder behaviors, the therapist must strive to understand both the common building blocks of eating disorders as well as what is specific to each individual. The underlying mechanisms across eating disorders are similar, but gathering individualized information from each person is crucial to the implementation of appropriate interventions and, more specifically, to the crafting of targeted exposure exercises. A case conceptualization form (available in the Clinician Resources at www.newharbinger.com/42235) can help in collecting specific individualized data relevant to the implementation of IMT interventions.

The numbering (0–16) of the sections that follow corresponds to the numbering in figure I.6, which presents an outline of the functional conceptualization of eating disorders. Note, however, that the behaviors listed in the figure and discussed in the following sections do not all occur or unfold for everyone, in real time, in the order presented here and in the figure. The information in the figure and in the following sections is intended to provide a framework for understanding how eating disorder behaviors relate to one another. It is easiest to foster this kind of understanding by placing the behaviors next to one another and discussing their reinforcing relationships. In short, the behaviors listed in the figure and in the correspondingly numbered sections that follow do not occur in the same linear fashion in which they are presented. Rather, they have been ordered in such as way as to foster a conceptual understanding of the functional mechanisms of eating disorders.

Figure 1.6. Outline of the Functional Conceptualization of Eating Disorders

0. Some patients have linked emotions (or emotion states) associated with fear of fatness.

    - Linked emotions could include specific fears or emotion states such as dysphorias.
        - Examples of linked fears:
            - Fear of failure
            - Fear of rejection or being ostracized
            - Fear of abandonment
            - Fear of imperfection
            - Fear of being unlovable
            - Fear of being attractive to a predator
            - Fear of death, dying, or illness
            - Fear of losing a competitive edge
        - Example of linked emotion state:
            - Gender dysphoria
    - Emotions or emotion states are linked with fear of "fatness" through learned associations.
    - Linked emotions do not necessarily precede the onset of the eating disorder.
    - Here is a sample list of associative links:
        - Regarding fear of failure, weight gain is defined as a failure: "I fail at my diet if I don't lose weight."
        - Lack of rejection becomes concretely linked with thinness: "If I'm thin, I'll be accepted and popular."
        - Prevention of being abandoned becomes concretely linked with attractiveness, which is linked with thinness: "If I'm thin, I won't get dumped."
        - Being perfect becomes linked with being pretty, which is linked with eating cleanly: "Being fat is wrong, and eating right is good."
        - Being lovable becomes linked with thinness: "If I'm thin, I will be desired and lovable."
        - Being a target for sexual abuse becomes linked with attractive fatty breast tissue: "If I am attractive, then I will get abused, so I just want to fade into the background."
        - Regarding gender dysphoria...
            - Having fatty breast tissue could trigger gender dysphoria because it is experienced as more feminine. Alternatively, having less breast tissue could lessen the experience of gender dysphoria (that is, via negative reinforcement).
            - Having a lack of muscles could trigger gender dysphoria because it is experienced as less masculine. Alternatively, having more muscle mass could lessen gender dysphoria (that is, via negative reinforcement).
    - Further, for some patients, we theorize that some linked emotions (or negative emotional states) can be particularly difficult to directly mitigate or control through means currently available to the patient. For a few examples:
        - *Fear of being attractive to a predator*: Particularly in the context of past trauma, it is difficult to learn to feel safe from predators in the environment.
        - *Gender dysphoria*: As a child or adolescent, it can be difficult to gain access to means of decreasing gender dysphoria (such as gender confirmation procedures), or one can be born into a specific culture that is hostile to any expression of being nonbinary (such as cutting hair short).

1. Fear of fatness and weight gain is the common emotional bedrock of eating disorders.

    - The primary function of most eating disorder behaviors is experiential avoidance of fear of fatness and weight gain.

2. Engaging in food restriction and food avoidance can provide the person with...

- Internal negative reinforcement = reduction in fear of fatness and weight gain

- Internal positive reinforcement = elevation in positive emotions (such as a feeling of accomplishment)

- Social negative reinforcement = reduction in negative social comments (about eating junk food, for example)

- Social positive reinforcement = elevation in positive social comments (such as praise for "healthy" eating)

3. Person becomes physically hungry and/or craves food, which serves as an eating prompt.

4. Some variant on the following belief exists: "If I eat food, I will be fat."

5. In the absence of eating essential foods and judging them negatively, food preoccupation occurs:

- Food-related thought suppression—that is, an active attempt to avoid thinking about food—occurs. This can be conceptualized as experiential avoidance of the negative internal experiences that accompany thinking about food or eating.

- Rather than eating, the person may also engage in experiential avoidance through food obsession (for example, ruminating about food or looking at pictures of food), which produces the positive reinforcement (that is, rewarding experience) of thinking about food without the calories.

6. Stressful outside events and negative emotions can destabilize a person putting energy toward food restriction and food avoidance.

7. The behavior of eating occurs because a person...

- Engages in binge eating, which provides temporary reduction in negative emotions and sensations (that is, negative reinforcement; for example, anxiety and hunger) as well as positive experiences (that is, positive reinforcement; for example, exhilaration and eating forbidden foods) because with any combination of these factors, the person...

  ○ Cannot maintain rigid dietary restraint.

  ○ May be physically very hungry.

- Simply must eat eventually for sustenance.

  ○ Provides temporary internal negative and positive reinforcement.

8. A physical feeling of fullness occurs.

9. Thoughts about being "fat" occur.

10. Distorted perception of seeing and proprioceptively feeling oneself as "fatter" occurs.

11. Regardless of any evolutionarily adaptive positive reinforcement felt from eating, because of an intense baseline fear of "fatness," the negative emotions of anxiety, guilt, disgust, and so forth increase after the behavior of eating.

12. For some, an intolerance behavior occurs (for example, purging, exercising, vowing to restrict, and so forth) to decrease aversive internal experiences such as negative emotions (that is, negative reinforcement) and/or to produce a feeling of being "high" (that is, positive reinforcement).

13. The thought *I will not gain weight* occurs.

14. Distorted perception of seeing and proprioceptively feeling oneself as "thinner" occurs.

15. If the patient ever loses weight or perceives that they have lost weight, the collective eating disorder behaviors are reinforced along with an entrenchment of the belief system.

16. The collective eating disorder behaviors are reinforced because of multiple and varied opportunities for reinforcement. The maintaining of an intense fear of "fatness" and weight gain occurs primarily through the reinforcement provided by weight loss, food restriction and avoidance, intolerance behaviors, and binge eating.

- As for linked emotions, if they are in play for a person, they can also become mitigated and reinforced, to some extent, through the eating disorder. Therefore, the eating disorder serves the function of fostering experiential avoidance of linked emotions.

0. Linked Emotions

For many (but not all) people, we conceptualize eating disorders as having two important emotional components at the foundation:

1. A universal *fear* of "fatness" as well as fear of weight gain

2. *Other emotions* linked to fear of "fatness" through associations that are specific to the individual

"Fatness" is not terrifying in itself. Therefore, it often means something specific to an individual. For instance, a given person may fear abandonment and, as a result, fear that "fatness" would result in abandonment. In this case, fear of abandonment would be considered to be an emotion linked to fear of "fatness." In short, linked emotions are those that a person has come to associate with fear of "fatness." Therefore, such eating disorder behaviors as restricting food intake may serve the function of avoiding a linked emotion in addition to avoiding the fear of "fatness."

It is very important to note that not everyone needs to have linked emotions. Because not everyone will have linked emotions and they are individual to the patient, they are labeled here and in figure I.6 with the number 0. In practice, clinicians should explore the possibility of linked emotions with patients at the start of treatment when conceptualizing the case; however, if linked emotions do not appear to be present, the investigation should be terminated. Clinicians coming from models where the thinking is that eating disorders exist only if there is a deeper reason may run the risk of searching, for instance, for trauma that never happened. This invariably has the effect of very much invalidating the many patients with eating disorders with no such history. It is important to check in a routine manner for the presence of linked emotions so that an accurate conceptualization can be formed and exposure exercises crafted, but not to press the issue if nothing emerges.

Further, it may also be the case that the patient does have linked emotions but is not disclosing them at the start of treatment. This is OK. As the saying goes, Rome was not built in a day. It is the patient's prerogative to disclose what they wish when they are ready. It is not 100 percent necessary to have a perfect conceptualization at the start of treatment, particularly in respect to linked emotions. Regarding trauma, one study (Brewerton, 2007) found that 37 percent of outpatients with eating disorders had co-occurring post-traumatic stress disorder (PTSD), by comparison with 12 percent of patients without eating disorders—a statistically significant difference. As for the reporting of traumatic events, as distinct from a diagnosis of PTSD, an earlier study (Gleaves, Eberenz, & May, 1998) had found that 74 percent of people hospitalized with eating disorders reported traumatic events. The incidence of trauma has significance, but it must be noted that not every person with an eating disorder has a history of trauma. When people do not have trauma, we should not go looking for something that is not there. When people do have trauma, it must be treated in due course.

In regard to trauma and the treatment of eating disorders specifically, eating disorders are life-threatening, and resources are often limited, and so the clinician can be faced with a choice between treating either the eating disorder or any *linked* (not necessarily *underlying*) trauma. In this situation, a triage mentality must be employed, and the physical threat that the eating disorder poses may very well need to be neutralized first. The treatment of the eating disorder should use behavior therapy techniques to directly target behaviors that interfere with the patient's health. Treating trauma eventually is extremely important for the person, of course. Such treatment is also very likely to be an important component of long-term recovery from the eating disorder.

1. Fear of "Fatness" and Weight Gain

Although each individual patient will have a different set of linked emotions, the common emotional bedrock among eating disorders is fear of "fatness" and weight gain. Because fear of "fatness" and weight gain is shared among people with eating disorders, it is the number one component of the functional conceptualization. Research conducted by Deliberto, Jacobs, Novak, Grabicki, et al. (2013) suggests that experiential avoidance of this fear is an extremely important component underlying such eating disorder behaviors as food avoidance, food-related thought suppression, and binge eating. Moreover, heretofore unpublished research by one of the coauthors of this manual (Tara Deliberto) highlights the importance of conceptualizing the experiential avoidance of fear of "fatness" and weight gain as the common cornerstone among eating disorders. In view of this conceptualization, all eating disorder behaviors, thoughts, thought processes, perceptions, and internal experiences are subsumed under the umbrella of experiential avoidance of fear of "fatness" and weight gain. Each individual patient will present with a slight variant of these eating disorder–related internal experiences, but they can all be conceptualized as serving the primary purpose of avoiding this particular negative emotion.

2. Food Restriction and Food Avoidance

Given this framework, the behavior of food restriction and food avoidance occurs in an effort to experientially avoid fear of "fatness" and weight gain along with other aversive experiences (such as physically feeling full) and linked emotions. Food restriction and food avoidance, once engaged in, provide four different types of reinforcement:

1. *Internal negative reinforcement:* reduction in the negative emotion of fear of "fatness" and weight gain

2. *Internal positive reinforcement:* a sense of internal satisfaction (achieved through "dieting")

3. *Social negative reinforcement:* removal of negative social comments (no more food-shaming)

4. *Social positive reinforcement:* increase in positive social comments ("Good job eating healthy")

Over the longer term, after any food restriction and avoidance behavior has been reinforced either internally and/or socially, a person simply learns that this behavior is "good." Over time, the eating disorder behavior also becomes ego-syntonic, and the patient has difficulty understanding why this behavior, which has been so reinforced, is suddenly considered maladaptive. In this theoretical framework, it stands to reason that once an eating disorder is in place, social messaging about dieting, and so forth, likely contributes to further reinforcement of eating disorder behaviors.

3. Hunger and Craving

Shortly after engaging in food restriction and food avoidance behavior, people may have some degree of physical hunger and/or craving, which serves as a prompt for eating.

4. Judgments About Food

Considering the context of baseline fear of "fatness" and weight gain, negative judgments about food and eating exist. These negative judgments are connected to "fatness." Some variant on the thought *If I eat food, I will be fat* is triggered.

5. Thought Processes: Ironic Processing and Obsessing

From here, one or both of the cognitive processes relating to food preoccupation will be triggered:

1. Food-related thought suppression

2. Food obsession

Because thinking about food may trigger anxiety, people may make active attempts to avoid thinking about food. This process is called *food-related thought suppression* (Barnes & Tantleff-Dunn, 2010). As the person attempts to experientially avoid both eating and even thinking about food, thoughts about food increase in frequency and intensity (Deliberto, Jacobs, Novak, Grabicki, et al., 2013). For instance, thoughts about that apple pie in the refrigerator might pop into someone's mind twenty times in the span of fifteen minutes. On the surface, this behavior appears to be obsessive, but we think it more clearly falls under the category of food-related thought suppression. Often, however, food-related thought suppression can be the driving force toward food-obsessive behaviors. For instance, one may try to prevent oneself from thinking about the apple pie but end up looking at food-related social media accounts for two hours.

Because actually eating would trigger a host of aversive internal experiences, food obsession (for example, watching online videos of other people eating) can be selected as an alternative behavior (Polivy, 1996; Franklin, Schiele., Brozek, & Keys, 1948). This choice produces the rewarding internal experience (internal positive reinforcement) of thinking about food without the need to feel anxious.

6. Negative Emotions and Outside Events

The eating disorder also sets up strong urges to binge eat through the culmination of restricting food and being hungry, avoiding specific foods and craving them, preoccupation with food through thought suppression and obsession, and generally putting monumental amounts of energy into avoiding food. Under these circumstances, if any sort of negative emotion occurs as a result of an event in the environment (such as a fight with a friend), a person may not be able to continue putting energy toward the eating disorder behaviors.

7. Behavior: Eating or Binge Eating

A binge may help reduce the current negative physical, cognitive, and emotional experiences (via negative reinforcement) with food. For research on the causal relationship between food restriction and binge eating, read the work of Polivy (see, for example, Polivy & Herman, 1985; Polivy, 1998; Polivy & Herman, 2002; Polivy, Coleman, & Herman, 2005). Eating is felt as a release from all the restrictive rules of the eating disorder and can be a pleasant experience, providing internal positive reinforcement. This relief is short-lived, however, and the chain of eating disorder events can continue. Binge eating does not necessarily have to occur for these events to continue similarly. Over time, a person with an eating disorder, just like anyone else, needs to eat. The consequences of even a non–eating disorder episode of eating often still prove difficult for people with eating disorders in the context of having intense fears of "fatness" and weight gain. For instance, a person with an eating disorder can have a normal lunch with a friend but may feel guilt afterward and engage in subsequent eating disorder behaviors.

8. Physical Feeling of Fullness

Following the behavior of either eating or binge eating, or simply eating, a physical sensation of fullness occurs. This fullness is often interpreted by the eating disorder as instantly "gaining weight."

9. Thoughts About Being "Fat"

Rigid thoughts about being "fat" occur.

10. Perception: Seeing and Physically Feeling Oneself as "Fatter"

Further, the patient perceives that they have gained weight. Many patients report visually seeing themselves as having "gained weight," or they proprioceptively "feel" that they have "gained weight."

11. Anxiety, Guilt, and Disgust

Intense feelings of anxiety, guilt, and disgust occur. Note that patients have very little willingness to tolerate these negative emotions at the start of treatment. Because there is a strong belief that eating is "bad," there is also a belief that one should have these helpful negative emotions. Therefore, there is a belief that negative emotions are justified and helpful for the purpose of weight loss.

12. Intolerance Behaviors

In the context of aversive internal experiences (physically feeling full, thoughts about being "fat," proprioceptively feeling oneself as "fatter," having negative emotions, and so forth), combined with the ever-present fear of "fatness," the patient may engage in intolerance behaviors (purging, exercise, vowing to restrict, and so forth). These are negatively reinforcing (that is, the behaviors reduce these aversive experiences).

These behaviors can be particularly compulsive and dangerous in nature. Often the patient has little to no awareness that these behaviors are unhealthy. In fact, at times these behaviors can be life-threatening and still be viewed as healthy by the patient. Therefore, education about the dangerous nature of these behaviors must be provided (Belak et al., 2017). Patients can feel panicked after eating and may have a sense of urgency around needing to get rid of the calories, "or else." This fuels the intense desire to do something in order to feel better. These behaviors, if engaged in, decrease the negative emotions prompted by eating (negative reinforcement). Regardless of whether a given episode of purging is actually effective at immediately eliminating calories consumed, this dangerous intolerance behavior *is* effective at providing reinforcement. In addition to being negatively reinforcing by providing relief from intense negative emotions, intolerance behaviors also are positively reinforcing. For instance, just as runners often report feeling a high, patients often report a similar sort of feeling after purging.

13. Thought: I Will Not Gain Weight

Patients may also believe that, after an intolerance behavior, they can no longer gain weight from the food eaten.

14. Perception: Seeing and Feeling Oneself as "Thinner"

After an intolerance behavior, there may also be a visual and proprioceptive perception that one is "thinner," even though physically this cannot be possible. In this framework, this perception may be very reinforcing of the intolerance behavior.

15. Collective Eating Disorder Behaviors and Beliefs

If weight is actually lost, or is perceived to have been lost, the collective eating disorder behaviors that have been engaged in are also reinforced:

1. *Internal negative reinforcement:* reduction in negative emotions and self-assessment ("I'm not fat")

2. *Internal positive reinforcement:* elevation in positive emotions and self-assessment ("I look good")

3. *Social negative reinforcement:* reduction in negative social attention (patient is no longer bullied about weight)

4. *Social positive reinforcement:* elevation in positive social attention (patient receives increased romantic attention)

16. Reinforcement of Collective Eating Disorder Behaviors

They are reinforced because of the multiple and varied opportunities for reinforcement that eating disorder behaviors provide. The maintaining of an intense fear of "fatness" and weight gain occurs primarily through the reinforcement provided by weight loss, food restriction and avoidance, intolerance behaviors, and binge eating.

As for linked emotions, if they are in play for a person, then they, too, to some extent, can become mitigated and reinforced by the eating disorder. Therefore, the eating disorder serves the function of fostering the experiential avoidance of linked emotions.

Further, eating disorder beliefs are left unchallenged. Through the felt reduction in aversive experiences and other types of reinforcement, the belief system and the associative network around the notion that weight gain is "bad" are fortified. For instance, the following associative pathway can be strengthened: *I literally feel better when I weigh less; therefore, weighing less must be good, and weighing more must be bad.*

From this perspective, given the impact of reinforcement on eating disorder behaviors and beliefs, it is extremely important to have a functional understanding of eating disorder behaviors and to be able to implement interventions targeting these functions.

TIP: A LITTLE GUILT AFTER AN INTOLERANCE BEHAVIOR MAY NOT BE A BAD SIGN

If a patient initiates a self-report of guilt after an intolerance behavior, this may actually suggest that the patient is aware that the behavior is destructive and/or dangerous. In this framework, an appropriate degree of experienced and freely communicated guilt has the potential to interrupt the reinforcement of the intolerance behavior. Of course, a patient should never be made to feel guilty for engaging in such behavior. Further, if the patient takes a self-flagellating stance, this would be rather detrimental.

Functional Conceptualization of Eating Disorders and IMT Interventions

To ensure that an eating disorder is treated in a thorough behavioral manner from all angles, the various components of the IMT interventions across therapeutic modalities are intended to address the aforementioned areas of the functional conceptualization of eating disorders that are common transdiagnostically (that is, the areas represented by numbers 1 through 15).

Therapy for Linked Emotions

Later in treatment, linked emotions can be partially addressed with BAE interventions. It is largely beyond the scope of this manual to discuss therapy for linked emotions at any length, but we can make the following recommendations:

- Linked emotions (such as fear of imperfection), that can be targeted with imaginal exposures from the BAE material should addressed in the context of eating disorder treatment.

- If linked emotions exist as a result of trauma, then trauma-focused cognitive behavioral therapy (Cohen, Mannarino, & Debliner, 2012) is recommended once health has been stabilized from the eating disorder and/ or perhaps once the eating disorder has remitted.

- If gender dysphoria is present, we recommend addressing it directly with specialized care. We also recommend that patients explore the *Gender Quest Workbook* (Testa, Coolhart, & Peta, 2015).

- External referrals (to dialectical behavior therapy, for example) are sometimes needed when a comorbid diagnosis is related to linked emotions (as when fear of abandonment is also related to borderline personality disorder).

Functional Conceptualization and Etiology: Biology and Eating Disorders

In the context of the functional conceptualization of eating disorders, questions about initial onset of eating disorders may arise. There is evidence that the onset of an eating disorder, like the onset of any other kind of disorder, can be attributed to biological factors (genetics, neurobiology, temperament, and so forth) as well as to environmental factors. In the area of biology, much interesting work has elucidated the genetic underpinnings of these disorders (Klump et al., 2001; Mazzeo & Bulik, 2009), their epigenetic mechanisms (Frieling et. al., 2010), and factors related to temperament (Bulik, Sullivan, Weltzin, & Kaye, 1995). The biological aspect of eating disorders' etiology is largely beyond the scope of this behavioral manual, but we also refer you to Hill and Dagg (2012).

Externalization and Etiology

Readers familiar with the treatment of eating disorders will be accustomed to the concept that the eating disorder is external to or outside the person. In regard to thinking of the eating disorder as *actually* being separate from the person, as clinicians we find it helpful to think of the eating disorder more deeply, in terms of its being a *neurobiologically based habit circuit* that is set off in the brain by a combination of external beliefs and learning history, a habit circuit whose onset, associated beliefs, and learning history are all influenced by genetics. Therefore, we conceptualize an eating disorder as a culminating outcome of four factors:

1. A person's unknowing acceptance of toxic beliefs from the environment

2. The person's acquisition (via trauma, and so forth) of learned associations with "fatness"

3. The formation of habit circuits in the person's brain

4. The hardwired genetic components of the person's brain and temperament

In this way, the eating disorder actually *is* something like an external force that becomes internalized and expressed. As clinicians, we have experienced interactions with patients who had eating disorders and who later recovered, and it certainly *feels* as if an eating disorder is an external entity that inhabits a person's mind. The contrast is quite striking between a person with an active eating disorder and a person who has recovered.

Regarding the Environment's Role and Implications

From this perspective, *the person with the eating disorder is not at fault for the development of the disorder, nor is anyone else. We take a nonjudgmental stance toward the patient and everyone else involved.* If the patient is not to blame for unknowingly having accepted toxic beliefs, then who is to blame? No one is to blame. We can't know why one person develops an eating disorder and another does not. What we do know, however, is that biological factors such as a child's genetics and temperament play a role in the onset of the eating disorder. Therefore, a given family member simply cannot *cause* an eating disorder. There is a much larger set of factors at work.

But what about the contribution that the environment *does* make to the onset of an eating disorder? So many people have unknowingly accepted toxic beliefs about "fatness" and accepted them as facts that *no one person is at fault*. To blame one person's toxic beliefs about "fatness" for influencing the development of an eating disorder is to be myopic and miss the mark. This is particularly the case where carers are concerned, given the sad history of blaming parents for the development of eating disorders. Not only is it false to say that carers are to blame, it is also neither effective nor compassionate to focus on persecuting a treatment ally. We must have compassion for *anyone* who has detrimental beliefs about "fatness." People who hold such beliefs may very well benefit from education themselves, and as they do, they become people with healthy attitudes toward "fatness" who can contribute to the stabilization of the larger emotional ecosystem.

Thankfully, not everyone develops an eating disorder, even though the environment is so toxic, and science is helping to elucidate the characteristics of those who do develop eating disorders. It is becoming clearer that biology and genetics play a role in the onset of eating disorders. At the same time, however, we cannot discount the role of the larger toxic environment in which we all take part. Fat-shaming, objectification, and reinforcement for dieting behaviors are all too common. Because our collective environment is so toxic, we must all work together and do our part to fortify the emotional ecosystem.

Core Behavioral Concepts

In addition to the behaviors outlined in the functional conceptualization of eating disorders, we must discuss two more types of behaviors that are key to the treatment of eating disorders:

1. Eating disorder–protecting behaviors

2. Eating disorder–exacerbating behaviors

Eating Disorder–Protecting Behaviors

As mentioned earlier, people with eating disorders experience intense negative emotions, which include but are not limited to fear of "fatness" and weight gain, guilt, and disgust. Once the eating disorder is in place, behaviors such as food restriction, food avoidance, purging, calorie counting, compulsive exercise, and so forth, serve to decrease these negative emotions temporarily.

Probably because these behaviors are so effective at reducing negative emotions, it quickly becomes apparent in treatment that patients are resistant to change when they are pushed to meet treatment goals. Patients display behaviors that serve to protect the eating disorder from treatment. More specifically, patients display behaviors that block reinforcement of recovery-oriented and non–eating disorder behaviors. For instance, after a patient finishes a meal, the therapist may say, "Good job finishing the meal," to which the patient may respond, "I *hate you* when you say that." The therapist's "good job" remark was intended to reinforce the patient's recovery-oriented behavior, but patients with ego-syntonic (self-eclipsing) eating disorders often react rather aggressively to the tried-and-true behavioral intervention of providing praise (see "Self-Eclipsing Versus Self-Acknowledged Disorders," later in this general introduction). From this perspective, the emotional escalation is interpreted as an effort to block reinforcement of the meal completion, in service of protecting the eating disorder. If the eating disorder is protected, the person is also protected from feeling all the negative emotions that the eating disorder regulates (fear of weight gain, guilt after eating, disgust with one's body, and so forth). We have even heard patients say, "If you keep saying 'good job,' it will make me fat."

Eating Disorder–Exacerbating Behaviors

Just as eating disorder–protecting behaviors involve the deflection of recovery-fostering reinforcement, and therefore block progress in treatment, other types of behaviors appear to actively exacerbate the eating disorder. In particular, we have noted a disturbing phenomenon in the context of eating disorders—namely, patients asking for others to body-shame them about their weight. Specifically, patients report seeking out abusive comments about their body as "motivation" to further restrict caloric intake, avoid foods, exercise, and engage in other eating disorder behaviors. For instance, on pro-anorexia (pro-ana) websites, people can post pictures of themselves and ask others to "guess" their weight in a mean-spirited way. Other participants in the forum will then intentionally "guess" clearly higher weights. There is even a term for this, *meanspo*, which is a variant on the more popular *thinspiration* (*thinspo*) or fitspiration (*fitspo*). The latter two terms are certainly maladaptive, but thinspo or fitspo content is not as disparaging and abusive as meanspo content is. *Do not introduce these terms to patients, because they may look them up and start engaging in these behaviors or participating in online meanspo forums.* Further, introducing the specific term *meanspo* to carers may also be unwise, because some carers may discuss this term with the patient. It is best to avoid introducing this term into any conversation in which the patient hasn't used it first.

From a behavioral perspective, actively soliciting abusive statements to fuel eating disorder "motivation" is particularly insidious. It represents the seeking out of reinforcement for the maladaptive behaviors, distorted beliefs, and perhaps even perceptions that comprise the eating disorder. Therefore, we refer to the behavioral seeking out of feedback that reinforces eating disorder behaviors, thoughts, and potentially perceptions as *eating disorder–exacerbating behaviors* (EDEBs). EDEBs also include intentionally tricking "oneself" into proprioceptively perceiving oneself to be physically larger than one is. For instance, a patient may wear extremely tight clothing, which produces the physical feeling of being "fat," and in this way the patient may be miscalibrating their proprioceptive awareness of the body. Other examples of how patients may alter proprioceptive awareness is to drink fluids in order to feel "fat" or weigh themselves on a scale that is skewed toward numbers that are higher than accurate.

In this model, the active seeking out of reinforcement for eating disorder behaviors is viewed as particularly toxic. Therefore, if these behaviors are occurring, we strongly encourage carers to set parental controls on all electronic devices to block the eating disorder from receiving reinforcement in the form of meanspo on social media, pro-ana websites, pro-bulimia (pro-mia) websites, and the like. It is important for the therapist to concretely follow up on this issue with carers by asking to view parental controls, for instance. Again, it is important to keep in mind that the main goal of this treatment is to eliminate the eating disorder while increasing the adolescent's sense of self and agency.

Reinforcement of Perception

We theorize that the process of soliciting body shaming may reinforce not only maladaptive eating disorder behaviors but also distorted beliefs, as per relational frame theory (Hayes 1991; Törneke, 2010). Further, we theorize that *perceptual disturbances*, as in visually seeing and proprioceptively feeling oneself as "fatter," may be behaviorally shaped, at least in part, through reinforcement as well.

It is not a perfect analogy, but the process of soliciting body shaming may be somewhat akin to asking someone to set all the clocks in your house ahead so as to trick yourself into being on time. With the clocks all set several minutes forward, you're tricked into perceiving the current time as being several minutes in the future. Behaviorally, this translates into leaving the house at a time that would result in your being early rather than late for meetings. Similarly, if a person solicits disparaging remarks about their body fat, that person may learn to perceive their current size as larger than it is, given the feedback coming from the environment. This may result in a visual misperception of reality and may fuel eating disorder behaviors.

We theorize that in order for anorexia nervosa to be exacerbated, perception may necessarily be distorted over time so that the person continues to see themselves as "fat" even as weight decreases. Without the continual distortion of perception, such that the person sees themselves as "fat" over time, regardless of actual weight, the person might just be able to lose some weight and experience reinforcement for the weight loss, and that would be the end of it. But a continually distorted perception may drive the engine of anorexia nervosa forward. Further, because behaviors in anorexia nervosa are reinforcing by nature but *also* extremely aversive (starvation, fatigue, extreme exercise, vomiting), this miscalibration in perception may be a necessary condition for the compulsivity to continue. In other words, anorexia nervosa *requires* the distorted perception to persist. To maintain a fear of "fatness" when one's weight is objectively low, one must continue to experience distorted beliefs about weight that are inconsistent with reality. When distorted perception exists in disorders other than anorexia nervosa, it stands to reason that this perception may have also been reinforced and may underlie compulsive behaviors.

Relational frame theory, simply described, posits that just as behaviors can be reinforced, thoughts (or associations) can be reinforced. As we view our theory, *perception* can also be reinforced as an extension of relational frame theory. Nevertheless, because this is currently just a theory, broad research in this area is needed. Specifically, we strongly encourage researchers to examine the effect of reinforcement on one's perceptual experience of one's body.

Self-Eclipsing Versus Self-Acknowledged Disorders

The terms *self-eclipsing* and *self-acknowledged* are used to refer broadly to different *classes* of disorders. Within the class of self-eclipsing disorders, each person will have a different degree of eclipsed self. Further, without evaluation, a disorder cannot be classified as either self-eclipsing or self-acknowledged. There may be types of disorders (such as eating disorders) that tend to be self-eclipsing, but disorders need to be evaluated on a case-by-case basis. For instance, one person can have a self-eclipsed version of bulimia nervosa, and another can have a self-acknowledged version. Over time, a disorder can also shift from having a self-eclipsing quality to having a self-acknowledged quality. In treatment, when behaviors begin to remit, the self begins to emerge, the disorder can become acknowledged by the self, and the self can find motivation to recover. Therefore, a disorder moving over time from being self-eclipsing to being self-acknowledged is favorable.

Ego-Syntonic Disorders Reimagined

An informal class of disorders described as *ego-syntonic* warrants discussion here. Although there are formal Freudian descriptions of the term *ego-syntonic* with specific theoretical implications, the term has been co-opted by behavior therapists in practice to describe disorders that are characterized by the following four phenomena:

1. *A belief that the behaviors should be performed:* "Regardless of my current weight, I should attempt to lose more weight through restriction and purging."

2. *An apparent intention to continue performing eating disorder behaviors:* "I want to keep running fifteen miles a day. You can't stop me."

3. *Inability to recognize functional impairment and ramifications of the disorder:* "My doctor is overreacting. She says I'm at risk for a heart attack, but I'm not."

4. *Marked lack of insight:* "I don't care what my treatment team says. I don't have an eating disorder."

One manifestation of the ego-syntonic nature of eating disorders is the pro-ana online community, which touts anorexia nervosa as a lifestyle. Ego-syntonia goes beyond merely lacking motivation to actively work on ameliorating the disorder. There is a quality to ego-syntonia of the person believing that maladaptive behaviors are positive and desirable. In fact, people with ego-syntonic disorders reject the idea that they have a disorder at all and are notoriously unlikely to seek treatment. Facts regarding functional impairment are also rejected. In the case of eating disorders, a portion of a person's functional impairment is objectively measurable in the form of weight, growth chart height, lab results, and so forth. But this objective data is not recognized by a person with an ego-syntonic eating disorder. The evidence is dismissed because it is inconsistent with the belief that the eating disorder behaviors are healthy and positive. The rejection of objective data regarding the negative impact of the disorder, accompanied by severe lack of insight regarding one's illness, is known as *anosognosia*.

The term *ego-syntonic* is widely used in practice by clinicians. Nevertheless, because of the formal definition's lack of behavioral specificity, we choose instead to say that eating disorders are *self-eclipsing*. We have chosen the term *self-eclipsing* because in this conceptualization, a healthy self with an adaptive set of values (related, for example, to health, family, friends, and school) exists separately from the eating disorder, which has its own set of maladaptive values (such as thinness). The nature of the eating disorder is such that it prevents a person from making a connection with an adaptive set of values. Therefore, the disorder has eclipsed the person's self and subverted their ability to act in accordance with preexisting adaptive values. In fact, the disorder causes a person to engage in an obsessive thought process regarding a maladaptive value (thinness) and engage in compulsive behaviors (such as maladaptive "committed actions" like restriction and purging) in line with that value. The term *self-eclipsing*, as we use it to describe eating disorders, is consistent with the depiction in family-based treatment of the eating disorder covering the person (Lock et al., 2001), and the rationale for this coinage where values are concerned is influenced by acceptance and commitment therapy (Luoma et al., 2007).

As a person emerges from the self-eclipsing disorder, maladaptive values and associated compulsive behaviors are abandoned, and the ability to connect with pre–eating disorder adaptive values is presented. Once a person is able to cite their preexisting values (health, creativity, and so forth), they are able to commit to taking action in line with those values (eating a healthy amount of food, painting, and so forth). Before a person is able to connect with an adaptive set of preexisting values, it is not feasible to expect that they will be able to start behaving in line with those values. It is difficult enough to behave in line with one's values when they are all adaptive. For instance, if one values self-care, it can still be hard to find time for oneself. Just imagine how little self-care one would engage in if it were not currently valued at all and if thinness were the only thing that mattered.

The degree to which any given person's disorder eclipses the self changes over time. Further, each given patient with a self-eclipsing disorder will have a different degree of eclipsed self. Not everyone with an eating disorder comes into treatment with a self that is completely and utterly eclipsed. Therefore, the concept of a self-eclipsing disorder includes the four phenomena already listed in connection with ego-syntonia (belief that eating disorder behaviors should be performed, apparent intention to continue the behaviors, inability to recognize one's functional impairment and the disorder's ramifications, and severe lack of insight) in addition to the understanding that everyone with a self-eclipsing disorder will display varying degrees of these behavioral phenomena.

A Note on Language In our conceptualization of an eating disorder, the person's *self* is being *eclipsed* by the disorder. At the same time, it is still the person with the eating disorder who is visibly enacting the behaviors that are being driven by the eating disorder. The person with the eating disorder is the person who is visibly displaying eating disorder behaviors. This person, not anyone else in the world, is the identified person with the eating disorder. Therefore, although we understand that the behavior is being driven by the eating disorder, in this manual we refer to the behavior as "the patient's behavior" or "the patient's eating disorder behavior." Because this is a behavioral family manual intended for therapists, it is imperative that we verbally explain who is displaying the behaviors. But to observe and state that a particular person is enacting a behavior—a behavior driven by the eating disorder—is not in any way to imply blame or fault. It is simply to make an observation. In this manual, the phrase "the patient's behavior" should always be understood as implying that the eating disorder is driving the behavior displayed by the patient. In the material for carers, however, this behavior is referred to as "eating disorder behavior."

Ego-Dystonic Disorders Reimagined

Not only is there utility in reimagining ego-syntonic disorders as self-eclipsing, it is also important to behaviorally conceptualize *ego-dystonic* disorders. Instead of using the term *ego-dystonic*, in this manual we use the term *self-acknowledged*. A self-acknowledged disorder is one characterized by the person's awareness of functional impairment and by the ability to express a relatively stronger desire for the disorder not to be present than for it to endure. Most disorders that clinicians in training learn to treat (anxiety disorders, depression, and so forth) are in this category.

Treating Self-Eclipsing Eating Disorders

Why is it so crucial to distinguish behaviorally between self-eclipsing and self-acknowledged disorders? Although broadening our conceptual understanding of the former term is important in itself, it serves a larger purpose in this manual. It has been our experience that many therapists find it difficult to understand why others must take control of food in the treatment of severe eating disorders. For instance, one of the coauthors (Tara Deliberto) once ran a workshop attended by thirty therapists with experience treating eating disorders, but only two reported having training in working with people with anorexia nervosa, the more notoriously ego-syntonic (or, in this conceptualization, self-eclipsing) disorder. These clinicians and others have also been quite resistant to the suggestion that carers should take control of food. This reaction has made it apparent that a deeper understanding of the behavioral rationale for this type of family therapy is needed. The concept of self-eclipsing disorders is key to that rationale.

Conceptualizing Recovery

In addition to conceptualizing how eating disorders impact a given individual, it is important to conceptualize the path to recovery. From this model, the overall goal of treatment is not simply to decrease eating disorder behaviors but to increase recovery behaviors and adaptive skill implementation.

For Clinicians

It is the role of the eating disorder behavior therapist to set up a framework for the patient in which healthy reinforcement is occurring. First, it is important to block eating disorder–exacerbating behaviors, or the active seeking out of reinforcement for behaviors, beliefs, and perhaps perceptions that comprise the eating disorder. Second, eating disorder–protecting behaviors must be circumvented and reduced so that appropriate reinforcement can be directly targeted at increasing the frequency of recovery behaviors. Once the eating disorder's protection against healthy reinforcement is weakened, targeted and steady reinforcement of recovery behaviors, reaffirmation of healthy beliefs, and provision of feedback about accurate perceptions must be put into place. From this theoretical framework, reinforcement from the environment (therapists and carers) is internalized over time until the patient is self-reinforcing, engaging in recovery behaviors, and ultimately using skills to cope with the negative emotions lying at the center of the eating disorder—fear of "fatness," disgust, guilt, and any related linked emotions.

For Patients and Carers

Because it is also important for the patient and carers to understand the path to recovery, several handouts are aimed at clarifying this. For instance, RAE Handout 4: The Road to Recovery from an Eating Disorder, in the individual therapy modality, depicts a sequence of events similar to a chain analysis in dialectical behavior therapy, with the difference that the subject of analysis is not a maladaptive behavior but an *adaptive* behavior. In this way, the building blocks to recovery are elucidated. Further, all handouts including tables that show eating disorder behaviors in the left-hand column and recovery behaviors in the right-hand column provide explicit information about adaptive counterparts to eating disorder behavior. In addition, all IMT measures relevant to treatment modalities are aimed at providing the patient with clear adaptive objectives relevant to the modality administered. This is intended to help patients and carers with setting intentions to focus their efforts on specific goals. Observing progress toward these goals over time is also reinforcing.

Acceptance That Recovery Is Inevitable

The concept of what we call *inevitability acceptance* is core to the IMT philosophy. Inevitability acceptance is coming to terms with the fact that the eating disorder is a destructive force that is incompatible with living a full and healthy life, and that one must therefore recover or else face severely negative consequences. Over time, the eating disorder becomes increasingly exhausting and consuming, to the point where nothing else matters. The eating disorder causes not only social, educational, and professional dysfunction—with ramifications for oneself and others—but also bodily harm and potentially death. Although the eating disorder seems as if it solves problems, it actually creates many more of them for oneself (and loved ones). Even though thinking about recovery is tough, it only gets harder to recover over time. There is no better time than the present to start working actively on recovery. Because the alternatives to *not* recovering are so severe, one comes to terms with accepting the inevitability of recovering.

Technically, a person could continue down the destructive eating disorder path. Focusing on that potential outcome misses the mark, however. The concept of inevitability acceptance is not to be interpreted literally but used *functionally*. Adopting an adaptive attitude that one *must* and *can* recover, because the alternative is not feasible, can foster an initial willingness to participate in treatment. Particularly because ambivalence about recovery is so common in this population, we view inevitability acceptance as important, at a foundational level, to building motivation for future treatment.

This concept is woven into the interventions in all three therapy modalities. Therapists are also encouraged to work statements that reflect this concept into dialogue with patients. Here are some examples of such statements:

- Having an eating disorder is very difficult. Eating is necessary for survival. Feeling negative emotions after each time you eat can be compared to feeling negative emotions each time you take a breath. You can avoid inhaling for a little while in order to delay those feelings, but eventually you *have* to take a breath. Eating is no different. Because eating is an essential part of living, learning to confront negative emotions and manage them is necessary. Treatment can help with this. It can get much easier over time, and with practice.

- Eating disorders can kill. We have to work together to kill this before it kills you.

- Can you imagine yourself at ninety years old with an eating disorder? How about at seventy? If not, how will you recover between now and then? It doesn't just go away. After about fifty years of doing the same thing, it will be hard for you to just stop the disorder. And it can cause a lot of destruction from now until whatever age it is supposed to just go away on its own. Are you willing to risk all that living for the eating disorder? If not, we have to start working on recovery *now*.

The concept of inevitability acceptance is similar to the concept of creative hopelessness in the literature on acceptance and commitment therapy (Luoma et al., 2007) as well as to the "gift of desperation" from the Alcoholics Anonymous literature (Bill W., 2014). These concepts reflect that a person has been trying to get through life by using a particular strategy that simply is not working, and that a new way of doing things must now be adopted. Because of the specific nature of eating disorders, this concept has slightly different qualities from its predecessors. To start, anosognosia brings with it the accompanying beliefs that maladaptive behaviors are healthy and that food is unhealthy. Therefore, from within the eating disorder mind-set, not only is recovery aversive, but the person may also believe that it is *against* their best interests. As a result, an outside party (such as a therapist) typically fosters the idea that eating disorder behaviors are untenable over time, and that recovery is both necessary and inevitable. Because this notion is aversive from within the eating disorder mind-set, *acceptance* that one must recover is the other key aspect of this concept. Taken together, the terms *inevitability* and *acceptance* reflect the idea that acknowledging the need for recovery is difficult, but recovery is a necessary condition for leading a full and healthy life.

TIP: BELIEVE IN YOUR PATIENT'S ABILITY TO SUCCEED

By adopting the attitude that your patient's recovery is simply inevitable, you express inherent belief in your patient's potential. If you model the belief that your patient can do it, your patient may start to believe it, too. Go beyond not fragilizing the patient. Go a step farther by modeling confidence in your patient's inherent potential to succeed. As an eating disorder behavior therapist, it is important not only that you know how to reinforce recovery behaviors but also that you model faith in your patient's ability to tolerate all the internal experiences that come with recovering. People are tough and resilient. They can handle a lot more than the eating disorder lets on. It's paramount that you maintain an attitude that fosters recovery by encouraging your patient to confront the eating disorder.

PART 1

Individual Therapy Modality

Section 1.1

Introduction to the
Individual Therapy Modality

This part of the manual is dedicated to describing how to conduct one-on-one therapy with the IMT individual handouts. Special considerations pertaining to specific disorders and comorbidities are discussed. Information on suggested administration, the individual IMT measures, and essential IMT individual handouts is reviewed. A section on thinking like a behaviorist while treating eating disorders is also provided. The remainder of this part of the manual, comprising the IMT individual therapy modality, will focus on describing how to use each IMT individual handout in practice.

As explained in the general introduction to this book, the IMT individual therapy modality is split into two distinct sections: *regular and appetitive eating* (RAE), and *body acceptance and exposure* (BAE). All RAE and BAE handouts in both sections will be covered.

How to Use This Manual for IMT Individual Therapy

It is recommended that you read in linear fashion through the following material:

- The general introduction to this manual, if you have not done so already

- This portion of the manual, through section 1.7, which covers the RAE and BAE handouts

- All IMT individual handouts, including those for Regular Eating (RE) and Regular and Appetitive Eating (RAE); download at www.newharbinger.com/42235 (see page 303 for download details)

As you are reading through the IMT individual handouts, it will be helpful to use this clinician's manual as a reference guide for the administration of particular handouts.

Other Relevant Sections of This Manual

If you have not yet read the general introduction to this book, it is highly advisable to do so prior to proceeding. It covers essential topics such as the core treatment philosophy and which treatment modality to use with which diagnoses. Additionally, it is recommended that therapists read the introductory section to the family portion of this manual prior to providing care with the IMT individual interventions because it discusses concepts relevant to individual therapy (such as recovery-specific positive attention, managing behavioral outbursts in session, and so forth). Further, many adolescent patients in individual therapy may benefit from incorporating carers into treatment at some point. Therefore, familiarity with the IMT family handouts is important.

About the Individual Therapy Modality

This section provides a further explanation of regular and appetitive eating (RAE, pronounced "ray") and body acceptance and exposure (BAE, pronounced "bay") needed prior to administering the material. This section begins by providing a rationale for the particular ordering of the material in both RAE and BAE.

About RAE

Regular and appetitive eating combines the concepts of eating at regular intervals throughout the day and eating according to appetitive cues of hunger and fullness. Taking a broad view, the *regular* eating interventions are aimed at decreasing eating disorder behaviors through the establishment of routine. In a manner that complements this aim, the *appetitive* eating interventions are designed to provide the patient with adaptive alternative behaviors.

Regardless of diagnosis, decreasing the eating disorder behavior of food restriction—limiting the overall amount of food consumed—is the first treatment goal in RAE for all patients enrolled. (The caveat, however, is that all adolescents with anorexia nervosa, and many with atypical anorexia nervosa, are not eligible for this treatment until their health has been restored.) It is generally suggested here that patients eat three meals and two snacks per day. Once regular eating is established, as evidenced by the patient eating appropriately sized meals and snacks throughout the day, the eating disorder behavior of food avoidance, or avoiding specific types of foods (such as carbohydrates), can be addressed. Feared foods can be eaten in session as exposures as well as incorporated into meals at home. Taken together, decreasing food restriction is the primary goal of the *regular* portion of RAE, and decreasing food avoidance is the secondary goal.

The next major RAE component is the *appetitive* piece. Appetitive eating, or eating when hungry and stopping when full, is the next major treatment goal. In line with this larger goal, the first aim is to simply start to become mindfully aware of hunger and fullness. Over time, patients begin to eat at regular intervals in accordance with appetitive cues. For instance, a patient might eat lunch at noon, notice they are somewhat hungry, and stop eating when they are appropriately full. As long as health and weight are maintained and restriction is not reported, this practice is continued. Initially a patient may not be hungry at the scheduled meal and snack times. Regular eating is still adhered to and is primary. Generally, over time, bodies adjust to the schedule and start to become hungry at the scheduled meal and snack times. In short, a person is encouraged to eat at the scheduled meal and snack times.

RAE for Various Populations

For patients who have difficultly identifying hunger and fullness cues because of the effects of the eating disorder, the period of mindful observation of these cues will be longer than for those who can readily identify them. Further, if a patient's eating disorder is currently self-eclipsing (see the general introduction to this book for an explanation of this concept), and if the patient has a recent history of engaging in food restriction and avoidance, then the appetitive eating interventions are not yet recommended. More information regarding the use of RAE with specific populations is provided in greater detail later in this manual.

RAE for Adults in Evidence-Based Practice

We are acutely aware that, given the lack of resources for people with eating disorders, therapists adhere to evidence-based practice models and implement what seems most likely to work for their particular patients, given the current literature. Therefore, it is very likely that this manual, which is intended for therapists who are treating adolescents, will be repurposed in practice for therapists working with adults. Given this, please note that eating in an appetitive way *may* not be appropriate for adults, particularly those who have had very long-standing illnesses. As described in this manual, appetitive eating is intended only for people with anorexia nervosa who have been health-restored. Even for adults with anorexia nervosa who have been weight- and health-restored, identifying and eating according to appetitive cues may be difficult. Notably, there is emerging evidence that appetitive eating approaches such as intuitive eating (Richards et al., 2017) reduce eating disorder symptoms in adults.

About BAE

The BAE handouts can be loosely categorized into three types: behavior-shaping work, exposure exercises, and compassion-focused work. A brief overview of the BAE handouts is provided here along with a review of each of these three broad categories. A description of how the IMT individual handouts are to be used with people who have different disorders is provided in the next section.

How the BAE Material Fits Together

Although formal exposure therapy exercises are the second component of three in the BAE material, they are the focal point of the treatment around which the other two categories of interventions are situated. The first category of BAE handouts focuses on behavior-shaping work. With an eating disorder comes a set of maladaptive behaviors that generally interfere with the efficacy of exposure exercises. Therefore, the first set of interventions is focused on stabilizing these behaviors. Once these behaviors are stabilized, exposure therapy exercises can be conducted to target fear of "fatness" and weight gain as well as select linked emotions. Once the foundation to tolerate negative emotions has been built, compassion-focused work can begin. The rationale for the ordering of the material is presented later in the manual.

In the RAE material, *food-related behaviors* (such as food restriction, food avoidance, binge eating, and purging) are addressed, whereas in the BAE material, *body-related behaviors* (such as body investigating, body avoidance, body comparison, and exercise) are addressed. Through a behavioral lens, both food-related and body-related behaviors can be conceptualized as *safety behaviors* if performed in the context of exposure therapy exercises. Safety behaviors are maladaptive strategies used to try to decrease negative emotions (or other internal experiences). The aim of the exposure therapy exercise is for the patient to experience and learn to tolerate negative emotions. Therefore, if the patient engages in safety behaviors during or after an exposure exercise, negative emotions may be decreased because of the safety behaviors, *not* because of the patient's learned ability to tolerate negative emotions.

For instance, if a patient challenged themselves with a pizza and purged, there is little opportunity for the emotion to rise and fall, and for the patient to learn that they can tolerate eating pizza. Instead, the reduction in anxiety comes after the purging behavior. Therefore, purging is reinforced as an anxiety reducer. Pizza is also reinforced as an anxiety trigger. By engaging in the safety behavior of purging, the patient is robbed of the opportunity to experience negative emotions.

Because safety behaviors interfere with the efficacy of the exposures, they need to be addressed first. Of course, in the context of eating disorder treatment, safety behaviors could include behaviors such as purging and taking laxatives. Therefore, these behaviors must first be addressed for the patient's safety. Body-related behaviors, such as body avoiding (for example, covering up one's body), are not as dangerous; however, they still interfere with exposure exercises. Therefore, both food-related and body-related behaviors must be somewhat mitigated before embarking on the exposures. The patient must be able to refrain from engaging in behaviors *after* the exercise. The patient must also agree to refrain from vowing to engage later in safety behaviors. For instance, a patient may internally vow to engage in exercise after an exposure exercise causing a decrease in negative emotion, not from the tolerance of negative emotion but because of the later promise of escaping it. Even though the negative emotions fell, that was due to the planning of a later safety behavior. This vowing or planning of engaging in later safety behaviors must also be addressed in treatment.

Once behaviors are mitigated enough to conduct exposure exercises without safety behaviors, exposure exercises commence. By targeting fear of "fatness" with exposure exercises, as in any other exposure exercise, the intensity of the targeted fear most often reduces. With decreased food- and body-related behaviors occurring, and a reduction in the intensity of fear of "fatness" experienced, the stage is set for acceptance of the body. Ultimately, the BAE material focuses on self-compassion and gratitude for the body.

EXPOSURES IN EATING DISORDER TREATMENT

Regarding discrete *in-session* exposure exercises (such as imaginal exposure to fear of "fatness," eating a feared chocolate cupcake with the therapist, and so forth), safety behaviors should be discussed, and the patient should be explicitly told not to engage in these behaviors during or after the exercise. Although safety behaviors can be mitigated in this fashion during in-session exposures, other types of exposures throughout treatment will not be as controlled. Because every meal and snack is essentially an exposure, it is to be expected that safety behaviors will be engaged in during eating disorder treatment. They simply cannot all be prevented. Unlike in the treatment of trauma or obsessive-compulsive disorder, where exposure exercises occur in outpatient therapy about once per week and behaviors can be relatively controlled, people with eating disorders must eat approximately thirty-five times per week and are tasked with tolerating all subsequent feelings of fullness. Safety behaviors are going to happen! Eating disorder treatment cannot be as controlled and precise as the treatment of other disorders. By comparison, it is rather messy. This does not mean, however, that behaviors cannot be shaped over time. All is not lost if a safety behavior is engaged in after a meal or snack. It is up to the therapist to find the behaviors in line with recovery that the patient *did* engage in and verbally reinforce those. It is also important to discuss the function of the safety behavior that occurred and how it can be prevented in the future.

Shaping Body-Orienting Behaviors

In the BAE material, the eating disorder behaviors of exercise, body avoidance, and body investigating (called *body checking* in other literature) are addressed, as is making comparisons to others. As previously explained, the collective behaviors and thought processes (such as obsessions) of the eating disorder serve the function of allowing the patient temporary experiential avoidance of negative emotions regarding the body. In other words, when under the eating disorder's influence, patients are not coming into contact with their fear of "fatness" and linked emotions (such as fear of rejection by peers). Instead, all the eating disorder behaviors, such as restriction, and all the obsessing serve to keep the person from confronting their fear of "fatness" and linked emotions (such as fear of imperfection). Therefore, fostering tolerance of negative internal experiences (such as emotions, thoughts, and so forth) in response to any body-related stimuli (such as thoughts about the body) is the crux of these interventions.

Although interventions aimed at decreasing behaviors are not formal exposure therapy exercises, a whole host of negative internal experiences will arise and must be tolerated when these behaviors are not engaged in. Therefore, decreasing behaviors can be viewed as the first phase in the wave of tolerating negative internal experiences. These behaviors, of course, keep negative internal experiences at bay. When they are not engaged in, these negative internal experiences are brought front and center into a person's awareness.

Considering the External Environment

Taking a broad view, behaviors occur in response to negative internal experiences *and* in reaction to stimuli from the external environment. When we work collaboratively with patients to decrease behaviors, we are asking patients to tolerate a host of these negative experiences. It is important to understand not only the context in which these behaviors occur but what, exactly, we are asking patients to tolerate.

When decreasing body-related behaviors, we are asking patients to foster tolerance of internal experiences:

- Having negative thoughts about their body (for example, that it's a "fat" body)

- Having negative emotions in response to the body (such as anxiety when looking in the mirror)

- Distorted visual perceptions of the body (such as seeing oneself as "fat" in the mirror)

- Distorted proprioceptive cues (such as physically feeling the midsection as "fatter" after eating)

- Urges to engage in eating disorder behaviors (such as restriction)

Moreover, we are asking them to foster these kinds of tolerance in the following social contexts:

- Being a participant in a society that generally reinforces the patient's disordered behaviors (such as seeing a video of another person being praised for weight loss)

- Being a participant in a society in which it is socially acceptable to comment on one another's bodies both online and in person

- Being a participant in a "culture of one" that has particular reinforcement contingencies for disordered behaviors (such as when a wrestling coach unwittingly reinforces an eating disorder behavior by saying "Nice job dropping down a weight class")

And we are asking them to do these things while they also potentially lack the following skills:

- The skill of *separation* or *defusion* between the body and the self ("I *am* fat"); there is fusion between the self and the body as the self is reduced to the body throughout the course of the eating disorder

- The skill of *fostering a positive attitude* toward the body ("If I nourish my body, it will help support me")

- A practice of *gratitude* for the body ("I am thankful for my body and health")

It is no small feat to shape behaviors in the context of the circumstances just described. That, however, does not mean that it cannot be done! If possible, addressing some of the preceding issues can be done prior to setting out to decrease body-related behaviors. Regarding the social factors, it is important to monitor patient responses on the IMT individual measures (such as in the "Body Commenting" section).

If maladaptive social reinforcement is coming in from the outside, implementing plans to cut down those reinforcements (such as by suspending social media use, having an intervention with a family member who is engaging in "fat" talk, and so forth) is necessary. It is also important to intervene if the patient is actively participating in social behaviors that reinforce the eating disorder (such as engaging in judgmental conversation about other people's bodies).

These behaviors are at odds with the goal of fostering body acceptance. Next, it is important to teach tolerance of the negative internal experiences (thoughts, emotions, physical sensations, distorted perceptions, behavioral urges). To the extent possible, directly target thoughts with cognitive restructuring techniques. These techniques may help reduce the degree of belief in specific types of thoughts (such as negative automatic thoughts, rules, and core beliefs) as well as the intensity of related negative emotions. Handouts for tolerating internal experiences and working on directly changing the content of thoughts are found in the IMT individual and group handouts. Regarding fusion between the body and the self, negative attitudes toward the body, and an absence of adaptive attitudes toward the body, the self-compassion and gratitude interventions are aimed at addressing these factors. Before the factors having to do with a lack of adaptive internal processes are directly addressed in treatment, these conditions often simply exist. And that is OK! Rome was not built in a day.

Taken as a whole, the preceding material describes a collection of factors that are present; however, not everything can or will be solved prior to decreasing body-related behaviors. These factors are often addressed concurrently in treatment. For instance, as part of the NIFTY skills (BAE Handout 9), which are used to teach patients to cope with body avoidance, patients are encouraged to feel negative emotions. Therefore, the factor of having negative emotions is addressed concurrently with decreasing the behavior of body avoidance. After the goal of decreasing body avoidance is introduced, it is completely acceptable to add in other supporting handouts over the course of treatment that will help the patient build the skills necessary to decrease this maladaptive behavior. When addressing minor, non-life-threatening treatment targets (such as body avoidance), treatment is not linear. A therapist focuses on these targets when possible, given other priorities. In this way, the behaviors subside and are decreased over time. The main aim is to get the body-related behaviors addressed prior to the next phase of BAE so that they do not interfere with exposure exercises. Body-related behaviors do not have to be completely decreased prior to body-related exposure exercises.

Although decreasing maladaptive behaviors brings avoided *momentary* internal experiences to the surface, there are often more pervasive fears and negative emotions that persist. Although patients may learn to tolerate negative internal experiences as they arise, there is still deeper work to be done. Is fear of "fatness" extinguished? What about fear of future weight gain? Have the linked emotions, such as fear of abandonment and failure, been addressed? The next step is to use targeted exposure exercises aimed specifically at evoking these negative emotions.

Directly Confronting Fear of "Fatness"

The primary aim of BAE work is to bring confrontation of fear of "fatness" front and center. Eating appropriately sized meals and feared foods is resoundingly not the same thing as confronting fear of "fatness." Food is not "fatness." Food is food. Food is only tangentially related to "fatness" through an associative network that may be something like this: *I am afraid of being "fat." One way I could potentially get "fat" is through eating. Therefore, I should restrict and avoid food.* Fear of food is only an aspect of fear of "fatness." It is not the direct treatment target itself. The reason why food is so important to target first, however, is that food is a necessity of life. We have to target it first or the patient may die. But the fact that food is the primary treatment target does not mean it is the bull's-eye. Fear of "fatness" is the bull's-eye of the eating disorder.

Figure 1.2.1 depicts the eating disorder treatment target with "fatness" as the bull's-eye. The first ring ("food") can be targeted in treatment by using techniques that address such behaviors as food restriction and avoidance. The second ring ("own body") can be targeted by using techniques to decrease such behaviors as exercise and body avoidance. This target suggests that "fatness" can be targeted as well. But how can "fatness" be targeted in behavior therapy? "Fatness" is an amorphous concept. Advanced behavior therapists reading this may know the technique: imaginal exposure. Imaginal exposure may be the single most powerful and underutilized transdiagnostic therapeutic tool we have today. Studies examining its usage indicate that only a small minority of clinicians implement this technique in practice, despite the evidence of its therapeutic strengths (see, for example, Becker, Zayfert, & Anderson, 2004). With this manual, we hope to make a contribution toward increasing the use of imaginal exposure in the specialty of treating eating disorders.

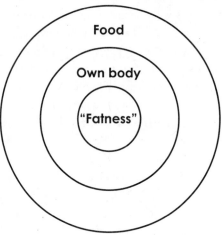

Figure 1.2.1. Treatment Target for Eating Disorder Fears

Imaginal exposure is a technique whereby a patient imagines a feared outcome that cannot be created in the real world at that time. For instance, if a person with generalized anxiety disorder has a fear of the world ending because of a specific political conflict, there would be no logical way to create this scenario. In this case, the therapist would help the patient write out a brief story regarding the particular feared scenario. The patient would be instructed not to engage in any safety behaviors during or after the exercise. Anxiety ratings would be given by the patient throughout the exercise. Anxiety rises and then falls during each session. This is done over the course of many sessions until the patient learns through experience that the anxiety is tolerable. Although the end of the world remains a troubling thought, related stimuli, such as a brief story about this scenario, no longer trigger intense anxiety.

Similarly, if a person fears that they will, for instance, gain weight and be unlovable, a scenario in which this happens (for example, a person gains a significant amount of weight and then all loved ones stop contacting them) can be written and confronted in session over time until it no longer elicits the feared response. In this way, fear of "fatness"—the bull's-eye of the eating disorder—can be directly targeted in treatment. Linked emotions are also targeted in this example because the concept of being unlovable is addressed. This concept is depicted in figure 1.2.2.

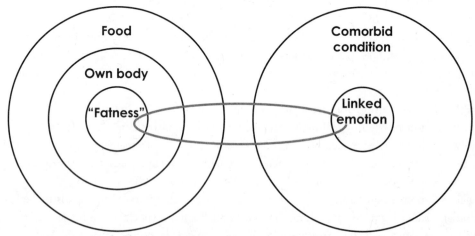

Figure 1.2.2. Treatment Target for Eating Disorders and Co-occurring Conditions

Why does a person fear "fatness"? "Fatness" is certainly not something to inherently fear in itself. Through learning, "fatness" becomes associated with something frightening. What is that thing for the individual? Although fear of "fatness" is a common bull's-eye for eating disorders, linked emotions play different roles for everyone. Some linked emotions serve a secondary function in eating disorder behaviors. Further, some linked emotions serve a primary function in other comorbid disorders. For instance, a person's avoidance of fear of "fatness" may be the primary function of eating disorder behavior, and avoidance of fear of failure may be the secondary function. Further, the linked emotion may be present in both the eating disorder and a comorbid illness. For instance, a person with an eating disorder may have fear of "fatness" *and* fear of abandonment. Although avoidance of fear of abandonment may be a secondary function to avoidance of fear of "fatness" in eating disorder behaviors, avoidance of fear of abandonment may be the primary function of the behaviors of borderline personality disorder. Taken together, the BAE handouts and measures will help uncover linked emotions.

TIP: DO NOT GET CAUGHT UP IN THE "FACTS" ABOUT EMOTIONS REGARDING "FATNESS"

Learning through reading science papers that obesity can be associated with medical issues is very different from carrying around the emotion of generally fearing "fatness." For instance, a physician can be aware of certain associations between obesity and medical illnesses, but that does not mean they should fear "fatness" on a daily basis. There is a difference between cognitively understanding science and experiencing the emotion of fear. When the emotion of fear of "fatness" is felt, sequelae of maladaptive thoughts and behaviors occur.

TIP: READ THE LITERATURE ON HEALTH AT EVERY SIZE

If you are still getting tripped up on the "facts" that having a body in the overweight range is unhealthy and people *should* fear it, read the Health at Every Size literature by Linda Bacon. You may learn that having a body in an above-"normal" weight range is not nearly as unhealthy as the myopic studies we extrapolate from suggest. By contrast, being out of tune with one's body and having pejorative attitudes about one's "fatness" appear to be rather damaging to physical health.

TIP: MODEL FEARLESSNESS OF "FATNESS"

A lot of people have some degree of fear of "fatness." If you do, do some work on this yourself. After all, it's only fair if you're asking patients to do it. An important component of classic behavior therapy is modeling. Therefore, the more a therapist can embody and model fearlessness of "fatness," the better. Try your best to imbue your attitudes and interventions with fearlessness of "fatness."

Self-Compassion, Gratitude, and Reconnection

After decreases in both eating disorder behaviors and fear of "fatness," the groundwork is laid for the introduction of something new. Rather than simply decreasing eating disorder behaviors in treatment, the aim of BAE is to restore balance. With the eating disorder largely in remission, the introduction of adaptive attitudes toward the body and self can be introduced. In clinical practice, interventions from the compassion-focused therapy literature seemed a natural fit. Fostering gratitude for the body, honoring oneself, and forming meaningful connections with others are the basis of this work.

The Timing of Introducing Self-Compassion Work

The content of the internal dialogue that comprises the eating disorder is harsh and rather cruel. Introducing a soft and compassionate tone appears to be both desperately needed and heavily protected against by the eating disorder. When introducing self-compassion work with patients who have not yet learned to tolerate negative emotions, an internal struggle appears to be initiated between the person and the eating disorder. On the one hand, the person needs self-compassionate words the way a person dying of dehydration in the desert needs water. On the other hand, the eating disorder protects itself against the invading compassion by setting off internal thoughts such as *These seemingly nice things are lies* and *You aren't worth anything*. In this way, the more a clinician attempts to foster self-compassion, the more the eating disorder pushes back. In our clinical practice, patients in earlier stages of recovery have reported experiencing more harsh and cruel thoughts during self-compassion exercises than prior to the intervention. If patients are not yet ready for these exercises, they may be left feeling vulnerable, triggered, or shut down at the end of the session.

This does not mean, however, that self-compassion should be abandoned as a treatment target! Quite the contrary. Given the harsh and cruel nature of the eating disorder, it stands to reason that developing the ability to show oneself compassion is a crucial part of recovery. It is therefore recommended that self-compassion interventions be administered after behaviors have been stabilized, after the patient can implement the skill of tolerating negative internal experiences (such as emotions), and after negative thoughts can be managed. In this way, treatment priories are addressed, patients are relatively more receptive to self-compassion interventions, and the likelihood of the intervention resulting in a triggering behavior is mitigated. For the reasons just stated, the self-compassion material appears toward the end of the BAE handouts.

Administering BAE Alongside RAE

The administration of BAE will vary for each patient. Some patients will have to work their way in linear fashion through all the RAE material prior to the introduction of any BAE material. Other patients may be focusing mainly on RAE with the exception of select BAE handouts (such as the exercise handouts). For still other patients who have the resources, RAE handouts can be administered in one session while BAE handouts (for example, on body avoidance, body investigating, and exercise) are focused on in the other session. The only major stipulations are that RAE treatment targets must be primary and that all major eating disorder, self-destructive, impulsive, alcohol abuse, and substance abuse behaviors must be substantially decreased prior to the beginning of the exposure portion of BAE.

Section 1.3

Individual IMT for Specific Disorders

This section describes the specifics about implementing individual interventions with people who have various eating disorder diagnoses as well as people who have comorbid borderline personality disorder.

Using RAE with People Who Have BOB Disorders

This section describes how to use RAE with patients who have BOB disorders. Recall that the term *BOB disorders* denotes a category that includes bulimia nervosa (BN), other specified feeding or eating disorder (OSFED), and binge eating disorder (BED), largely with the exclusion of atypical anorexia nervosa.

Bulimia Nervosa and Other Specified Feeding or Eating Disorder

LeGrange and Lock's evidence-based family-based treatment for bulimia nervosa is based on their groundbreaking treatment for anorexia nervosa (see LeGrange & Lock, 2007). This treatment is clearly helpful for many adolescents with BN. At the same time, a clinician can run into a couple of practical obstacles when administering this evidence-based treatment. The first hurdle is that carers are not always available for treatment. The second obstacle, less obvious, is that patients with BN often present as less self-eclipsed (ego-syntonic) than patients with AN. Of course, when this occurs, it is of benefit to the patient. In terms of implementing a family-based treatment, however, carers are not required to be involved to quite the same degree as in the treatment of AN. If the carer is taking a less active role, the question for some patients becomes "What, exactly, does a therapist *do* when meeting with the adolescent individually?" Because enhanced cognitive behavioral therapy is the gold standard for treatment of adults with BN, using techniques from this treatment is the natural choice for motivated adolescents who can tolerate individual therapy. Because there is no treatment we know of considered to be the gold standard for adolescents with BN, this sort of hybrid is what results when operating in the trenches from an evidence-based practice model. Further, because evidence supports the approaches of intuitive eating (Tribole & Resch, 2012), Health at Every Size (Bacon, 2008), and Appetite Awareness (Allen & Craighead, 1999; Craighead, 2006), we have also used appetitive eating techniques in practice. Therefore, our treatment of BN in adolescents often involves a hybrid of family therapy as well as regular and appetitive eating. Of course, this manner of treatment also applies to the lesser defined OSFED. Because no treatment manuals we are aware of have been written for adolescents with OSFED, clinicians are more in the dark. In our evidence-based clinical practice, however, the aforementioned combination of approaches is typically implemented.

Because IMT is a reflection of what is done in the trenches from an evidence-based practice model, we offer a collection of interventions intended to be used flexibly with guidelines rather than a set of stringent rules. Therefore, clinical judgment must be used in deciding the degree to which to involve family versus individual work for patients with BN and OSFED. (Guidelines for incorporating family are provided later in the manual.) If you are unclear regarding the degree to which to involve family for particular cases, it is suggested that you seek consultation or supervision. The network of clinicians through the Academy for Eating Disorders (www.aedweb.org) is recommended. In addition to seeking consultation and supervision regarding specific cases, examples of factors that play into the decision regarding the degree of family involvement are outlined in what follows.

Discontinuing Individual Treatment

As with all other patients, if a significant decrease in weight occurs, health declines, or mental health deteriorates, a higher degree of family intervention should occur or a higher level of care should be considered. BN and OSFED are dangerous disorders with high mortality rates. Physicians must be monitoring patients regularly.

Binge Eating Disorder

As in other eating disorders, people with BED report overvaluation of shape and weight, and some (such as Grilo et al., 2013) suggest this cognitive feature should be considered a diagnostic feature of the disorder. In clinical practice as well as research, we have found that adolescents and young adults who engage in binge eating also report fear of "fatness" (Deliberto, Jacobs, Novak, Grabicki, et al., 2013). From this fear stems a sequence of eating disorder behaviors (such as food avoidance, food obsession, and food-related thought suppression) culminating in binge eating.

Fear of "Fatness": Never Judge a Book by Its Cover

It should be noted that it is never apparent from looking at a patient that they have fear of "fatness." A therapist must always assess for this. For instance, to a novice eating disorder behavior therapist, it may seem counterintuitive that a patient who has a BMI in the underweight, normal, or overweight range would be afraid of "fatness." When first coming across a person in the underweight range, a novice therapist may assume that this person would not be worried about their weight. Of course, people with anorexia nervosa have bodies in the underweight range as well as an ever-present fear of "fatness." Similarly, a novice therapist may erroneously make the same assumption if a patient with a BOB disorder has a body in the normal weight range. If the novice therapist does not take the perspective of the patient, the assumption may be that a person in the normal weight range would not worry about their weight. Eating disorder pathology, however, exists completely independently of a person's weight. People in the normal weight range can and do engage in extremely destructive, even life-threatening, eating disorder behaviors secondary to intolerance of fear of "fatness." Similarly, a novice therapist may assume that a person who has a body above the normal weight range doesn't care about their weight and is therefore certainly not afraid of weight gain. This kind of attitude completely overlooks the experience the person may be having. These attitudes are rooted in the therapist's judging from their own experience and not taking the perspective of the patient. Therefore, on intake, we suggest that therapists pose the following screening question to all patients: "On a fear scale of 0 to 10, with 10 representing the greatest amount of fear, how afraid are you of gaining weight?"

No Fear of "Fatness" Present

If fear of "fatness" does not appear to be present in BED, it is suggested that a thorough assessment be conducted with the IMT BAE measure as well as with other reliable and valid measures, such as the Eating Attitudes Test-26 (EAT-26; Garfinkel & Newman, 2001) and the Eating Disorder Examination Questionnaire (EDE-Q; Fairburn & Beglin, 1994). If fear of "fatness" is not present but loss of control over eating is, implementing the RAE interventions from this manual is recommended. It is important to identify whatever negative emotions are being avoided and target them with specialized interventions (such as imaginal exposures).

Discontinuing Individual Treatment

Although BED typically poses less of a risk relative to other eating disorders, if the patient's mental or physical health deteriorates for any reason, implementing family interventions or higher levels of care may be necessary. This, of course, must be determined on a case-by-case basis.

Reevaluating Individual Treatment

Physicians must be monitoring BED patients with a regularity that they set in order to detect changes in physical health conditions. If, however, the therapist has reason to suspect that there has been an onset of or relapse to health-interfering eating disorder behaviors (such as purging) over the course of treatment, the therapist may assert that a medical visit is necessary for continued treatment.

Using Individual Interventions with People Who Have Anorexia Nervosa and Atypical Anorexia Nervosa

This section discusses topics pertaining to the administration of the IMT individual interventions.

Outpatient Individual Treatment with People Who Have Anorexia Nervosa and Atypical Anorexia Nervosa

As stated in the general introduction to this manual, family therapy is the recommended modality for patients with AN and for most with AAN if these patients have been cleared for an outpatient level of care. If family treatment cannot be administered, a higher level of care should be sought. In outpatient settings, IMT individual therapy handouts are to be used in this population only for patients who have the RAN distinction (recall that the term *RAN* refers to weight- and health-restored AN and AAN).

Discontinuing Outpatient Individual Treatment with People Who Have Anorexia Nervosa and Atypical Anorexia Nervosa

If a substantial amount of weight is lost for any reason, or if health declines during the administration of individual interventions, the reimplementation of family interventions or a higher level of care must always be considered. Close monitoring of whether each person is progressing or backsliding in treatment is important during this phase of treatment, even though the patient is no longer at imminent risk. It should be made clear to the patient that if weight is not maintained, and if health indicators (such as lab work) reveal medical issues, the current course of treatment (such as treatment goals) will either be adjusted or changed. For each individual patient, it is important to have a discussion with the physician regarding which weight and what indicators of poor health would warrant intervention. In patients with the RAN distinction, even if weight is lost for a reason other than the eating disorder (such as influenza) and needs to be regained, the individual portion of the treatment must stop, and either family interventions or a higher level of care must be pursued. Individual interventions are not designed for weight gain (that is, pushing past the point of being comfortably full while eating quantities of food large enough to cause an average gain of two pounds per week). Individual interventions are aimed at helping patients eat in a regulated manner that will likely have the effect of stabilizing rather than increasing weight.

USING INDIVIDUAL INTERVENTIONS IN FAMILY THERAPY WITH PEOPLE WHO HAVE ANOREXIA NERVOSA OR ATYPICAL ANOREXIA NERVOSA

In view of work by Levinson and her colleagues (Levinson, Rapp, & Riley, 2014; Levinson & Byrne, 2015; Levinson et al., 2015), further examination of imaginal exposure for patients with non-health-restored AN and AAN is a particularly exciting area of study. We encourage readers who are scientists to conduct research on imaginal exposure exercises targeting fear of "fatness" and/or weight gain in this population, along with imaginal exposure exercises targeting fear of *recovery*; see, for example, BAE Handout 18: Pretending It's Forever and BAE Handout 19: Imagining Recovery. For each of the proposed exercises, the same script can be used across participants (that is, one script for fear of "fatness" can be written and used with every participant in a study who has AN or AAN). Given a common pathology, participants will have relatively similar emotions evoked in response to the same script. We also encourage research using individually crafted imaginal exposure exercises to target linked emotions, given that each participant will present with a unique learning history and a different set of associations with "fatness." In addition, if a scientist-practitioner is interested in incorporating imaginal exposure into the treatment of non-health-restored AN and AAN, it is highly recommended that these exercises be incorporated into (not used as a substitute for) family therapy or treatment at a higher level of care. In all experiments involving imaginal exposures with this population, participants should be instructed not to engage in safety behaviors, and the level of personality pathology should be measured.

Using Individual Interventions with People Who Have Anorexia Nervosa or Atypical Anorexia Nervosa at Higher Levels of Care and in Family Therapy

If an adolescent with AN or AAN is in treatment at a higher level of care, it is very often the case that they will receive individual therapy in addition to the package of other treatment services that are offered (such as group therapy, medical management, nutrition counseling, and so forth). Because the adolescent is already safely and securely in a setting with meals and health being monitored, if the person is able to take on additional challenges, note that only select BAE material should be incorporated into individual sessions, since imaginal exposures may be too overwhelming. This must be determined on a case-by-case basis.

At higher levels of care, because a person is already going through almost constant exposures (three meals per day, two snacks per day, feeling full after eating, actually gaining weight, and so forth), adding further exposures may be overwhelming to some patients. For other patients, this process may be similar to the behavioral technique of flooding and may have the effect of expedited recovery. Research in this particular area is not only needed but also encouraged. Questions such as "Does adding in imaginal exposure exercises targeting fear of 'fatness' and/or weight gain, recovery, and linked emotions at higher levels of care have an impact on recovery?" and "What role does personality pathology play in outcome?" require formal examination.

RAE at Higher Levels of Care in People Who Have Anorexia Nervosa or Atypical Anorexia Nervosa

Unlike BAE material, which may be incorporated into individual therapy sessions at higher levels of care, depending on the circumstances, RAE material is not suitable for patients with AN or AAN until health restoration has been reached.

Using RAE with People Who Have Health-Restored Anorexia Nervosa

There are several administration specifics regarding the use of RAE interventions with adolescents who have the RAN distinction following a relatively more perilous stage of AN or AAN.

Regular Eating Is Already Established

Some adolescents with AN or AAN will, fortunately, be entering RAE after a very successful course of family intervention or after being at a higher level of care. If this is the case, the patient may not need to be logging their own food intake in order to establish regular eating, because regular eating has already been established in the prior treatment. For these patients, rather than going through the regular eating interventions, it will likely be appropriate to transition to the appetitive eating interventions. For patients receiving IMT family interventions, they will likely already be familiar with the concept of appetitive eating, since it is introduced in stage 2 of IMT family therapy.

Strong Eating Disorder Urges

Alternatively, some people with RAN will have strong eating disorder urges to restrict and avoid foods. This may be due, for instance, to the course of their former treatment. For instance, in the United States, even though the patient was doing relatively well at a residential treatment program, insurance may have been cut off right after health restoration was achieved but before the eating disorder urges largely subsided. Although the patient could benefit from more support, there are, unfortunately, no available carers. This situation is clearly not ideal for the patient, but they are health-restored and can enter RAE. In this case, it would be important to get completed food logs from the patient each week. This will give the therapist a sense of how much food is actually being consumed. In addition, the therapist would do weekly weigh-ins to help assess for the degree of food restriction and avoidance. Although weight is certainly not a perfect measurement of food restriction (let alone food avoidance), if the patient's weight suddenly drops, it may be possible to infer (in the absence of confounding variables, such as illnesses) that the patient is limiting food intake secondary to the eating disorder.

Regular Eating Is Established but Cannot Be Moved Past

In clinical practice, it has been our experience that that are some patients with the RAN designation for whom regular eating will readily be established, but for whom the goal of appetitive eating appears to be currently contraindicated. For instance, patients who have rigid and inflexible cognitive styles may do quite well with concrete goals of eating specific volumes of food at specific times. The introduction into treatment of the relatively less concrete concept of eating in general accordance with a range of appetitive cues can feel chaotic for these patients. The patient may, for instance, start to have strong urges to restrict. Patients may also report, quite rightfully, that they are not ready for these interventions. In these cases, it is important to roll with resistance. Ensuring that food restriction does not return as a behavior is the priority. There is no need to push the agenda of appetitive eating. For some patients, it is best to table the monitoring of appetitive cues indefinitely. For other patients, it is appropriate to monitor hunger and fullness cues for extended periods of time before taking the step toward eating in accordance with those cues. After all, becoming more flexible over time is an important goal. It does not, however, need to be achieved in full immediately. Each child or adolescent patient will be different. In the time it takes for the patient to be ready for appetitive eating goals, the focus of treatment is on maintaining regular eating, decreasing food avoidance, and moving on to the BAE material when ready.

If a Person with Anorexia Nervosa or Atypical Anorexia Nervosa Backslides in Outpatient Treatment

Of course, patients with the RAN distinction should be medically monitored during treatment. It is also helpful to take the patient's weight at the start of each weekly therapy appointment. If a patient's health is declining significantly, they should be enrolled either in family treatment or in a higher level of care, depending on the severity of the health issues. If, however, the patient is in the appetitive eating portion of the treatment and has a minor setback (such as losing three pounds while maintaining a weight that is healthy), appetitive eating should be suspended, and regular eating should be implemented. The patient should be closely monitored until the condition improves. If the condition worsens, family intervention or a higher level of care will be needed. If you ever have questions about cases, you can consult the network of specialists at the Academy for Eating Disorders (www. aedweb.org).

Using BAE with People Who Have Borderline Personality Disorder

Certain BAE handouts should be implemented with consideration and forethought with people who have borderline personality disorder or traits. Because BPD is characterized by emotion dysregulation, emotion intolerance, and impulsivity, exposure to negative emotions can prompt self-destructive thoughts and behaviors if the person is not properly prepared. Therefore, it is recommended that patients learn skills to cope with emotion dysregulation, emotion intolerance, and impulsivity before they receive treatment with any of the BAE handouts for which this manual provides notes advising caution in use with patients who have BPD or traits.

In clinical practice, we have found that for some patients with comorbid BPD or traits, the self-compassion-focused material can also be quite triggering. People fused with believing the content of their self-destructive thoughts may not be ready to process self-compassion material that is totally on the other end of the spectrum. They may respond to self-compassion interventions by refuting outright the content of self-compassion material, thereby seeming to burrow further into their own maladaptive beliefs. Therefore, it is not recommended that the compassion-focused material be administered until the person is able to tolerate the negative internal experiences that may arise in response to the self-compassion-focused material. If they can tolerate these negative responses and avoid engaging in attempts to refute the content with the help of the therapist, an opportunity for the interventions to be effective is opened. Undoubtedly, the imaginal exposure self-compassion material is quite relevant to people with BPD and traits. It is, however, a matter of timing and readiness.

Section 1.4

Thinking Like a Behaviorist

This section explains core behavioral concepts that are salient in the individual therapy modality.

FEELING TEMPTED TO DEVIATE FROM THE GOAL OF REGULAR EATING?

Generally, targeting food restriction is the starting point of any evidence-based treatment. Although there are often many underlying issues present for the patient, rest assured that addressing food restriction is a helpful place to start. When the thread of food restriction is pulled, the eating disorder tapestry will start to come undone. Food restriction is one of the main seams holding the tapestry together. When the food restriction seam starts to unravel, all connected internal experiences holding the eating disorder together are weakened. For instance, if a person with bulimia nervosa is no longer restricting, then binge eating does not occur, which cuts purging off at the pass. In simplified terms, targeting restriction has a very beneficial effect on both mental and physical health. Often many temptations to deviate from this goal will arise, but it must be adhered to for the safety and well-being of the patient.

"It's Boring"

Sometimes helping a patient through the concrete goal of establishing regular eating is boring. It just is! When a person envisions becoming a therapist, they typically think of having meaningful conversations and connecting with people. Well, there is nothing deep about a food log. The connection with the patient, however, comes through working together to make real change over time. When the patient makes progress, the therapist is there to cheer them on and root for them. By combating the eating disorder together, a relationship is built. Once the eating disorder has been defeated, the person can emerge. Work can then be done to address any underlying issues that remain when the patient is physically healthy and equipped with skills learned in the battle against the disorder. The patient's basic need for food must be put above the clinician's desire to connect. Food intake must be shaped directly with reinforcement; it is not to be circuitously targeted through traditional talk therapy.

Treatment Drift in RAE

Because addressing food restriction is so important for both psychological and physical health reasons, it is important not to allow the focus of treatment to drift *away from* addressing the goal of food restriction and *toward* working on decreasing food avoidance prematurely. In other words, patients may often present as preferring to work on the less threatening goal of eating scary types of food rather than increasing the overall amounts of food eaten. Although certain foods are feared, the patient is likely cognizant of the often touted "fact" that it is "really" the overall *caloric amount* you eat that will cause you to gain weight, rather than *what* you eat. Therefore, patients may present as willing to working on the goal that, according to the eating disorder's logic, is least likely to actually cause weight gain but is still pleasing the therapist—eating challenge foods! Therefore, it is important that the therapist, to the best of their ability, initially guide treatment in the direction of addressing food restriction with regular eating. Encourage patients to eat within given reasonable time frames. Clearly outline these time frames and agree upon them.

Behavior Therapy and the IMT Individual Measures

The IMT measures navigate both the therapist and the patient through treatment. Reading through an IMT measure prior to a session is similar to the practice of setting an intention at the beginning of a mindfulness practice—the aims of the present endeavor are considered. The IMT measures are essentially summaries of the current treatment intentions. For each measure, a summary of the behaviors, beliefs, social interactions, and physical symptoms that are to be either increased or decreased over the course of treatment are written out in detail. Therefore, as the patient reads through the list, it is made clear what is maladaptive and what is adaptive. Reading through the measure each week, the patient is reminded of what the concrete treatment targets are and may be better able to steer their own behavior away from the maladaptive behaviors and toward the adaptive targets. After all, the ultimate goal of the treatment is to empower the person with the eating disorder to take recovery and their life into their own hands.

At the same time, the IMT measures provide the therapist with a clear picture of what to reinforce. If recovery behaviors are endorsed, the therapist is to provide recovery-specific positive attention (Rec-SPA) (reinforcement), thereby helping the patient shape their behavior. The IMT measures are also useful tools in catching spikes in eating disorder behavior and steering treatment toward the needed direction. For instance, if a patient completing the measure suddenly reports purging, the focus of the session could shift to addressing this behavior. In short, the IMT measures are clinical tools that state the intentions of each treatment modality, provide a roadmap for the patient, highlight areas to reinforce for the therapist, and are intended to focus the treatment.

Reinforcing What Is Adaptive

The eating disorder behavior therapist is always looking for opportunities to shape adaptive behavior. Reviewing the IMT individual measures with patients provides a rich opportunity to provide reinforcement for engaging in recovery behaviors, tolerating emotions, actively challenging beliefs, engaging in appropriate social interactions, and taking action to improve one's health. This section reviews this skill.

Recovery Behaviors

For any recovery behaviors (such as eating meals, or eating foods that were challenging) that the patient records, the therapist should provide Rec-SPA. For instance, a therapist might say, "It looks like you did a really great job this week with eating challenging foods."

Tolerating Negative and Positive Emotions

It is also important to provide feedback about the experience of both negative and positive emotions. If the patient reports feeling negative emotions, the therapist should make clear that the experience of negative emotions is a very desirable state of affairs in treatment. For instance, a therapist might say, "Along with eating challenging foods this week, you wrote that you were experiencing intense negative emotions. This is a very good sign! The only way through to recovery is to eat challenging foods and tolerate the emotions that come afterward. This tells me that you were really pushing yourself. Good job tolerating these negative emotions this week."

If the patient reports feeling any positive emotions whatsoever after eating, it is worth inquiry. It is important to discern whether the positive emotions are coming from the eating disorder ("I feel accomplished that I was able to avoid all carbs in this meal") or if they are coming from the recovered self ("I feel accomplished because I pushed myself to eat carbs at this meal"). If the positive emotions are coming from the eating disorder, point out that the eating disorder is holding on to wanting the experience of positive emotions around restricting and avoiding food intake. If, however, any positive emotions are being expressed from the recovering self, this is to be appropriately acknowledged in session. For instance, a therapist might say, "Let yourself feel any positive feelings, however small, after you eat. Underneath the eating disorder, your healthy self is celebrating your hard work. Those positive feelings are a message from *you*, telling you to keep up the good work."

For many patients, experiencing positive emotions in response to engaging in recovery behaviors is a complicated experience. The eating disorder will attempt to subvert these experiences. In clinical practice, patients have often reported negative reactions (for example, "feeling like a fat failure") in response to having positive emotions for completing meals. Therefore, it is particularly important to provide feedback and reinforcement for adaptive and appropriate responses to recovery. If patients have negative reactions in response to their positive emotions, encourage tolerance of both the negative and the positive experiences. It is not advisable to back down from providing feedback that the experience of positive emotions is adaptive simply because a patient has experienced negative emotions. Patients will experience negative emotions very often in eating disorder treatment in response to healthy and adaptive feedback because the eating disorder pushes back. This does not mean that the feedback should not be given. Withholding intervention because the eating disorder causes a person to feel negative emotions keeps people sick. Remember not to fragilize patients. Fragilizing patients serves the eating disorder.

Reinforcing Knowledge and Recovery Attitudes

If a patient has shown movement in the direction of adopting healthy beliefs, the eating disorder behavior therapist reinforces this by providing feedback and praise. For instance, if during the beginning of treatment a patient with binge eating disorder has reported that there was no degree of belief in the connection between restricting food and losing control of eating, and then, upon later assessment, endorses understanding the connection, the therapist can point out that throughout treatment the patient has learned a substantial amount through psychoeducation.

Body Commenting

Although no item under the "Body Commenting" section of an IMT measure represents an adaptive behavior, a decrease of behaviors in this section of a measure is to be praised. A therapist might say, "When you first started treatment, you engaged in a lot of body-commenting behaviors, and this week you haven't marked down any. You have done a really great job working on this." Note that making flattering comments about someone else's body is not an adaptive behavior. Regardless of whether a patient is making positive or negative judgments about another person's body, judgments are still occurring. The aim to is move toward a place of nonjudgment. Therefore, in the context of this treatment, all commenting on another's body, positive or negative, is part of the judgmental mind-set of the eating disorder. Occasionally, however, a patient may be viewing prorecovery content online and writing things like "You are beautiful" to other recovered patients. Since this is a general statement, it is not specifically pointing out the body (as in, for example, "Your legs are *so* toned"). This type of comment is intended to be encouraging and uplifting and is acceptable.

Physical Health Improvements

Although the patient cannot be praised directly for improved health, the recovery behaviors they took that collectively added up to improvements in health can be praised. Parallels between eating disorder behaviors and sickness can be drawn as well as between recovery behaviors and health. It can be helpful to ask patients to remember how they physically felt when the physical symptoms were worse and compare that experience to what it physically feels like today. For instance, a therapist might say, "When the eating disorder was at its worst, you went through all these checked-off physical problems because of it. Remember what that felt like. How did you feel? Now compare how you felt back then to how you physically feel now. A lot better, right? Through all the hard work you put into eating three full meals a day, completing two snacks per day, tolerating negative emotions, filling out food logs, going to group, completing homework, and practicing skills, you were able to improve your health." In this way, the patient's behavior is linked to the alleviation of physical symptoms and then verbally reinforced by the therapist.

In reviewing an IMT measure, however, it may not be advisable to point out to a patient with a self-eclipsed eating disorder at the start of treatment that the eating disorder is causing all these physical ailments. This discussion should largely be tabled until the review of RAE Handout 3: Medical Consequences of Eating Disorder Behaviors.

Values

Values are listed in the Body Acceptance and Exposure (BAE) Measure. Although there is a values handout in the group material (see MAC Handout 11: The Eating Disorder's Impact on Values), it is advisable to administer it in individual therapy as well. Over time, as thinness falls lower and lower in the ranking of importance, this can be reinforced by the therapist in treatment. The focus of taking action in line with pre–eating disorder values can be emphasized in individual sessions as well.

Addressing What Is Not Adaptive

After what is adaptive on an IMT measure has been addressed, the remainder of the session is largely devoted to discussing and solving problems in relation to the behaviors that are *not* adaptive and to introducing handouts relevant to the patient's treatment. For instance, if a patient reports a lot of restrictive behavior, the remainder of the session is spent on addressing the restrictive eating and on planning to establish regular eating for the coming week. If necessary, past handouts on the topic may be reviewed (for example, RAE Handout 1: Information on Eating Disorder Behaviors), or new ones can be introduced from the IMT individual handouts or even from the IMT group handouts, such as MAC Handout 4: Coping with the Urge to Restrict (EAT MEALS Skills). Prior to moving on to the main session topic, it is important to briefly review the IMT measure and cover any major red flags.

Generally, the priorities that need to be addressed are as follows:

- Any medical issue that has been newly reported and not previously addressed

- Restricting

- Purging, taking laxatives, and other intolerance behaviors

- Providing or receiving solicited disparaging remarks about one's body online (meanspiration, or meanspo)

- Avoidance of food

Although responses regarding linked emotions (thought of by some as *underlying issues*) and self-compassion may pull for the therapist to respond to in session, it is important to understand when these treatment targets must be addressed in the hierarchy of the patient's needs. If any of the issues just listed are present, those must be dealt with first—*safety first*. Further, the patient may not yet be ready to address linked emotions and self-compassion. Clinical judgment must be used.

"Body Commenting" Section of the IMT Measure

All questions in the section on body commenting have to do with the patient making comments about other people's bodies or being the recipient of comments about their own body. The first two items in the "Body Commenting" section pertain to intentionally hostile comments. The other items in this section pertain to comments ranging from negative to flattering.

As discussed in the "Core Concepts" section of this manual, meanspiration is a particularly concerning topic. So as to not draw attention to this behavior, meanspiration is not asked about directly on the IMT measures. Instead, the items are phrased as follows:

- For *any* reason, did people say negative or mean things about your *body* online?

- For *any* reason, did you say negative or mean things about another person's *body* online?

Therefore, in addition to inquiring about unsolicited bullying and victimization behavior, these items aim to obtain information about solicited remarks of a disparaging nature. If either of the first two behaviors in the "Body Commenting" section is endorsed with a number other than 0, further inquiry is required.

Depending on which answer was endorsed, a therapist may use either of these open-ended prompts with the patient:

- Tell me more about what happened when someone said something negative or mean about your body online.

- Tell me more about what happened when you said something negative or mean about another person's body online.

If it appears that the patient was engaging in solicited body-commenting behavior, it is important to have a discussion with carers and make this a primary treatment target. Internet permissions should be implemented. *Psychoeducation should not be provided to the patient regarding the reinforcing nature of soliciting or providing disparaging feedback on the body*. Instead, this behavior should be shaped down by preventing access and providing verbal reinforcement for not engaging in the behavior.

If the patient endorses other items, it is also important to follow up. If the patient endorses the statement that others in the environment are making comments about their body, then efforts should be made to mitigate this. If, upon inquiry, it is discovered that family members are making comments about the patient's body, then (for instance) the therapist may administer FAM/PT Handout 1.23: Stop the "Fat" Talk! (found in the IMT family handouts) with family members present in a particular session. Another example could be that the patient is using social media to post many pictures of their body in minimal clothing (such as a bathing suit) while flexing, and others are commenting. Therefore, a treatment target could be to decrease posting pictures of this nature.

The "Physical" Section of the IMT Measure

It is important to monitor medical problems to see whether anything troubling arises and to notify the patient's carers and physician, if appropriate.

It may be helpful for patients with BED to complete the "Physical" section once, and thereafter infrequently.

The Four IMT Individual Measures

This section explains the four separate IMT individual measures.

1. The Regular Eating Measure

The Regular Eating Measure is a weekly measure administered at the start of IMT individual therapy during the period when regular eating is the focus. It is administered only in the period prior to the introduction of the appetitive eating material. Even though core treatment concepts presented in the Regular Eating Measure may not yet have been covered in treatment, this assessment may still be administered at baseline (for example, in an intake packet). If patients have any questions about the items, simply review the items with the patients.

Patients Receiving Family Support If a patient who is receiving some regular eating interventions is also receiving family support, the Regular Eating Measure can be administered at the same time as the relevant family measure. This may be done if carers are supporting only a portion, rather than all, of the meals and snacks. Just as family support and individual therapy are not incompatible, neither are the family measures and the Regular Eating Measure. In both measures, the "Physical" and "Body Commenting" sections are the same. Therefore, if a patient is also completing a family measure on the same day as the Regular Eating Measure, they do not have to complete the portion of the Regular Eating Measure that has both of the redundant sections.

2. The Appetitive Eating Measure

The first iteration of the Appetitive Eating Measure, created in 2011 by Tara Deliberto and her colleagues (Deliberto, Reinharth, & Sanderson, 2012), was further developed with Stephanie Jacobs and Thomas Hildebrandt (Deliberto, Jacobs, Sanderson, & Hildebrandt, 2014). The measure was initially named the Eating Beliefs and Behaviors Questionnaire (EBBQ), and it incorporated a study examining food-related thought suppression and binge eating. It has been repurposed for clinical use in this manual.

The Appetitive Eating Measure is meant to catalogue maladaptive thoughts and behaviors as they pertain to the adaptive practice of appetitive eating. If eating when hungry and stopping when full are psychologically healthy behaviors, then pathology can be behaviorally defined around these anchors. In the context of an eating disorder, these four behaviors can be thought of as psychologically maladaptive and thus as treatment targets:

1.   Stopping oneself from eating when hungry

2.   Eating past the point of being full

3.   Stopping oneself from eating before being full

4.   Eating when not hungry

Therefore, these four behaviors are assessed in the Appetitive Eating Measure. To be thorough, other behaviors consistent with this framework have also been included. (Of course, this measure also includes the *adaptive* behaviors of eating when hungry and stopping when full.)

In addition to assessing for behaviors, a section on beliefs regarding eating behaviors was developed. The beliefs listed in this section reflect a mind-set at odds with an adaptive appetitive eating style and in accordance with an eating disorder mind-set (Deliberto et al., 2014). Because the items are intended to be used individually in clinical practice, no subscales were developed, and a total score is not calculated. Each individual item is important to note. These beliefs are to be targeted with psychoeducation from the IMT handouts and behavior therapy targeting appetitive cues. From the behavioral perspective, behavior change precedes thought change.

Recommended Use

It is recommended that the Appetitive Eating Measure be given before the decision is made to administer appetitive eating interventions in the context of RAE, that it be given again as needed throughout treatment, and that it be given once more at the conclusion of treatment. But it can also be administered weekly, if desired, along with the Regular and Appetitive Eating Measure. Progress should be reviewed with the patient over time.

Using the Appetitive Eating Measure in Decision Making

In keeping with the clinical practice–based model of this manual, assessing for when a given patient may be ready for the appetitive portion of RAE is not an exact science. That said, administering the Appetitive Eating Measure may provide information that is helpful in making a decision. For instance, if a patient with a history of purging has endorsed about 75 percent of the "Beliefs" items with a 5, 6, or 7, then the person may not be ready to eat in accordance with hunger and fullness cues. Perhaps spending a longer time eating regularly would be helpful in addition to providing psychoeducation about appetitive eating. After a couple of weeks of psychoeducation, perhaps try readministering the Appetitive Eating Measure to see if the numbers have come down. If so, perhaps taking on appetitive eating goals is likely to be more fruitful. For patients who have BED, the risk for the engagement in intolerance behaviors is very likely not as high as for those who have a history of these behaviors. Therefore, although psychoeducation is helpful in fostering willingness, it is not as necessary to take a conservative approach and employ an extended period of psychoeducation prior to tackling the behavioral treatment targets of eating when hungry and stopping when full.

By itself, the Appetitive Eating Measure is a rather crude tool for helping the clinician decide whether a patient is ready to embark on appetitive eating as a goal. In context, however, and together with other factors—such as the level of carer support, the patient's history of intolerance behaviors, the patient's medical history, and the patient's cognitive flexibility—this measure can help provide support to the clinician in the trenches.

3. The Regular and Appetitive Eating Measure

The Appetitive Eating Measure is intended to help a clinician get a comprehensive idea of all beliefs and behaviors related to appetitive eating that may be present during critical periods in treatment (for example, prior to administering appetitive eating interventions, and at the conclusion of treatment). By contrast, the Regular and Appetitive Eating Measure is intended to be a weekly measure. This measure is to be administered after the appetitive eating interventions have been introduced. Once the Regular and Appetitive Eating Measure has been administered, the Regular Eating Measure is no longer administered, but the Appetitive Eating Measure can be administered in conjunction with the Regular and Appetitive Eating Measure.

4. The Body Acceptance and Exposure Measure

It is not advisable to conduct BA exposures from the first day of IMT individual therapy, and so it is also not advisable to administer the Body Acceptance and Exposure Measure from the first day of treatment. The measure's questions may be overwhelming to some patients who are not yet ready for this type of emotional processing. Some questions are like a mini-imaginal exposure. If patients are at the point in treatment where food-related behaviors are under control and they are ready to take on body-related behaviors, then the concept of BAE in treatment must be addressed before this measure is administered. Once the patient understands that they will be asked to confront negative emotions and underlying fears in this portion of treatment, the measure can be administered.

Homework   Each week, patients will be assigned about five to ten minutes of homework to be completed every day. Completion of homework is essential to the successful generalization of the skills and concepts taught in session. When patients do complete their homework, be sure to provide Rec-SPA, such as saying, "Good job completing your homework" and giving a thumbs-up. If patients do not complete their homework, a brief intervention is required. If the therapist happens to be familiar with dialectical behavior therapy (Linehan, 1993, 2014a, 2014b), conducting a chain analysis is recommended. If the therapist is not familiar with dialectical behavior therapy, not to worry! A great starting point is simply to ask, "What got in the way of completing the assignment this week?" From there, doing some problem solving around the roadblocks to homework completion is recommended.

Suggested Administration: Moving Through the IMT Individual Material

As will be explained in greater detail, regular eating must be the first treatment goal to be addressed. Everyone will take a different amount of time to complete the regular eating portion of RAE. Because this is a clinical practice–based model rather than a strict protocol, a predetermined number of sessions in which to provide the regular eating inventions is not offered here. How long regular eating takes to establish will vary according to a variety of factors, including severity of illness, the degree to which the patient's disorder is self-eclipsing (ego-syntonic), motivation, resources, and so forth. The following information is also important to consider in determining whether a patient is ready to progress to appetitive eating as a treatment goal:

- Patient's history of health stability

- Information recorded on food logs

- Patient's reported urges to restrict and avoid food

- Patient's answers on the IMT measures

- Patient's self-reported readiness to begin taking on new treatment goals

Criteria for Moving Through the IMT Individual Material

The following guidelines are intended to help the clinician move through the IMT individual handouts. Not all cases will fit neatly into the various parts of the framework that is outlined here, but the information is nevertheless intended to provide the clinician with appropriate pacing.

Administer the *regular eating* material from RAE if...

- The patient is not underweight relative to what is healthy for their individual body

- Health restoration has been achieved (AN and AAN patients)

- The patient has been medically cleared for the appropriate level of care

- The patient has an active eating disorder in which food restriction is present

Administer the *appetitive eating* material from RAE if...

- Regular eating has been established

- Challenge foods are being incorporated into meals

- The patient can label emotions

- The patient can tolerate emotions

- The patient eats food they like and find delicious

- Mindfulness has been practiced

- The patient displays a somewhat flexible cognitive style

- The Appetite Eating Measure has been administered

- The patient has rated a substantial portion of the "Beliefs" items on the Appetitive Eating Measure at 5 or lower

Administer the *body-related behavior* (exercise, body avoidance, and so forth) portions of the BAE material if...

- This material becomes necessary at any point in treatment *after* the treatment target of food restriction has been introduced (for example, if compulsive exercise is a problem, introduce these portions of the BAE material at the start of treatment)

- The regular eating material has been mastered and the appetitive eating material has at least been introduced (unless there is a need to introduce these portions of the BAE material earlier)

Administer the *exposure exercises* in the BAE handouts if...

- The regular eating material has been mastered

- Intolerance behaviors have been significantly reduced

- Body-related behaviors have been introduced

- The concept of safety behaviors has been reviewed

- Personality pathology has been assessed

- Self-destructive behaviors have been significantly decreased

- The patient has practiced skills from dialectical behavior therapy if personality pathology is present

Administer the *self-compassion exercises* in the BAE handouts after...

- The regular eating material has been mastered

- Challenge foods have been mastered

- Body-related behaviors (such as compulsive exercising) have been significantly reduced

- Exposure exercises targeting fear of "fatness" and/or weight gain have been conducted

- Appropriate linked emotion–related exposure exercises have been conducted

- Relevant real-life exposure exercises have been conducted

Criteria for Skipping the IMT Individual Material

The *regular eating* material (RAE Handout 5 and RAE Handout 6) can be skipped if the patient meets the following criteria:

- Eats regularly without a struggle

- Denies moderate to strong urges to restrict or avoid food

- Denies acting on urges to restrict or avoid food

- Is weight- and health-restored (in cases of anorexia nervosa and atypical anorexia nervosa)

The *appetitive eating* material (RAE Handout 12, RAE Handout 13, RAE Handout 14, and RAE Handout 15) can be skipped if the patient meets the following criteria:

- Readily identifies hunger and fullness cues

- Is readily able to eat when hungry and stop when full

- Is able to identify the type of food desired and allows self to eat it

The *appetitive eating* material (RAE Handout 12, RAE Handout 13, RAE Handout 14, and RAE Handout 15) can be postponed if the patient meets the following criteria:

- Currently displays a rigid and concrete cognitive style

- Reports they will very likely give in to eating disorder urges if they are not given direction regarding the quantity of food to eat

- Reports that they are not ready for appetitive eating

The BAE *exposure* exercises can be put on hold if the patient meets the following criteria:

- Has significant personality pathology

- Engages in self-destructive behavior

- Engages in moderate to severe food-related eating disorder behaviors (such as restriction, avoidance, and purging)

- Engages in moderate to severe body-related eating disorder behaviors (such as compulsive exercising)

Treatment Objectives in RAE and BAE

If the *regular eating* material is administered, then ensure that...

- Health and weight are maintained

- Food logs are completed

- Urges to restrict are decreased over time

- Regular eating is a focus of treatment for at least two months (but take as long as necessary while actively targeting the regular eating–related treatment goals)

- Food exposures are conducted

- Urges to avoid are decreased over time

If the *appetitive eating* material is administered, then ensure that…

- Health and weight are maintained

- Appetite is monitored

- Logs are completed

- Patient is actively committed to working on not acting on the urge to override hunger

- Patient is actively committed to working on not acting on the urge to stop before full

- Appetitive eating is a focus of treatment for at least two months (but take as long as necessary while actively targeting the appetitive eating–related treatment goals)

If the *BAE material* is administered, then ensure that…

- Fear of "fatness" and weight gain are decreasing over time

- Fear of recovery is decreasing over time

- Avoidance of linked emotions is decreasing over time

- Health and weight are maintained

- Regular eating is established

- Appetite is monitored

- Patient is not acting on the urge to override hunger

- Patient is not acting on the urge to stop eating before full

- Logs are completed

BAE Material in Session Versus Separate BAE Sessions

Although it is paramount to address food restriction first, and then food avoidance, a point is typically reached in treatment where there is time left in session for the discussion of other issues. For instance, after the patient has developed a routine of eating regularly, confronted many challenge foods, and been stabilized for some time, the therapist's role in RAE is to continue to reinforce adaptive recovery behaviors and simply monitor for signs of relapse. When this stage has been reached, it is time to start introducing BAE handouts in individual sessions.

If the patient is at a point in treatment where it is appropriate for BAE material to be introduced, but if there never seems to be enough time in session to get to it, it may be appropriate to set up an additional session later in the week for the BAE material alone. This can sometimes happen when it is just too much to get to both RAE and the BAE material in one session. For instance, in the middle of a course of treatment, RAE material may take up twenty-five minutes of a session, and meeting with the family may take up another fifteen minutes. In this scenario, no time remains to cram in imaginal exposure exercises. Therefore, a second session is established where the sole focus is on the BAE material.

Ordering BAE Interventions in Treatment

It is important to assess what body-related behaviors are most disruptive to the patient and then start there. The behavior-shaping BAE handouts are not meant to be administered in linear fashion. For instance, if a patient is really struggling with body investigating (body checking), but not with exercise, then be sure to administer, as soon as necessary, BAE Handout 10: Body Investigating Behaviors and BAE Handout 11: ROCKS Skills for Decreasing Body Investigating.

Mixing Individual and Group Treatment

It may often be the case that patients are not able to attend groups where IMT material is being taught. Therefore, IMT group handouts may be used in individual therapy sessions. It is not advisable, however, to use the IMT individual handouts in IMT groups, because many of the IMT individual handouts were designed to be more personal in nature, and answers to questions in the IMT individual handouts may be triggering to other patients in a group setting. In short, IMT group handouts can be used in individual sessions, but IMT individual handouts should not be used in group settings.

In addition, for patients with BOB disorders, individual interventions may be used during the same stage of treatment as family and group interventions. This is *not* the case for anorexia nervosa, however, and often it is not the case for atypical anorexia nervosa, either. (Please note that although AAN technically falls under the diagnosis of OSFED, it is grouped with anorexia nervosa here.) Either a higher level of care or family interventions must precede the implementation of individual interventions with AN and often with AAN as well.

Section 1.6

Administration Considerations

Concurrent Family and Individual Therapy

This section discusses how to incorporate family members into individual therapy for eating disorders. Guidelines for the degree of carer involvement are provided and are based on the patient's current presentation. Discussion of how carers can support the treatment of various disorders is also reviewed here.

Family Involvement for People with Bulimia Nervosa or Other Specified Feeding or Eating Disorder

With respect to BN and OSFEDx (recall that the "x" notation indicates the general exclusion of atypical anorexia nervosa), patients will benefit from the support of willing and able carers. This section provides guidelines for the degree of carer involvement, based on patient presentation.

In context, for patients with BN or OSFEDx, any of the following examples of factors and behaviors may play a role in constituting grounds for *full-scale family involvement in an outpatient setting* (that is, at least one session per week devoted only to family work, and excluding individual work until a later time):

- Purging many times per week, but medically cleared for outpatient treatment

- In addition to purging, engaging in other intolerance behaviors, such as taking laxatives

- Severe restriction

- A more severely self-eclipsing (ego-syntonic) eating disorder

- Engaging in pro–eating disorder behavior online, such as soliciting or providing meanspiration, or meanspo (disparaging and abusive remarks about a person's body)

- Denying motivation to recover

- Reporting that their number one value is thinness

For patients with BN or OSFEDx, here are examples of the types of factors and behaviors that would constitute grounds for *partial family involvement* (that is, presence of carers for a portion of the weekly session, with family interventions implemented at home) along with implementation of some individual interventions:

- Purging once or twice per week, but medically cleared for outpatient treatment

- Reporting only partial motivation to recover

- Reporting that they have more important values than "thinness," but that thinness is still very important

- Presence of at least moderate impairment in functioning

For patients with BN or OSFEDx, here are examples of the types of factors and behaviors that would constitute grounds for *little family involvement* (touching base with carers each week):

- Little to no current intolerance behaviors (such as purging)

- No severe restriction or fasting

- Reporting motivation to recover

- Reporting that they have more important values than thinness

- Reporting mild impairment in functioning

Family Involvement for People with Binge Eating Disorder

Typically, family members do not need to be involved in the treatment of BED. It is always helpful, however, to have regular communication with carers, who can provide collateral regarding the patient's food- and body-related behaviors at home. When the symptoms of BED are quite severe and impairing, however, we have found it helpful for carers to be involved in supporting meals and snacks.

Family Involvement for People with Health-Restored Anorexia Nervosa or Atypical Anorexia Nervosa (RAN)

This section discusses family involvement in largely individual treatment for people with health-restored AN or AAN. As explained earlier, patients with AN or AAN who are not health-restored are not appropriate for individual therapy in an outpatient setting. Either family treatment or a higher level of care is required.

Here are examples of factors and behaviors that would call for *partial family involvement* (that is, presence of carers for a portion of the weekly session, with family interventions implemented at home) concurrent with individual therapy for RAN:

- Recent discharge from a higher level of care after a period of stabilization, with some support or supervision during meals and snacks needed in the home to target food restriction and avoidance

- Recent completion of intensive family treatment, but presence of urges to engage in eating disorder behaviors, such as food restriction or food avoidance, with intolerance behaviors (such as purging) still intense

- Recent health restoration outside the context of treatment (for example, on their own, with family support outside treatment), but extra support with meals and snacks at home may be useful

- Any factor listed earlier as constituting grounds for *partial family involvement* in the treatment of patients with BN or OSFEDx

Factors that would constitute grounds for *little family involvement* in the individual treatment of RAN are largely the same as those for patients with BN or OSFEDx. Additionally, if a patient with RAN recently completed a course of family treatment and is ready for individual therapy, there is no need for active family involvement. Touching base with carers each week for collateral largely suffices, in most cases.

Implementing Concurrent Family and Individual Interventions

The degree to which family interventions will be integrated into individual therapy will vary. Clinicians must select the most appropriate family interventions to weave into individual therapy on a case-by-case basis. The IMT family handouts designated for BOB disorders were created so that they are not at odds with the IMT individual therapy handouts. These handouts were designed to complement the individual therapy modality. Note that for patients with the RAN designation, the BOB versions of the family handouts should be used, not the AN and AAN versions.

Splitting Treatment Between Family and Individual Therapy

It may seem that implementing family interventions would be at odds with individual therapy. How can carers take control of foods while the patient is also learning to eat on their own in individual therapy? In short, as is the case with many learning endeavors, initial support results in later autonomy. When learning to ride a bicycle, a carer may walk behind a child, holding their seat to steady them as they learn to pedal. In this way, the carer supports the child before they can ride the bicycle themselves. Combining family and individual interventions is no more at odds with individual therapy than a carer holding a bicycle seat while a child pedals. How, exactly, to implement both, though, is currently a clinical art. This section aims to provide the clinician with guidance in creating that art.

In regard to incorporating the family, the behavioral treatment of eating disorders in adolescents is not entirely removed from the treatment of other disorders. For instance, in the behavioral treatment of obsessive-compulsive disorder in adolescents, a primary carer may be brought into treatment for collateral, to help construct an accurate fear hierarchy, and to ensure that exposure exercises are being completed for homework at home. The same is true in the treatment of eating disorders. Carers can provide the clinician with collateral regarding the patient's food- and body-related behaviors at home, play an active role in meal and snack planning, ensure that portion sizes being served are appropriate, support the patient at meal and snack times as often as possible, provide recovery-specific positive attention to the patient at home, monitor technology use for eating disorder–exacerbating behaviors, help construct challenge food hierarchies in session, and help incorporate a reasonable number of challenge foods into meals and snacks at home during the week. All of this can be done while the patient logs their own food intake and monitors their appetitive cues. It is recommended that you read the IMT family handouts and choose the best interventions for your patient.

 Researchers are encouraged to establish more specific protocols for incorporating family interventions into individual therapy for mild and moderate bulimia nervosa, OSFEDx based on symptom presentation, severe binge eating disorder, health-restored anorexia nervosa, and health-restored atypical anorexia nervosa.

Necessary Interventions in an Outpatient Setting

Although IMT interventions can largely be used flexibly, there is a small number of handouts that *must* be implemented in outpatient settings in a given modality. This section lists those IMT interventions.

Necessary Regular and Appetitive Eating Interventions

For almost all patients receiving RAE interventions, the following handouts must be administered in due course:

- RAE Handout 1: Information on Eating Disorder Behaviors

- RAE Handout 3: Medical Consequences of Eating Disorder Behaviors

- RAE Handout 4: The Road to Recovery from an Eating Disorder

- RAE Handout 5: How Does Regular Eating Work? (plus the Regular Eating Log and the Regular and Appetitive Eating Log)

- RAE Handout 9: Challenges: Hard Work That Is Worth It

Exceptions to Administering Certain RAE Handouts

In the following cases, the necessary RAE interventions do not need to be administered:

- RAE Handout 3: patients with BED

- RAE Handout 5 and the Regular Eating Log: patients with health-restored AN or AAN who are coming from previous treatment where regular eating patterns were established

Necessary Body Acceptance and Exposure Interventions

For most patients receiving BAE Interventions, the following handouts must be administered in due course:

- BAE Handout 1: How Does My Eating Disorder Impact Body Image?

- BAE Handout 6: When Exercise Is Unhealthy (except for patients who have never struggled with the issue of exercise as an unhealthy activity)

- BAE Handout 8: Body Avoidance Behaviors

- BAE Handout 9: NIFTY Skills for Decreasing Body Avoidance

- BAE Handout 10: Body Investigating Behaviors

- BAE Handout 11: ROCKS Skills for Decreasing Body Investigating

Once all life-threatening eating disorder behaviors have decreased, all minor eating disorder behaviors have been addressed, no other self-destructive behaviors are present, and the concept of safety behaviors has been reviewed, the following BAE handouts are required:

- BAE Handout 13: Real-Life and Imaginal Fears

- BAE Handout 14: Getting to the Bottom of Things

- BAE Handout 18: Pretending It's Forever

- BAE Handout 19: Imagining Recovery

Section 1.7

Using IMT Materials in Individual Therapy

RAE Handouts

This portion of the manual describes how to incorporate RAE handouts into individual therapy sessions. Each handout is discussed individually.

RAE HANDOUTS

RAE Handout 1: Information on Eating Disorder Behaviors

RAE Handout 2: Psychological Consequences of Eating Disorder Behaviors

RAE Handout 3: Medical Consequences of Eating Disorder Behaviors

RAE Handout 4: The Road to Recovery from an Eating Disorder

RAE Handout 5: How Does Regular Eating Work?

RAE Handout 6: Five Non-RE Eating Disorder Behaviors and Five RE Recovery Behaviors

RAE Handout 7: Anxiety, Guilt, and Disgust in Recovery

RAE Handout 8: Accepting the Food You Have Eaten

RAE Handout 9: Challenges: Hard Work That is Worth It

RAE Handout 10: Try Not to Think of a Pink Cupcake

RAE Handout 11: Distraction and Mindfulness

RAE Handout 12: Regular and Appetitive Eating

RAE Handout 13: How Does Appetitive Eating Work?

RAE Handout 14: Your Stomach Is Like a Gas Tank

RAE Handout 15: Six Non-RAE Eating Disorder Behaviors and Six RAE Recovery Behaviors

RAE Handout 16: I Can't Tell If I'm Hungry or Upset

RAE Handout 17: Food Is Everywhere, All the Time

RAE Handout 18: Why Dieting Doesn't Work

RAE Handout 19: Honoring Your Food Every Day

RAE Handout 1: Information on Eating Disorder Behaviors

Administration of this handout is required for all patients.

The concepts presented in RAE Handout 1 are core and essential to the behavioral treatment of eating disorders. It is imperative that both therapist and patient be fully versed in the language and concepts presented here. This handout should be administered early on in individual treatment. Presenting eating disorder behaviors individually and then in a sequence, as this handout does, fosters an understanding of the solitary pieces of the eating disorder puzzle as well as an understanding of the greater whole. Unlike the usual experience of being caught up in the whirlwind of eating disorder experiences, reviewing this handout fosters a sense of anchoring. Knowledge about what experiences are happening and how they tie together helps a person foster separation, rather than fusion, with the eating disorder experience. This handout is also intended to be used to help the patient further understand behavioral treatment targets. The therapist is encouraged to concretely state in treatment, "The behaviors presented here are going to be what we target in treatment over time." The information is chunked so that the patient can better understand not only the mechanisms of the eating disorder from a behavioral perspective but also the mechanisms of recovery. With the eating disorder broken down into its parts, recovery is less overwhelming.

Food Restriction and Avoidance

Food restriction and food avoidance are separate behaviors. It is very important to know the difference and distinguish between the two in clinical practice. For more information as to why, see the general introduction to this manual.

In this section, cognitive processes are also examined. The concept of thought suppression (that is, attempting to avoid thinking about something) is briefly introduced, as is obsession. These concepts are later explored in more depth in the RAE Handout 10: Try Not to Think of a Pink Cupcake. Briefly, thought suppression feeds obsession, and vice versa. By trying not to think about something, in essence one is fueling thinking about it more. This is called *ironic processing* (Wegner, Schneider, Carter, & White, 1987; Wegner & Zanakos, 1994). In turn, the more it is thought about (obsessed over), the greater the attempts at suppression may become. In short, suppressing thoughts and obsession are related and influence one another. Food-related thought suppression and obsession have been shown to play a role in eating disorder pathology in this way (Lavender et al., 2009; Barnes & Tantleff-Dunn, 2010; Deliberto, Jacobs, Novak, McVey, et al., 2014).

Avoiding Internal Experiences

Depending upon a variety of factors, such as the patient's level of experience in treatment, the distinctions among the four types of internal experiences may not be readily understood by the patient. This information will have to be returned to throughout treatment. For instance, patients often conflate the thought *I'm fat* with negative emotions. Further, patients may also confuse feeling physically sated or full with the thought *I'm fat*. Therefore, although a brief review of the four internal experiences is warranted here, it will be important to revisit this information throughout treatment. Lastly, in reviewing the eating disorder sequence of behaviors later in this handout, it will be helpful to point out the internal experiences listed along the left-hand side of the figure on the last two pages of the handout.

Questions (Part 1)

Go through these questions with the patient in session, and have them write in answers. If they are conflating any concepts (for example, food restriction and food avoidance), ask them to refer back to the beginning of the handout for clarification. If they appear to be struggling after that, provide feedback. It is important, however, for patients to get into the practice of referring to the handouts themselves, both in and outside of session. The therapist can help guide this process early on in treatment.

Specific Notes on Certain Questions:

- Question 13: This question starts to probe for the patient's current insight into the connection between food restriction and/or avoidance and binge eating. If the patient endorses all the aforementioned behaviors but denies a connection, psychoeducation in this area should be emphasized.

- Question 14: This question prompts the patient to begin to contemplate the concept of inevitability acceptance (that is, the idea that the eating disorder behaviors are so self-destructive that they simply cannot be sustained). Because food is needed to nourish the body, deprivation is not a long-term option. At this stage in treatment, the statement "Something has to give" will mean different things. For people with anorexia nervosa, restricting type, this may mean that their physical health is deteriorating and that engaging in food restriction and food avoidance is therefore not sustainable. For people with other disorders, this may also be true, with the addition that these behaviors backfire into the behavior of binge eating as well as other intolerance behaviors (such as purging).

Types of Binge Eating

The information provided about the behavior of binge eating may be helpful to patients for several reasons. For patients who eat an objectively large amount (for example, an amount that one would eat across the span of a day) in one sitting, it can be reassuring to know that they are not alone. Eating this quantity of food has a name, and it is called an *objective binge*. As treatment progresses for patients who engage in objective binge episodes, it is helpful to label the shift from objective to subjective binges. Conversely, if a patient, in an out-of-control manner, eats an objectively small amount of food that they perceive to be large (for example, a normal meal, a few pieces of candy, and so forth), it can be helpful for them to know that they are not engaging in an objective but rather a *subjective* binge episode. Like objective binges, subjective binges are defined by loss of control. This helps to frame their experience. It may be helpful to briefly describe to patients that the word "objective" has to do with data and the word "subjective" refers to a person's experience. That said, loss of control is experienced in both types of binge eating episodes. It is important to emphasize the loss-of-control aspect of the behavior because this, more than the quantity of food consumed, is the defining feature.

A description of internal experiences follows the more academic distinction between objective and subjective binge episodes. This introduces the idea that after episodes of binge eating, internal experiences that are unpleasant do not have to be "gotten rid of" with subsequent behaviors (such as purging) and instead can be tolerated.

TIP: DON'T WORRY TOO MUCH ABOUT THE TYPE OF BINGE

It is important not to get caught up in "correctly" classifying binge episodes as objective or subjective. Precious time should not be wasted on attempts to determine this, nor is it clinically indicated to have the patient count calories to obtain an estimated amount. It is best to focus on the loss-of-control piece and get a general idea of the volume of food consumed. For patients who have episodes of binge eating that involve large quantities of food at baseline, it will be important to track a decrease in food volumes consumed during binge episodes because this is a marker of decreased impulsivity. Generally, the volume of food during binge episodes should trend down.

Intolerance Behaviors

What are called *intolerance behaviors* here are elsewhere referred to in the eating disorder literature as *compensatory behaviors*. This term was relabeled because, although *compensatory behaviors* describes the rationale for the behavior from an eating disorder perspective, *intolerance behaviors* describes the function from within a behavioral framework. For instance, from within the eating disorder mind-set, if the "mistake" of eating was made, guilt is felt, and the error should be corrected, or "compensated for," through a "corrective" action, such as purging. Conversely, the term *intolerance behaviors* reflects an unwillingness or current inability to tolerate negative internal experiences (emotions, thoughts, physical sensations, and/or behavioral urges), and so a maladaptive behavior is performed. For these reasons, the term was relabeled here.

Further, as they are defined here, intolerance behaviors are those that come after eating and produce the effect of decreasing negative internal experiences. Therefore, an action such as vowing to restrict in the future technically fits the definition of an intolerance behavior. If a person makes this vow immediately after a binge episode and it decreases negative internal experiences, then the behavior of binge eating is negatively reinforced (that is, an aversive experience is reduced). Therefore, making a vow to restrict in the future would be a necessary treatment target.

Because this handout was written for people with various eating disorder diagnoses, examples of intolerance behaviors were not given. If a patient asks for an example of an intolerance behavior, give an example that they have previously reported. Another alternative is to ask about eating disorder behaviors they may have heard of. Later on in the handout, the example of "exercise" is given because it is a widely known strategy attempted by people desiring weight loss. Therefore, depending on the context, we have found this example to be rather benign.

Questions (Part 2)

Even if the patient does not have a history of binge eating or losing control while eating (that is, if the patient answers no to question 1), go through each item together in session, and have the patient fill in answers. If the patient has truly never lost control while eating, they may skip the questions pertaining to binge eating (questions 2, 4, 6, and 9). The majority of patients, however, have likely lost control of their eating at some time. All the points in the following paragraph regarding inevitability acceptance will still apply to patients who have never lost control over food.

If a Patient Answers the Eating and Binge Eating Questions Similarly

For many patients, in the context of the eating disorder and fear of "fatness," negative internal experiences (such as emotions) can result after eating regardless of whether a binge occurred. This is especially true for patients who are eating with supervision or in the context of treatment; however, it also can apply to patients who have been feeding themselves. Although internal experiences can certainly be more *intense* after a binge, it is still important to highlight that negative internal experiences can occur even after eating without loss of control in the context of the eating disorder. This information can help the patient comprehend that the eating disorder is an unsustainable way of life and inevitably must be abandoned. Life cannot possibly be lived in such a way that every single time a person engages in the vital act of eating, a host of negative thoughts, emotions, physical sensations, and self-destructive behaviors occur. Therefore, new ways of thinking and being *must* be adopted because the old eating disorder way is not only not working, it is also dangerous and life-threatening. In short, the seeds of inevitability acceptance are planted early. (This is a philosophy akin to "creative hopelessness" in the acceptance and commitment therapy literature, or to the idea of the "gift of desperation" from the Alcoholics Anonymous literature.)

If a Patient Answers the Eating and Binge Eating Questions Differently

At the start of treatment, if a patient reports they are *not* having negative internal experiences after eating, there is likely something awry. Recovery behaviors produce negative internal experiences. Therefore, if there are no negative internal experiences, there are likely also no recovery behaviors. No pain, no gain. In the absence of negative internal experiences after eating, it is very likely that highly restrictive behaviors are occurring.

If a person is highly restrictive, going through the eating disorder sequence of behaviors will help elucidate the connection between highly restrictive behavior and loss of control regarding food. Although the person is getting an internal reward (reinforcement) from the restriction, there can *also* be a backlash in the form of later loss of control and all the negative internal experiences that go with it. In line with the concept of inevitability acceptance, a cycle of careening between restricting and binge eating is unsustainable and *must* be changed.

Specific Notes on Certain Questions

- Question 7: Being afraid of weight gain causes people to be on high alert. They are very often looking for things to go wrong. If people were not afraid of weight gain, they likely would not have the same kinds of thoughts.

- Question 13: Intolerance behaviors directly reinforce the fear of weight gain and/or "fatness" and the belief that a person cannot tolerate internal experiences. Engaging in intolerance behaviors can also be physically dangerous.

Tying It All Together

This section simply explains that eating disorder behaviors are all tied together. It also sets the stage for the eating disorder sequence of behaviors.

Eating Disorder Sequence of Behaviors

The eating disorder sequence of behaviors is a sample cross-section of how the behaviors could all tie together. This is not the be-all and end-all in terms of the ways that eating disorder behaviors link together. Because the matrix of behaviors is so complex, this depiction is meant as a learning tool to help people understand a "clean" version of eating disorder behaviors in something of a vacuum. In reality, the behaviors could present as more complicated. There are two sequences presented, the first for patients who *do* report having engaged in any sort of intolerance behavior (even occasionally), and the second for patients who report *never* having engaged in an intolerance behavior. More on this follows in the next section.

Because this eating disorder sequence of behaviors maps onto what was presented in the general introduction to this manual, please review that for deeper reference. Regarding the precipitants of binge eating, negative emotions can either follow eating or be triggered from the outside. Further, the only internal experience presented here that is not previously listed is perception. In this context, it can be explained that perception is at work when one of our senses, such as sight, can be influenced by our internal experiences. For instance, because someone is afraid of gaining weight and has the thought *I'm fat*, they can actually see themselves, with their eyes, as bigger than they really are. If the patient appears to understand, you might ask, "Do you think that happens to you?" If they still seem confused, you might ask, "Do you know of anyone who thinks about themselves differently than you do? Maybe someone who says, 'I'm so fat' all the time, but you don't see them that way?"

Binge Eating

It is likely that the majority of patients will relate to the first sequence. The second sequence is available for patients who present without any report of avoidance behaviors (including internal ones, such as vowing to restrict in the future), something that will happen occasionally. The second sequence is the same as the first except for the exclusion of intolerance behaviors.

RAE Handout 2: Psychological Consequences of Eating Disorder Behaviors

RAE Handout 2 naturally follows the first handout in the series. This handout starts by externalizing the eating disorder. It states that it is the eating disorder that keeps people focused on the details rather than on the larger picture. For each person, a different combination of values that are in line with the eating disorder (such as thinness), negative emotions, obsessions, and a rigid cognitive style interact to create a pathological attention to detail and numbers (such as calories). From within this inflexible cognitive style, without guidance it is often difficult for the patient to recognize larger behavioral patterns at play.

Understanding the eating disorder sequence of behaviors is the first major step forward in treatment in line with moving toward a broader, more flexible, and adaptive cognitive style. Comprehending the concepts presented in RAE Handout 2 is the second step in line with this goal. In short, this handout explains that the function of eating disorder behaviors is primarily to avoid negative internal experiences and that recovery will involve tolerating these experiences. This handout focuses on the negative internal experience of *fear*. Although it is likely different for each individual patient, we have found it to be largely the case that this is one of the chief negative internal experiences being avoided. That said, other negative internal experiences (such as thoughts, physical sensations, and behavioral urges) are often stated as well. In an effort to make things clearer, a description of the model using fear is offered to patients in this handout. Further, at the beginning of treatment, patients must learn to tolerate negative emotions, and it can be helpful to focus on this area.

Regarding the section of the handout called "Psychological Consequences," patients may dispute that they will have a worsening body image over time in the context of the eating disorder. It is important to take a moment to explain the difference between having a long-term positive body image and temporarily feeling "better" after having met an eating disorder weight goal that will just keep getting lower and lower. In the first instance, a person *accepts* themselves unconditionally. In the second, a person will *approve* of themselves only for a period of time, and that approval depends on whether a certain condition is met. There is a big difference! In the second scenario, the person's body image actually worsens over time as the conditions get harder and harder to meet. BAE Handout 1 also addresses this issue.

RAE Handout 3: Medical Consequences of Eating Disorder Behaviors

This handout should not be administered to patients with binge eating disorder.

Although patients may already have been presented with information about medical complications, either in family sessions or at the doctor's office, during an individual therapeutic session it is important for them to have an opportunity to process emotions regarding medical complications. Therefore, we recommend administering this handout even if the patient may already have been made aware of the medical consequences. Prior to administering this handout, be sure to familiarize yourself with all the issues listed, in the event that a basic question should arise. Again, if you are the primary therapist, it is unlikely that you have a medical degree or are in a position to give medical advice, but it is important to be knowledgeable about potential issues that can arise in the context of eating disorders.

Ask the patient what emotions they may be feeling. If the patient is feeling a host of negative emotions, encourage them not to push those emotions away but to express what they are feeling in session. Have them answer the three questions that follow the list of medical issues. Ask for specific, concrete behaviors a patient can engage in that are in line with recovery (for example, coming to session, not opposing supervision of meals, completing treatment-related homework assignments, completing meals, and so forth). If a patient does not show any negative emotions, this may be an indication of *anosognosia*, or inability to recognize functional impairment and the ramifications of the eating disorder (for more information, see part 3, section 1, of this manual, and specifically FAM Handout 1.6). The patient may not be emotionally connecting with these interventions because there may not be an understanding that they have an eating disorder or that their behavior is problematic. Another reason could be that the patient is aware of medical consequences and is not concerned, either because the eating disorder has such a strong hold or because of suicidal ideation. In either case, further assessment may be warranted. The outpatient level of care without active family supervision of meals may not be indicated. In these instances, a clinician should refer to guidelines for level of care and exercise clinical judgment.

RAE Handout 4: The Road to Recovery from an Eating Disorder

Administration of this handout is required for all patients.

This handout is simply the recovery version of the eating disorder sequence of behaviors. Not only is it important for the patient within the eating disorder mind-set to understand the broader perspective on the disorder, it is also important for the patient to understand recovery from the same vantage point. The handouts in the individual therapy modality are meant to embody the broad and flexible cognitive style rather than the narrow, fear-based, inflexible cognitive style. The idea here is to get the patient's mind accustomed to processing in this manner. In addition to being a part of this larger goal, RAE Handout 4 itself is meant to practically and concretely display the steps a patient needs to take to move toward recovery. There is a dialectic here. On the one hand, the individual tasks may seem ridiculously insurmountable to the patient, and therefore overwhelming; on the other hand, concrete steps toward recovery are laid out, and these can inspire hope. Therefore, it is important to ask the patient to process their thoughts and emotions regarding this handout in session. It may also be important to point out that the last internal experiences on the right are not *thoughts* but rather three underlying *beliefs*. The implication here is that over time, rather than instantaneously, a person's beliefs change after long-standing behavior change. Whereas thoughts pop into our minds automatically, underlying beliefs are formed over time.

RAE Handout 5: How Does Regular Eating Work?

This handout explains how regular eating will be implemented. Its administration is often straightforward. It is important to agree in advance on time frames within which to eat and on appropriate amounts of food. This also must be logged. The appropriate amount of food depends on the specifics of the diagnosis and the case. In some cases it may be appropriate to defer to the carers or to the patient; in other cases, it may be appropriate to defer to a dietitian; in still other cases, the appropriate amount of food can be estimated in session.

TIP: Increasing Food Variety Is Not a Substitute for Increasing Quantity
Eating disorders may influence patients to steer away from the goal of regular eating and toward the goal of eating challenge foods early in treatment. In particular, it is important to watch for *treatment drift* away from targeting food restriction and toward food avoidance. For some

---

patients, it is less threatening to eat scary types of food than to increase the overall amount of food eaten. Although certain foods are feared, the patient is likely cognizant of the often touted "fact" that what "really" causes weight gain is not what foods are eaten but rather the overall caloric amount of what is eaten. As a result, patients may appear willing to work on the goal that, according to the eating disorder's logic, is least likely to actually cause weight gain but is still pleasing to the therapist—eating challenge foods. Therefore, it is important that the therapist, to the best of their ability, initially guide treatment in the direction of addressing food restriction with regular eating. Encourage patients to eat within given reasonable time frames. Clearly outline these time frames and agree on them.

RAE Handout 6: Five Non-RE Eating Disorder Behaviors and Five RE Recovery Behaviors and Regular Eating Log

This handout summarizes both the regular eating targets. Examples of eating disorder thoughts that might go along with each maladaptive behavior are provided on the left. On the right, examples of adaptive attitudes that would go along with each adaptive behavior are provided. The arrows between the columns symbolize the fact that patients are not expected to immediately start thinking and believing all the thoughts listed in the right-hand column. These adaptive attitudes and behaviors are simply intended as helpful guides. Similar to the IMT measures, the IMT material lists behaviors in this fashion so that they can serve as a roadmap for the patient. The patient is encouraged to set intentions regarding recovery behaviors—for instance, to select a recovery behavior and aim to behave in accordance with that behavior. Patients are encouraged to use the blank rows in the left-hand column of the handout to list eating disorder behaviors they struggle with and then write down accompanying eating disorder thoughts in line with each maladaptive behavior, and then to use the blank rows in the right-hand column to list corresponding recovery behaviors and attitudes that are in line with those behaviors. The adaptive attitudes that patients construct for themselves can be used somewhat like mantras to help focus their recovery. As they are working on shaping their own RAE behaviors, they can remind themselves of what they wrote.

Regular Eating Log

Administration of this handout is required for all patients unless regular eating patterns were established in prior treatment.

In the individual therapy module, patients log their own eating throughout treatment. In this modality, it is more important for patients to log their own food intake and for the therapist to review the food logs on a weekly basis. This helps establish regular eating. Read the directions carefully with the patient, and ensure comprehension. Also, ensure that patients have enough copies of the log to last until the next session. Ask the patient to make an entry in the log after each meal and snack so they do not forget the information.

Completed Food Logs

When patients bring a completed log to session, be sure to provide recovery-specific positive attention (Rec-SPA) for homework completion. For instance, a therapist might say, "Really nice job completing the food logs this week." Active engagement in treatment is to be reinforced. Further, Rec-SPA is to be provided for all meals and snacks completed as well as for challenge foods eaten. Compare weekly progress to the progress shown in previous weeks and to the baseline.

Incomplete Food Logs

If the patient has not completed the food log before coming to session, be sure to explore the reasons why the log was not completed. Problem solve for what got in the way, to ensure that the same roadblocks do not hinder treatment in the coming week. Ask the patient for a commitment to complete the log in the future. Next, and most important, take time in session to reconstruct the log to the best of the patient's recollection and ability. Point out that if the log had already been completed, more time in session could have been spent talking about other topics. Then provide Rec-SPA for the patient's completion of the log in session. Lastly, be sure to provide Rec-SPA to the patient for all the meals and snacks completed as well as for challenge foods eaten.

Problems with the Food Log

Although it may be tempting to offer verbal praise for a food log completed to absolute perfection, perfection is never to be praised. Patients completing food logs in a highly perfectionistic manner is problematic because perfectionism is part of the eating disorder. It is important to obtain information, however, so do not ask the patient to log information any less accurately. Instead, ask the patient to sully the log in some way—by crumpling the paper, tearing a corner, or making a mark across it with a marker. Then be sure to praise the willingness to make the log imperfect as well as the logging of behavior.

In a similar vein, another problem that can arise is that patients may be tempted to log specific caloric amounts or to measure food. Because it is important to know what a patient is eating and to have an opportunity to shape behavior, it is often helpful to frame the task of logging food without caloric content as an extra treatment challenge.

RAE Handout 7: Anxiety, Guilt, and Disgust in Recovery

At the start of treatment, patients often present with *alexithymia*, the inability to distinguish which emotions they are feeling. They may use vague words to describe how they feel, such as "upset" or "overwhelmed." Over time in treatment, it is important to shape the labeling of specific emotions and their intensity (for example, "I feel anxious at an 8, guilty at a 5, and disgusted at a 7"). Although patients may feel any emotion, positive or negative, after eating, to start chipping away at alexithymia, this handout starts by introducing three—anxiety, guilt, and disgust.

The introduction of this handout externalizes the eating disorder and describes how, in response to the patient's doing things in line with recovery, the eating disorder triggers a host of negative experiences. Rather than feeling good for having accomplished something in line with recovery, patients often feel intense negative emotions. This handout prepares patients for this experience. It also provides the feedback, in written format, that when the eating disorder appears to be "punishing" a person (by telling them, for example, that they did the wrong thing, initiating the feeling of guilt), it is actually because the patient is doing the *right* thing in recovery.

The last section of the handout focuses on judiciously using distraction as a skill. Because food is an essential component of living and must be eaten multiple times throughout the day in order for the patient to thrive and survive, in the eating disorder world we must take a practical approach to the implementation of exposures. The priority at the start of treatment is getting nourishment. Unlike in the treatment of other disorders, where the feared stimuli can be approached over time, there is no time to waste in the treatment of eating disorders. The feared stimuli must be approached by a patient with a self-eclipsing (ego-syntonic) disorder multiple times per day, or else. Under such conditions, the priority is not to feel every little last bit of negative emotion during each exposure (such as a meal or snack) and the period afterward, until fullness subsides. The current clinical wisdom holds that if a patient with a self-eclipsing eating disorder and alexithymia were to spend time feeling confusing negative emotions before, during, and after breakfast, then it would be too difficult for the patient to muster the motivation needed to complete lunch a couple of short hours later. Therefore, at the start of treatment, patients practice eating, labeling emotions, experiencing some tolerable portion of those emotions, employing distraction, and moving on to the next meal or snack. In this way, a person is able to engage in treatment without ever becoming nutritionally deprived. When, however, a person is ready to face the challenge of full exposure without distraction or negative emotion, that phase of treatment can be mindfully started.

In session, go through distraction strategies with the patient that they might be able to use. Examples include talking with a friend, watching a movie, listening to an audiobook, and listening to music. Distractions could be things the patient finds particularly pleasant (such as music the patient likes) so that eating is paired with positive experiences over time.

RAE Handout 8: Accepting the Food You Have Eaten

When the patient has better established a normal eating pattern and has demonstrated some ability to label and tolerate negative emotions, it is time to administer RAE Handout 8. This handout explains the *"nonacceptance of the food I've eaten" cycle*. In essence, engaging in intolerance behaviors is framed as taking a nonaccepting stance toward the food that was just eaten. One line of the handout says "Once you have eaten the food, you have eaten the food. Work on not looking back."

With respect to the six questions under the heading "The 'Nonacceptance of the Food I've Eaten' Cycle: Sequence of Events," typical answers are that patients can continue eating regularly, use the skills presented in the handouts in the group therapy modality, practice tolerating negative emotions, and lean on others for support to cope. With respect to the question under the heading "Accepting the Food You Have Eaten," answers typically are in the vein of "The negative emotions go down over time," but some patients will write that they believe they will continue having to cope with negative emotions, as well as other aversive internal experiences, forever. It is important to provide psychoeducation about the rise and fall of emotions when confronted in exposure therapy.

It is important that patients attempt to start decreasing distraction after meals and tolerating negative emotions. The section of the handout under the heading "Leaning In" sets the stage for this. It is important to note that if emotions are high, short-term distraction can be useful. When emotions are in the manageable range, however, attempting to tolerate them is appropriate. When exposures are conducted with non–eating disorder populations, tolerating negative emotions rated at around 6 on a scale of 0 to 10 is considered a reasonable place to start. For patients with eating disorders, however, given the multiple exposures that are required throughout the day, starting at 6 can be somewhat aggressive, depending on the context. But patients with eating disorders are often feeling negative emotions in the middle to high range of such a scale. Therefore, it is not often possible or practical to begin at a lower point.

RAE Handout 9: Challenges: Hard Work That Is Worth It

Administration of this handout is required for all patients. The aim of this intervention is to extinguish fear of foods. This intervention must be implemented over the course of treatment until foods are no longer feared. It is *not* advisable to use this handout as a guide to conducting food exposures *before* intolerance behaviors have significantly decreased. Until then, it may be helpful simply to administer the handout as a way of getting an idea of what foods the patient fears most. The list of challenge foods that the patient creates can be discussed with carers, and the benefits of holding off on incorporating feared foods into meals and snacks until the patient is ready can be reviewed. The benefits would be the patient's greater likelihood of completing meals and snacks that excluded the highly feared foods, faster establishment of regular eating, and the patient's tolerating negative emotions as opposed to engaging in intolerance behaviors.

After major health-interfering intolerance behaviors (purging, laxative abuse, excessive exercise, and so forth) have significantly decreased, RAE Handout 9 can be used to conduct food exposures. Before moving toward the treatment goal of reducing food avoidance with food exposures, it may also be helpful to bring the EAT MEALS, NO BINGE, and NO PURGE skills from the group therapy modality into individual sessions to help patients decrease restrictive eating, binge eating, and purging.

Handouts from the individual therapy modality should not be used in group, because they can be triggering, but any handout from the group therapy modality can be used in an individual session.

Fear of Food Exposures

This work was influenced by Joanna Steinglass and her colleagues at Columbia University Medical Center.

When a patient has established a pattern of regular eating, and when intolerance behaviors have decreased, it is time to start introducing challenge foods. In essence, this handout prompts therapists and patients to collaboratively create a *fear hierarchy* (that is, a list of feared stimuli—in this case, a list of feared foods ordered from most to least challenging). This fear hierarchy is used to guide both the patient's incorporation of challenges into meals and snacks at home and the selection of foods to be worked on as challenges in session.

It is often advisable for patients to select foods rated at 8 or below to eat as challenges outside session. It is also helpful to bring in carer support for challenges. For instance, a therapist and a patient may invite a carer in at the end of a session and tell them the plan to eat a particular food on a particular day. Ways in which that carer could be supportive of the patient during the challenge can be discussed. Regarding foods that are ranked high on the fear hierarchy, for some patients it may be best to bring these food items into session.

Conducting Food Exposures in Session

Conducting food exposures in session with a willing participant in individual therapy is straightforward. If you have never done exposure therapy before, it may be helpful to think of it just as eating a snack with a patient. From there, you can work on technique.

In-Session Technique

Patients constructing the fear hierarchy (that is, completing RAE Handout 9) typically have a general idea of what is challenging for them, but they may get caught up in exactly which food goes where. In this case, let them know that a general picture will suffice and that the information will change over time. To help the patient with ranking, it may be useful to start by having the patient list easy, medium, and difficult foods and then compare the relative degree of challenge associated with the foods in each category. For instance, if pizza, cookies, and cake are all difficult for the patient, but pizza is more difficult than cookies, and cookies are more difficult than cake, then the patient's ranking would look like this:

10. Pizza

9. Cookies

8. Cake

Once a fear hierarchy is constructed, it is advisable to select a reasonably feasible stimulus for the patient and plan to conduct an exposure exercise around it in session. In typical exposure therapy outside the eating disorder world, a stimulus ranked at about 6 on a scale of 1 to 10 is typically appropriate. Our patients, however, may be routinely eating foods at home that are ranked in the range of 6 to 7. Therefore, sometimes it is more appropriate to pick a food in the range of 8 or 9 for an exposure in session, but this depends on many factors, including the patient's current degree of self-eclipsing, their current ability to tolerate negative emotions, and their history of intolerance behaviors. In individual therapy, of course, the patient's stated preference is usually the deciding factor when it comes to determining which stimuli will be worked on. Once the food is selected, ask the patient or the patient's carers to ensure that this food is provided for the next session. If possible, also arrange for yourself to have that food (or a similar food) to eat during the session, since an important part of behavior therapy is modeling adaptive behavior for the patient.

Before, during, and after the exercise, the therapist asks the patient to rate their distress on a scale of 0 to 10, with 10 representing the highest degree of distress and 0 representing no distress at all. These ratings constitute the *subjective units of distress* (SUDs) scale. When this concept is introduced to the patient, the therapist should say, "Before, during, and after eating the snack together today, I'm going to ask you how much distress you are feeling on a scale of 0 to 10, with 10 being the highest. To start, on a scale of 0 to 10, how distressed are you feeling now?" Record the first rating, or SUD level. Halfway through the snack, ask the patient again, "On a scale of 0 to 10, how much distress are you feeling now?" Record the SUD level. Ask the question again after the snack is completed, and record the SUD level. Continue to ask the same question periodically, and record the SUD level until it is lower than 4. During this process, ensure that no safety behaviors (such as distraction, body investigating, and so on) are being engaged in if they would interfere with the patient's experience of negative emotions. Ask the patient to sit with the negative emotions and process them. It is important to keep a record not only of the patient's SUD levels but also of the food eaten, how the patient ranked it in the fear hierarchy, and the date.

By confronting feared stimuli during the exposure exercise, the patient comes to have a decreased emotional reaction in response. The chance to confront rather than avoid feared stimuli provides an opportunity for new learning. As the patient completes more and more exposures to food, the fear hierarchy will shift. Foods that were once scary will no longer be scary after the exposure has been conducted. The foods that have not yet been confronted will likely start to take a higher position in the fear hierarchy. Because of this evolution, it is important to continue to create new fear hierarchies frequently (for example, every week or every few weeks) as challenges are completed both at home and in session. Further, each patient will require a different number of in-session exposures in order to extinguish fear of food. For instance, some patients may have very supportive carers who can introduce feared foods at home and thus greatly reduce the need to do in-session exposures. Other patients, however, may require greater support from the therapist in session. Still other patients will have eating disorders that are more self-eclipsing in nature, and the patients will need support both at home and in session. In short, the number of exposures will vary. *Exposures must continue to be conducted at home, in session, or in both settings until fear of food is eventually extinguished.*

It is recommended that the process of introducing foods in treatment sessions and at home continue for as long as necessary. While this process is under way, other material may sometimes be introduced. For instance, a food exposure does not always take the entire session. Therefore, perhaps additional handouts can be reviewed in the time available. If the therapist thinks a particular issue other than food exposure should be addressed in a given week, then coordinating with a carer so that more challenge foods are incorporated at home may be an option. The process of extinguishing most fear of foods will take some time, and so clinical judgment must be used in introducing other treatment goals that will deviate from the goal of extinguishing fear of foods. Ultimately, it *is* a treatment goal to completely extinguish fear of foods. Just as in any other exposure therapy, all items in the hierarchy will eventually be addressed. Therefore, it is advisable at this stage not to stray too far from the treatment target of food avoidance. Once fear of food is under control, other treatment targets (such as appetitive eating, body image, self-compassion, values work, and building a life after the eating disorder) can be addressed.

RAE Handout 10: Try Not to Think of a Pink Cupcake

This handout is for patients who have experienced a loss of control when eating, and for patients who currently display traits of *asceticism*, or self-denial of perceived indulgence.

For patients who have experienced loss of control when eating, RAE Handout 10 is a complement to the fear hierarchy in RAE Handout 9. Often patients fear a food not simply because they have made a direct connection between that food and gaining weight. At times the association between the food and weight gain is more complex. In particular, the more *delicious* a food is to the patient, the more concern they may have about bingeing on the food. For instance, a patient may fear rice because it is associated with weight gain, but they may not actually like the taste of rice, and so they may be more willing to eat rice in treatment. But because the patient *likes* the taste of cookies, they may show resistance to eating them. On top of being associated with weight gain, some foods are associated with the additional fear of being potential binge foods. If a feared food is also feared as a potential binge food, then the patient's fear may be compounded, and their willingness to eat that food may be decreased.

Further, studies with the Eating Disorder Inventory-3 (Garner, 2004) have shown that *asceticism*, or self-denial of perceived indulgence, is a characteristic of many people with eating disorders (see also Clausen, Rosenvinge, Friborg, & Rokkedal, 2010). In other words, patients may have a tendency to deprive themselves of foods they enjoy. Thus, there may be an underlying propensity to deny themselves the pleasure of eating those foods in addition to fear of gaining weight from those foods and fear of bingeing on those foods. Therefore, it is particularly important to focus on foods the patient currently perceives as delicious or has found delicious in the past. It is essential to get a carer report of foods that the patient liked prior to the onset of the eating disorder. This, of course, is because the eating disorder clouds the perception of patients. Patients may earnestly report, for instance, that they *never* liked cookies and *always* preferred the *taste* of diet soda, but a conversation with the carers quickly reveals that this is not the case.

RAE Handout 10 was constructed around the concept that patients who engage in binge eating have a more fraught relationship with foods they perceive or have perceived in the past as delicious. Connected to this concept is that of *thought suppression* (attempting not to think of an aversive stimulus). In the case of people with eating disorders who have underlying asceticism, pleasurable stimuli *are* aversive stimuli. In other words, if a person is in the practice of deriving satisfaction from denying themselves perceived indulgences, then the thought of something pleasurable is something to be avoided. As mentioned earlier, research on ironic processing (Wegner et al., 1987; Wegner & Zanakos, 1994) has shown that the more a person deliberately attempts to avoid thinking about something, the more likely they are to think about it. Research by Lavender et al. (2009) and unpublished work by one of this manual's coauthors (Tara Deliberto) show that this occurs with food-related thoughts for people with eating disorders.

Along with tolerance of negative emotions, mindfulness of *thoughts* is the natural choice for targeting ironic processing. The alternative to suppressing thoughts is allowing and noticing thoughts. This intervention also begins to target asceticism in a behavioral fashion. Allowing oneself both to have thoughts of pleasurable stimuli and to eat foods that (in behavioral terms) are pleasurable stimuli starts to target this practice.

RAE Handout 11: Distraction and Mindfulness

This handout is an extension of RAE Handout 8 and explains the nuances of when to distract and when to use mindfulness in therapy. Encourage patients to try to use "7 or above and distract" and "6 or below and be mindful" as loose guidelines. This is not a precise practice. As mentioned in the handout, if patients do not have experience with mindfulness and are not enrolled in group, it can be helpful to bring the mindfulness handouts from the group therapy modality into individual therapy.

Handouts from the individual therapy modality should not be used in group, because they can be triggering, but any handout from the IMT group therapy modality can be used in an individual session.

Regarding the last two questions at the end of the handout, patients (and therapists) are strongly encouraged to incorporate mindfulness into their daily routine. It is helpful to frame mindfulness as an essential part of a person's daily routine, like brushing your teeth. Encourage patients to commit to taking five mindful breaths in the morning, no matter how chaotic the morning may be. For instance, after jumping in the shower and brushing your teeth, stand in the bathroom with your eyes closed, and take five mindful breaths before leaving home for the day. For more, see the Mindfulness and Acceptance (MAC) handouts in the group therapy modality as well as part 2, section 1, of this manual.

RAE Handout 12: Regular and Appetitive Eating

Prior to the administration of this handout, ensure that patients meet the criteria for starting appetitive eating, as outlined in the general introduction to this manual (see "Criteria for Moving Through the IMT Individual Material"). RAE Handout 12 aims to introduce the concept of appetitive eating. It also introduces the dialectical concept of eating both regularly *and* according to appetitive cues. These concepts are not at odds. Lastly, the idea of eating what you want to combat asceticism is further addressed.

RAE Handout 13: How Does Appetitive Eating Work?

RAE Handout 13 aims to introduce the concept of appetitive eating. Inform the patient that the anchors on the scale regarding hunger and fullness are general guidelines. There is no precise way to eat exactly according to the numbers. They are a helpful tool; they do not represent black-and-white goals. Patients should be encouraged to stay between 2 (at the very lowest) and approximately 8 on the scale. It should be clearly expressed that going a little bit over an 8 to a 9 is within healthy limits. This emphasizes the point that it is not helpful for people to allow themselves to become too hungry; however, it is acceptable to go slightly *past* the point of being full. The eating disorder's aim is to calibrate the patient to override hunger and have an intense emotional reaction to fullness after eating or binge eating. Because we must do the opposite of whatever the eating disorder does, our recovery calibration is set in the opposite direction. It is not healthy for patients with eating disorders to get to the point of extreme hunger. Therefore, they should not let their hunger dip below 2 on the scale. Patients should be eating regularly so as to prevent this. Additionally, over time, if they are eating regularly and notice that they are below 2 on the scale, they should flexibly learn to eat a snack. On the other end of the scale, if a patient occasionally eats slightly past the point of being comfortably full (8 on the scale), *this is no cause for concern or panic*. An eating disorder behavior therapist must model fearlessness of both fullness and weight gain. The patient is to tolerate the physical sensation of being slightly overfull along with any negative automatic thoughts that may come up about potential weight gain, any negative emotions (such as anxiety), and any urges to engage in intolerance behaviors. Eating slightly past the point of being full is to be normalized. It happens. It is normal. It is certainly healthier than engaging in intolerance behaviors. And as RAE Handout 14 explains, eating slightly past the point of being full is just like topping off your car's gas tank.

RAE Handout 14: Your Stomach Is Like a Gas Tank

RAE Handout 14 is intended to help foster acceptance of occasionally eating slightly past the point of being full. Rather than thinking about eating past the point of being full as a terrible mistake, this handout reframes it as no big deal—it will just take a longer time before you are hungry. In this handout, the stomach is compared to a gas tank. If you have just a little more gas in your car, it will run for longer. From a healthy appetitive eating perspective, having slightly more fuel on board is not a problem.

If we indulge in considering the worst-case scenario, it is true that too much food in the stomach *can* backfire. If a patient eats way past the point of being full, involuntary vomiting could occur. If, however, anxiety is triggered in response to any degree of fullness, then voluntary vomiting could occur at much lower points on the scale. Therefore, it is crucial to foster tolerance of negative internal experiences for the occasions when a patient eats slightly past the point of being full. Further, the same mind-set is to be carried over to a rank of 10 after a binge or a holiday dinner, for instance. If tolerance of internal experiences is not fostered at the higher ends of the scale, then a backfire into intolerance behaviors is likely.

This is not to say, of course, that the aim in general *should be* to eat past the point of being full. The patient's eating disorder has already provided them with an excess amount of this particular "should," which has ended in behaviors such as restriction, avoidance, binge eating, and purging, not to mention health consequences. We have had quite enough of this "should," thank you! In recovery, a balance must be struck. To counteract the eating disorder's asceticism and rigidity, treatment must introduce flexibility and acceptance.

RAE Handout 15: Six Non-RAE Eating Disorder Behaviors and Six RAE Recovery Behaviors and RAE Log

This handout summarizes both the regular and the appetitive eating targets in an integrated way. As in RAE Handout 6: Five Non-RE Eating Disorder Behaviors and Five RE Recovery Behaviors, patients are to use the blank rows on the left to provide their own examples of disordered attitudes and the blank rows on the right to provide their own examples of adaptive attitudes. This helps clarify treatment targets and guides the patient in this portion of treatment. The arrows between the columns symbolize the fact that patients are not expected to immediately adopt all the behaviors listed in the right-hand column.

The top part of the three-part Regular and Appetitive Eating Log is to be completed in the same manner as the Regular Eating Log (see RAE Handout 6). The bottom two parts are used to help the patient self-reinforce toward RAE behaviors and away from non-RAE eating disorder behaviors. Patients are very much to be encouraged to complete all three parts of the Regular Eating Log immediately after meals and snacks. Checking off the RAE recovery behaviors helps foster this internal reinforcement. This, of course, also helps to ensure accuracy. If the logs are completed, not completed, or too perfectly completed, the same protocol is to be followed as with the Regular Eating Logs (see that portion of the manual).

Once a patient is able to demonstrate that they can eat when they are generally hungry and stop once they are generally full, a more nuanced mindfulness practice of these subtle cues may be in order. Each week, one copy of the Belly Signals Log should be given to patients, since it accounts for seven days (unlike the daily Regular and Appetitive Eating Log). As per the directions on the Belly Signals Log, patients are to record their approximate appetitive cues after each meal and snack. Initially, patients are *not* to adjust the volume of food being eaten to match their reported levels of hunger and fullness. The aim of tracking these appetitive cues is simply to track these cues to foster mindfulness of them. When a patient is reporting greater ease in identifying these cues and is no longer reporting urges to engage in food restriction, food avoidance, binge eating, intolerance behaviors, and other eating disorder behaviors, the patient may begin to use hunger and fullness cues to gauge the appropriate volume of food to eat. At this time, it might be helpful to track the volume of food being eaten by having patients also complete the Regular and Appetitive Eating Log. If a backslide occurs, regular eating *without* the appetitive component is to be resumed.

RAE Handout 16: I Can't Tell If I'm Hungry or Upset

In addition to alexithymia of emotions, patients with eating disorders display a similar disconnection to the physical sensation of appetitive cues. Patients are driven by the eating disorder to override both hunger and fullness. Over time, these cues become harder to identify. In this disconnection from both emotional and appetitive cues, there also seems to be a cross-wiring of sorts—patients cannot tell if they are physically hungry or emotionally distressed. Hunger is the inborn cue to initiate eating, but in the context of binge eating disorder, negative emotions become the prompt for eating. During an episode of binge eating, the behavior of eating immediately follows emotional distress. After many episodes of binge eating, the pairing of emotional distress with eating becomes stronger. The inborn cue of hunger as a prompt to eat becomes replaced with emotional distress. Further, in the context of the eating disorder, patients are overriding hunger cues and restricting. Therefore, hunger cues become subverted. The most salient prompt to eat becomes emotional distress. While all of this is going on beneath the surface, the patient's experience is one of confusion. They cannot identify whether they want to eat because they are distressed or because they are hungry.

This handout is an intervention aimed at addressing this issue. In the regular eating portion of the material, patients begin to tackle alexithymia by labeling emotions. The patient is taught to replace words like "upset" and "overwhelmed" with specific emotion words, such as "anxiety," "guilt," and "disgust." Once the patient has spent some time labeling these emotions after eating, they should be better able to identify emotional experiences. Likewise, at the start of appetitive eating interventions, patients are instructed to label appetitive cues. This helps reconnect the patient to the physical sensations that naturally guide the process of eating. These cues have been handed down through the process of evolution to help keep us alive. These cues are inborn. For adolescents, even after several years of disconnection, it is likely that reconnection to these inborn drives is possible.

Regardless of whether every patient with an eating disorder might ever be able to reconnect to these evolutionary drives, fostering an attitude of inevitability acceptance is essential to this work. If we foster within ourselves an attitude that most adolescents will be able to reconnect to these drives because they are inborn and reconnection is inevitable, then we can set out on this course with hope. But if we start out with the mind-set that the eating disorder has done irreparable damage, and that several years of subverting inborn appetitive cues means they are gone forever, we limit the patient's opportunity for recovery. We cannot let our own inflexible thinking sabotage a patient's chance of making a full recovery. Decreasing the eating disorder symptoms is not enough. Restoring psychological health must be the new bar we set for treatment.

RAE Handout 17: Food Is Everywhere, All the Time

RAE Handout 17 is a complement to RAE Handout 10 on thought suppression and ironic processing. Thought suppression and obsession go hand in hand. The more one attempts to suppress a thought, the more one thinks about whatever one was trying *not* to think about. If we zoom out of this situation and take a bird's-eye view of it, the whole ordeal of attempting to suppress a thought about something, and then thinking about that thing even more, *is* essentially obsession. This type of obsession would be akin to the concept of *ego-dystonia*; in other words, the patient is obsessing, but they do not *want* to be obsessing. There are other types of obsessions, however, that have a more ego-syntonic flair; the content of the thoughts that comprise these obsessions is not aversive to the patient. In fact, the patient may very much enjoy the obsessions. Getting lost in fantasy or obsession may serve many functions, such as avoidance of other aversive stimuli in the physical world. RAE Handout 17 begins to address some of the latter types of obsessions. Some patients report an obsession with collecting recipes, watching videos about food, and following food-related social media accounts. If these behaviors arise, they must be addressed, targeted, and decreased in treatment.

At the end of World War II and the Holocaust, it became clear that more information was needed on severe caloric deprivation because famine and malnourishment were widespread. RAE Handout 17 starts by summarizing the results of the Minnesota Experiment, in which men without eating disorders were semistarved (see Franklin, Schiele, Brozek, & Keys, 1948). The original report from 1948 is fascinating and is freely available online (as if you didn't have enough to read with this manual). It can be surmised from the results of this study that many of the symptoms often attributed to the eating disorder (narrowed interests, depression, obsession with food, and so forth) can actually be attributed to caloric deprivation. This provides strong support for a behavioral interpretation of eating disorders. In short, if the patient is depriving themselves of food—in this case, secondary to fear of "fatness" and/or the drive for thinness—then a predictable set of circumstances will result. The same circumstances were present even for adult men *without* eating disorders who were given a limited-calorie diet. Therefore, the behavior of eating should be the target of treatment. The takeaway to discuss with patients is that many of the issues present in the eating disorder are helped by eating.

The handout goes on to home in on food obsession. The "Eat Whenever You Want" and "Eat Whatever You Want" exercises should be conducted in session when there is enough time left to process emotions. The aim of these exercises is to start breaking down the psychological barrier that limits access to food. Pointing out that food is readily available and can be accessed aims to undermine obsessional processing. Although the patient is still eating regularly, the idea is to start thinking of food as accessible at any point. Food is not off limits.

Each individual patient will need to try something different for homework. There are three main behavioral areas that this handout addresses:

1. The handout may bring this more ego-syntonic type of food obsession to the surface. If patients are engaging in such behaviors as collecting recipes, watching videos about food, and following food-related social media accounts, it is important to start setting homework assignments like throwing out recipes, watching alternative videos, and unfollowing food-related social media accounts in favor of recovery accounts.

2. It may be appropriate for some patients to start trying to eat snacks more flexibly when they are hungry. It is important, however, to stick to the scheduled mealtimes. To help ensure that the patient's day-to-day hunger needs are met, mealtimes will be more fixed, and snacks will be more flexible.

3. For other patients, who continue to struggle with asceticism and eating foods they like, it will be helpful to carry out an "Eat Whatever You Want" exercise in real life. Have the patient eat their favorite "off limits" food (for example, a Snickers candy bar) every single day for two weeks. Over time, the desired food becomes less desired, and the patient grows tired of it.

Whatever is determined to be the best plan with the patient, write it out on the lines provided in the homework portion of the handout. A "behavioral experiment" is a patient's trying out something new to test how it goes. It is then discussed in the next session. Adjustments are made as needed. If it was too challenging, an easier target is picked. If the experiment went well, another challenge is added. Be sure to check the homework during the next session. Also ensure that the patient's willingness to try a new challenge and take a chance is verbally reinforced in session.

✖ RAE Handout 18: Why Dieting Doesn't Work

Toward the end of RAE, patients may still have the lingering question "If I need to lose a little weight, can I diet?" The answer is *no*. RAE Handout 18 addresses this issue. Go through the question with the patient. Instruct them to refer to this handout in the future if they ever have the urge to "diet."

RAE Handout 19: Honoring Your Food Every Day

In keeping with the IMT custom of offering alternatives to maladaptive behaviors and attitudes, RAE Handout 19 discusses taking the stance of honoring food. Most often this handout goes off without a hitch. If any negative emotions do come up, patients who are toward the end of treatment are able to tolerate and appropriately express emotions in response to this handout. Some patients have such thoughts as *I was not grateful enough* and feel negative emotions, such as guilt. At this later stage of treatment, it is encouraged to allow the patient to process negative emotions in session. Rather than jumping in and externalizing the eating disorder *for* the patient, the therapist should encourage patients to process the experience themselves. Patients are usually able to disentangle the eating disorder from themselves. They may, however, need some direction in this separation if they are caught in a cycle of self-blame. The patient should also be encouraged to tolerate any negative emotions that arise in session. After emotions are processed, an emphasis should be placed on *moving forward* with gratitude.

BAE Handouts

This portion of the IMT individual therapy modality describes how to incorporate BAE handouts into individual sessions. Each handout is discussed individually. It is important to read each handout before reading in this section about its administration.

BAE HANDOUTS

BAE Handout 1: How Does My Eating Disorder Impact Body Image?

BAE Handout 2: Body Acceptance and Exposure

BAE Handout 3: Positive Body Image and Acceptance

BAE Handout 4: Exposure: Seeing the Light

BAE Handout 5: Eleven Non-BAE Eating Disorder Behaviors and Eleven BAE Recovery Behaviors

BAE Handout 6: When Exercise Is Unhealthy

BAE Handout 7: Exercise and the Illusion of Improved Body Image

BAE Handout 8: Body Avoidance Behaviors

BAE Handout 9: NIFTY Skills for Decreasing Body Avoidance

BAE Handout 10: Body Investigating Behaviors

BAE Handout 11: ROCKS Skills for Decreasing Body Investigating

BAE Handout 12: Comparing Yourself to Others

BAE Handout 13: Real-Life and Imaginal Fears

BAE Handout 14: Getting to the Bottom of Things

BAE Handout 15: Being Compassionate Versus Hurting Yourself

BAE Handout 16: Treating Yourself with Kindness

BAE Handout 1: How Does My Eating Disorder Impact Body Image?

BAE Handout 1 sets the tone for BAE. It explains how eating disorder behaviors make body image worse, not better. The assumption that patients (and some therapists) have about such change strategies as restricting diet and increasing exercise is that if we just did these things, we would be *happier* with ourselves. But attempting to make many changes to one's appearance does not lead to happiness, only to a temporary feeling of achievement that soon fades into the need to achieve something else. Attempting to stay afloat from achievement to achievement is no way to live. Instead, the inclination toward change must be decreased, and steps toward acceptance must be taken. Therefore, the first major treatment target in BAE is body acceptance. This is fostered through decreasing such change strategies as the behaviors of exercise, body investigating, and body avoidance (for example, hiding one's body to change its presentation to others and to the self).

In line with the IMT custom, this handout presents two sequences of behaviors, one maladaptive and the other adaptive. The maladaptive sequence depicts how eating disorder behaviors worsen body image over time. Here, body image is conceptualized as an interplay among negative emotions, perceptions, and beliefs. In the first sequence of behaviors in BAE Handout 1 there is fear of weight gain along with seeing and feeling oneself as "fat" and believing that one must change one's appearance. In the second sequence of behaviors, body image improves as fear of weight gain subsides; the belief that change is necessary is abandoned, and perception is clarified.

BAE Handout 2: Body Acceptance and Exposure

This handout simply frames the targets of body acceptance through exposure for the patient. Most likely, the patient is already familiar with the concept of exposure, but this handout can be a helpful refresher. The handout does not need to be reviewed in session and can be given as homework.

BAE Handout 3: Positive Body Image and Acceptance

BAE Handout 3 delves further into the concept of body acceptance. After the patient has spent some time in the change-oriented eating disorder mind-set, the concept of acceptance can be unfamiliar. This handout, like BAE Handout 2, may be given as homework. In session, however, it is helpful to review the core concepts of how body acceptance is conceptualized and how it will be addressed in treatment.

BAE Handout 4: Exposure: Seeing the Light

BAE Handout 4 further explains the concept of exposure. BAE Handout 4, like BAE Handout 2 and BAE Handout 3, can be given as homework.

BAE Handout 5: Eleven Non-BAE Eating Disorder Behaviors and Eleven BAE Recovery Behaviors

This handout, like the tables of behaviors in other IMT modalities, is used to help ground the patient in the current treatment goals. In the left-hand column, the patient finds a list of maladaptive behaviors. In the right-hand column, the patient finds a list of adaptive behaviors. This handout, conceived as a roadmap through BAE, is intended to guide the patient from where they are to recovery. In the blank portions of the handout, patients can write their own examples of maladaptive and adaptive behaviors. The arrows between the columns symbolize the fact that patients are not expected to immediately adopt all the behaviors listed in the right-hand column.

BAE Handout 6: When Exercise Is Unhealthy

This handout, as well as BAE Handout 7, can be introduced earlier than any other BAE material in the context of RAE and the IMT family therapy modality, if needed. Again, it is usually not as helpful to administer in group, because patients tend to share about their personal behavior, which can be triggering.

Because exercise is usually the most destructive body-related behavior, it is listed first here. It should be addressed early on in treatment. As already noted, this handout can be introduced as early as necessary.

Although patients often have some pushback to the opening paragraph of this handout, going through the checklists is often clarifying. Because patients are coming to treatment with such strong eating disorder beliefs, it can be confusing to them to start to think in another way. Being confused is a great place to be in treatment! Confusion is the beginning of thinking in a new way. Encourage patients to embrace confusion. Point out that, over time, confusion will subside as these concepts clarify. They do not have to understand everything completely in this very moment.

Encourage patients to complete the homework exercise at the end of the handout. When the patient brings the completed homework to session, be sure to provide verbal reinforcement for engaging in adaptive alternative behaviors to exercise. Reinforce the concept that attempting to change the body is in line with the eating disorder, and that accepting the body is in line with recovery. As noted in the general introduction to this manual, when patients complete their homework, be sure to provide Rec-SPA, such as saying, "Good job completing your homework" and giving a thumbs-up. If patients do not complete their homework, a brief intervention is required. If the therapist happens to be familiar with dialectical behavior therapy (Linehan, 1993, 2014a, 2014b), conducting a chain analysis is recommended. If the therapist is not familiar with dialectical behavior therapy, a good starting point is simply to ask, "What got in the way of completing the assignment this week?" From there, doing some problem solving around the roadblocks to homework completion is recommended.

BAE Handout 7: Exercise and the Illusion of Improved Body Image

It is often helpful to administer BAE Handout 7 along with BAE Handout 6. This handout explains the bottomless pit of attempting to change the body to derive satisfaction. This handout encourages patients to take a further look at how body change–oriented and eating disorder–consistent strategies work to keep them stuck in an unhealthy cycle.

BAE Handout 8: Body Avoidance Behaviors

This handout describes body avoidance behaviors (BABs), the function of which can be to hide the body's appearance from others *or* oneself. For instance, a patient could sit at home alone in a hot apartment wearing a sweatshirt in order to avoid seeing their own midsection. Although body avoidance is not aimed at changing the body itself, it is aimed at changing the appearance of the body. As such, it is at odds with acceptance of the body.

BAE Handout 9: NIFTY Skills for Decreasing Body Avoidance

The NIFTY skills are used to address BABs. As is depicted in BAE Handout 9, the NIFTY skills are as follows:

Notice the urge to avoid your body (such as by wearing baggy clothes).

Instead of avoiding your body, challenge yourself (for example, by wearing appropriately fitting clothing).

Feel negative emotions (shame, worry, and so forth).

Thank yourself and acknowledge that you took a step that is in line with recovery.

By now, patients should be familiar with the skill of mindfulness. If they have not been introduced to this skill, it is recommended that the mindfulness handouts from the group therapy modality be pulled into individual therapy. Once the foundation of mindfulness is laid, the patient is better able to notice the urge to avoid their body.

Instead of avoiding their bodies, patients are encouraged to do something, *however small*, to challenge themselves. To modify behavior even slightly is an achievement. For instance, rather than covering their midsection with their arms, attempting to sit on their hands even for thirty seconds while at school is a good start.

Patients should also be familiar with the skill of tolerating negative emotions. Thanking themselves, however, may be newer. It is very important that patients learn to reward themselves. In the beginning of treatment, the reinforcement often is external (for example, from carers, the treatment team, or the therapist). As treatment progresses, however, patients are to internalize the reinforcement process and learn to reward themselves for recovery behavior. As such, the "thank yourself" skill is not to be overlooked or underestimated.

Homework   Patients are to complete the NIFTY Skills Log for homework, to the best of their ability. They will likely not be able to log every single urge to engage in body avoidance that occurs. Therefore, they are only to log the instances in which they use the NIFTY skills. When the completed log is brought to session, the therapist is to reinforce the implementation of the skills.

BAE Handout 10: Body Investigating Behaviors

As is explained in BAE Handout 10, body investigating (called "body checking" in other literature) happens frequently and can be influenced by a variety of factors (such as mood). Body investigating is not an accurate way for a patient to gather data about whether they have gained weight. Regardless, whatever the results of a patient's body investigating test are, these results can determine their mood, moving forward. Considering that body investigating can happen impulsively at any point throughout the day or night, this creates a great deal of instability for the patient. Suddenly a patient can be feeling very down or very up, all because of the perceived results of a body investigating examination. This handout explains that process in greater detail. The next handout outlines skills to address this behavior.

BAE Handout 11: ROCKS Skills for Decreasing Body Investigating

The ROCKS skills were designed to address body investigating behaviors (BIBs, known as "body checking" in other literature):

Remove temptations (hide scales, cover mirrors, throw out skinny jeans, and so forth) until urges are less intense.

Observe urges to engage in BIBs pass by when they do happen.

Catch negative and positive determinations about your body ("I look good because I lost weight") if BIBs happen.

Know that, after BIBs, negative and positive determinations about your body are part of the eating disorder.

Stay the course. Don't let the roller coaster of thoughts, urges, and emotions triggered by BIBs get you off track. Continue doing whatever it was you were doing before you had the urge to engage in BIBs.

First, it can be helpful to discuss a plan of action that involves *stimulus control* or, in this case, limiting access to triggering stimuli such as mirrors, scales, and old clothing, in service of decreasing BIBs. Taking preventive measures is what the "remove temptations" skill is all about. Often, involving carers in implementing these interventions is required, or at least very helpful.

The remainder of the ROCKS skills are to be used in real time. The "observe" and "catch" skills in the ROCKS skills are similar to the "notice" skill in the NIFTY skills. A previous education in mindfulness is helpful here. Group handouts on the topic are suggested. The "know" skill here, however, is a bit more intricate. In the context of engaging in BIBs, making both negative *and* positive determinations about the body is problematic. Acceptance involves moving away from judgment *of any kind* and toward a nonjudgmental stance. Therefore, it is important for patients to catch both negative and positive judgments and *know* that they are part of the eating disorder mentality.

The following two lists distinguish between making psychologically unhealthy positive judgments and healthy body assessments:

PSYCHOLOGICALLY UNHEALTHY POSITIVE BODY JUDGMENTS

- In the eating disorder mind-set, a positive judgment about their own body is made in the context of fearing weight gain.

- If a BIB was just engaged in and a patient makes a positive judgment, the BIB is reinforced.

- If the patient just engaged in any eating disorder behavior (such as avoiding food), then making a positive judgment about their body after engaging in a BIB also reinforces the eating disorder behavior.

- Positive judgments are made in response to perceived *change* and are not *acceptance*-oriented.

- The positive judgment temporarily quells a fear.

- The positive judgment disallows the patient an opportunity to sit with negative emotion.

- The positive judgment has the ability to make a person feel an exhilarating high of sorts.

- Passing judgments keeps the person in a critical mind-set.

- Whereas a positive judgment can make a person's whole day, a negative judgment can ruin it, causing chaos.

Psychologically Healthy Positive Body Assessments

- A person does not fear weight gain and makes a positive assessment after seeing, not checking, their body.

- A person accepts how they look and does not feel a compulsion to change how they look.

- The basis of the positive assessment has nothing to do with a number on a scale.

- The positive feeling does not have a "high" quality to it.

- A feeling of satisfaction or joy can result.

- A positive or negative assessment does not make or break the person's day.

After taking a moment to consider that both negative and positive judgments are trouble, the patient must carry on with whatever they were doing. BIBs can occur so frequently that it just does not seem practical to ask patients to engage in an elaborate skill each time they have an urge. Rather, taking a moment to acknowledge what is going on, and why it is not helpful, seems more appropriate. Further, because BIBs can be so disruptive, it appears that the alternative is to urge patients to keep a steady pace and focus on whatever is at hand—hence the "stay the course" skill.

Homework The ROCKS Skills Logs are to be completed similarly to the NIFTY Skills Logs. Rather than logging each BIB urge (because there would likely be hundreds), each time the ROCKS skills are used, it is to be logged. The usage of the skills is then reinforced. Patients may also thank themselves for completing the ROCKS skills.

BAE Handout 12: Comparing Yourself to Others

In keeping with the idea that both negative and positive judgments keep the patient in the judgmental eating disorder mind-set, BAE Handout 12 prompts patients to notice thoughts and foster accepting attitudes.

BAE Handout 13: Real-Life and Imaginal Fears

Before moving on to the exposure portion of the BAE work, all major food-related behaviors (such as restriction, avoidance, binge eating, purging, and so forth) need to be addressed. Prior to embarking on body-related exposure exercises, regular eating should be established, and the patient should be able to implement skills to decrease food-related intolerance behaviors (such as purging and taking laxatives) as well as body-related intolerance behaviors (such as exercise and body avoidance). In the context of exposure exercises, both food-related and body-related behaviors should be framed as safety behaviors if engaged in after the exercise.

Additionally, the patient should display an ability to implement skills at decreasing any other maladaptive behaviors that can be used as safety behaviors in the context of these exercises, such as self-injurious behaviors (for example, nonsuicidal self-injury, suicide attempts, and so forth) prior to targeting fear of "fatness" and linked emotions with exposure exercises in treatment. If a patient currently displays features of borderline personality disorder without the ability to use skills to decrease self-injurious thoughts and behaviors, exposure exercises may be inappropriate until the patient has completed a course of dialectical behavior therapy.

Patients should be instructed to refrain from all safety behaviors after the exposure exercise. If necessary, it may be helpful to review BAE Handout 4, which briefly explains the concept of exposure therapy and safety behaviors to the patient.

In addition to completing the Body Acceptance and Exposure (BAE) Measure (included in the online Clinician Resources downloadable at www.newharbinger.com/42235), the patient should complete the exercises related to real-life and imaginal body fears. Both will help the therapist in constructing fear hierarchies and exposures. As is standard with other measures, the questions on the BAE measure are asked on a 0–4 scale, the linked emotions items are relatively expanded, and the exposure items are relatively limited. In BAE Handout 13, however, more exposure items are listed, and a 0–10 scale is used, which matches that of the fear hierarchy. As such, both measures are useful in different ways at this particular junction in treatment.

My Real-Life Body Fears List

With respect to completing the list of real-life body fears, the same concepts as were present in RAE Handout 9 on food challenges apply. Examples on this list should include only stimuli that the patient could actually confront in the real world. An example of a fear hierarchy a patient might complete here would be the following:

10. Wearing a bathing suit in public

9. Wearing tight clothes (such as a dress) in public

8. Going out in public without wearing a shirt tied around my waist

7. Looking in the mirror in therapy with regular clothes on

6. Looking in a mirror alone in my house with regular clothes on

5. Bending over and having my midsection touch my thighs

4. Sitting down and having my thighs touch

3. Going outside in sweatpants

2. Going outside without applying a hair product

1. Going outside wearing glasses

Creative *In Vivo* Exercises   Creativity is encouraged here. Clinicians have done such things as having a patient stand on a scale with a heavy book so that the scale reads a higher number, finding pictures of scales with feared numbers displayed, digitally altering pictures to make patients' bodies appear larger, and so forth. Feel free to work collaboratively with the patient to come up with creative and doable examples to put on the hierarchy.

Real-Life Body Exposure Plan

The patient does not have to pick four behaviors to work on just because four lines are available. One behavior is just fine. The behavior can be worked on at home or in session. If an exposure is conducted in session, the same rules from the food exposure section apply to real-life body exposures. Be sure to take the time to complete this portion of the handout with the patient in session, and follow up on what the patient did over the course of the week in the next session. Further, it is also imperative to follow through on in-session plans.

For practitioners interested in mirror exposure therapy, we refer you to the work of Thomas Hildebrandt (see, for example, Hildebrandt et al., 2012).

Imaginal Fears List

A hierarchy of imagined fear is generally a bit more difficult to construct than one of concrete fears. The patient has to *imagine* what would be anxiety-provoking to *imagine*. Therefore, the hierarchy really does not have to be constructed perfectly. In fact, the goal is really to simply get a target in the range of five to seven fears to work with and advance to the next page of the handout—Practicing Imaginal Exposure.

For reference, here is an example of an imaginal exposure hierarchy for fear of weight gain:

10. Imagining gaining 50 pounds

9. Imagining gaining 25 pounds

8. Imagining gaining 20 pounds

7. Imagining gaining 15 pounds

6. Imagining gaining 10 pounds

5. Imagining gaining 8 pounds

4. Imagining gaining 5 pounds

3. Imagining gaining 3 pounds

2. Imagining gaining 2 pounds

1. Imagining gaining 1 pound

Here is an example of an imaginal exposure hierarchy incorporating the linked emotion of fear of judgment:

10. Someone calls me "fat," and the whole school laughs at me in the auditorium.

9. Someone calls me "fat" while I'm eating lunch.

8. Someone calls me "fat" in front of my English class.

7. In front of my group of friends, someone asks, "Have you put on weight?"

6. Alone in the bathroom, someone asks, "Have you put on weight?"

5. Someone I consider "not skinny" compares their body to mine by saying, "We are about the same size."

4. Someone comments about clothes I am wearing, which makes me self-conscious.

3. Someone sits right next to me on the bus.

2. Someone sits across from me on the bus.

1. Someone looks at me for what seems like a second too long on the bus.

Here is an example of an imaginal exposure hierarchy incorporating fear of social ostracism and abandonment:

10. My significant other dumps me because they think I'm fat now.

9. My significant other lost interest in me because they think I'm fat now.

8. My significant other made comments that other people are more attractive than me.

7. My friends are all ashamed to hang out with me and have stopped calling because they think I'm fat.

6. One friend thinks I'm fat and calls less because they do not want to be associated with me.

5. One friend said behind my back that I'm not good looking enough to hang out with our group.

4. Someone in my school said that they didn't know why I was popular any more.

3. Someone said my clothes were really lame.

2. My friend didn't call me back.

1. My friend didn't text me back.

Practicing Imaginal Exposure

To conduct an imaginal exposure, follow the directions provided in this portion of BAE Handout 13. Read through the steps together with the patient. Regarding the constructing of a story, it is usually not that difficult to construct. Patients often describe a little bit about what their fears would be. Work those fears into the story. A couple of sentences will do the trick. Here are some straightforward examples of imaginal exposures for fear of weight gain:

- You wake up in the morning and step on the scale. The scale reads 145 pounds. You've gained 10 pounds. Having to get ready for school, you try to put on clothes, but they are all tight.

- Knowing that you've suddenly gained weight, you go to the doctor. The doctor's scale reads 175 pounds. You have gained 15 pounds overnight.

- Before going to bed at night, you step on the scale. The scale reads 165 pounds. You've gained 20 pounds. You knew that you had gained some weight over time, but you did not know the amount.

The story does not have to be particularly involved. Each of these stories would likely be enough to trigger intense enough anxiety for patients to have an opportunity to tolerate in session.

Along with conducting straightforward fear-of-weight-gain exposures, working on a linked emotion is also an option *when* the patient is ready. The following examples would suffice:

- You wake up in the morning and step on the scale. The scale reads 150 pounds. You gained 15 pounds. In disbelief, you go to school. That day, you notice that your friends are less interested in talking to you. One of your friends stops calling you to hang out.

- Your significant other was away for the summer, during which time you gained 25 pounds. Upon seeing you when they return, they immediately dump you.

- You were the star of your soccer team at the start of the season. As the season went on, though, you gained 15 pounds and started to lose your magic touch. Everyone could see that your performance suffered.

These types of exposures are a double whammy of sorts—they get to fear of weight gain *and* a linked fear of social isolation, abandonment, and losing a competitive edge, respectively. For some patients, it will be ideal to do imaginal exposures that target both fear of "fatness" and linked emotions. For others, however, linked emotions are too intense for targeting in eating disorder treatment (for instance, when they are associated with trauma). In these instances, it may be appropriate to do separate imaginal exposures relating to the eating disorder and trauma or refer the patient to a specialist.

Regardless of the content of the exposure chosen, it is imperative to keep reviewing the narrative in session after session until the patient has no fear response to the story any longer. When the story gets boring, it is time to pick a new story that is higher on the hierarchy. When the short stories are no longer cutting it, it is time to lengthen the stories and make them more detailed. *Continue this process until fear of "fatness" is eventually extinguished.* This may take some time in treatment (for example, on average six to eight sessions per hierarchy constructed). It is, however, imperative to treatment that fear of "fatness" and feasible linked emotions be confronted.

Decreasing Fear Does Not Increase Desire   Extinguishing fear of "fatness" does not promote a *desire* to gain weight (anything that could foster an actual desire to gain weight in this population would be quite remarkable). The precise goal of any exposure exercise is to extinguish *fear*. Decreasing experiential avoidance of fear of "fatness" does not unhinge eating behaviors. It is experiential avoidance of fear of "fatness" that results in out-of-control eating disorder behaviors such as binge eating as well as food restriction, food avoidance, and intolerance behaviors. In treatment, engaging in regular and appetitive eating, in unison with confronting fears, promotes recovery.

⊘ BAE Handout 14: Getting to the Bottom of Things

After the imaginal exposure therapy portion of treatment has kicked off, BAE Handout 14 is administered to dig a little bit deeper. The downward arrow technique (Beck, 2011) is used to further explore what it might mean for patients in a more open-ended way if they gained weight. Often, further ideas for imaginal exposure exercises come from the completion of this handout. Two other topics—whether a patient feels as if they deserve food, and whether they struggle with putting themselves first—are explored. Although some patients struggle in these two areas, not all patients do. If, however, a patient does endorse that these topics are salient for them, then the compassion-focused interventions that come next will be of particular importance. MAC Handout 6: Lessons from Cute Stuff, in the group therapy modality, will be important to administer in the context of individual therapy for these patients as well as for many others.

BAE Handout 15: Being Compassionate Versus Hurting Yourself

This handout goes farther than BAE Handout 14 by beginning to home in on concepts explored in that handout (in particular, the distinction between being compassionate toward others and hurting oneself). Actions that on the surface appear prosocial but actually have eating disorder functions are listed (such as giving away food to people who are homeless). Recovery behaviors, for the first time, are framed as being compassionate toward oneself. Lastly, compassionate deeds toward others that do not have an eating disorder function are listed. The patient is encouraged to be honest with themselves and the therapist about behaviors they engage in that could be classified as prosocial actions with eating disorder functions. They are also encouraged to engage in compassionate deeds toward both themselves and others. It is pointed out that engaging in compassionate deeds toward the self is not mutually exclusive with showing compassion toward others. In fact, the more kindness one shows to oneself, the more kindness one can show to others. If a patient is particularly philosophically inclined, it may be useful to take some time to muse on whether prosocial actions with eating disorder functions are more or less kind than the compassionate deeds.

BAE Handout 16: Treating Yourself with Kindness

Ask patients to complete the questions at the top of the handout. It is often helpful to make a link between the first two questions: "It certainly would be difficult to show yourself compassion if you did not believe you deserved it." Without getting into a debate with the patient regarding whether they deserve compassion, it is best to proceed with reading the handout. As is evident at the beginning of the handout, it addresses myths about self-compassion that are reframed with the intention of addressing the eating disorder population. The double-standard technique from the cognitive therapy literature (Beck, 2011), which asks patients to consider how they might respond to a friend, is then employed in the portion called "Self-Compassionate Thoughts."

Patients are to complete the assignment under "Homework (Part 1)."

In the portion called "Behaviors Change, and Then Beliefs Change," the handout focuses on making recovery behaviors compassionate as well as increasing compassionate behaviors that are not related to the eating disorder. The patient is *also* to complete the assignment under "Homework (Part 2)," at the end of the handout.

BAE Handout 17: Body Gratitude

BAE Handout 17 on body gratitude is an essential part of the therapy. If we think of the brain as hardware and the eating disorder as software, the eating disorder inserts destructive coding into the brain. Exercises such as this work to do the opposite. Practicing body gratitude fosters adaptive attitudes and can be conceptualized as healthy coding. Because it is so important for the patient to internalize this new coding, a mindfulness exercise is conducted in session. It is best to read from the following script for in-session work. Have the patient reread the exercise on the handout for homework.

Therapist script: Settle into your seat with your back straight up against the chair and your feet planted firmly on the ground. Gently allow your eyes to close, and take three anchoring breaths in and out. Now let yourself just breathe. Call your attention to your feet. Think of the ways that they help you to get around. Think of where your feet have carried you. Take a moment and thank your feet for their service to you. Next, call your attention to your legs. Think of what your legs have helped you to accomplish. Take a moment to acknowledge your legs and thank them for all they have done. Now call your attention to your midsection. Think of all of the things your midsection has done for you. Take a moment to thank your midsection. Next, bring your focus to your arms. Think of the ways your arms have helped you. Take a moment to thank your arms. And last, call your attention to your head. Think of the ways your head has benefited you. Take a moment to thank your head for all it has done. Take a moment to notice how you feel and what emotions you may be experiencing. Breathe. And when you are ready, you may open your eyes.

After the body gratitude mindfulness exercise has concluded, ask the patient to process the experience in session. Be sure to remind them to do this exercise for homework and to ask them about how it went at the following session. As ever, provide reinforcement for the completion of homework and the practicing of a skill learned.

 It is essential to administer MAC Handout 11: The Eating Disorder's Impact on Values (from the group therapy modality) to all patients in the context of individual therapy. The eating disorder disrupts a person's values to the point where thinness moves to the top of the list. Over the course of treatment, patients need to align their behaviors with what their values were prior to the onset of the eating disorder. Over time, the patient's values start to reflect their values prior to the onset of the eating disorder. As the eating disorder recedes, it is important for the patient to know where to go next. Doing values work is essential because it provides the patient with direction for taking action in recovery that is in line with what is most important to them.

BAE Handout 18: Pretending It's Forever

This handout should be implemented once major intolerance behaviors (such as purging, laxative use, and so forth) have decreased. Further, for patients with borderline personality disorder or traits, treatment with dialectical behavior therapy is recommended to stabilize symptoms prior to the administration of this handout.

Considering the self-eclipsing (ego-syntonic) nature of eating disorders, behavioral interventions should be aimed at decoupling the patient from the disorder. Eating disorders are often compared to abusive romantic partners, and the reason why is clear—the patient is emotionally attached to the eating disorder, which provides it with some reinforcement, but it is ultimately extremely harmful. In the context of this type of relationship to the disorder, the patient has difficulty letting go. In clinical practice, many patients who have stabilized their behaviors still hold on to the idea that they can fall back on eating disorder behaviors "just in case." In other words, they do not psychologically let go of the eating disorder even though things appear to be fine on the surface. That cord must be cut. The emotions that come with severing ties can be painful, but they must be confronted and processed.

This handout prompts patients to imagine what it would be like if nothing they did could *ever* change their body size, shape, and weight. Framed in another way, this handout is asking patients to imagine that they would forever be cut off from experiencing any reinforcement from the eating disorder. By imaging that the body cannot change, no matter what, the patient starts to imagine a world in which they ultimately must let go of eating disorder behaviors. After all, attempting to change the body in this imaginary world is totally futile. Within this framework, the patient can then start to experientially explore what it would feel like to *completely* let go.

Regardless of the emotion the patient encounters, whether anxiety or relief, in the imaginary world of being completely free from the disorder, the experience is an important one. If the patient experiences anxiety, it is important for them to tolerate any anxiety that remains about separating completely from the eating disorder. If the patient experiences relief, it is important information for the patient to have that being completely disconnected from the eating disorder would be experienced as freeing. Regardless of whether the patient experienced anxiety or relief, this exercise should be practiced multiple times throughout treatment. If a patient experienced anxiety, this exercise should be practiced until the patient has habituated completely from fear of complete separation from the eating disorder and has moved fully into the experience of feeling relief. If the patient experienced relief, doing the exercise again is a nice reminder that completely cutting ties with the eating disorder is freeing.

If the patient is generally on board with the exercise and has moved into a place of acceptance, it will be time to do the in-session mindfulness exercise. If the patient is *not* ready, this exercise will be much more like a full-on exposure. If the patient is resisting the idea of acceptance, it is best not to move on to the mindfulness exercise and to repeat the first part of the handout during another session. Once the patient has moved into acceptance, doing the mindfulness exercise is appropriate.

Administering This Handout Too Early in Treatment   If this handout is administered too early in treatment, this exercise causes intense negative emotions that the patient may not yet have the skills to manage. Further, patients with a history of suicidal behavior may immediately jump to a thought such as *I would want to kill myself rather than live in a world where I could not have the eating disorder.* Therefore, it is important that this be administered when the nature of the eating disorder is more self-acknowledged and the patient's emotion dysregulation symptoms have been addressed with the proper treatment.

 ## BAE Handout 19: Imagining Recovery

BAE Handout 19 is very similar to BAE Handout 18 in that the intention is to confront fear of recovery. The objective, however, is more obviously stated. Patients are asked to imagine what it would be like to live life without the eating disorder. All of the same concepts from the previous handout apply to this one. Rather than a mindfulness exercise, though, a visualization is conducted. If the patient is still very attached to the eating disorder, this will be an exposure exercise. If, however, the patient has a self-acknowledged disorder, this will be more of an opportunity to process the experience that occurs.

If the patient has a particular feared outcome about recovery, the eating disorder behavior therapist is encouraged to write out an individualized imaginal exposure exercise about what recovery would look like for that person. For instance, if a patient fears recovering and then "not having a life," this scenario would be a useful topic to construct an imaginal exposure around.

BAE Handout 20: Building a Life Without the Eating Disorder

Whether in the throes of the illness or in treatment, the eating disorder can become the sole focus of a patient's life. Toward the end of recovery, it can be very scary to step into a life, especially after being absent from it for so long. For instance, patients are often pulled out of school, lose connections with friends, and are unable to participate in their favorite sports or hobbies. Getting back into the swing of things can be really difficult. This handout is meant to help patients with this transition. Help patients answer the questions at the end of the handout and build a plan to reengage. Revisit this plan in future sessions.

BAE Handout 21: Your Body Is Your Temple

This handout can be administered to patients at any point in recovery, but it should also be administered prior to the end of treatment.

The eating disorder reduces a person and their worth down to the body. It creates a fusion between the self and body: "I am 'fat.'" BAE Handout 21 emphasizes that a person is *not* their body. This handout can really emotionally resonate with some patients. It is important to allow patients to process both emotions and thoughts about this handout in session. At times, a therapist may want to "save" a patient from experiencing negative emotions. Particularly if a patient cries while reviewing this handout in session, it is important to allow them to have that experience.

BAE Handout 22: Feeling Connected Again

This handout reviews how the eating disorder disrupts a person's connection with themselves at the physical, emotional, psychological, and spiritual (values) levels. When a person with an eating disorder loses connection with themselves, they also appear to lose connection with others. Now that patients have largely reconnected with themselves in treatment, it is time to start thinking more specifically about reconnecting with others. Like the previous handout, this one can emotionally resonate with some patients. Again, it is important to allow these experiences to happen without interference.

BAE Handout 23: Acknowledging the Impact on Others

This handout should be implemented at the end of treatment. Further, patients who have or display traits of borderline or narcissistic personality disorder will likely benefit from appropriate treatment prior to the administration of this intervention.

Similar to the handouts in the family therapy modality on repairing the relationship between carers and the patient after a course of family treatment, this handout prompts patients to consider how the eating disorder may have impacted their loved ones. Although getting an eating disorder in the first place was not the patient's fault, since the disorder is a neurobiological illness influenced by a great number of factors outside the patient's control, this does not mean that the patient's interpersonal relationships would not benefit from repair. This handout compares the eating disorder to a hurricane—it is a destructive force of nature. All the same, if hurtful things were said and done during the course of the illness, it is likely best to address them. If it is fair and relationships could benefit, the patient is encouraged to assume accountability for their actions. In doing so, the patient is encouraged to honor themselves and respect others by being honest about the future. It is easy when apologizing about the eating disorder to promise that everything is going to be just perfect in the future. Instead, patients are encouraged to make a realistic commitment to recovery.

Because of the already large volume of material in the individual therapy modality, more interpersonal connection work was not included here. If patients could benefit from continued interpersonal skill development, adolescent dialectical behavior therapy will likely be helpful.

BAE Handout 24: Cultivating a Daily Gratitude Practice

Extending the analogy of the brain as hardware, this handout encourages patients to continue installing adaptive programming on the machine. As the handout describes, the intention is to cultivate an upward spiral on the basis of acceptance and gratitude.

BAE Handout 25: Eighteen Tips for Continued Recovery

This handout is a summary of the major points of both RAE and BAE. Patients should be encouraged to review it as often as is necessary.

PART 2

Group Therapy Modality

Introduction to the Group Therapy Modality

This portion of the manual focuses on conducting group therapy with handouts from the group therapy modality. It contains general guidance for using IMT in a group setting as well as some situation-specific topics, such as handling rule-breaking behaviors. It also includes explanations of how to administer the IMT group interventions.

Sections of the Group Therapy Modality

The material in the group therapy modality is separated into two distinct sections:

1. Mindfulness and acceptance (MAC)

2. Cognitive behavioral therapy (CBT)

This separation exists only for the sake of administering outpatient comprehensive IMT for anorexia nervosa and many cases of atypical anorexia nervosa. For patients who are not in comprehensive IMT, this distinction is not necessary.

Rolling Admissions

Patients may enter an IMT group at any time, whether in an outpatient setting or at a higher level of care. Please note that because groups have rolling admissions, the handouts are numbered mainly for the sake of convenience. The decision to make group admissions rolling was initially made because group material is sorely needed at higher levels of care, where group admissions *must* be rolling. Further, in the outpatient treatment of eating disorders, there is often a need to begin treatment as soon as possible. Therefore, if a patient is new to a group, simply make efforts to introduce the newcomer with icebreakers, explain the homework from the previous session, and fold them into the group conversation to the extent that they are comfortable.

"Groups" of One

Although the IMT individual interventions should not be administered in a group format, because of their sensitive and personal nature, IMT group interventions can be administered in "groups" of one or in individual sessions, if needed. For instance, in rural areas there may not be enough patients to create a whole IMT group, but these interventions can still be administered to a patient even if there are not any other group members. Lack of fellow patients should not keep an individual from learning the skills.

The IMT Group Measure

We recommend that outcomes be measured across administration of the IMT group interventions. The IMT Group Measure was designed to measure progress toward treatment goals over time. Patients are not expected to be familiar with all the material presented in the IMT Group Measure. For instance, the IMT Group Measure asks about the frequency of practicing mindfulness exercises. It's OK if this concept has not yet been introduced. The frequency will simply be 0. Any increase in this skill after its introduction will then be reflected on future measurements. Ask patients to complete the measure to the best of their ability, and clarify any questions they may have while completing it.

For patients in an outpatient setting, it is definitely recommended that the IMT Group Measure be filled out upon admission to the group and at discharge. The IMT Group Measure should also be administered during the interval between intake and discharge, since it is a clinical tool intended to help guide treatment. The IMT Group Measure not only provides the therapist with important information, it provides the patient with feedback about their own progress. As such, the IMT Group Measure should be administered about once per month. (Note that weekly administration may feel taxing and may address too short a time for the patient to notice measurable changes.) On days when the IMT Group Measure is being administered, bring patients' previously completed measures for reference. It can be very encouraging for patients to see the progress they have made. This also provides the therapist with an opportunity to praise patients for treatment gains and provide verbal reinforcement for group participation, homework completion, attendance, and working hard in recovery. Alternatively, if patients appear not to be meeting treatment goals, important conversations regarding treatment may be prompted.

For patients enrolled in comprehensive IMT, there is one IMT Group Measure that has items for all IMT skills. No need to fret, however—the measures are clinical tools, not exact research measures. In due time, patients in comprehensive IMT will learn all the skills listed in the IMT Group Measure.

The Eating Disorder Group Therapist

This section provides general information and tips for the therapist about the challenges of conducting group therapy from a behavioral perspective for adolescents with eating disorders.

Redirecting Intolerance Behaviors in Session

Patients will be engaging in all sorts of eating disorder behaviors during your groups, and other patients will notice. Not only will these other patients be mildly triggered by this behavior, they may also start to engage in the same behavior if it is not addressed. To prevent this scenario and provide the best treatment for all patients, it is important to direct patients who are engaging in eating disorder behavior to engage in a recovery behavior instead. As the group leader, it is your duty to redirect the behavior of the patient who is in violation of group rules and to provide reinforcement for compliance. Do this as many times as necessary during the group. This provides a safe healing environment for everyone.

For instance, patients will often covertly exercise by letting their feet hover just above the floor. An example of a simple verbal redirection might be "Please sit in a relaxed, seated position with your feet on the ground." Using the same term ("relaxed, seated position") as in the group rules ("During group sessions, all members must assume a relaxed, seated position, without engaging in any form of exercise whatsoever"; see "IMT Group Rules" in section 2.3, "Administering IMT Groups") is a reminder that the rule is being broken. If the patient accepts the redirection, reinforce that behavior both verbally and nonverbally. You can provide verbal reinforcement by saying "Thank you for sitting in a relaxed, seated position" and nonverbal reinforcement by smiling. This has a tendency to relax the other patients in the group, inspire confidence in your group leadership, and prevent the spread of the eating disorder behavior to other patients in the milieu.

From this perspective, reinforcement is very effective and has the power both to heal and to destroy. The eating disorder is an automatically reinforcing system (for example, purging is reinforced through reduction in negative internal experiences). If this automatically reinforcing system is left unchecked, it can become even more entrenched over time. The reinforcement of healthy behaviors can change that course. Reinforcement can literally be lifesaving. The eating disorder is what is causing the exercise in group, and your verbal reinforcement of the patient's decision to sit with a relaxed posture is an agent of recovery. In fact, if the patient behaves in a way that is in line with recovery rather than with the eating disorder, then that recovery behavior must be reinforced. The machine of the eating disorder provides all too much reinforcement, and we must seek out opportunities to counter this whenever possible. Do not think of yourself as a schoolmarm reprimanding children for "bad" behavior in class. You are a healthcare provider administering the treatment of verbal reinforcement to foster recovery from a serious illness.

Particularly when you're running an eating disorder group for the first time, you can very easily become frustrated with the constant rule breaking and "bad" behavior. It is easy to take it personally and feel disrespected. You know intellectually that this behavior is occurring because of the eating disorder. But when rules are constantly being broken, when this behavior dysregulates the other members of the group, and when chaos ensues on your watch, your compassion can start to wane. And from here, the psychological transition from therapist to schoolmarm is not a hard one. This is a tough job. What can often combat these negative emotions and less effective behavioral patterns is to remember that, as part of your job, you are actually looking for real-time opportunities to redirect eating disorder behavior and reinforce recovery behavior. It is all well and good to talk to patients about changing their own behavior in individual therapy, or to carers about shaping behavior in family therapy, but group therapy is *your* opportunity to contribute to shaping behavior. When you lead a group, you play an active role in guiding patients toward recovery-oriented decision making and in reinforcing healthy behavior. Of course, you are doing this while teaching patients skills and discussing how they can shape their own behavior outside the group.

REDIRECTION AND REINFORCEMENT

One group member will inevitably trigger other group members by blurting out something that is against the group rules—for example, "I lost twenty-five pounds by eating nothing but protein!" Once a patient triggers other patients, you will be in the delicate position of having to address the patients who were triggered while redirecting the patient who broke the group rule, but without shaming them. Because you have already done a fantastic job of introducing the group members to the rules, everyone knows that a rule was broken. In fact, the patient who broke the rule probably knows it, but the temptation to discuss weight loss can sometimes be too strong in the context of an eating disorder.

We must have compassion for this through our understanding of reinforcement; that is, if a patient is engaging in this type of behavior in the group, then they have probably received such an overwhelming amount of social reinforcement for it (such as praise, or people's interest in their weight-loss strategies) that they can hardly be blamed for attempting to use a social forum to seek reinforcement again. But what do we do instead of reinforcing the eating disorder behavior? We focus on redirection and reinforcement.

In this case, you can start by objectively stating that it is against the rules to discuss numbers in terms of calories, pounds, and so forth (see "IMT Group Rules" in section 2.3, "Administering IMT Groups"). You can then explain that numbers are not discussed because that kind of discussion is triggering for others and is part of the eating disorder mentality that the group is trying to move away from. You can redirect the patient (and prevent social positive reinforcement) by simply asking them not to mention numbers in the future. That patient will now have experienced enacting an eating disorder behavior and *not* being reinforced for it.

If any group members were triggered, encourage them to tolerate their negative internal experiences by using skills during the group until urges pass. If they are still experiencing urges at the end of the group session, have a brief check-in to discuss which skills to use and a plan to avoid engaging in eating disorder behaviors.

Group Derailment with Eating Disorder–Protecting Behaviors

Some IMT group interventions are psychoeducational, and others are more emotionally experiential. The latter category of exercises can engender a range of responses within a group. IMT group interventions, as we've conceived them, challenge the eating disorder in the moment instead of equipping the patient to challenge it later on, and this is why eating disorder–protecting behaviors can occur in session. Therefore, although behaviors that are relatively difficult to manage may arise during a group session, they may present the very opportunities that are best for shaping the eating disorder behavior. Two handouts in particular—MAC Handout 6: Lessons from Cute Stuff, and MAC Handout 12: False Promises—can prompt a variety of challenging interpersonal behaviors.

Here are some examples of in-group eating disorder–protecting behaviors:

- Getting caught up in the specific phrasing of a question or an exercise

- Accusing the therapist of trying to make patients feel bad

- Reporting disagreement with an exercise "on principle" but appearing to be emotionally avoidant

- Refusing to participate

If any eating disorder–protecting behaviors occur in session, listen to the patient's description of their experience. It can be helpful to take a moment to find your footing and remind yourself that you, not the adolescent, are the person leading the group. Luckily, this gets easier over time. Take a brief moment to calmly address the seemingly logical aspect of the patient's argument against, for example, participating in an exercise. Be sure to move on quickly so as to not reinforce the eating disorder's taking hold. Without leaving too much room for discourse, proceed with your agenda of running the exercise. Remember that the squeaky wheel does *not* get the oil. There are other patients in the group who have eating disorders and need to learn the skills you're trying to impart. If you spend too much time indulging the eating disorder of the person who is struggling, then you not only reinforce their eating disorder, you also allow an opportunity for other members of the group to be triggered. If a group leader allows one patient's eating disorder to be in control of the room, other patients' eating disorders will start to express themselves and join in on the derailing of the group.

TIP: Don't Let Them See You Sweat

If a patient engages in an eating disorder–protecting behavior that has the effect of derailing the group, don't let them see you sweat. For example, a patient with anorexia nervosa in an inpatient setting might say something like this during group: "You must be a really terrible therapist for making us do something that makes us feel so bad. You're supposed to make us feel better, not worse." It is important not to get defensive. At the same time, you must calmly stand your ground and keep the conversation moving in a helpful direction. Remember, you, not the eating disorder, are the group leader. In response to this comment, a group leader might say, "Part of this exercise does involve feeling bad because experiencing negative emotions is an important component of treatment. In fact, avoiding negative emotions is considered to be at the root of many disorders. Therefore, we need to do the opposite. Moving on, let's turn our attention to question 6 of the handout. Can I have a volunteer to read it, please?" If no one volunteers, keep the conversation moving by quickly calling on someone other than the patient who engaged in the eating disorder–protecting behavior. This will show the patient that they can't ruffle your feathers. It will also inspire confidence in your leadership abilities among the other group members—who are, after all, adolescents and need to feel secure.

Mindfulness in an Eating Disorder Group Setting

Each session should start with a brief mindfulness exercise. Because people with eating disorders can be triggered in specific ways by mindfulness exercises, we offer suggestions here for conducting such exercises as well as guidance regarding standard mindfulness exercises that should be avoided.

We do not recommend doing mindfulness exercises involving food (such as mindfully eating a piece of chocolate, mindfully eating one raisin, and so forth) in a group setting. Introducing unplanned food is more of an opportunity for opposition to an unplanned exposure than an opportunity for mindfulness. This will derail the group and may cause a mutiny. Mindful eating is a generally advisable practice for people, but this crowd may turn on you. Even the introduction of a single raisin can be problematic. For instance, the standard exercise of mindfully eating a single raisin in an eating disorder group can appear to be promoting a restrictive mind-set and thus be triggering. Therefore, we generally advise against conducting mindfulness exercises involving food.

Patients with eating disorders often report that mindfulness involving attention to somatic experiences (breathing, noticing the body, and so forth) can trigger intense negative emotions, thoughts about "fatness," and eating disorder urges. It would be ideal to be able to practice such exercises in the group, with the aim of building tolerance for negative internal experiences, but with a given group, that can sometimes be too ambitious an undertaking. In an outpatient group setting, we recommend starting with exercises for adolescents that are more concrete (such as writing thoughts) before moving to exercises with a focus on somatic experiences. Once a particular group of patients can tolerate mindfulness with a focus on somatic experience, we encourage you to select these types of exercises. There is no reason to avoid mindfulness of the breath, for instance, if it will not cause dysregulation and derailing of the group.

For patients starting out in treatment, it is best to think of in-group mindfulness exercises more as an opportunity to cognitively sharpen focus than as an opportunity to tolerate intense internal experiences. Of course, learning to tolerate intense internal experiences will be an essential component of treatment, but there is a time and a place. Think of mindfulness exercises that do not involve somatic experiences as helping patients build a foundation for being able to mindfully tolerate negative emotions.

In our experience, practical nonsomatic exercises include having patients mindfully observe art or items in the room, mindfully listen to sounds, mindfully play a game of catch, and mindfully remain as still as a statue, without fidgeting, for a short time (say, one minute). Further, instead of introducing a new exercise each session, we have sometimes found it more suitable to have patients practice the same exercises over consecutive sessions and then remark on their progress.

In the IMT group intervention material, there are two exercises that are the focus of entire group sessions. One involves examining the specific thoughts that arise during a written mindfulness exercise. The other concretely introduces mindfulness of physical sensations. We have slowly introduced mindful experience of physical sensations by playing nature sounds, using imagery, and having patients write down any physical sensations that arise (such as having the belly expand and contract during diaphragmatic breathing). This gradual introduction can then be followed by more somatically focused exercises. Once patients have shown that they can tolerate these exercises, mindfulness of internal experiences and the breath can be incorporated.

If patients verbalize a judgment or an eating disorder thought during a mindfulness exercise, the therapists can ring a mindfulness bell, as in dialectical behavior therapy (Linehan, 1993). This is a wonderful way to increase awareness of judgments and eating disorder thoughts, since it conditions patients to monitor their thinking.

Section 2.3

Administering IMT Groups

This section provides general information about conducting IMT groups with adolescents who have eating disorders.

A Patient's First Group

Here is a list of things to do before patients' first IMT group:

- Inform patients that they must arrive early on the first day because of paperwork.

- Be sure to administer choice assessments (such as IMT measures).

- Briefly introduce members to the idea that they will be receiving homework from the group, and set the expectation that the homework is to be completed and practiced outside the group during the week.

- Inform members that the purpose of the group is specifically for them to learn skills.

- Go over the IMT group rules.

IMT Group Rules

Here is a sample of rules that we recommend. You may want to modify them to fit your setting. Each rule should be discussed with any new group member.

- Group members must be on time to group sessions.

- Attendance is mandatory.

- Unless otherwise stated, electronic devices cannot be used in the group.

- The assigned homework (usually between five and ten minutes' worth) must be completed each week.

- Everything discussed in the group is confidential. Sharing a group member's name or any other personal information regarding another group member outside the group is strictly prohibited.

- Commenting on another group member's appearance in any way is strictly prohibited.

- No numbers in relation to food or the body (in terms of calories, pounds, and the like) can be discussed in the group.

- The terms *restriction*, *food avoidance*, and *binge eating* are permissible in the group.

- We use the term *intolerance behavior* to refer to eating disorder behaviors that occur after eating.

- No details about any intolerance behavior (such as how the behavior was carried out) may be shared with the group.

- During group sessions, all members must assume a relaxed, seated position, without engaging in any form of exercise whatsoever.

- Details of *non*–eating disorder behaviors that may be triggering (such as self-injurious behavior, use of substances, and so on) cannot be shared with the group under any circumstances.

- In outpatient, intensive outpatient, day treatment, and partial hospital settings, no communication between two or more group members is allowed outside the group. Once treatment has concluded for both or all patients, this rule no longer applies.

- If a group leader deems a group member to be at imminent risk for self-harm or hurting others, appropriate people (such as carers) will be notified.

- Any group member who arrives to a group session under the influence may not participate in the group.

- Group members must treat one another in a respectful manner.

TIP: AVOID USING SPECIFIC EXAMPLES OF INTOLERANCE BEHAVIORS IN GROUP SESSIONS
It is exceedingly common knowledge that people exercise in an effort to lose weight. Therefore, if it happens that a specific example of an intolerance behavior has to be used in order to illustrate the concept of intolerance behaviors, we suggest using the very general, relatively uncreative idea of exercising to lose weight. This mitigates the risk of introducing new ideas that the patient may not have considered (such as using a new herbal version of a laxative). We have found that patients are largely not triggered by hearing other patients name intolerance behaviors ("I purged last night"). Even for patients who struggle with purging, hearing that another patient has purged does not appear to have a triggering effect, unless specifics about the behavior are divulged ("I ate a gallon of ice cream, stuck my fingers down my throat, played music loudly so no one could hear, and purged"). Further, because patients in the group will all be well aware that purging and exercise are eating disorder behaviors, we have found that it is acceptable and helpful on occasion to discuss these specific behaviors by name during a group session. For example, in a group exercise examining the relationship between emotions and behaviors, it is instructive to say that the emotion of guilt may trigger an eating disorder urge to purge. But when it comes to any other, less common intolerance behavior, we simply tell patients to label it broadly as an "intolerance behavior."

What Is Permitted in an IMT Group

Discussing specific ideas for carrying out various eating disorder behaviors (such as taking a certain brand of laxative a given number of minutes after a meal) is strictly prohibited. At the same time, in order to communicate about important group topics, it is necessary to discuss broad categories of eating disorder behaviors. Because our aim is to maximize therapeutic effects while minimizing any potential negative outcomes, we address two parallel concerns: spreading ideas about carrying out eating disorder behaviors, and triggering urges to engage in eating disorder behaviors.

IMT groups are not recommended for patients with binge eating disorder and no prior history of emotional intolerance behaviors (such as purging), and so we mitigate the risk of onset of intolerance behaviors by excluding people who do not already engage in them. Because this group is largely for patients with BN, AN, and OSFED who already have engaged in intolerance behaviors to some degree, the aim is to directly address these behaviors without exacerbating them. Although it is true that adolescents have access to the Internet, and therefore to a huge amount of information about various intolerance behaviors, we must do our best to curb access to this information any way we can in treatment, including in group discussions.

Group Homework with Rolling Admissions

Patients will receive between five and ten minutes' worth of homework to complete each week. Completion of homework from the IMT group is essential to the successful generalization of the skills and concepts taught during the group session. We recommend spending ten minutes at the beginning of each group session to review the homework from the previous session.

TIP: INCLUDE NEW GROUP MEMBERS IN THE DISCUSSION

New group members will be lost during homework review because admission to IMT groups is rolling. Therefore, provide a copy of the IMT group handout from the previous session to the new member. The therapist can then ask a volunteer to explain the basic concepts from the handout and the homework to the new member. It would then be the group leader's job to verbally reinforce the participation of the group member who volunteered ("Thank you so much for explaining the homework to our new group member, getting them up to speed, and making them feel welcome"). From there, the therapist can fill in any gaps in the explanation the volunteer provided. If the new member is willing, the group leader can ask them to listen to the answers of the other group members during the homework review and then simply attempt to complete the handout during the time allotted for homework review. But because this is the new member's first time in the group, they will not be asked to share their answers. Nevertheless, it is not advisable to say, "You don't have to share your answers if you don't want to," because this puts the new member on the spot. Instead, we recommend that you simply say it's not necessary for the new member's answers to be shared with the group. If the new member then offers to participate in the group discussion, the group leader warmly welcomes their participation.

Materials Needed

In each session, the group leader will need to provide the following materials and items:

- Choice outcome measures, such as IMT measures and the Eating Disorder Examination Questionnaire (EDE-Q; Fairburn & Beglin, 1994)

- A copy of the group rules for each new member

- A Tibetan singing bowl (that is, a mindfulness bowl or bell) or small xylophone

- Copies of new handouts to be discussed during the group session

- Copies of any handouts being reviewed for homework that new members did not receive

- Writing utensils

- Special materials mentioned at the beginning of some handouts

Using IMT Materials in Group Therapy

Mindfulness and Acceptance (MAC) Handouts

This portion of the manual describes how to incorporate MAC handouts into group therapy sessions. Each handout is discussed individually.

MAC HANDOUTS

MAC Handout 1: The IMT Model of Eating Disorders

MAC Handout 2: Full Is Not Fat!

MAC Handout 3: Eating Disorder and Recovery Behaviors

MAC Handout 4: Coping with the Urge to Restrict (EAT MEALS Skills)

MAC Handout 5: Eating Disorder Monsters

MAC Handout 6: Lessons from Cute Stuff

MAC Handout 7: The Eating Disorder Triad

MAC Handout 8: The Eating Disorder's Anxiety

MAC Handout 9: The Eating Disorder's Disgust

MAC Handout 10: The Eating Disorder's Guilt

MAC Handout 12: False Promises

MAC Handout 13: Noticing the Thoughts in Your Head

MAC Handout 14: Mindfulness and Leaves on a Stream

MAC Handout 15: Staying Motivated in Your Recovery (RECOVERY Skills)

MAC Handout 16: Telling Others About Your Eating Disorder

MAC Handout 17: Why You Might Despise Supervised Eating

MAC Handout 18: Coping with the Urge to Binge (NO BINGE Skills)

MAC Handout 19: Coping with the Urge to Purge (NO PURGE Skills)

MAC Handout 1: The IMT Model of Eating Disorders

Main Take-Home Points

- Mindfulness is about practicing focusing the mind.

- The gray globe in MAC Handout 1 represents the environment.

- Internal experiences include thoughts, behaviors, physical sensations, and emotions.

- The environment influences these four types of internal experiences.

- These internal experiences all influence each other.

- The Eating Disorder Sequence of Internal Experiences shows one way in which these internal experiences can interact.

- It is helpful to write out sequences of internal experiences.

Group Opener (If Needed)

For groups running linearly through the material, this will be the first session. If so, be sure to administer all relevant measures, review the group rules, and conduct a group icebreaker.

Mindfulness

Therapist script: Quick show of hands—who has done mindfulness before?

Therapist script: Who can tell me what mindfulness is?

To Do

- Explain that mindfulness is not about relaxing per se but about practicing focusing the mind.

- Explain that mindfulness is going to be practiced at the start of every group.

- Explain that each exercise will take about one to two minutes.

- To begin the exercise, strike a singing bowl, bell, chime, or small xylophone three times.

- Conduct a mindfulness exercise for about one to two minutes.

- To conclude the exercise, strike a singing bowl, bell, chime, or small xylophone twice.

- Share experiences.

- Ask patients what thoughts, emotions, physical feelings, and behavior urges they had during the exercise.

- Ask patients if the exercise was easy or difficult to focus on.

- Remind patients that minds wander and that bringing attention back to the exercise is a skill.

- Verbally reinforce (praise) willingness to participate in the mindfulness exercise.

Homework Review (If Needed)

For members who are enrolled in group and not attending for the first time, review the homework assignment from the previous week.

The IMT Model of Eating Disorders

Therapist script: This [*indicate the illustration at the top of the handout*] is the IMT Model of Eating Disorders. There are thoughts, behaviors, physical sensations, and emotions represented here. We call these things *internal experiences* because they are things that happen inside us. There are arrows connecting each of the four internal experiences. There is also a gray globe in the background. Can anyone guess what this diagram might represent?

To Do

- Have patients discuss specific stressors or triggers in the environment (represented by the gray globe) that can influence internal experiences.

- Discuss the differences among the internal experiences.
  - Thought: an idea or belief in our heads (such as *I should not eat*)
  - Behavior: an action (such as taking a selfie)
  - Body sensation: a physical sensation in the body (such as a full stomach)
  - Emotion: a positive or negative feeling (such as sadness) that is not a body sensation

- Have patients discuss how the environment, represented by the gray globe, may affect their internal experiences (thoughts, behaviors, body sensations, and emotions). Ask for specific examples (for example, seeing a diet ad in the environment can prompt the thought I *should restrict*).

- Have patients write answers to the first set of twelve questions. If patients are having difficulty understanding the differences among the internal experiences, go through the first several questions with them aloud. Then have them complete the rest of the questions on their own. When everyone is finished, ask patients to share their answers.

Eating Disorder Sequence of Internal Experiences

Therapist script: Now that you have an understanding of how internal experiences interact with one another, let's take a look at how they may interact specifically in an eating disorder.

To Do

- Tell patients that this is only a diagram, and that everything may not apply to them.

- Read the Eating Disorder Sequence of Internal Experiences aloud to group members.

- Be sure to emphasize that some people engage in binge eating behavior, but others do not.
  - For people who do engage in binge eating, a negative emotion often precedes binge eating. Hunger and craving often play a role as well.
  - For others, a negative emotion does not necessarily precede nonbinge types of eating.

- Explain that, regardless of whether people simply eat or binge eat, in the context of having an eating disorder, people may feel full, have negative thoughts, and have negative emotions.

- Emphasize that not everyone will experience everything displayed in the diagram, but that sometimes people with eating disorders do experience everything depicted in it.

Therapist script: Raise your hand if this diagram does *not* reflect the typical eating disorder behavior pattern for you.

Therapist script: Of those of you who raised your hands, who would like to volunteer to work out what sequence of internal experiences best fits your own experience?

To Do

- Help the willing participant construct a sequence on the board.

- If there is time left in session, do this with other patients as well.

TIP: RESISTANCE MAY BE AN EATING DISORDER–PROTECTING BEHAVIOR

Some adolescents will provide a lot of extraneous details when reviewing the diagram, losing the core concept of the exercise. There can be a desire to prove the therapist "wrong" with information. Treat this as an instance of an eating disorder–protecting behavior.

Homework Assignment

Therapist script: For this week, please complete the homework section of this handout. Any questions?

MAC Handout 2: Full Is Not Fat!

Special Materials

You will need three or four easily accessible pictures (saved on a device or printed) of people who have bodies of different sizes. Include two or three extra pictures of people expressing different emotions (joy, sadness, and so forth).

Main Take-Home Points

- The eating disorder equates feeling full with instantly gaining weight.

- The eating disorder makes you perceive that you have gained weight, even though you haven't.

- You cannot tell if someone is hungry or full just by looking at them.

Group Opener for New Members (If Needed), Mindfulness, and Homework Review

See the relevant portions of MAC Handout 1.

Full Is Not Fat!

Therapist script: Today we're going to talk about how to cope with feeling full. To start us off, let's talk about why feeling full can trigger the eating disorder. Does anyone have any ideas?

To Do

- Ask patients for their general thoughts about the Fullness Trap. Ask which parts of it sound familiar to them.

- Have them answer the two questions that follow the illustration of the Fullness Trap.

- Answer to question 2: This chain of events is a trap because feeling full doesn't make someone immediately "fat." Thinking that it does keeps people from recovery and trapped in eating disorder behavior.

Therapist script: Now we're going to move on to the exercise.

To Do

- Display one photo at a time of people who have different body sizes as well as those making different expressions. Ask patients if the person in each photo is hungry or full.

- Ask patients (if they can remember) how they used to feel, emotionally, when they were hungry *before* the eating disorder started.

- Ask patients (if they can remember) how they used to feel, emotionally, when they were full *before* the eating disorder started.

- Address cognitive distortions as they arise in discussion.

Questions (Part 1)

To Do

- Go through these five questions one by one, aloud with the group.

- Clearly state that it is impossible to tell if someone is hungry or full by looking at them. People who have overweight bodies can be hungry, and people who have underweight bodies can feel full. You simply cannot tell if someone is hungry or full by looking at them.

- The eating disorder is so used to associating "full" with "fat" that it seems as if you can just tell by looking. But you can't.

When you ask patients which people in the photographs are hungry and which are full, they will probably comment that some people look hungry because they are skinny, and full because they are fat. Patients may also say that some people are hungry because they look happy, and that some are full because they look sad.

Therapist script: Now we're going to move on to the next set of questions.

QUESTIONS (PART 2): ANSWERS

- Question 1: Your stomach may feel full of food to you, but this does not mean that your belly area looks "fatter" to anyone else. Only you can discern your feelings of being full or bloated.

- Question 2: Just as having a full stomach does not mean weight gain, having an empty stomach does not mean weight loss. Feeling empty does not mean you look any thinner on the outside. No one can tell if you're hungry or full.

- Question 3. Having food in the organ that is your stomach is not the same thing as having fat on your body. That is not the way it works. No one can instantly have more fat on their body from eating.

- Question 4. Associating an empty stomach with weight loss can lead to serious health consequences if a person does not properly nourish themselves, and it can backfire into binge eating (as in MAC Handout 1). Further, this sets you up to feel triggered every time you feel full. Everyone needs to feel full several times throughout a given day because we need to eat to survive. If you think you are gaining weight every time you feel full, you are set up for having a hard time in life.

- Question 5: No! A person does not gain weight each time they eat. Many people maintain a stable weight over time, and they eat three square meals and two snacks every day. The food gets used up.

- Question 6: When feeling "fat," many people are actually feeling the emotions of anxiety, guilt, and disgust. Many times other emotions, like shame and sadness, are also experienced. People can also wrongly perceive themselves as "fat" just because they feel full.

- Question 7: If you let yourself experience negative emotions (anxiety, guilt, disgust, and so forth), they will subside over time. The perception that weight was instantly gained just because food is in the stomach fades. The idea that one is fat just because one has eaten is no longer believed.

TIP: RESPOND TO RESISTANCE TO CHANGE DUE TO FEAR OF "FATNESS" AND WEIGHT GAIN
At this point, some patients will insist that without their negative emotions, distorted perceptions, and erroneous beliefs, they would gain weight. When this inevitably happens, you can respond by saying, "In order to recover, a person must tolerate these negative emotions as well as the distorted perceptions and beliefs that comprise the eating disorder. With that comes a decrease in intensity of these negative experiences. Once this occurs, a person can leave behind the compulsion to keep a very close watch on their weight. But this does not mean that your weight will absolutely skyrocket. In treatment, a method of eating is taught that naturally prevents weight from skyrocketing. This manner of eating is psychologically healthy and also does not cause weight to career (barring medical anomalies). Behaviors that can influence weight in one direction or the other are typically erratic eating disorder behaviors—for instance, restriction backfiring into binge eating—not consistent recovery behaviors."

Therapist script: Now we're going to move on to the section of the handout called "Eating Disorder Assumptions."

To Do

- Have patients take turns reading the assumptions.

- Be sure to mention the points in the following script.

Therapist script: Think of your stomach feeling full as being like getting Novocain at the dentist's. Your mouth feels really big, but it actually doesn't *look* very big. An eating disorder can work the same way—your stomach feels really full, but you actually don't *look* any bigger. Does this make sense?

Homework Assignment

Therapist script: Now that this session has come to an end, it's time to assign homework. Please complete the homework section of MAC Handout 2. Any questions?

 ## MAC Handout 3: Eating Disorder and Recovery Behaviors

Main Take-Home Points

- There are eating disorder behaviors that occur in the context of treatment.

- The goal is to work toward recovery behaviors.

- There is a certain mentality that is associated with both eating disorder behaviors and recovery behaviors.

- Group members are to practice having a recovery mentality over time.

Group Opener for New Members (if Needed), Mindfulness, and Homework Review

See the relevant portions of MAC Handout 1.

Eating Disorder and Recovery Behaviors

Therapist script: Today we are going to zero in on behaviors. We're going to talk about both eating disorder behaviors and recovery behaviors. We're also going to talk about the different types of thoughts that can go along with each eating disorder and recovery behavior.

Therapist script: The first chart in MAC Handout 3 shows examples of behaviors and examples of thoughts (statements) that can go along with the behaviors. On the left-hand side there are examples of eating disorder behaviors with related eating disorder thoughts. On the right-hand side there are examples of recovery behaviors and acceptance thoughts that go with them. Please note that we don't necessarily expect you to believe all the acceptance thoughts associated with the recovery behaviors right this instant. The idea is that you can get there eventually, and that's what the arrows between the columns represent. These are the kinds of recovery-oriented attitudes to foster over time.

Therapist script: Let's take turns reading aloud from the items on this list. I'll go first, and then we'll go around. Circle the items that apply to you as we go.

Therapist script: Would anyone like to share what the most difficult eating disorder behavior is for them to fight?

Therapist script: How would practicing the type of acceptance thinking listed on the right-hand side of the handout help you engage in recovery behaviors?

Moving Toward Recovery Behaviors with Acceptance Thoughts

Therapist script: Let's take a look at the second chart in the handout. It's just like the first one except that it has blank spaces under the different eating disorder and recovery behaviors. Use the first chart as a guide, and fill in the blank spaces with your own eating disorder thoughts and your own acceptance thoughts for each item that applies to you.

To Do

- Help craft acceptance thoughts for any patient who is having difficulty.

Therapist script: Who would like to share three of their answers?

Therapist script: What was difficult about this exercise?

Recovery Promise

Therapist script: At this point, you may not feel ready to fully commit to recovery. In treatment, though, you are expected to work on it. So that means if you're struggling, you should start by making a small recovery promise. If you are ready to take on something bigger, by all means, go ahead!

To Do

- Have a volunteer read the directions and the first two items in the numbered list.

- Have group members complete the sheet.

- If they are struggling, go around and help them choose a manageable goal.

- Have members go around and share their promise.

- When patients make their promise, make sure that you warmly encourage them to work toward the goal. Acknowledge their effort and provide warmth and support.

Therapist script: Sticking to that promise is going to be really difficult. Sometimes the eating disorder will get so strong that it may be practically impossible for you to stick to your promise. But if you fall off the recovery horse, you can always get back on. Making one mistake doesn't mean you've completely failed. Can you think of some reasons why a mistake does not equal failure?

EXAMPLES

- Recovery is a process.

- People are expected to make mistakes—in life, and when beating an eating disorder.

- The eating disorder can be a really strong opponent.

Homework Assignment

Therapist script: Your homework for this week has two parts. First pick one of the eating disorder behaviors that you circled on the first chart, and practice saying the corresponding acceptance thought to yourself when you need to. Then reread your recovery promise before meals that you expect to be difficult.

MAC Handout 4: Coping with the Urge to Restrict (EAT MEALS Skills)

This handout may take more than one session to complete. That's OK. Give it as much time as it needs.

Main Take-Home Points

- There are many skills that you can use to help you cope with the urge to restrict.

- Putting those skills into practice is essential to recovery.

Group Opener for New Members (if Needed), Mindfulness, and Homework Review

See the relevant portions of MAC Handout 1.

Coping with the Urge to Restrict

Therapist script: Today we're going to talk about more ways to help us cope with the urge to restrict. Who can tell me what "restrict" means?

To Do

- Explain that restricting means limiting the overall *amount* of food consumed. Explain that food avoidance refers to not allowing oneself to eat a certain *type* of food (such as fats, carbohydrates, and so on).

- Have patients take turns reading each of the skills.

EAT MEALS Skills

- **Encourage yourself**
  - Explain that motivating yourself in treatment is important. Of course, having social support is also paramount, but developing a sense of being accountable for recovery over time is essential. The things on the "Encourage Yourself" list can help in taking recovery into your own hands.

- **Act as if you will succeed**
  - First, ask what the group thinks succeeding at a meal or snack means for them. Help patients to define what success would be at a given meal.
  - For patients in RAE, success in this context ultimately means eating regularly and according to appetitive cues.
  - For patients on a weight-restoration protocol, meal completion is ultimately success in this context.
  - Patients receiving meal and snack support may have intermediate goals (such as sitting through a meal without having an emotional outburst and finishing most of the food).
  - Discuss how motivation to recover most often comes after, not before, starting to engage in recovery behaviors. For instance, at the start of treatment, there can be no motivation at all to eat a meal. After some time in treatment, however, motivation can build to eat meals and recover. This is why the strategy of "fake it till you make it" is so helpful.

- Turn your thoughts in another direction

  - Note that emotions can be experienced at different intensities. If one is at 8 or higher on an intensity scale of 0 to 10, it can be helpful to use thought distraction until emotional intensity decreases.

  - Explain that thought distraction is not a helpful strategy in every situation, because not thinking about problems certainly doesn't make them go away. This strategy is reserved for times of intense emotion.

  - Also explain that in recovery, negative emotions can be at an intensity level of 7 or above at most meals for several months, and it is OK to use thought distraction during this time. Even though a period of several months might feel like forever, it is not.

  - Emphasize that if patients choose to use thought distraction by going on the Internet, they should plan with their therapist to visit specific sites and use specific apps. Just going on the Internet without a plan can easily lead down a triggering path, but using one specific gaming app can be a very effective distraction.

- Make effective decisions

  - In session, ask patients how restricting food will impede recovery.

  - Ask them also to list consequences for not completing meals.

- Externalize and separate the eating disorder

  - Ask if anyone knows what it means to externalize the eating disorder.

  - Explain that this fancy language basically means thinking of the eating disorder as an entity that is separate from them.

  - It is easiest to fight the eating disorder when it is thought of as separate.

- Accept that food must be eaten in recovery

  - Explain that the eating disorder will trigger negative thoughts and emotions about eating and feeling full. Although thought distraction is a good strategy when emotions are at 7 or higher on an intensity scale of 0 to 10, experiencing and accepting emotions without attempting to push them away is the way to go when your emotions are at an intensity level of 6 or lower.

  - It is helpful to foster the following attitude from RAE Handout 8: "Once you have eaten the food, you have eaten the food. Work on not looking back. To the extent that you are currently able, let yourself experience the anxiety, guilt, disgust, and whatever else happens to come up. Rather than trying to get out of feeling uncomfortable, a goal of recovery is to work on accepting the distress that currently comes along with eating. Learning to tolerate your negative internal experience is absolutely necessary to your recovery."

  - For patients with anorexia nervosa or atypical anorexia nervosa who are at a higher level of care or who are all in comprehensive IMT, you can foster inevitability acceptance: "Remind yourself that once you're in treatment, your family and team will not let you get below a certain weight again. The days of being malnourished are over."

- Let go of judgments

  - First ask what a judgment is. Then explain the difference between a judgment and a fact.

- Explain that you can judgmentally describe a marshmallow by saying it is a gross junk food that will make you fat. Alternatively, a marshmallow can be described nonjudgmentally, with objective language, as a small white squishy food.

- Emphasize that describing food nonjudgmentally can help make the negative emotions triggered by the eating disorder more manageable.

- Have the group do one of the following two activities: (1) have each patient take a turn stating their challenge food and describing it judgmentally, and have the other group members counter with a nonjudgmental description, *or* (2) have each patient describe their challenge food nonjudgmentally, without stating what the food is, and have other group members try to guess the food item.

- Soothe yourself

  - Remark that although the self-soothing ideas in the handout may seem obvious, unless you actually use the skill, it will not be helpful.

  - The example of smelling peppermint is given because it is said to decrease nausea.

  - Take a "brain break" by doing such things as listening to soothing music, safely lighting scented candles, snuggling up in a comfy blanket, or practicing mindfulness.

To Do

- Once you're done describing the various skills, ask patients for examples of how they might use a particular skill.

- Have patients answer the questions in the "Preparing for Homework" section.

Homework Assignment

Therapist script: Your homework for this week has two parts. First practice the skills we reviewed, and then complete the section called "Homework."

 ## MAC Handout 5: Eating Disorder Monsters

It is best to administer this intervention after all patients have been exposed to the EAT MEALS and/or RECOVERY skills.

Main Take-Home Points

- The eating disorder is separate from you.

- The eating disorder takes many forms.

- The eating disorder has taken many things from you.

- There is a battle raging between the Eating Disorder Monsters and the Superheroes.

- You can call upon each Superhero to help you save yourself from the Eating Disorder Monsters.

Group Opener for New Members (If Needed), Mindfulness, and Homework Review

See the relevant portions of MAC Handout 1.

Eating Disorder Monsters

Therapist script: The main topic of today's group is thinking about the eating disorder as separate.

To Do

- Ask for reasons why the eating disorder *feels like the same entity as* the person.

- Write these reasons on the board.

- Reasons given for why the eating disorder and the person are the same might include those that follow:
  - "I started to diet."
  - "I wanted to lose weight."
  - "The eating disorder is inside me".
  - "I like how I feel when I don't eat."
  - "I feel proud (happy, perfect…) when I don't eat."

- Ask for reasons why the eating disorder *is separate from* the person. These are examples of topics to discuss:
  - There is a genetic component that contributed to your getting an eating disorder.
  - You had dieting under control at first, but now the eating disorder has control.
  - A lot of people go on diets at some point, but only a few people develop eating disorders.
  - Having an eating disorder is not a choice. It is a psychiatric condition.
  - An eating disorder is influenced by genetics, like other diseases.
  - You value other things, like school and friendships, but the eating disorder is focused only on your body.

- Look for opportunities to reinforce the idea that the eating disorder is separate from the person.
  - If a patient reports that the main reason they want to recover is to get their interests back, but they also completely believe that they and the eating disorder are the same entity, point out that they will get their interests back *from the eating disorder.*
  - Also mention that this indicates some thinking about the idea that they and the eating disorder have separate interests.

Therapist script: The eating disorder can be viewed as a monster that causes mayhem in your life. Let's take a look at MAC Handout 5. Can I please have a volunteer to read the first set of directions?

To Do

- After they have finished the labeling exercise, ask them to go around and share. Encourage participation.

- Make sure to link the strength of the Eating Disorder Monsters with past difficulties patients may have had in achieving treatment goals. Provide validation.

- Also be sure to mention that there are ways to beat the Eating Disorder Monsters.

Superhero Helpers

Therapist script: Take a look at the next part of the handout. Next to each Superhero, write down something that can help you beat each Eating Disorder Monster. Can I please have another volunteer to read this set of directions?

To Do

- After they have finished the labeling exercise, ask them to go around and share. Encourage participation.

- Point out how this handout integrates the skills. The intention of this handout is to help patients decide which skills work best for which eating disorder manifestations (for example, guilt about eating).

Homework Assignment

Therapist script: Now that you have some concrete ideas about which skills to use for which manifestations of the eating disorder, your homework is to pick three skills to practice using this week, to save yourself from the Eating Disorder Monsters.

TIP: REINFORCE RECOVERY-ORIENTED BEHAVIORS AND DECISIONS

In the battle between the Eating Disorder Monster and the self, the self needs as much reinforcement as it can get. Every time the person uses a coping skill or engages in a recovery behavior, you can verbally reinforce the recovery-oriented decision. For instance, you can say, "It's fantastic that you chose to use an EAT MEALS skill in that moment. You didn't let the Eating Disorder Monster win. You won!"

 MAC Handout 6: Lessons from Cute Stuff

Main Take-Home Points

- The eating disorder can be viewed as verbally and physically abusive.
- It can be a very emotional experience to think of the eating disorder in this way.
- Other people who love you view the eating disorder as abusive, and they are trying to stop it.
- You can help put a stop to your own eating disorder behaviors.

Administering this handout to patients with personality pathology may be particularly challenging.

Group Opener for New Members (If Needed), Mindfulness, and Homework Review

See the relevant portions of MAC Handout 1.

Lessons from Cute Stuff

Therapist script: Today I'm going to ask you to complete the eight questions in this handout one by one, on your own. Once we have all finished, we will have a discussion.

- This handout is best administered by having patients answer all the questions in session by themselves and then share their answers later. If patients were to read ahead while a group discussion was occurring, some of the gravity of the exercise could be lost. Patients could also derail the group discussion. Therefore, do not have patients take turns reading the questions in this handout.

- Be sure to allow enough time for all group members to complete the exercise.

- After the patients have answered the questions in the handout, we often find it very helpful for group leaders to share their personal thoughts and feelings about the idea of the eating disorder "abusing" the patients (see the following script).

Therapist script: OK, this exercise was a little heavy. Thank you, everyone, for completing it. Let's walk through some of the answers together. It's OK to share only what you feel comfortable sharing. Also remember that it's important not to mention any numbers or triggering behaviors. Who would like to share their answer to the first question?

To Do

- Question 1. Patients will likely have a somber mood and may be hesitant to answer this question. It can be helpful to start by sharing your own ideas of what you would do if you could spend time with this puppy.

- Question 2. Share with patients that many people have feelings of anger and sadness when they think of the puppy having a mean owner. There can also be a feeling of moral outrage at the injustice.

- Question 3. Share your answer about how you might treat the puppy with kindness and love.

- Question 4. For this question, remind patients to use general terms for eating disorder behaviors. In addition to writing about eating disorder behaviors, people sometimes write that the eating disorder has led them to be secretive, dishonest, and isolative.

- Question 5. We have found it particularly powerful for group leaders to say something like this before asking patients how they answered this question: "As a therapist who treats people with eating disorders, I have seen eating disorders abuse many people. It can make me feel really sad and frustrated sometimes. It seems unfair that some people go through this. How does it make you feel to think about the ways the eating disorder mistreats you?"

- Question 6. Ask what group members wrote down for this question. Then share that some other people have also written that it is important to eat well, go to medical appointments regularly, and be patient with oneself.

- Question 7. Most of the time, patients respond to this question with positivity. Sometimes, however, patients may remark that being self-compassionate sounds daunting:

  - If a patient gives this response, encourage them to start with small steps.

  - If patients report feeling confused, provide feedback that confusion can be a good thing. The eating disorder was certain it was right. When we are working on ways to think about things differently, we can feel confused. But this means that progress is being made. Encourage this type of confusion in therapy!

- Question 8. Patients typically provide a wide variety of responses to this question:
  - Some patients say that poor body image and lingering eating disorder thoughts and urges will get in the way of self-compassion. Be sure to note in session that poor body image and remaining eating disorder thoughts are to be expected over the course of treatment, and that practicing self-compassion can help ease symptoms.
  - Others will say that they have negative associations with self-compassion—that it's selfish, self-indulgent, and so forth. Be sure to address these beliefs in session.

TIP: Resistance to MAC Handout 6 Can Be an Eating Disorder–Protecting Behavior

Eating disorder–protecting behavior may be expressed as resistance to this exercise. Patients can be driven to start derailing group conversation in any number of ways. It is important to remain calm when this happens and remember to stand your ground. For instance, if patients are resistant because they are experiencing negative emotions, remind patients that feeling negative emotions is helpful in recovery, and continue with the exercise.

TIP: If MAC Handout 6 Goes Over Well, Use It as an Opportunity to Join with the Patient

If this intervention happens to go particularly well, and if patients have a moment of insight here regarding their carer's concern, it can be a joining opportunity. For instance, if a patient's behavior in comprehensive IMT has been oppositional toward the treatment team and carers up until this point, the group leader has an opportunity to speak to the recovering self of the patient and explain that the carers are attempting to fight the eating disorder, out of the same type of concern the patient would have for the puppy in the exercise.

Homework Assignment

Therapist script: Your homework this week is to complete the homework section of this handout.

 ## MAC Handout 7: The Eating Disorder Triad

Main Take-Home Points

- Often people feel anxiety, disgust, and guilt in the context of having an eating disorder.
- Other emotions can be felt as well.
- It is important to consider positive emotions in the context of eating disorder recovery.

Group Opener for New Members (If Needed), Mindfulness, and Homework Review

See the relevant portions of MAC Handout 1.

The Eating Disorder Triad

Therapist script:　　Today we're going to be discussing the Eating Disorder Triad. The triad consists of three negative emotions—anxiety, disgust, and guilt. Although your eating disorder will probably prompt you to feel other emotions as well, it can be helpful to start practicing coping with these three. Let's start going through the questions together. First, what does the eating disorder prompt anxiety about? Examples might include eating high-calorie, fatty, or fried foods, wearing a bathing suit, or having a full stomach.

Therapist script:　　Now what does the eating disorder prompt disgust about? Examples might include looking in the mirror, eating until you're full, or eating something fried.

Therapist script:　　Disgust is an interesting emotion. One can feel the emotion of disgust. But disgust also can involve the body sensation of nausea. Sometimes a person can be so disgusted with someone's else's behavior that they can feel physically nauseated. Eating disorders are particularly tricky because they can mix up our emotion of disgust and our physical sensation of nausea. For instance, you may have started out life thinking that fried foods are delicious, but then, over time, the eating disorder taught you to think of fried foods as disgusting. After learning that fried foods are disgusting, you started to feel physically nauseated when eating fried foods. Something like this probably happened [*write this on the board*]:

1. You learned that being _fat_ = _bad_.

2. Therefore, eating food = _bad_.

3. You avoided food.

4. When you did eat this _bad_ food, you felt
   - anxious
   - disgusted
   - guilty

5. Furthermore, the negative emotions from eating contributed to being physically nauseated, which led to feeling even more negative emotions for having the _bad_ food.

In short, maybe you were so afraid of eating "bad" fried foods that eating actually made you feel physically nauseated. This is a very unfortunate consequence of the eating disorder—it makes treatment particularly difficult. But it's not impossible to recover! Over time, you will start to think of food as less disgusting and feel less guilty about eating it. Your body will also get used to it. We are going to go into detail about each of these emotions and how to lessen the impact of each of them.

Therapist script:　　Now let's consider guilt. What does the eating disorder prompt guilt about? Examples might include eating what you think is too much, eating high-calorie, fatty, fried, or other "bad" foods, or stopping your workout at a point that you think is too early.

Guilt is also a very interesting emotion. Under what circumstances do we feel guilt? If you were going to explain the emotion of guilt to an alien from outer space, how would you describe it? We feel guilt when we think we've done something wrong or immoral. Let's discuss other times when people feel guilt. Let's rate these examples on a scale of 0 to 10, with 10 representing the most guilt. Here are some examples:

- Telling a lie, such as telling your carer you did not have any homework when you did

- Telling a lie that could hurt someone, such as making up a story about someone you don't like

- Setting a trap to kill a mouse

- Borrowing and losing your friend's favorite sweater

- Accidentally killing a person—probably around a 10, right?

- Eating a chocolate bar—is that a 10 as well?

Now, how could you explain to an alien that you would feel just about as guilty for accidentally killing a person as you would for eating a chocolate bar? Why is eating a chocolate bar just about as bad as killing a person? When we feel the third emotion in the Eating Disorder Triad—guilt—it is because we've judged ourselves harshly as having done something morally wrong. Is eating a chocolate bar immoral?

Therapist script: What other emotions does the eating disorder prompt?

Patients often report shame, sadness, anger, confusion, and hopelessness.

Therapist script: Now let's move on to the next portions of the handout, starting with the first set of questions about the last meal you ate.

To Do

- Have a volunteer read the directions for answering the first set of "Before the Meal" and "After the Meal" questions.

- Have patients rate the three emotions before and after the remembered meal.

- Ask the patients to consider why it might be important for them to separate their experience into different emotions.

- Offer the explanation provided in the following script.

Therapist script: Let's examine that question more closely. Just being able to identify your emotional experience as "upset" is overwhelming. By understanding the various emotional components, you can break down your experience into manageable pieces. It is also easier to willingly tolerate an emotional experience when you are aware of its components.

To Do

- Have a volunteer read the directions for answering the second set of "Before the Meal" and "After the Meal" questions.

- Ask the patients to answer the second set of "Before the Meal" and "After the Meal" questions.

TIP: Reinforce the Rating of Recovery-Oriented Positive Emotions

Some patients will report having no positive emotions whatsoever. If possible, encourage them to rate any positive emotion at all, even if it involves using decimal points (for example, .01 on a scale of 0 to 10). Any positive emotions from eating reflect expressions of the recovered self. Therefore, reinforce the rating of any positive emotion, regardless of the magnitude. For instance, a group leader might say this to a patient who writes ".01" next to "Sense of accomplishment" under "After the meal": "It's really good that you were able to write down any number higher than 0. This is a start! This means that someone deep down underneath the eating disorder—your recovered self—is feeling something. This can grow over time. Keep working on it." The patient may roll their eyes at you now, but that does not mean that the reinforcement was not received. In this case, you are reinforcing the patient's willingness to experience positive emotions—which the eating disorder often blocks—regarding actions they have taken that are in line with recovery. The therapist must always be looking for opportunities to foster the growth of the recovered self through reinforcement.

Homework Assignment

Therapist script: Can I have a volunteer to read the homework assignment?

Therapist script: Be sure to practice the mantra this week, and complete the written section of the homework.

 # MAC Handout 8: The Eating Disorder's Anxiety

Main Take-Home Points

- The eating disorder causes a lot of anxiety.

- The eating disorder makes you focus on worst-case scenarios.

- You can handle worst-case scenarios.

- People do not keep gaining weight forever without the eating disorder.

Group Opener for New Members (If Needed), Mindfulness, and Homework Review

See the relevant portions of MAC Handout 1.

The Eating Disorder's Anxiety

Therapist script: Today we are going to focus on anxiety.

To Do

- Go through each of the thirteen question together, with patients taking turns reading the questions.

- This handout is largely self-explanatory.

- Clearly, the idea of questions 1 and 2 is to show that anxiety is likely to increase as the eating disorder takes over.

- The idea behind questions 3, 4, and 5 is to show that the eating disorder is likely to trigger more anxiety than the person is aware of.

- Questions 6, 7, 8, and 9 are precursors to imaginal exposure work.

- Questions 10, 11, 12, and 13 help foster a sense that a patient could manage if the worst were to happen.

Will I Keep Eating and Gaining Weight Forever?

To Do

- Have a volunteer read the directions for answering the five questions under "Will I Keep Eating and Gaining Weight Forever?"

- Have patients answer the questions.

- If there is time left in session, dispute any negative automatic thoughts that may have arisen or been expressed during the discussion or the answering of questions (for example, "If the eating disorder isn't around to help me, I will gain weight").

Homework Assignment

Therapist script: For homework, complete all the questions in the homework section of the handout.

 MAC Handout 9: The Eating Disorder's Disgust

Main Take-Home Points

- The eating disorder causes a lot of disgust.

- The eating disorder mixes the emotion of disgust and the physical sensation of nausea.

- Disgust and nausea decrease over time in recovery.

Group Opener for New Members (If Needed), Mindfulness, and Homework Review

See the relevant portions of MAC Handout 1.

The Eating Disorder's Disgust

Therapist script: Today we will be discussing disgust. Let's go through the first thirteen questions in MAC Handout 9 together.

Questions 1, 2, 3, 4, and 5 can be answered only by the patient. Questions 10, 11, and 12 are similar to questions 7, 8, and 9.

- Go through the questions one by one in session, and ask patients to share their answers.

- Question 6: If patients get stuck, ask them to think back to any early associations they may have learned to make with weight gain. For instance, perhaps they were bullied at school for being overweight and afterward started to become disgusted with themselves.

- Question 7: Pick something from the list under question 4, and ask for evidence that this thing is disgusting. (Patients' answers to question 6 can help provide such "evidence.") Another answer that should be verbalized in session, if not by patients then by the group leader, is that the experience of the negative emotion of disgust is not in itself evidence that something is disgusting.

- Question 8: Make the point that the eating disorder distorts information and causes people to believe that something is disgusting when it is not. Then collect evidence against the idea that whatever was chosen from the list under question 4 is disgusting.

- Question 9: It can be helpful to ask patients to imagine how people they know *without* eating disorders might react to the item chosen from the list under question 4. If they can remember a time before the eating disorder, you can ask them how they themselves used to perceive things then. This may help them answer this question.

- Question 13: The group leader should take a moment to acknowledge that recovering does involve experiencing disgust. For instance, in order to recover, patients must eat, feel full, and feel disgust. Therefore, patients will have to practice coping with disgust. It can be helpful to remember that it is the eating disorder causing feelings of disgust, and that the things the eating disorder feels disgust about are not inherently disgusting.

Disgust Versus Nausea

Therapist script: Now let's talk about the difference between disgust and nausea.

Answers

Question 5 can be answered only by the patient.

- Question 1: Disgust is an emotion that can be described as revulsion for something unpleasant.

- Question 2: Nausea is a physical sensation that involves feeling sick.

- Question 3: Disgust is an emotion and nausea is a physical sensation.

- Question 4: Disgust and nausea are similar because one can trigger the other.

Homework Assignment

Therapist script: For homework, complete the eight questions in the homework section of the handout.

MAC Handout 10: The Eating Disorder's Guilt

Main Take-Home Points

- The eating disorder has its own morality.

- The morality of the eating disorder drives unhealthy behavior.

- In recovery, it will be important to rediscover your own morality.

Group Opener for New Members (If Needed), Mindfulness, and Homework Review

See the relevant portions of MAC Handout 1.

The Eating Disorder's Guilt

Therapist script: Today we'll be focusing our attention mainly on the emotion of guilt. Let's go through the first six questions together, one by one. Can I have a volunteer to read the first question?

The questions in this handout are intended to introduce the concept of morality and the idea that it is at least partially influenced by one's environment. The answers to these first six questions are later contrasted with answers to a set of eleven questions about how the eating disorder's "morality" developed (that is, how patients learned that being "fat" is "wrong" or "bad").

To Do

- Question 5: If group members are having difficulty answering this question, say something like "Let's start by examining why people have emotions." Provide brief psychoeducation about the evolutionary reasons we experience emotion (for example, it is adaptive to have anxiety because it signals us to fight or to flee; emotions communicate to others and ourselves; emotions can validate us, and so forth). Then explain that guilt can help us

- Question 6: This is a tough question. Ask patients to do their best with it, and offer to explain the question if necessary. This question attempts to get at the concept of losing one's moral way. It is intended to postulate that people can get morally confused and start behaving in a way that is inconsistent with their true values. Considering that this material is for children and adolescents, the example of stealing here is intentionally simplistic. The idea is to get patients thinking about indicators that they may have morally gone astray if they engaged in the behavior of stealing.

Eating Disorders and the Difference Between Right and Wrong

Therapist script: While the first portion of this handout focused generally on guilt, the second part focuses on guilt specifically in the context of the eating disorder. Can I have a volunteer to read the first question?

The second portion of MAC Handout 10 prompts the patient to think about what we call *eating disorder–related morality*. Eating disorder–related morality refers to the notion that being "fat" and eating certain foods is immoral, but that eating disorder behaviors such as restricting, purging, excessively exercising, and so forth, are moral. We conceptualize this set of morals as deriving from the primary value of "thinness." In other words, in eating disorders, thinness as a value eclipses all others. Therefore, a set of morals that would naturally derive from the primary value of thinness would be, for instance, that while gaining weight and eating are immoral, losing weight and restricting are moral.

QUESTIONS UNDER "EATING DISORDERS AND THE DIFFERENCE BETWEEN RIGHT AND WRONG": ANSWERS

- Question 1: Be ready to undermine eating disorder thoughts when opportunities arise. For instance, if patients answer the first question by saying they learned from diet advertisements that eating certain foods is wrong, take the opportunity to point out that weight-loss ads are intended to sway people's minds for profit.

- Questions 2, 3, 4, and 5: The general idea of these questions is to convey the fact that people eat solid foods for many years before suddenly developing ideas that eating certain foods is "bad." Further, basic morality (for instance, about stealing) develops prior to the development of ideas that certain foods are "bad."

- Question 6: Emphasize that while many people hold idiosyncratic beliefs about which foods are "good" and "bad," not everyone develops an eating disorder. Once an eating disorder is in place, there is a morality about foods.

- Question 7: Group members might respond to this question by saying, "They want to make me fat" or "They're punishing me." A group leader can dispel these ideas by explaining that if a person's sole objective is to lose weight, it may seem to that person as if the treatment team has such aims, but the picture is much broader. The treatment team aims to move a person's focus beyond weight loss and toward health. That involves viewing food as good and healthy.

- Question 8: Let patients answer with what they currently think about this question. There is no reason to engage in a discussion about who is right and who is wrong. The question is intended more to have patients think this through than to prompt the therapist to engage in a discussion. Patients' answers also provide the therapist with information about whether patients are able to verbalize being currently in line with the treatment team. If a patient does admit that the treatment team is "probably right," it can be helpful to reinforce this acknowledgment in nonverbal ways (such as with a nod). Verbally reinforcing the behavior in this situation can backfire.

- Question 9: Encourage patients to discuss the feedback they have received from the environment about how the eating disorder is unhealthy. At higher levels of care, "I would be hospitalized" would be an appropriate answer to this question. At lower levels of care, "My doctors would tell me I was unhealthy" is appropriate.

- Question 10: Like question 8, this question is for the patient to answer. The therapist is not to debate, but the patient's response can provide interesting information to the therapist.

- Question 11: Patients need to answer this question, but it can be thought of as asking, "What else needs to happen before you will believe that this is unhealthy?" Let patients work out for themselves what other evidence they might need in order to be convinced that food is good.

Eating Disorder Morals Versus Recovery Morals

Therapist script: In this section of the handout, we have a visual representation of the difference between eating disorder morals and recovery morals. For the eating disorder, food is bad, and I am bad if I eat. But recovery morals say that food is good, and that I will be healthy if I eat.

Therapist script: Because food is so essential to our survival, having a set of morals telling us that food is bad is like having a set of morals telling us that breathing is bad. Think about how unhappy we would be if we thought we were bad every time we took a breath. That would be one upsetting set of morals! Eating disorder morals are the same.

Therapist script: Although this handout makes these concepts look simplistic, the point is that the eating disorder has its own set of morals. The eating disorder's morals tell us that food is bad and that if we eat it, we are bad. These morals are distinct from your morals and values, but the eating disorder can be powerful enough to make you believe that you share its values.

To Do

- If there's time, you may ask group members for their reactions to this section of the handout.

Homework Assignment

Therapist script: For homework, complete all the questions in the homework section.

MAC Handout 11: The Eating Disorder's Impact on Values

Main Take-Home Points

- The eating disorder takes over your values.

- The eating disorder takes over your time.

- Recovery will involve living life according to *your* values, not the eating disorder's.

Group Opener for New Members (If Needed), Mindfulness, and Homework Review

See the relevant portions of MAC Handout 1.

The Eating Disorder's Impact on Values

Therapist script: The experience of guilt can be tied to our value system. Can anyone explain why feeling guilty provides information about our values?

To Do

- Explain or review that we feel guilty when we believe we have behaved in a morally wrong manner.

- Explain that our morals are guided by our values.

- Reiterate that sometimes we can prioritize our values in a really harmful way. Explain that the eating disorder negatively impacts our values.

- Before moving on, ask patients to complete the three values/enjoyment-ranking exercises at the beginning of the handout.

- If patients cannot remember a time before they had an eating disorder, have them imagine what they would value if they did not have an eating disorder.

- When group members are finished, ask if anyone would like to share their answers. To expedite this process, you can ask patients to discuss their top three rankings from all three exercises.

- Be sure to acknowledge how the eating disorder can reprioritize what is really important to us.

- Strongly make the case that *thinness is not a legitimate value.* You may want to write this on the board in big letters with lots of exclamation points.

- Also say it out loud: "Thinness is *not* a legitimate value for a human being!"

- Humans must value health, not "thinness," in order to survive.

- The eating disorder values thinness in order to survive, but this so-called value is unrealistic and certainly unhealthy.

- Make the point that thinness and health are *not* the same. In fact, they're exact opposites in this case.

Therapist script: Let's move on now to the two pie charts. Please read the directions on your own, and complete the two charts. If you have any questions about how to complete the exercise, please ask.

To Do

- If patients cannot remember a time before they had an eating disorder, have them imagine how they would spend their time if they did not have an eating disorder.

- When they have completed the pie charts, ask them to share their answers. To expedite the process, ask patients to discuss those items that show the biggest gap between the time before the eating disorder and now.

Tying It All Together

Therapist script: Now, how does all of this stuff fit together—guilt, morals, and values?

To Do

- Explain that we feel guilty when we believe we have done something that is morally wrong or something that goes against our values.

- Explain that people can get confused about what is right and wrong in life. Because of this, people can start feeling guilty for things that are totally normal, natural, and healthy—like eating. When this happens, the guilt is not based on facts, and so it's not justified.

- Because we start to think of food as "bad," over time we lose our moral way.

- The eating disorder confuses our sense of morality and what is important.

- The eating disorder takes us away from what we really value.

- A big part of recovery is getting back in touch with our real values.

- Your real values are what's important to *you*, not to your eating disorder.

Homework Assignment

Therapist script: Your homework this week is to complete the homework section of the handout.

 MAC Handout 12: False Promises

Main Take-Home Points

- Eating disorders promise you whatever you want to hear.

- Eating disorders deliver on some promises but take a lot from people.

- Eating disorders behave like con artists

Group Opener for New Members (If Needed), Mindfulness, and Homework Review

See the relevant portions of MAC Handout 1.

False Promises

Therapist script: Today I'm going to read these eight questions from the handout aloud and have you write your answers on your copy of the handout. Then we will all talk about them. Just a reminder—if you write down anything like specific numbers or things that can be triggering to others, please don't share those answers aloud. Let's get started now with the first question: What is a promise?

To Do

- Patients are to quietly write their answers on their handouts and then discuss them.

- Discuss the answers to each question before moving on to the next.

Answers

- Question 1: A promise expresses a commitment to doing something in the future.

- Question 2: A false promise expresses a commitment to doing something in the future that you actually have no intention of doing. In another type of false promise, you follow through on what you said you would do, but you also cause a lot of harm. The classic example is that of the genie who grants wishes that end up hurting people who did not specify exactly what they wanted.

- Question 3: The eating disorder promises that being thin will lead to all sorts of positive things for you, such as romantic attention, popularity, and so forth.

- Question 4: Often the eating disorder delivers on some portion of the promise. For instance, perhaps initially losing some weight did bring you increased romantic attention.

- Question 5: The problem is that the eating disorder can also really hurt the body physically, cause you psychological turmoil, cause distress in your family, isolate you, keep you from engaging in your favorite sports, and so forth.

- Question 6: This is for patients to answer for themselves. Probably the majority of patients will answer yes. On occasion, however, a patient will report that they intentionally developed the eating disorder to hurt themselves, knowing full well the repercussions. This can happen in the context of treating patients with comorbid features of personality disorders. For instance, the behavior of purging can be reported as serving the same type of function as nonsuicidal self-injurious behavior. If this type of response arises in session, we suggest that you validate this as the patient's experience.

- Question 7: Often patients report feeling angry or cheated. But if patients report that they intentionally began engaging in eating disorder behavior for the purpose of inflicting pain, then you might ask how it makes them feel to think about how the eating disorder is harming others.

- Question 8: Most often patients will have a justifiably emotional response to this question. That is OK. Let it happen in session. Validate the negative emotions in session.

To Do

- Encourage patients to reflect.

- If patients report confusion, confirm that this is OK. Confusion in therapy means that different thinking is occurring.

Therapist script: Now I'm going to read a little bit about how eating disorders can be viewed. Afterward, I would like you to write down your reactions to question 8 and then share.

TIP: RESISTANCE TO QUESTION 8 CAN BE AN EATING DISORDER–PROTECTING BEHAVIOR

If a patient is resistant to question 8, this can sometimes be conceptualized as an eating disorder–protecting behavior. Patients can start derailing the group. For instance, patients can accuse the group leader of making them feel negative emotions. It is important to remain calm and in control whenever you're facing eating disorder–protecting behaviors. For instance, you can assert that feeling negative emotions is not a negative thing and then redirect attention back to the exercise.

Writing a Letter to All Eating Disorders

To Do

- Read the directions for this activity.

- Make sure that patients understand that the objective of the activity is not to write a letter to their own eating disorder per se but to all eating disorders. They can draw from their own experience, but the idea is to have patients write about what they have learned about how eating disorders operate.

- As patients finish writing, ask to privately read their letters. While you are reading, ensure that nothing in the letters is triggering. If the content appears appropriate for sharing, ask the patient if they feel comfortable sharing.

- After letters have been shared, you can process emotions about the activity in session.

Homework Assignment

Therapist script: Your homework this week is to answer the three questions at the end of this handout.

 MAC Handout 13: Noticing the Thoughts in Your Head

Main Take-Home Points

- We have many thoughts in a short span.

- It is best to accept thoughts now, although they may change over time.

- Thoughts do not need to be acted on.

Group Opener for New Members (If Needed), Mindfulness, and Homework Review

See the relevant portions of MAC Handout 1.

Noticing the Thoughts in Your Head

Therapist script: The main topic of today's discussion will be noticing your thoughts.

To Do

- Ask for a volunteer to read the directions.

- Start timing two minutes and thirty seconds while patients write down their thoughts.

- The group leader is encouraged to participate in the exercise as well.

- When the window of two minutes and thirty seconds is up, ask patients to stop writing.

Therapist script: Now we are going to take a closer look at our thoughts. Please do your best to answer all the questions, and then we will discuss our answers together. Some thoughts can be counted more than once. For instance, question 2 asks you to count eating disorder thoughts, and question 3 asks you to count judgmental thoughts. You may have a thought that can be counted as both an eating disorder thought and a judgmental thought.

This exercise is meant to extend over the entire group session. There are opportunities for teachable moments when each question is reviewed. Take your time.

Answers

- Question 1: The objective is simply to count the number of thoughts. Foster a discussion about how sometimes one can have as many as twenty thoughts or as few as seven thoughts in a period of two minutes and thirty seconds. You can ask patients if they think they had a lot of thoughts or only a few in that period. You can also go on to ask why they may be having a particular number of thoughts. For instance, anxiety may prompt a speeding up of thoughts, and being calm may prompt a relative slowing of thoughts.

- Question 2: To help foster externalization of the eating disorder, patients are to count the number of eating disorder thoughts they had. Ask patients to compare their overall number of thoughts to the number of eating disorder thoughts they had. If you have a smartphone easily accessible, calculate basic percentages. For instance, if someone had twenty thoughts, and eighteen were eating disorder thoughts, comment that 90 percent of the person's thoughts in the period of two minutes and thirty seconds were eating disorder thoughts. Ask patients if this ratio of eating disorder thoughts to overall thoughts is normal Ask them to reflect on this ratio. How does it make them feel to have such a high percentage of eating disorder thoughts?

- Question 3: Patients may need a description of what a judgmental thought is. Explain that a judgment is not a fact but an opinion. For instance, the thought *I am tired* is simply a fact, whereas the thought *I am fat* is a judgment. In this case, judgmental thoughts about oneself or others should be included in the count.

- Question 4: Worried thoughts can be described as thoughts connected to the emotion of anxiety: *What if I don't have enough time to finish homework tonight?*

- Question 5: Note the number of positive thoughts that patients have, compared to the number of eating disorder, judgmental, and worried thoughts.

- Question 6: Note the number of neutral thoughts that patients have, compared to the number of eating disorder, judgmental, and worried thoughts.

- Question 7: This question is not just for good measure. Patients do have interesting thoughts or questions that come up at this time.

- Question 8: Patients often reflect that the eating disorder has taken over their minds. Take the opportunity to support these insights with nonverbal feedback (such as head nods) and verbal statements (such as "Wow, 90 percent—that's a large percentage").

- Question 9: Patients can provide a variety of responses to this question. Be sure to state that one's mind will generate a lot of unsolicited thoughts that cannot be controlled. Trying to push thoughts away doesn't work. Pushing thoughts away just makes you think about them more. But if one practices mindfulness, thinking nonjudgmentally, and catching negative thoughts, then the content of thoughts can change over time. It is also very important to make the point that changing behavior changes thoughts over time. For instance, a big part of the eating disorder is having eating disorder thoughts. But if one works on recovery behaviors in addition to skills like the ones taught in group, then the eating disorder thoughts go away over time. In short, although it is pretty much impossible to immediately change your thoughts, thought patterns can change over time.

- Question 10: Because thoughts cannot immediately change, there are some things that must be accepted. The fact that thoughts are negative often arises.

- Question 11: Trying to change the thought *I'm fat* can involve engaging in a lot of eating disorder behaviors that, paradoxically, just make the thought *I'm fat* stronger over time. People can spend a lot of time trying to change thoughts in very ineffective and harmful ways. Accepting thoughts allows people to break unhealthy patterns of behavior and move toward psychological health.

- Question 12: People definitely do not have to act on their thoughts. Over time, people can learn to be mindful of their thoughts, use skills, and choose to behave differently. It is very difficult and often requires a lot of support, but it can be done.

- Question 13: People *have* eating disorder thoughts. They *are not* these thoughts, but they can mindfully *notice* eating disorder thoughts. When patients circle thoughts that are in line with recovery, such as *I love my family even though they have control over food*, reinforce that these thoughts are in line with the self rather than the eating disorder.

Homework Assignment

Therapist script: This week for homework, complete the homework portion of the handout.

〰〰 MAC Handout 14: Mindfulness and Leaves on a Stream

Special Materials

You will need a nature sounds app, such as Noisli.

Main Take-Home Points

- Mindfulness is the practice of noticing your own experience in a nonjudgmental way.

- Mindfulness helps build awareness of the eating disorder's influence.

- Mindfulness can help a person make recovery-oriented choices and decisions.

Group Opener for New Members (If Needed), Mindfulness, and Homework Review

See the relevant portions of MAC Handout 1.

Mindfulness and Leaves on a Stream

Therapist script: Today's group will focus on broadening our mindfulness practice to include noticing the four types of internal experiences. Can anyone name the four types of internal experiences?

Therapist script: The four internal experiences are thoughts, behaviors, physical sensations, and emotions. Now we're going to be reading about mindfulness. Can I have a volunteer to read the first paragraph?

To Do

- Have patients take turns reading the three sections at the beginning of the handout.

- Ensure that patients understand what an urge is, and elicit examples (such as an urge to walk out of the room, an urge to exercise, and so forth). Urges can be thoughts or body sensations.

Therapist script: Imagine that you are on the bank of a river, next to a big tree full of leaves. As a thought, behavior, emotion, or body sensation comes up, write it down on the picture of a leaf that you see on this handout.

To Do

- Set a timer for two minutes and thirty seconds.

- Use a nature sounds app (such as Noisli) to create sounds for this exercise.

- Once the period of two minutes and thirty seconds has passed, ask patients to stop writing.

- Have volunteers share their experience and observations.

Developing a Daily Mindfulness Practice

To Do

- Have patients answer the first set of four questions in session.

- Have volunteers read through the section called "Developing a Daily Mindfulness Practice."

- Now have patients answer the second set of four questions in session.

  - Question 1: The exercises in the first of the two lists are less challenging. But if patients would like to start with the more somatically focused exercises, this can be encouraged.

  - Question 2: Focusing on the breath can prompt eating disorder thoughts and emotions and thus trigger behaviors.

  - Question 3: After a meal, the eating disorder can be particularly challenging because there are distorted thoughts about being "fat" simply because there is food in the stomach. The emotions of anxiety, guilt, disgust, and shame can occur, and eating disorder behavior urges can be stronger.

  - Question 4: We encourage group leaders to take time to ask each patient what they can do. If you have a daily mindfulness practice, we encourage you to share your practice. For instance, one of the coauthors (Tara Deliberto), as part of her daily routine, takes five mindful breaths every morning before leaving the house, no matter how hectic the morning is. The idea is to begin working a small amount of mindfulness into one's daily schedule.

Homework Assignment

Therapist script: Your homework this week is to practice the mindfulness exercises on both lists.

Tell patients that it will take them two minutes and thirty seconds to complete the homework portion of the handout, and that they will have to complete it in a quiet place.

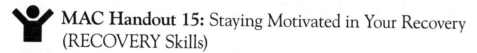 MAC Handout 15: Staying Motivated in Your Recovery (RECOVERY Skills)

Main Take-Home Points

- Motivation waxes and wanes in recovery.

- Coping skills can help you on the way to recovery.

Group Opener for New Members (If Needed), Mindfulness, and Homework Review

See the relevant portions of MAC Handout 1.

Staying Motivated

Therapist script: It can be very difficult to stay 100 percent motivated in treatment all the time. Luckily, there are some coping skills that can help us along the way. In today's group, we will be reviewing the RECOVERY skills.

Depending on the time and resources available, this intervention can be spread out over the course of several sessions. For instance, the RECOVERY skills can be reviewed, and then a whole session can focus on just one of the skills.

Unless group sessions are taking place at a higher level of care where there is an art group available, we do not suggest spending an entire outpatient group session on recovery inspiration. In an outpatient setting, encourage patients to make recovery scrapbooks or boards and bring them in to show others.

RECOVERY Skills

- **R**ecovery inspiration
  - Encourage patients to create a visual representation of all the things motivating them to recover. Some patients like to make a scrapbook and others like to make one board.
  - Encourage patients to bring in their recovery boards to share with other group members.
  - If it is too difficult to bring the whole project in, tell them to take a picture of it and bring that in for the next session.

- **E**valuating the pros and cons of your eating disorder
  - List on the board the pros and cons of having the eating disorder and of recovery.
  - Talk patients through the benefits (for example, the eating disorder provides a distraction, makes one feel good about oneself temporarily, and so forth) as well as the negative medical, psychological, social, and familial consequences.
  - Do not be afraid to provide patients with information (about medical consequences, for instance) in addition to soliciting information about how the eating disorder has negatively impacted them.
  - An interesting area of conversation can be to ask patients about how their carers have been impacted by the eating disorder.

- **C**oping plan
  - Depending on how much time there is in session, a group leader may choose to have patients develop coping plans in session.
  - One way of doing this is to have patients write the words "coping plan" at the top of a sheet of paper and then list the major triggers of their eating disorder behaviors.
  - Next to each trigger, patients can write out a coping skill that can be useful for that trigger.
  - If patients have more than five triggers, ask them to select the five most common or important triggers.

- **O**penness about eating disorder behaviors, urges, and thoughts
  - This skill is self-explanatory, but the group leader does have the opportunity to verbally reinforce the recovery behavior of verbally disclosing eating disorder behavior and soliciting help in recovery.
  - The group leader can go around the room and ask each patient about a time they asked for help in coping with an eating disorder urge.
  - Afterward, provide each patient with specific verbal reinforcement: "Telling your father that you had an urge to purge was a really effective way of managing that eating disorder. Nice job making a recovery decision, Jared. Keep it up in the future."

- Validate yourself

  - Having a therapist and carers provide reinforcement and validation is helpful, but more is needed to fight the eating disorder.

  - It is important to convey the message that it's necessary to start validating yourself by internalizing the messages provided in treatment (that is, taking them to heart).

  - This skill encourages patients to start to take treatment into their own hands.

- Even more effort to work even harder in your recovery

  - The overall idea of this skill is to emphasize that recovery is a long process that requires continued work.

  - If carers have responsibility for food, they will turn over responsibility to the child over time. If carers are not involved, the patient has more and more of a recovery mind-set in treatment. Either way, the patient will have to take an active role in their own recovery.

  - It is important for patients to understand that they will have to work even harder in the future—and this statement, of course, validates that the patient is already working hard.

- Remember what the eating disorder has taken away

  - Encourage patients to use this skill when the temptation to engage in an eating disorder behavior is present or it is simply easier not to put the work into treatment. Go around the room and ask patients to name three things the eating disorder has taken away from them. As a task in group, writing the three things on index cards and having patients carry them can be helpful. Additionally, it can be useful for encouragement to have patients write what the eating disorder has taken away and/or what their motivation is to recover on the top of their meal plans.

- You can beat the eating disorder

  - Many adolescents are told that people can never recover from eating disorders. It is astounding how pervasive this belief is.

  - It is imperative that therapists exude confidence that adolescents can recover from eating disorders. If patients believe that they cannot recover, why bother trying? Particularly in an adolescent population, the patients simply have not been alive long enough for the eating disorder to have rooted itself in place for decades. Further, by virtue of the fact that the patient has received this handout, they are in treatment. Therefore, confidence must be instilled at this phase that recovery is possible.

  - At other points in this manual, the concept of inevitability acceptance is discussed. This item is part of that concept. In short, inevitability acceptance is the idea that one cannot live a full and healthy life with the eating disorder.

  - The eating disorder is a destructive force that causes bodily harm as well as social, educational, and professional dysfunction, all of which have ramifications for the family. Therefore, it is inevitable that the eating disorder cannot coexist with a full and healthy life.

  - Because the eating disorder only gets harder to treat over time, there is no better time than right now to start working actively in recovery to establish a healthy and full life with the help of a therapist.

To Do

- Have patients answer the questions in the "Preparing for Homework" section.

- Ask patients to name the specific *skills* they will use, and how.

- Before the session ends, try to help patients solve problems involving barriers to using the skills.

Homework Assignment

Therapist script: This week for homework, complete the homework portion of the handout.

MAC Handout 16: Telling Others About Your Eating Disorder

Main Take-Home Points

- Telling others about the eating disorder is tricky business.

- Shame is often involved.

- If treatment involves going away, an explanation of where the person has been may be needed.

Group Opener for New Members (If Needed), Mindfulness, and Homework Review

See the relevant portions of MAC Handout 1.

Telling Others about Your Eating Disorder

Therapist script: It can often be tricky to decide to tell others about the eating disorder. Sometimes it is best if people don't know. But sometimes it is best if they do know. Also, it can be really emotionally difficult to tell people about the eating disorder. Because of how hard making the decision to tell someone can be, and because of how difficult telling someone can be, we are going to talk about it today in group.

To Do

Only the patient can answer questions 1, 2, 3, 4, and 5.

- Go through the set of seven questions with the patients, one by one.

- Question 6: This question is intended to help patients think judiciously about telling others. Patients can help protect their privacy by asking the other person to keep it a secret, to tell only trusted people, and so forth.

- Question 7: This question is designed to make patients think about some people who may not have fully earned their trust.

- After the questions are answered, have patients take turns reading the three disclosure strategies aloud.

- Ask which of the three strategies best suits the patients.

- If any judgmental thoughts are expressed (for example, "Having an eating disorder is shameful, and I will definitely be an outcast if I disclose my diagnosis"), ways to cope with these thoughts should be reviewed in session.

- Discuss the pros and cons of telling a small number of trusted friends and family members about the eating disorder.

- Especially if shame is preventing them from sharing, patients may be encouraged by the group leader to tell a small number of trusted family members and friends about the eating disorder.

- If patients are worried about their friends who are engaging in similar behaviors, examples of how to relay information about eating disorders in a nontriggering way can be discussed. For instance, a patient might say something like "I am struggling with self-esteem and body image issues right now."

- Discourage patients from sharing very specific details about how they managed to restrict calories, hide food, compulsively exercise, and purge.

- Encourage patients to solicit support from a select number of trusted people.

- Further disclosing information about struggling can (but does not always) help deter "fat" talk and triggering statements.

Homework Assignment

Therapist script: Read and complete the homework assignment for this week by next session.

 ## MAC Handout 17: Why You Might Despise Supervised Eating
This handout should be administered only to patients who have others in control of food (such as patients with anorexia nervosa in comprehensive IMT, inpatients, and so forth).

Main Take-Home Points
- The eating disorder has reasons for not liking supervised eating.
- People have their own reasons for not liking supervised eating.
- Reasons why people do not like supervised eating are valid, but supervised eating is still helpful.

Group Opener for New Members (If Needed), Mindfulness, and Homework Review
See the relevant portions of MAC Handout 1.

Why You Might Despise Supervised Eating

Therapist script: Today we're going to talk about accepting something really difficult—having your eating supervised. Let's take turns reading the list of eleven reasons why people don't like supervised eating. I'll go first, and then we'll go around. As we go, check the reasons that apply to you.

To Do

- Once the reading aloud has ended, ask patients to count how many reasons they checked on the list.

- Ask why the first two reasons in the list are different from the rest. Explain that the first two reasons are coming from the eating disorder, and that the other reasons are coming from the self.

- Spend some time discussing the separation between eating disorder reasons and their own reasons for not liking supervised eating.

- Before offering statements that support the logic of supervised eating, be sure to validate the patients for all of the non–eating disorder reasons they checked for not liking supervised eating. If a patient is expressing negative automatic thoughts regarding an item, it is also important to say something in support of supervised eating.

  - Reason 3. *Validation:* "It feels really crummy to be nauseated from eating so much." *Support of supervised eating:* "At this point, there is no other way to recover than to pass through this phase involving nausea. It's a necessary phase. Luckily, it's only a phase."

  - Reason 4. *Validation:* "Supervised eating is so restrictive that it can really seem like a punishment." *Support of supervised eating:* "Because the eating disorder only feels good when it is losing weight, it feels like supervised eating is a punishment because it takes away the thing that the eating disorder likes the most. But in treatment we are concerned with what is healthy instead of what the eating disorder wants. It is the eating disorder that likes losing weight, not you. Supervised eating isn't a punishment for bad behavior at all. It is designed to keep you safe from the eating disorder, and healthy. It is protecting you."

  - Reason 5. *Validation:* "Because little kids have their eating supervised, and so do you, it is understandable that you feel like you are being treated like a little kid." *Support of supervised eating:* "Of course, everyone knows that you are not a little child. When someone of *any* age is struggling with a serious illness, they need more support. Sometimes that support can be around basic things like eating. In the case of eating disorders, people of *any* age with eating disorders need support around food."

  - Reason 6. *Validation:* "It must be really difficult to have an adult supervise your eating at every meal and snack at a time in your life when most of your peers in school are gaining independence. For someone your age, in your position, feelings of embarrassment are totally normal." *Support of supervised eating:* "It is really unfortunate that supervised eating is a necessary part of treatment."

  - Reason 7. *Validation:* "Because so much responsibility is being taken away from you, it is understandable how you could feel not trusted." *Support of supervised eating:* "Of course, we can't trust the eating disorder to keep you safe. Eating disorders kill. That's why supervised eating is necessary right now."

  - Reason 8. *Validation:* "The supervised eating process is really, really hard. It makes total sense that you would want it to be over." *Support of supervised eating:* "I think everyone, including your carers, wants it to be over, too. The reason everyone keeps plugging away at supervised eating is that it's necessary to keep you healthy and safe from the eating disorder right now."

  - Reason 9. *Validation:* "In the context of having an eating disorder, it can be confusing to understand how much food is needed. It makes total sense that you think you are being given too much food. It's also hard to trust other people who are supervising your eating to give you the right amount of food." *Support of supervised eating:* "At the same time, you are being given the appropriate amount of food. Because eating disorders can kill, your carers have to be in charge of deciding what is an appropriate amount of food right now."

- Reason 10. *Validation:* "Treatment of the eating disorder is all-consuming. It leaves very little time for other things. Of course it feels like you have no life now." *Support of supervised eating:* "A stitch in time saves nine. If you beat the eating disorder now, that frees you up to have a life."

- After providing validation and support for supervised eating for each relevant item, ask patients to share what they think is their number one reason for not liking supervised eating.

Therapist script: Now let's take a look at the first pie chart. Before you begin, think about what percentage of your dislike of supervised eating is because of the eating disorder. For instance, if I thought that the eating disorder was the main reason I didn't like supervised eating, then I might draw a pie with 75 percent of the area covered by the words "eating disorder." Then, in the remaining 25 percent of the pie, I would write in the other reasons why I don't like supervised eating [*do this on the board*].

Therapist script: Would anyone like to share what they wrote on their pie chart?

Reasons Why Supervised Eating Could be Helpful

Therapist script: Now take a look at the list that follows the first pie chart. These are all reasons why some people actually appreciate supervised eating, even though there are valid reasons *not* to like supervised eating. Let's take turns reading these reasons. I'll go first, and then we'll go around. As we go, just like last time, check off the reasons that apply to you.

In your tone, do not imply in any way that patients at this point should be *appreciative* of having their eating supervised. It very well may be the case that the eating disorder is so strong that they are unable to get in contact with appreciation. Your job is to objectively present the material as options. Having an itemized list helps patients articulate their feelings. It is not intended to tell them what to feel.

To Do

- Ask patients to share their top three reasons for appreciating supervised eating.

- Be sure to provide nonverbal reinforcement (head nods, smiles, and so forth) as well as verbal reinforcement ("That is very insightful") if patients do disclose their appreciation for supervised eating.

- Have patients fill in the second pie chart.

Discussion: The Importance of Acceptance

Therapist script: Why do we need to accept the hard parts of recovery?

Therapist script: What are some of the hardest parts about recovery for you to accept?

To Do

- In your discussion, be sure to make the following points:
  - If the plan is not followed, you will be stuck in treatment and continue being sick. Being malnourished is not sustainable forever. Eating disorders make people very sick, and people can die from them. Eating disorders take over people's lives.

- There's no choice but to accept recovery. Accepting recovery makes things easier. We have to eventually recover anyway, so we might as well accept it.

- Can you imagine yourself as an older person with an eating disorder? At some point, the difficult recovery process has to happen. This thing can't last forever. Fighting against recovery causes fights in families, sadness, and hardship.

- Pain + nonacceptance = suffering. Having an eating disorder is emotionally and physically painful. Having a painful eating disorder, plus not accepting that recovery is inevitable if you are going to lead a full life, makes it worse. Pain is inevitable, but pain plus nonacceptance leads to suffering in life. If you don't accept recovery, you suffer more than necessary.

Homework Assignment

Therapist script: This week for homework, complete the homework portion of the handout.

When reviewing the homework in the next session, be sure to nonverbally (with a smile) and verbally reinforce any number higher than 0 on question 3: "On a scale of 0–10, with 0 representing no appreciation at all and 10 representing extreme appreciation, how much do you appreciate supervised eating?" Any ranking other than 0 is a reflection of the recovered self and must be reinforced. A therapist might say, "It's insightful to reflect any appreciation of supervised eating, so it's notable that you wrote down a 1."

MAC Handout 18: Coping with the Urge to Binge (NO BINGE Skills)

This handout should be administered only in groups where all patients have already disclosed in group that they struggle with subjective or objective binge eating. This handout has also been used successfully in individual sessions. This IMT intervention may take more than one session to complete.

Main Take-Home Points

- Binge eating can happen in any eating disorder.

- Developing skills specifically for binge eating is important in recovery.

Group Opener for New Members (If Needed), Mindfulness, and Homework Review

See the relevant portions of MAC Handout 1.

Coping With the Urge to Binge

Therapist script: Today we're going to be talking specifically about the eating disorder behavior of binge eating. Binge eating can occur in the context of any eating disorder. Therefore, it is worth taking the time to discuss it here. Can I have a volunteer to read the top paragraph, please?

To Do

- Once the top paragraph has been read, the group leader should provide an overview of the handout by briefly reading down the list of NO BINGE skills. Then the skills should be reviewed one by one with volunteer readers from the group.

NO BINGE Skills

- **N**ix all-or-nothing thinking

  - For this skill, first it is helpful to explain what all-or-nothing thinking is. All-or-nothing thinking can be described to adolescents as assuming that things are all one way or all another way, without considering the middle ground.

  - An example of all-or-nothing thinking related to binge eating is the thought *If I have one bite of something that I did not plan, everything is ruined, so I should binge.*

  - Explain that all-or-nothing thinking about food sets people up to binge eat.

  - Flexible thinking—for example, the thought *It's OK if I have something I wasn't planning on eating*—is much less likely to rebound into binge eating.

- **O**pt for out-in-the-open eating

  - Ask patients about the ratio of the number of times they've had a binge in secret to the number of times they've had a binge out in the open. The likelihood is that the number of times people have had a binge out in the open is very small in comparison to the number of times they've had a secret binge.

  - Encourage patients to eat out in the open as much as possible.

  - Patients may understandably push back on this item. They may report that they binge eat in secret because people in their family comment on their food or weight when they eat anything. If this is the case, validate this concern. Do not assume that patients definitely have family members who do not engage in triggering behavior. It is appropriate to ask a patient if they ever have anyone available who does not engage in triggering behavior. If so, tell the patient that it can be helpful if they simply increase the number of times they eat out in the open, even if it is not 100 percent of the time.

- **B**uild a bridge to eating disorder recovery

  - Ask patients to list ways in which their environment triggers them to restrict their food intake or to "diet."

  - Help them think about ways to avoid this.

  - Ask patients if they can identify anyone they can tell about their binge eating who does not already know.

  - Process any feelings of shame or other negative emotions that may come up.

  - Discuss the importance of confronting shame and other negative emotions for the purpose of recovering.

  - It is also important to discuss what the patient must leave behind. This would be anything that reinforces the eating disorder. Be sure to mitigate discussions of specific triggers.

- **I**ncrease fun activities to replace binge eating

  - Because binge eating can be experienced as enjoyable, it is important to replace this behavior with something that is fun so that the patient is not left feeling bereft.

  - This can be something to do in session. It may take up some time. That is OK. This intervention does not need to be completed in one session.

- **N**otice belly signals of hunger and fullness

  - Although this is actually quite an involved process, it is worth noting in session.

- Tell group members that although learning to do this is more an aim of individual therapy, it is an important part of not binge eating in the future.

- For patients who have bodies in the underweight range relative to what is healthy for them, stress that belly signals of hunger and fullness are not something to focus on until after weight restoration. In fact, eating past the point of being full is currently in order.

- Briefly mention that paying attention to hunger and fullness cues has been shown to curb binge eating.

- Give yourself time to eat
  - This item really is about making eating—and not restricting—a priority.
  - It can be difficult to find time to eat, and easy just to let time slip away, but finding time to eat is of the utmost importance.
  - Ask patients what can get in the way of giving themselves time to eat. Help them in session to think about ways to address this issue.

- Eat three square meals every day, plus snacks
  - Tell patients that this is the most important skill, and the one on which the majority of effort should be spent, although other items are very important as well.
  - Emphasize this in session.

To Do

- Have patients answer the questions in the "Preparing for Homework" section.

- Ask patients to name the specific skills they will use, and how.

- Before the session ends, try to help patients solve problems involving barriers to using the skills.

Homework Assignment

Therapist script: This week for homework, complete the homework portion of the handout.

MAC Handout 19: Coping with the Urge to Purge (NO PURGE Skills)

This handout should be administered only in groups where all patients have already disclosed in group that they struggle with purging. This handout has also been used successfully in individual sessions.

Main Take-Home Points

- Purging can happen in many eating disorders.

- Developing skills specifically for purging is important in recovery.

Group Opener for New Members (If Needed), Mindfulness, and Homework Review

See the relevant portions of MAC Handout 1.

NO Purge Skills

Therapist script: Today we're going to be talking specifically about the eating disorder behavior of purging. This behavior can cause a lot of physical damage, and it is worth spending extra time to address it. Can I have a volunteer to read the top paragraph, please?

To Do

- Ask if there are any questions about the top paragraph.

- The group leader should provide an overview of the handout by briefly reading down the list of NO PURGE skills. Then the skills should be reviewed one by one with volunteer readers from the group.

- The NO PURGE skills are all largely self-explanatory; however, we will make several specific notes here.

- Regarding the skill of being open about thoughts, have patients name specific people to whom they can disclose eating disorder thoughts, urges, and behaviors.

- Regarding the skill of postponing urges, list activities patients can engage in when having urges.

- Regarding the skill of relaxing, progressive muscle relaxation can be practiced in session. Many scripts are readily available on the Internet.

- Regarding the skill of emphasizing health consequences, patients can privately list any health consequences they experienced in session. The group leader can go around to each patient and provide verbal reinforcement for their participation in the group activity by saying something like "Good job making your list."

To Do

- Have patients answer the questions in the "Preparing for Homework" section.

- Ask patients to name the specific skills they will use, and how.

- Before the session ends, try to help patients solve problems involving barriers to using the skills.

Homework Assignment

Therapist script: This week for homework, complete the homework portion of the handout.

Cognitive Behavioral Therapy (CBT) Handouts

This portion of the manual describes how to incorporate CBT handouts into group therapy sessions. Each handout is discussed individually. It is important to read each handout before reading the discussion of the handout in this section.

CBT Handouts

CBT Handout 1: General Stressors and Eating Disorder Triggers

CBT Handout 2: Categorizing Types of Eating Disorder Thoughts

CBT Handout 3: Examining the Evidence For and Against Eating Disorder Thoughts

CBT Handout 4: Thought Record

CBT Handout 5: Weighing the Pros and Cons of Acting on Eating Disorder Urges and Impulses

CBT Handout 6: Positive Self-Talk

CBT Handout 7: Creating a Coping Card

CBT Handout 8: Active Eating Disorder Problem Solving

CBT Handout 9: Problems with Perfectionism

CBT Handout 10: Practicing Self-Care with an Eating Disorder

CBT Handout 11: Writing a Letter to Your Eating Disorder

CBT Handout 12: Relapse-Prevention Plan

CBT Handout 13: Remembering All You Have Learned

 ## CBT Handout 1: General Stressors and Eating Disorder Triggers

Main Take-Home Points

- There are general stressors and eating disorder–specific triggers.

- General stressors can contribute to triggering eating disorder behavior.

Group Opener (If Needed)

For groups running linearly through the material, this will be the first session. If so, be sure to administer all relevant measures, review the group rules, and conduct a group icebreaker.

Mindfulness

Therapist script: Quick show of hands—who has done mindfulness before?

Therapist script: Who can tell me what mindfulness is?

To Do

- Explain that mindfulness is not about relaxing per se but about practicing focusing the mind.

- Explain that mindfulness is going to be practiced at the start of every group.

- Explain that each exercise will take about one to two minutes.

- To begin the exercise, strike a singing bowl, bell, chime, or small xylophone three times.

- Conduct a mindfulness exercise for about one to two minutes.

- To conclude the exercise, strike a singing bowl, bell, chime, or small xylophone twice.

- Share experiences.

- Ask patients what thoughts, emotions, physical feelings, and behavior urges they had during the exercise.

- Ask patients if the exercise was easy or difficult to focus on.

- Remind patients that minds wander, and that bringing attention back to the exercise is a skill.

- Verbally reinforce (praise) willingness to participate in the mindfulness exercise.

Homework Review (If Needed)

For members who are enrolled in group and not attending for the first time, review the homework assignment from the previous week.

Questions (Part 1)

To Do

- Once the first paragraph has been read, go through the first set of questions, one by one, with the patients.

- During the exercise, patients may continue to give eating disorder examples. Simply state that we will focus more on eating disorder examples in the next part of the handout, and ask them to try to think of non–eating disorder examples for this particular exercise.

Questions (Part 2)

Therapist script: Now we're going to focus more on eating disorder–specific triggers. Let's go through the questions together, one by one.

To Do

Only the patient can answer questions 1, 2, 3, 4, and 5.

- Question 6: Although the two experiences are related, there is a big difference between feeling generally stressed and triggered. Everyone feels generally stressed by things in the environment that have an influence on emotions, thoughts, physical sensations, and behaviors. Unlike general stressors, eating disorder triggers influence a person with an eating disorder to have specific sets emotions, thoughts, physical sensations, and, perhaps most important, behaviors. Eating disorder triggers in the environment make it more difficult than usual to cope and not engage in eating disorder behaviors.

- Question 7: Avoiding triggers during the recovery process can be helpful because triggers make it more difficult to refrain from engaging in eating disorder behaviors. The longer someone goes without engaging in eating disorder behaviors, the easier it can be over time. Therefore, in a perfect world, if triggers could be totally avoided, eating disorder treatment would probably be a lot quicker and easier.

- Question 8: There is no such thing as a perfect world without triggers. Unfortunately, you will come into contact with triggers sooner or later. Therefore, it can be helpful to expose yourself to triggers while in treatment so you can learn to cope with them.

- Question 9: There is a time and a place for everything. It is best to minimize exposure to triggers at the beginning of treatment, if possible, so recovery is given a chance. If there are too many triggers at the start of treatment, it can feel like trying to stand up in the ocean, only to get immediately knocked down by another wave. You need a bit of a break to get your footing. Over time, it is best to try to systematically expose yourself to triggers, with the help of your therapist. When triggers are outside your control, you can practice coping with them and discuss them in therapy.

- Question 10: If you are already feeling generally stressed, a trigger may be more likely to cause intense emotions, eating disorder thoughts that are hard to shake, physical sensations (like feeling full) that are difficult not to interpret as being "fat," and eating disorder urges that are difficult not to act on.

Homework Assignment

Therapist script: Read and complete the homework assignment for this week by next session.

 ## CBT Handout 2: Categorizing Types of Eating Disorder Thoughts

Main Take-Home Points

- There are specific types of eating disorder thoughts.
- It is important to be aware of these different types of eating disorder thoughts.

Group Opener for New Members (If Needed), Mindfulness, and Homework Review

See the relevant portions of CBT Handout 1.

Categorizing Types of ED Thoughts

Therapist script: Today we're going to be talking about the different types of thoughts that make up the eating disorder. During your recovery, it will be really important to catch these different thoughts. We will also talk about the different categories of these thoughts. Knowing what category a thought falls into can really help in reminding you that a thought is part of the eating disorder.

To Do

- Having patients take turns, read through the chart of eating disorder thoughts.
- Ask the patients if they have questions.
- Clarify the questions.

Exercise

To Do

- Have patients complete the exercise alone.
- While they are working, go around to each patient and read over their list. Provide help and clarification where it is needed.

- Before asking patients to share answers, remind patients that nothing triggering can be shared in group.

- One by one, have patients share answers.

- Answer questions and clarify as you go.

Homework Assignment

Therapist script: Read and complete the homework assignment for this week by next session.

🔍 CBT Handout 3: Examining the Evidence for and Against Eating Disorder Thoughts

Main Take-Home Points

- Examining the evidence for and against eating disorder thoughts is a helpful coping skill.

- This coping skill fosters critical thinking about the eating disorder.

Group Opener for New Members (If Needed), Mindfulness, and Homework Review

See the relevant portions of CBT Handout 1.

Examining the Evidence

Therapist script: Being able to identify thoughts as part of the eating disorder is a really helpful coping skill. Beyond that, it is also helpful to develop critical thinking skills about our own thoughts. It is important to understand what parts of our thoughts are supported by facts, and what parts are not. In today's group, we will focus on examining the evidence for and against eating disorder thoughts. Let's go through the four eating disorder thoughts in the exercise together, one by one.

To Do

- Eating disorder thought 1

  - *Evidence for:* People typically do not gain weight without eating. It is usually a necessary component of weight gain. If one eats more than the body is using, then weight gain occurs.

  - *Evidence against:* Although eating is usually a necessary component of weight gain, it is not sufficient. One has to eat more than the body is using. If one eats generally as much as is required by the body, then weight gain will not occur. In fact, it would be preposterous if eating per se, which is something everyone is required to do multiple times per day, led to weight gain.

- Eating disorder thought 2

  - *Evidence for:* This thought seems true in the context of having an eating disorder. Negative emotions like fear of "fatness," guilt, disgust, and shame would likely be high.

  - *Evidence against:* Having negative emotions and thoughts would be very difficult to manage. But can you think of anything worse?

Be sure to be sensitive. Have patients generate their own ideas of other things that could be worse than gaining weight. Do not offer your own thoughts about what could be worse than weight gain.

- Eating disorder thought 3
  - *Evidence for:* It is very taxing and difficult to restrict food.
  - *Evidence against:* Restricting temporarily holds off fear of "fatness," which the eating disorder lives on. Restricting is difficult, but it also serves to help you avoid fear of "fatness." In the context of having an eating disorder, eating and facing your fear of "fatness" are *much* more difficult than restricting food.

- Eating disorder thought 4
  - *Evidence for:* For some people, losing weight can be healthy.
  - *Evidence against:* Even for people who have bodies in the obese range, research coming out of the Health At Every Size movement (Bacon, 2008) and the intuitive eating movement (Tribole & Resch, 2012) shows that it is not necessarily weight loss that contributes to better health in people who have bodies in the obese weight range. Some studies (see Bacon, 2008) have shown that eating when hungry, stopping when full, and reducing stress have resulted in better health outcomes than weight-loss programs for people in the obese weight range. For people not in the obese weight range, it certainly is not necessarily healthy to lose weight. In fact, it can be unhealthy. And eating disorder behavior is very unhealthy.

- If there is time left in group, ask patients for other eating disorder beliefs that they strongly hold. Examine the evidence for and against these beliefs.

Homework Assignment

Therapist script: Fill in your own eating disorder thoughts for homework, and examine the evidence for and against these thoughts.

 CBT Handout 4: Thought Record

Make two copies of this handout for each patient, one to be used during the group session and the other to be used for homework.

Main Take-Home Point

- Writing down, categorizing, and examining the evidence for and against eating disorder thoughts impacts emotions and recovery-oriented behavioral decision making.

Group Opener for New Members (If Needed), Mindfulness, and Homework Review

See the relevant portions of CBT Handout 1.

Thought Record

Therapist script: Today we are going to talk about thought records. Thought records are used to write down eating disorder thoughts, thought categories, and evidence for and against the thoughts. A thought record also helps us examine the impact that thoughts have on our emotions and behaviors. Using our first copy of this handout, let's create two examples together.

To Do

- It can be helpful to start out with a straightforward, non–eating disorder thought. For an example:

  - Situation or event: I forgot the answer to a question on an exam.

  - Thought: *I'm an idiot.*

  - Emotion you felt: Shame

  - Intensity of emotion: 7

  - Behavioral urge: Stay in bed

  - Evidence for thought: I forgot the answer.

  - Evidence against thought: I remembered all the other answers. I have done lots of other things right.

  - Intensity of emotion after considering evidence for and against thought: 3

  - Outcome of situation or event: Instead of staying in bed, I went outside.

- It can then be helpful to give the example of an eating disorder thought and solicit answers from the patients. For an example:

  - Situation or event: I noticed my reflection in a window.

  - Thought: *My thighs look huge.*

  - Emotion you felt: Anxiety

  - Intensity of emotion: 9

  - Behavioral urge: Exercise

  - Evidence for thought: I saw in the reflection that my thighs look big to me, and I feel anxious.

  - Evidence against thought: My eating disorder distorts perception. My thighs may look huge to me but not necessarily to everyone else. "Huge" is also an exaggeration.

  - Intensity of emotion after considering evidence for and against thought: 6

  - Outcome of situation or event: I decided to stick with my recovery plan of *not* exercising when I have an urge to exercise.

- After the first two examples of thought records have been completed with the group, have patients complete the third example on their own.

Therapist script: Now use the blank portion marked with the number 3 to create a thought record on your own.

It can be difficult sometimes to dispute eating disorder thoughts in the same way we dispute normal negative thoughts. Many eating disorder thoughts have to do with distorted perception. It can be useful to remind patients that the logic of the eating disorder causes distorted perception, and that it is not functional or helpful to have eating disorder thoughts. It can also be useful to focus on the more dramatic or exaggerated overtones of eating disorder thoughts (for example, the inaccuracy of the word "huge" in the preceding example).

Homework Assignment

Therapist script: For homework this week, complete a thought record for three examples of situations or events along with the eating disorder thoughts, emotions, emotional intensity ratings, and behavior urges that go with them. Be sure to include the evidence for and against the eating disorder thoughts as well as the emotional intensity ratings after you've considered the evidence. Don't forget to mention the outcomes of these situations and events.

CBT Handout 5: Weighing the Pros and Cons of Acting on Eating Disorder Urges and Impulses

Make four copies of this handout for each patient. There is usually time to complete three examples during the group session, and the first three copies of the handout will be used for this purpose. The fourth copy will be used for homework.

Main Take-Home Points

- Changing behavior is key to eating disorder recovery.
- Weighing the pros and cons of engaging in eating disorder behavior is a helpful coping skill.

Group Opener for New Members (If Needed), Mindfulness, and Homework Review

See the relevant portions of CBT Handout 1.

Pros and Cons of Acting on ED Urges and Impulses

Therapist script: In recovery, it is of the utmost importance to focus on changing our behavior. Without the behavior that keeps it going, the eating disorder would cease to exist, and once behavior has changed, thoughts and emotions start to change, too. For instance, only after people start to eat regularly do they come to think, over time, that regular eating is actually not so scary. This is why making behavioral changes before trying to change thoughts is the way to go. Does this make sense? Any questions?

Therapist script: One tool that can be really helpful in making recovery-oriented choices is weighing the pros and cons of engaging in an eating disorder behavior. This will be today's focus. Let's start by picking an eating disorder behavior from this list [*write the following items on the board*]:

- Restricting food intake
- Avoiding specific foods
- Binge eating
- Body investigating (or body checking)
- Body avoidance
- Exercising [*or another intolerance behavior*]

To Do

- Fill in the first five sets of blank lines for the selected eating disorder behavior.

- Ask patients to fill in the remaining set of blank lines with the best replacement behavior (recovery decision). For instance, if exercising is the behavioral urge chosen, then "Staying home and watching a movie with my support person" would be an appropriate recovery decision.

- Ask whether anyone would like to add another urge or impulse (such as not showing up to therapy appointments) related to the eating disorder behavior. Remind patients not to mention any specific intolerance behaviors that may be triggering.

- Pick two more eating disorder behaviors from the list on the board, and repeat this process for each one.

Questions

To Do

- With the group, go through the three questions preceding the homework section.

Homework Assignment

Therapist script: Follow the directions in the homework section, and use your fourth copy of this handout to complete an analysis of the pros and cons of acting on an urge or impulse related to an eating disorder behavior.

 CBT Handout 6: Positive Self-Talk

Main Take-Home Points

- Making body acceptance statements is important to recovery.

- The eating disorder will fight against body acceptance statements with negative emotions and thoughts.

- Body acceptance statements are important to practice anyway.

- Body acceptance statements feel more natural over time.

Group Opener for New Members (If Needed), Mindfulness, and Homework Review

See the relevant portions of CBT Handout 1.

Positive Self-Talk

Therapist script: Today we are going to focus on positive self-talk. In particular, we are going to focus on body acceptance statements, and on how the eating disorder gets in the way of practicing them. Let's take turns reading the list of body acceptance statements at the beginning of the handout.

To Do

- After the statements have been read, patients are to complete the first exercise and then read their answers aloud.

Answers

- Question 1: Patients may report feeling confident, relieved, calm, or proud. They may also report feeling no positive emotions, or struggling to feel positive emotions. They may report feeling as if repeating these phrases is insincere. In the context of having an eating disorder, these body acceptance statements are not the types of statements that are typical, familiar, or comfortable. Therefore, patients often understandably report struggling with these statements.

- Question 2: Patients can report feeling a range of negative emotions in response to body acceptance statements. They may report feeling hopeless, insincere, inauthentic ("fake"), anxious, disgusted, shameful, and angry in response to body acceptance statements. If patients report feeling hopeless, be sure to remind them that these are statements to be practiced and rehearsed over time, not believed immediately. Be sure to validate negative emotions and connect the experience to the eating disorder. For instance, you might say, "The eating disorder is going to fight against any positive and accepting statements, so of course you are going to feel negative emotions when trying this."

- Question 3: Patients will have negative thoughts like "Body acceptance will make me fat" or "I will never be able to accept my body."

- Question 4: It is acceptable to spend a large portion of group time examining the evidence for and against negative thoughts about body acceptance statements. These thoughts can be a major barrier to practicing body acceptance statements.

- Question 5: Patients may give practical reasons (such as not having time), but the idea here is that negative emotions and thoughts coming from the eating disorder may make it unpleasant to practice body acceptance statements.

- Question 6: In addition to negative emotions and thoughts, resistance to doing homework and in-session exercises may emerge. Weaving this idea into the conversation is a delicate matter. If group members tend to be more compliant, simply mention that not following up with homework and not doing in-session exercises may be expressions of the eating disorder. If group members tend to be more resistant, point out that resistance to homework and in-session exercises is probably part of the eating disorder. It may be helpful to say that in a room filled with people who do not have eating disorders, there probably would not be so much resistance to practicing body acceptance statements.

- Question 7: Patients may come up with a variety of answers to this question. Be sure to verbally reinforce accurate and insightful answers.

If someone offers an intentionally provocative response to question 7, practice active ignoring—move on to the next person, but do ultimately have every group member at least go through the motions of offering an appropriate response, if possible. The following script may help:

Group leader: Can I have another volunteer read their answer to question 7?

Tammy: "I shouldn't practice body acceptance statements. They're stupid."

Group leader: OK, Tammy. Next person?

Billy: "Tolerating negative experiences is a part of recovery, and I need to start practicing body acceptance statements to help me think more positively."

Group leader: Really well done, Billy. To summarize, recovery is difficult. It requires tolerating negative emotions and thoughts. Practicing body acceptance statements will help. So what I'd like everyone to do now is just write out a reason why it would help to practice body acceptance statements as you work toward your recovery. You don't have to believe this reason now, but just write it out for this question.

To Do

- Have patients complete the second exercise. Then ask them to share their answers to the question that follows the exercise.

Homework Assignment

Therapist script: Complete the homework assignment before next session.

 ## CBT Handout 7: Creating a Coping Card

Special Materials

You will need index cards along with materials for decorating them, such as markers, construction paper, glue, and stickers.

Main Take-Home Points

- It is important to have different coping statements at the ready as a reminder.
- You can make coping cards for yourself.
- You can make coping cards for other group members.

Group Opener for New Members (If Needed), Mindfulness, and Homework Review

See the relevant portions of CBT Handout 1.

Creating a Coping Card

Therapist script: Today we are going to be making coping cards for ourselves and for one another. Let's start by taking turns reading the first set of coping card statements.

To Do

- After patients have finished reading the first set of statements (under "Coping Card Statements for Myself"), say that patients who are struggling with binge eating and intolerance behaviors can also read the next set of statements (under "Coping Card Statements for Binge Eating and Intolerance Behaviors").

- For the first half of the session, patients will create and decorate coping cards for themselves, to help them stay on target with recovery behaviors and treatment goals.

- For the second half of the session, patients will create and decorate coping cards for the person sitting to their right (this procedure ensures that no one feels left out or ends up with too many cards).

- Patients may write other recovery statements, if they wish to, but the group leader should approve the statements.

- At the end of the session, group members should take turns presenting the coping cards they created for other members.

- Be on the lookout for opportunities to provide verbal reinforcement for recovery-oriented behaviors and attitudes expressed during the session.

Homework Assignment

Therapist script: Be sure to use your coping cards this week, and complete the homework section of the handout.

CBT Handout 8: Active Eating Disorder Problem Solving

Make three copies of this handout for each patient, two to be used in group and the third to be used for homework.

Main Take-Home Points

- Thinking strategically about the eating disorder is a skill.

- Active problem solving can help repair damage caused by the eating disorder.

- This skill, instead of focusing on eating disorder behaviors, helps you rebuild your life after the eating disorder.

Group Opener for New Members (If Needed), Mindfulness, and Homework Review

See the relevant portions of CBT Handout 1.

Active ED Problem Solving

Therapist script: Today we are going to be talking about active problem solving around the eating disorder. In other sessions, we've focused on changing eating disorder behaviors, but in this session we'll be focusing on repairing the damage caused by the eating disorder. For example, the eating disorder can strain relationships, make you unable to participate in your favorite activities and sports, leave you feeling disconnected from your peers at school, and cause health problems.

To Do

- Ask patients for examples of problems that the eating disorder has caused for them.

- List all these problems on the board.

- Provide verbal reinforcement for those patients who participated in generating the list of problems.

- Choose a problem that the patients all seem to share (for example, strained relationships).

- Have patients use the first copy of the handout to write the chosen problem on the blank lines next to item 1.

- Go through items 2, 3, 4, and 5 with the patients.

- Items 3, 4, and 5: Help patients think through which solution might be best for them to try. For example, if relationships are strained, possible solutions might include apologizing to carers for past resistance to treatment that was caused by the eating disorder, spending more time with loved ones, doing something nice for loved ones, and recovering. Point out that the solution may take a long time to implement, and help patients break it down into smaller steps.

- Item 6: Ask patients to select one portion of the solution to begin working on (for example, they might give loved ones a thank-you card for their support throughout treatment).

- Have patients use the second copy of the handout to complete items 1 through 6 on their own, identifying a different problem and then brainstorming and evaluating possible solutions.

- Encourage patients to help others who are having difficulty with the exercise.

- Ask patients to share their answers with the group.

Homework Assignment

Therapist script: Be sure to start working on your solutions this week, and complete the homework section of the handout.

CBT Handout 9: Problems with Perfectionism

Special Materials

For each patient, you will need a sheet of paper showing some kind of image that can be colored in (for example, a copyright-free illustration reproduced from a coloring book or printed from the Internet). You will also need colored pencils, markers, or crayons for patients to use.

Main Take-Home Points

- Perfectionism causes more problems than it solves.

- Perfectionism is part of the eating disorder.

- You have to practice being imperfect.

Group Opener for New Members (If Needed), Mindfulness, and Homework Review

See the relevant portions of CBT Handout 1.

Questions (Part 1)

Therapist script: Today we are going to be talking about problems with perfectionism. Let's start by going through the six questions at the beginning of the handout.

To Do

- Question 1: Patients may list general examples of perfectionism (such as needing to have a perfectly clean room) as well as eating disorder–related examples of perfectionism (such as needing to be the "perfect" weight).

- Question 2: Striving to be perfect can improve one's work, to an extent.

- Question 3: Teachers, parents, coaches, and similar figures can reward perfectionism with trophies and other kinds of recognition. It can also feel good internally to do something "to perfection."

- Question 4: Patients may report such problems as needing a long time to get things done, getting angry at others for not doing things perfectly, and so forth.

- Question 5: Once the belief exists that there is a perfect way to eat or look, if someone tries to eat or look perfect, it can become all-consuming and extremely unhealthy.

- Question 6: Perfectionism is problematic because no one and nothing can ever be perfect. Striving for perfection can cause a lot of anxiety and anger. It can also waste a lot of time.

Exercise 1

This exercise prompts patients to think about how to do things imperfectly. Patients may really struggle to come up with "perfectionism opposites." Despite having just reviewed the reasons why perfectionism is not helpful, patients may also struggle to understand why this brief exercise is being encouraged.

To Do

- If patients are having trouble understanding why they are being asked to do this exercise, point out that a theoretical understanding of why perfectionism is not helpful is a start, but that a person will continue to struggle unless perfectionistic behavior changes, and so it's useful to start thinking about how to concretely implement being *imperfect*.

Exercise 2

Therapist script: Now we're going to practice being imperfect. Take these coloring sheets, and let's practice coloring outside the lines.

To Do

- It is important to remain vigilant throughout this exercise, to ensure that patients are coloring outside the lines. They may need direction and encouragement.

- Patients will often ask for a new coloring sheet. Insist that they keep working with the same imperfect coloring sheet throughout the remainder of the exercise.

- If you are already aware that the group includes very highly perfectionistic patients who will probably refuse to color outside the lines, ask them to color on top of an already imperfect sheet, and to tolerate that experience. (You might consider making some kind of mark with a colored pencil on every one of the coloring sheets before you pass them out.)

- Allow seven to eight minutes for this exercise.

Questions (Part 2)

To Do

- Question 1: Provide verbal reinforcement to all patients for participating in the exercise and tolerating the negative emotion of anxiety.

- Question 2: Increasing emotional tolerance of imperfection is helpful because it builds emotional tolerance of perceived imperfections about oneself and one's environment. This can help in fighting the eating disorder.

- Question 3: A person does not always have to do the exact opposite of perfection, but we're doing that here as an exercise.

- Question 4: Finding a middle ground between perfection and the opposite of perfection is most functional.

- Question 5: An example of finding a middle ground is to type and proofread a text message *once* before sending it rather than spending ten minutes rereading and correcting it.

- Question 6: Help patients pick an exposure exercise (such as sending a text message that contains a typo) for the coming week.

Homework Assignment

Therapist script: Take on a perfectionism challenge this week, and answer the questions in the homework section of the handout.

 ## CBT Handout 10: Practicing Self-Care with an Eating Disorder

Special Materials

Bring in a variety of self-soothing materials for the five senses, such as lotions that have a pleasing fragrance, pictures of soothing landscapes, calming music or nature sounds, pictures of cute animals, and essential oils.

Main Take-Home Points

- Self-care is taking care of yourself.

- Routine self-care is essential to maintaining your health.

- Self-soothing practices are helpful when you are feeling distressed.

Group Opener for New Members (If Needed), Mindfulness, and Homework Review

See the relevant portions of CBT Handout 1.

What Is Self-Care?

Therapist script: Today we are going to talk about the importance of self-care. Can I have a volunteer to start reading the first part of the handout?

To Do

- Have volunteers continue reading the first part of the handout, including the examples of self-soothing practices.

- Ensure that the difference between routine self-care and self-soothing is made clear.

Questions

To Do

- With the patients, go through the list of five questions.

Self-Soothing Exercise

Therapist script: Here [*indicate the items you brought to group*] are some self-care items for us to use today. We'll try them out slowly.

To Do

- It is recommended that you start out with lotion. Everyone can either put the lotion on their hands or put some on a tissue.

- Walk the patients through the experience of mindfully smelling the lotion, noticing the fragrance, and feeling the lotion or tissue on their hands.

- Ask for reflections on the experience.

- Now pass around pictures of soothing landscapes.

- Ask patients to really look at the pictures and imagine themselves in the landscapes.

- Playing soothing music or nature sounds is also a good option.

Preparing for Homework

Therapist script: Before we end, we need to take some time to prepare for this week's homework assignment. Can I have a volunteer to read the directions under "Preparing for Homework"?

To Do

- Have patients write down their own examples of routine self-care and self-soothing.

- Go around and ask patients to read their examples aloud.

- Provide feedback to any patients who have answers that may need tweaking.

Homework Assignment

Therapist script: The homework assignment is to use routine self-care every day, to use self-soothing when you're distressed, and to log your use of these skills.

 ## CBT Handout 11: Writing a Letter to Your Eating Disorder

Special Materials

You will need enough sheets of paper for everyone, since patients will be writing letters.

Main Take-Home Points

- Eating disorders take a lot away.

- It can be helpful to write a letter to your eating disorder and tell it exactly how you feel.

Group Opener for New Members (If Needed), Mindfulness, and Homework Review

See the relevant portions of CBT Handout 1.

Questions

Therapist script: Today you are going to be writing letters to your eating disorders. Can I have a volunteer to read the paragraph at the beginning of the handout?

To Do

Almost all questions in this handout can be answered only by the patient.

To Do

- Question 7: This is an important but sensitive question. It is OK if patients do not want to share their answers, and it is not necessary to press them on this. But patients should at least consider this question privately.

Exercise: Writing a Goodbye Letter

Therapist script: Can I have a volunteer to read the directions for this exercise?

To Do

- As patients finish writing their letters, ask if you may read them. Scan for anything that may be triggering to other group members.

- Ask patients to read their letters aloud, if they're willing to do so.

Homework Assignment

Therapist script: The homework assignment is to reread your letter at least once during the coming week, and to share it with someone supportive if you feel like it.

CBT Handout 12: Relapse-Prevention Plan

This handout is for patients who are already enrolled in IMT group therapy and have received the interventions focused on practicing mindfulness, managing eating disorder thoughts, tolerating negative emotions, and monitoring eating disorder behaviors.

Main Take-Home Points

- Progress in treatment is not linear.

- It is important to have a relapse-prevention plan in place.

Group Opener for New Members (If Needed), Mindfulness, and Homework Review

See the relevant portions of CBT Handout 1.

Using Your Skills

Therapist script: Today we are going to be talking about making plans to prevent eating disorder relapse in recovery. Can I have some volunteers read the material at the beginning of the handout, up to the section "Identifying Your Triggers for Relapse"?

Therapist script: Thank you. You have already learned many skills. Today we are going to talk about integrating them into your daily lives to prevent relapse.

To Do

- Ensure that all skills are reviewed.

- Ask patients how they will use each set of skills in their daily lives to prevent relapse.

Triggers and Signs of Relapse

To Do

- Go through each of the potential triggers and signs of relapse.

- Be sure to emphasize that even unintentional weight loss (for example, because of catching the flu) can trigger a relapse.

Skill Use for Relapse Triggers

Therapist script: Now that we have reviewed some general coping skills, triggers, and signs of relapse, your task here is to list, from memory, as many coping skills as you can. When you are done, let me know.

To Do

- Ask patients to share their lists of the skills they remember they can use. The idea is that patients need to start remembering all the various tools at their disposal.

- For the task involving matching signs of relapse with coping skills, patients may refer to past handouts.

Homework Assignment

Therapist script: Your homework is to integrate your coping skills into your daily life and use your relapse-prevention plan if you need to.

If there are patients in the group who are to receive the next handout in this modality—CBT Handout 13: Remembering All You Have Learned—tell them to bring all their past handouts to the session or sessions where CBT Handout 13 is covered.

CBT Handout 13: Remembering All You Have Learned

This handout is only for patients who are already enrolled in IMT group therapy and have received all the previous interventions in more or less linear fashion. The material usually takes more than one session to cover. Patients receiving this handout should have been told to bring all their past handouts to this session.

Main Take-Home Points

- You have learned a ton in IMT group therapy.

- Now you have to use the skills.

Mindfulness and Homework Review

See the relevant portions of CBT Handout 1.

Remembering Skills

Therapist script: Today we are going to be talking about all the skills you've learned in IMT group therapy. Before you receive this session's handout, let's list on the board as many skills as you can remember learning.

To Do

- List on the board all the skills that patients remember having learned.

- After patients cannot remember any more skills, provide this handout.

- Comment on the difference between the number on the board and the number of skills (forty-two) listed in the handout.

- Go through the forty-two items, one by one.

- Ask patients to look back through their past handouts and ask any questions they may still have about using any of the skills.

- Tell patients to make short notes on this handout regarding how they can use the particular skills (for example, "I can use this skill to eat" or "I can use this skill after an intolerance behavior").

PART 3

Family Therapy Modality

Section 3.1

Introduction to the Family Therapy Modality

Part 3 of this manual describes IMT family therapy, including core concepts and language, an overview of the structure of family therapy sessions, and instructions for using the IMT family therapy material.

Core Family Treatment Concepts

Self-Eclipsing Eating Disorders and the Rationale for Family Treatment

Self-eclipsing eating disorders (SEEDs) are a different kind of animal. They are very much unlike the more common self-acknowledged class of disorder. Because the self is eclipsed, maladaptive values (such as thinness at any cost) are present along with an impairment in recognizing facts (such as those that disconfirm one's status as "fat"). Therefore, committed actions in line with adaptive preexisting values (such as health) are very likely to be self-initiated. Reinforcement from others for engaging in recovery behaviors (such as completing meals) is necessary. In order for that reinforcement to occur, however, a context must be set up in the environment by others so that the behaviors can be reinforced. In other words, there is not enough time to sit around waiting for a person with a life-threatening eating disorder to eventually eat a little something and shape that behavior over time. We need to ensure that sufficient quantities of food are being consumed, and quickly. Otherwise, the patient may literally die in the interim. Therefore, others must control the environment by taking control of food and providing reinforcement in that context. Once a person is medically stable, able to take committed action in line with recovery without reinforcement from others, and able to cite adaptive values (such as family) rather than eating disorder values (such as thinness), control of food is no longer necessary.

In short, this theoretical conceptualization is provided in an earnest effort to counter two attitudes: that it should be up to the patient to recover, and that the patient's wishes need to be respected during treatment for a life-threatening and self-eclipsing disorder. These attitudes may very well put the patient at risk. Active outside intervention is necessary. A self-eclipsing eating disorder is different, and its treatment should be different from that of a self-acknowledged disorder when a person's life is at stake.

"It Takes a Village": Treating Self-Eclipsing Eating Disorders

There is a vast difference between working with motivated people who have nonlethal self-acknowledged disorders (such as phobias) and people who are convinced that their life-threatening eating disorder behaviors are healthy. Treating a person whose self has been eclipsed by a deadly disorder requires an additional set of skills. One of these skills is training others in the person's environment to help them because they cannot yet help themselves. The eating disorder is too powerful. When the eating disorder has very much eclipsed the self of a person, it is too risky to leave the monumental task of recovering to the patient alone. The person simply needs help.

Help comes in the form of others in the environment providing reinforcement, setting boundaries, giving directives, and monitoring behavior with the goal of decreasing eating disorder behaviors and increasing recovery behaviors. This is a very hands-on approach. For instance, during a one-on-one session, a behavior therapist, rather than giving suggestions on how to eat a less restrictive lunch in the future, must provide a directive for the patient currently eating in the therapist's office to finish the last bites of the sandwich in front of them and must provide positive attention when the task is completed (such as by smiling and saying, "Good job").

A behavioral family therapist must also teach carers these kinds of skills and shape their behavior in session. The therapist provides reinforcement to the carer who is providing reinforcement to their child during in-session meals. Additionally, when interventions are being delivered by a behavior therapist or carer, a person with a SEED is likely to experience a range of negative emotions. In turn, the eating disorder can cause the person to have disruptive behavioral outbursts that are difficult to manage. These situations can be emotionally and intellectually taxing for therapists and families alike.

In short, patients as well as families learn from the therapist's in-session instruction, reinforcement, modeling, and provided resources. IMT family handouts, which describe how to implement rules, provide reinforcement, and manage oppositional behavior, are explained to the carers in session and are to be referred to at home for further study and as otherwise necessary.

The Skill Set Needed for Treating Self-Eclipsing Eating Disorders

Treatment of a SEED, as just mentioned, requires a specific skill set that needs to be employed prior to the skill set required for more self-acknowledged disorders. In the treatment of a SEED that seriously endangers a person's health, as is the case with eating disorders for some children and adolescents, the following specific clinical skills are needed:

- The clinician must be able to provide psychoeducation about the self-eclipsing nature of the disorder, such as by saying, "The eating disorder will not allow your child to care about anything else right now except losing weight, and they cannot be left to their own devices. They cannot recover without help."

- The clinician must have the ability to be direct regarding how physically destructive the disorder can be, such as by saying, "This eating disorder can kill your child."

- The clinician must be able to facilitate the setting up of a home environment that acts as a context in which adaptive reinforcement can be provided (that is, the clinician must help carers take control of food and implement rules).

- The clinician must be able to set treatment goals for the family on the basis of objective data, such as by saying, in a private conversation with a patient's carer, "Your child's doctor says he needs to gain at least ten more pounds to no longer be at risk. He is expected to gain about two pounds per week, which he has been doing. Therefore, you must remain in control of food for at least five more weeks."

- The clinician must be able to model adaptive behaviors in session for the patient and family, such as by eating in session with the family.

- The clinician must be able to model how to provide directives, such as by saying, "Sarah, you haven't started on your mashed potatoes. It's time to give them a try."

- The clinician must be able to teach others in the environment to decrease eating disorder behaviors by blocking their reinforcement—for example, by monitoring bathroom use to block purging from providing negative reinforcement.

- The clinician must be able to teach others in the environment to shape adaptive behavior with reinforcement—for example, by teaching carers to smile and say, "I'm proud of you" following meal completion.

- The clinician must be able to teach carers to manage disruptive behavioral outbursts by withholding reinforcement of the outburst and providing reinforcement of emotion regulation—for example, by ignoring the outburst until is over and then saying, "Thanks for sitting at the table."

In this conceptualization, these techniques can help shift disorders from self-eclipsing to self-acknowledging. By creating a context in which reinforcement of recovery behaviors is provided and reinforcement of eating disorder behaviors is mitigated, a person is guided over time toward taking their own self-initiated actions in line with adaptive values (such as health), which they were unable to at the start of treatment. In this way, taking control of food away from the child is a temporary and necessary measure taken toward the ultimate goal of treatment—empowerment of the child.

Power Dynamics of the Eating Disorder

Understanding the nature of eating disorders fosters a compassionate stance for people who have them as well as for their families. Taking a compassionate stance toward the treatment of this disorder is of the utmost importance, as is providing validation and support. In behavioral family therapy, this must be balanced with understanding and confronting the power dynamics a SEED introduces. Considering both the suffering of the family and the power of a SEED, a therapist must take a stance that balances warmth with firmness. The compassionate portion of treatment is just as important as the firm piece. Here, however, we are discussing the rather complicated power dynamics that a SEED introduces into treatment.

In IMT family therapy for eating disorders, a lot of consideration is given to who currently holds the power and to the nature of that power:

1. The therapist must consider who is currently in a position of power—the eating disorder, the child, the carer, or even the therapist.

2. The quality of that power—whether it is tyrannical, authoritarian, or benevolently authoritative—must also be examined.

3. The appropriateness of the current status of power must be determined.

Tracking these three variables is crucial to adaptively implementing behavioral interventions across time in treatment.

The Life Cycle of Power

At the beginning of treatment, a SEED can have tyrannical power over a family. Family members live in fear of the eating disorder. They may avoid any reaction associated with it. Whether they are afraid that the person with the eating disorder will have an angry outburst, become physically ill, or feel negative emotions (such as panic), this fear of the eating disorder dictates their behavior. It is clear that they are complying with the eating disorder's demands out of fear, dread, or defeat. At the start of treatment—as early as the intake session—point out what behaviors the family currently engages in to avoid their own negative emotions. Point this out as evidence that the eating disorder has control. Take a moment to acknowledge just how unfortunate this current dynamic is, and express both compassion and empathy for the family.

With the purpose of compassionately assisting the family toward the goal of decreasing symptoms of the SEED, the eating disorder must be disempowered. The tyrannical power should shift away from the eating disorder and diffuse appropriately. By the end of treatment, carers should have benevolent authoritative power relative to their child with the eating disorder in an age-appropriate manner. In turn, the patient should become empowered to freely decide to behave in line with their pre–eating disorder values rather than be caught in a loop of continually attempting to decrease fear of "fatness." Additionally, in an effort to foster appropriate modeling of healthy power dynamics in session for both the carer and the patient, the therapist is also appropriately empowered. The therapist is positioned as a teacher who has the potential to earn the respect of the family by providing guidance in the battle against the eating disorder. Ideally, the therapist, carers, and the patient are all on the same team and share the intention of not conceding their own empowerment by giving in to reinforcing the eating disorder. Through this concerted team effort of appropriate self-empowerment, the eating disorder is, ideally, left powerless by the end of treatment.

The Eating Disorder in Power

It is extremely important to work on disempowering a SEED because when it is in a position of tyrannical power, it allows for the unintentional reinforcement and condoning of the eating disorder. Therefore, it flourishes. This dynamic comes about *because of* the eating disorder; it does not *cause* the eating disorder. This dynamic simply allows the eating disorder to grow once it has already come into existence, and then to gain power. Because the eating disorder is so physically and psychologically destructive, it must be halted by being overthrown and diffused, and healthy individual empowerment must then be reestablished. It is never appropriate for an eating disorder to be in a position of power. It is expected, however, that an eating disorder will be in a position of power during the treatment weeks before carers implement the treatment rules.

Carers Taking Benevolent Authoritative Power

In a family where carers have the ability to put the needs of their child first—a factor that is not always a given—carers should be taught skills to overtake the eating disorder and have appropriate power with a benevolently authoritative quality. For instance, carers, not the child under the influence of the eating disorder, should be calling the shots regarding family meals. If there are two carers present, the carers should do this as a team. It can be extremely difficult for carers who have been living in fear of the tyrannical eating disorder to begin to take power away from the eating disorder. Through psychoeducation, skills, confrontation of their own fear of the eating disorder, and experiential mastery of implementing treatment rules, carers can gain an inherent sense of firm but kind empowerment over time.

FRAGILIZING THE ADOLESCENT

Unwittingly, carers can concede power to the eating disorder by fragilizing their child. This, in our experience, typically happens slowly, but once the adolescent is being fragilized, it is an important obstacle to overcome. Especially relatively early in the development of the illness, a person with an eating disorder can continue to function somewhat normally outside the single domain of eating. For instance, they may be a good student, a polite person, and so forth, but whenever the eating disorder is directly challenged by the carer (for example, in the carer's attempts to get the adolescent to eat more calories), the person can really snap. Especially in view of the contrast with the non–eating disorder self, a sudden eating disorder–driven outburst can be shocking and disturbing. Carers can come to learn that if the eating disorder is challenged, they are snapped at. In this way, they have learned to avoid addressing the illness. While keeping the intervention of others at bay, the eating disorder is freed to consume its host without interruption. Snapping at and alienating others is one of the defenses the eating disorder uses to keep the patient isolated and sick. As it becomes apparent that their child is quite ill, carers can become quite fearful for the patient's well-being. Any lashing out that occurs when the eating disorder is challenged can be viewed as "upsetting" the already distraught child. Therefore, some carers are often resistant to challenging the eating disorder, experientially having been shaped to avoid it and having developed the belief that "upsetting" their child is causing further damage. In this way, some carers overestimate the power of the eating disorder and underestimate their child. It is the *fragilizing* of the *person* with an eating disorder that helps keeps them sick, not the *challenging* of the *eating disorder*.

Challenging the eating disorder will not break a person. It will help them gain strength in recovery. Because this fact is not very obvious, however, asking carers to directly address the illness in family-based treatment can be very anxiety-provoking for them. In these instances, it is the clinician's responsibility to point out how the eating disorder has shaped the carer's fearfulness of it, address how much fearfulness of the eating disorder feeds its power, and discuss the importance of working through the carer's own anxiety in the best interests of the patient.

Empowerment of the Child

The empowerment of the child—not the eating disorder—should also be fostered over time in treatment. Often at the start of treatment, the eating disorder may be so powerful that it may be hard for a person to determine any personal values or goals. The only value may appear to be "thinness," and the only goal may appear to be "to lose weight." With the establishment of appropriate power dynamics and successful implementation of treatment interventions, a person with a set of healthy values (such as family, school, and so forth) who is able to take committed action toward their goals (such as spending time with siblings, finishing high school, and so forth) begins to emerge. When this happens, the behavior therapist must reinforce expressions of the healthy self and teach carers to do so as well.

The therapist must also foster healthy power dynamics in family sessions, allowing for the continued fortification of the empowered self at home. For instance, if an *authoritarian*-style carer, as opposed to a carer with the more adaptive *authoritative* style, shuts down the patient's healthy desire to explore their interests when appropriate, a therapist can provide education about the importance of empowering the child.

Further, each family will be different in regard to the degree of power given to children within the family, with some carers being very open to collaborating with their children and others being more hierarchical. Of course, it is not the therapist's place to advise the family on the degree to which children should be included in family decision making. It is, however, the therapist's role to point out the distinction between the child and the eating disorder. When the eating disorder appears to be usurping a carer's power as well as the child's power, it is necessary to decouple the child's wishes and opinions from decisions being driven by the eating disorder's fear of "fatness." The therapist must facilitate the joining of the carers and the children in the family, with the carers in charge, to fight the common enemy of the tyrannical eating disorder.

The Empowered Therapist

Working at higher levels of care with patients who have SEEDs, it has often been our experience that clinicians in training doubt themselves when personally faced with a challenge from the eating disorder. This is an unpleasant experience to begin with, and SEEDs often exploit this self-doubt. For instance, on a regular basis in the hospital, SEEDs drive patients to call attention to training clinicians' unlicensed status as well as to their age, inexperience, or uncertainty ("You're just a trainee—what do you know?") when in pursuit of reinforcement (such as going to the bathroom unattended, against the rules, to engage in a behavior). If a trainee does not feel grounded in their sense of skillfulness, this situation can very easily turn into the trainee feeling suddenly uncertain about their authority to implement rules and doubting their intelligence. This can even spiral into the reinforcement-allowing behavior (RAB) of letting a patient go to the bathroom unattended. (A reinforcement-allowing behavior is any action taken by any person—carer, hospital staff member, and so forth—in a current position of authority, and charged with implementing treatment rules, that results in the reinforcement of an eating disorder behavior.) But that RAB could have been avoided if that skilled clinician just had a little faith in their intelligence and ability to implement the rules. We can do it, everyone! We've got this!

Therefore, it seems that both education about eating disorders and a sense of self-empowerment are needed to come up against the eating disorder in person rather than just talking about doing it. One of the specialized skills required in treating SEEDs, from this conceptualization, is that the therapists themselves need to personally develop a sense of empowerment to enforce reinforcement-inhibiting behaviors (RIBs) as well as model the enforcement of RIBs for carers. (A reinforcement-impeding behavior is any action taken by any person—carer, hospital staff member, and so forth—in a current position of authority, and charged with implementing treatment rules, that results in reinforcement of the *blocking* of an eating disorder behavior.) In order to help establish healthy power dynamics within the family at home, the power dynamics within a given therapy session must be considered. In order to help play a role in overthrowing the eating disorder, a therapist must be able to model both being empowered and having station. Carers are living in fear of the eating disorder. Therefore, overthrowing the eating disorder will involve confronting their fears. Since implementing treatment rules will be an exposure for the carers, having a therapist model confidence, unflappability, and compassion in the face of eating disorder behaviors is an important component of treatment. It is important not only for a therapist to reflect that attitude in discussion and inspire confidence but also for carers to see a therapist interacting with the patient in session.

As mentioned earlier, a power move of the eating disorder can be to undercut the therapist's ability, authority, and even personality at the start of treatment, in an effort to avoid recovery. For instance, a patient may say to a carer that they just don't like "this stupid therapist." If the eating disorder is in a position of tyrannical power, a carer may defer to the eating disorder and drop out of treatment without ever hearing what the therapist has to say on the matter. If, however, the therapist presents themselves as (and believes themselves to be) a person with knowledge to be respected, there may be a fighting chance of getting through to the carers about the importance of family treatment and the likelihood that another excuse will be invented if they seek any type of therapy other than the type that actually involves eating. In this way, a respected therapist is viewed as a contender with the eating disorder. Carers *do* have the authority to decide whether their child will be in treatment, but they may not be fully using it yet. A therapist can help them tap into this authority from the beginning by appealing to their good judgment: "Is this really not a good fit? If not, OK. Or is this about avoiding eating and not addressing the very serious and life-threatening issue of the eating disorder?" If it is really not a good fit, insist that another family therapist be seen.

Regardless of how prone a given carer is to fold in the presence of the eating disorder, or how willing they may be to consider a therapist's rationale for family treatment, what every therapist has to contribute is their education, skills, and experience. In session, you can show carers in real time how to avoid reinforcement of the eating disorder, you can lay ground rules for treatment, and you can show what you know about how to fight the eating disorder. When you are of use to the carers and can help them help their child recover, they can choose to trust you on the basis of what they have experienced. This is how the therapist is appropriately empowered in this style of treatment. Empowerment of the therapist is not to be underestimated. It is our belief that if the therapist is respected, and believes this, it is easier for scared carers to make the choice to move away from avoiding the eating disorder and toward confronting it. Further, the stance of the empowered therapist is not at odds with empowering carers to take benevolent authoritative roles or with empowering the child's self-expression. In fact, it models appropriate behavior.

The Empowered Therapist: An Afterthought As we taught this material to clinicians in training, we were initially surprised that many of them were turned off by the idea of a therapist also being empowered and having confidence in their own skill set. Particularly because therapists teach the importance of having self-confidence all the time, this was particularly curious. If one has not been personally disempowered by a self-eclipsing eating disorder, it may be difficult to realize how important one's own empowerment can be. One's own empowerment is probably something that is taken for granted in treatment by those who treat primarily self-acknowledged disorders. One's empowerment is not something that is under attack on a daily basis. It is not something that a therapist needs to fight to hold on to. When being either verbally or in some way physically confronted (such as when food is thrown at them, a can of Ensure is dumped on their head, they are spit on, and so forth), a disempowered therapist is not only likely to end up feeling rather miserable but also liable to feel defeated and to concede to the eating disorder. An empowered therapist, however, can weather storms, effectively implement treatment in session, and model adaptive behavior for the family.

Influencing Shifts in Power Dynamics

Over the course of IMT family therapy, the eating disorder usually starts out with tyrannical power. The therapist must guide carers toward a benevolently authoritative stance that decreases the eating disorder's power. As the eating disorder loses power, the patient's self emerges and can become empowered over time. The therapist is also empowered through knowledge, experience, and confidence and is able to help by skillfully implementing interventions and modeling appropriate behaviors.

Power Struggles

The following material is strictly for professional use and is not to be shared in any way. This content is not for public consumption. The coauthors strongly discourage writing about this material online in blog posts and articles.

As the therapist attempts to work with the family on aligning a healthy hierarchy of power, the eating disorder will work against this. Throughout the supported recovery process, patients will engage in any number of the power dynamic behaviors that therapists must be aware of and address. Here are some ways to address the following power moves on the part of the eating disorder:

- *Cutting off the therapist from potential meal-support network:* Make sure to inform family members that the eating disorder is attempting to avoid treatment, that the eating disorder requires outside intervention, and that it could be very dangerous if not treated. Get good at detecting avoidance maneuvers and compassionately confronting them—for example, by asking, "How anxious are you about having your family members involved in care?" Communicate to carers that the reason for the patient's resistance and avoidance is fear that must be faced. Additionally, reaching out to carers with calls outside sessions can be helpful.

- *Withholding information and providing inaccurate information:* Let the patient know that you are aware of the information being withheld or misrepresented (such as evidence of purging, water loading, and so forth); let carers know, too, and provide reinforcement when the patient discloses accurate information about the eating disorder. Also encourage carers to provide reinforcement when the patient discloses accurate information about the eating disorder. Gather accurate data about the eating disorder from the family, and let the patient know that you are gathering accurate data about the eating disorder.

- *Aligning with those who collude with or enable the eating disorder:* Be aware of the degree to which each family member is colluding with or enabling the eating disorder, and why. Explain how they are reinforcing the eating disorder, how they have probably become fearful of outbursts, and why it is so important to confront the eating disorder.

- *Splitting:* If a patient is driven by the eating disorder to pit one authority figure against another, the treatment team and the carers must get back on the same page. It is important to explain that splitting is occurring, point out ways in which the eating disorder is getting away with behaviors when the front is divided (for example, when carers are busy fighting, no one is watching the patient eat), and decide from this point on to implement rules in a unified way.

- *Putting down:* If a patient is driven by the eating disorder to personally attack a therapist ("Your smile is ugly"), maintaining an unflappable approach is best. Showing irreverence can be helpful, both through non-verbal communication (such as lightly chuckling at the comment) and verbal communication (such as telling the patient, "Regardless of the ugliness of my smile, we are going to carry on eating this snack").

- *Sucking up:* This behavior may be difficult for the novice behavioral family therapist to detect, but when it comes to eating, and the patient cannot complete a meal or has a behavioral outburst, sucking up can be classified as a power move. A given patient may engage in excessive flattery or make overtures to falsely convince others of treatment adherence, but if they are failing to behaviorally meet treatment goals, they cannot earn freedom from carers' supervision of food. If a patient is displaying these behaviors, the behavioral family therapist can simply indicate that the patient can be as complimentary as they want, but they still must follow all the treatment rules.

- *Running out the clock:* A patient may be driven by the eating disorder to steer conversation in sessions with carers away from disempowering the eating disorder. If this happens, it is important to catch this early and redirect the conversation or ask the patient to sit outside.

- *Breaking the rules:* Work with carers to have a system in place to address rule breaking. In a therapeutic milieu at a higher level of care, it is up to the treatment team to enforce consequences if rules are broken.

- *Negotiating and making demands:* Shape down negotiating about food over time. Do not give in to demands. Make sure that the patient understands that demands cannot be made.

- *Engaging in an emotional outburst:* A patient may be driven by the eating disorder to have an emotional outburst to avoid eating or RIBs. By contrast with the other behaviors listed here, it is best to avoid reinforcement of the outburst, as well as of the eating disorder, by refusing to engage. If the function of the outburst is to pull a carer's attention away from the objective of eating, then the carer must remain focused on eating. If a patient escalates, the carer must remain calm. The patient's outburst must be ignored until it passes. Once it does, the patient must be redirected to eating. The patient must learn that having an emotional outburst is not an effective strategy for pulling a carer's attention away from the objective of completing the meal. When the patient has calmed down, reinforcement can be provided for emotion regulation. In short, carers must be trained to wait until the wind is out of the patient's sails and then simply redirect the patient to eating. If the carer does not do this and attends to the emotional outburst, the risk of engaging in an argument, and of the meal not being completed, is present. It is not advisable to try to overpower a person having an emotional outburst to avoid eating, because it can backfire. Attempting to overpower a patient in this state will result in a screaming match, or in the carer's need to punish the child in the moment. Both end in an incomplete meal. Contributing to the emotional escalation of the patient does not foster an environment suited to completing a meal and keeping it down. Having an emotional outburst in the context of eating disorder therapy is not "bad" behavior to be punished. It is an eating disorder behavior to be shaped. More specifically, having an emotional outburst to avoid eating is what is called a reinforcement-seeking eating disorder behavior (see FAM Handout 1.15: Ten Reasons Why Your Child Despises Supervised Eating).

Reinforcement Is the Key

By now, establishing adaptive power dynamics, disempowering the eating disorder, and empowering the child may all sound like rational treatment goals. But how does one go about doing all of that, exactly? The following material discusses the tool—the selective withholding and implementation of *reinforcement*.

Reinforcement-Allowing Behaviors

In any given family session, whether it involves eating or only discussion, a therapist watches for the patient's eating disorder behaviors as well as for the carers' RABs, which include their failure to take active measures to block eating disorder behaviors from being reinforced. One classic example of a RAB is allowing one's child with an eating disorder to engage in organized sports or activities that can double as eating disorder behaviors (such as running track, playing soccer, engaging in gymnastics or ballet, and so forth) when one is fully aware of the potential ramifications. In instances like these, the patient's eating disorder behavior is negatively reinforced through a temporary reduction in fear of "fatness." RABs also include more passive and inadvertent behavior, such as using one's cell phone during a meal rather than watching for food being hidden. If food is successfully hidden during this time, a carer inadvertently allows their child to experience relief, which reinforces the eating disorder behavior of hiding food. In both examples, eating disorder behaviors are reinforced in the context of a carer's action. In these cases, if carers were to take a different course of action, the reinforcement of eating disorder behaviors would be blocked. Here are some other common RABs:

- Allowing the child to dictate the type of therapy provided (such as choosing traditional talk therapy over behavioral family therapy) or allowing the child to avoid treatment altogether

- Allowing the child to dictate the treatment (such as insisting that a proportion of the family session be spent with just the therapist and the patient talking, because the child is strongly suggesting it)

- Allowing the child to engage in incidental exercise (such as walking around a city or mall all day) if the treatment team has advised against it

- Allowing the child to choose their own type and amount of food

- Allowing the child to prepare food

- Allowing the child to plate food

- Allowing the child to stop eating meals and snacks before completion without first adequately prompting them to finish and implementing skills

- Allowing the child to use the bathroom unsupervised immediately after meals

- Allowing the child unrestricted access to laxatives, diet pills, and so forth

- Allowing the child unrestricted access to maladaptive Internet communities

- Allowing the child's eating disorder behaviors to be reinforced by the carer's current inability to set firm limits

- Allowing the child to negotiate the treatment rules

- Allowing fear of confronting the eating disorder to result in general avoidance of the child

- Allowing the child's behavioral outbursts, splitting, insults, sucking up, and other power moves to distract from using skills to encourage the child to complete the treatment goal at hand

In a somewhat similar manner to how a patient's eating disorder drives their behavior, a carer's behavior may be driven by maladaptive avoidance of fear. There is no judgment in this. In fact, it is a therapist's duty to take an objective, nonjudgmental stance and aim to compassionately understand why a carer may be engaging in RABs. A given carer may be fearful of confronting the eating disorder for a variety of reasons, such as being yelled at, having discord in the home, making the eating disorder worse, and so forth. It is worth taking the time to explore. One needs to work on decreasing their experiential avoidance in treatment by following the treatment rules. Neither fault nor blame has anything to do with whether a carer's behavior is classified as allowing reinforcement. Objectively, a behavior is simply classified as a RAB if an eating disorder behavior is reinforced in relation to it.

Because eating disorders are a round-the-clock kind of disorder, and because carers cannot watch their children every second of the day, there will always be some number of passive RABs. That's OK. Perfection is never possible. The aim here is to decrease RABs to the most reasonable extent possible. When carers are presenting with any of the RABs already mentioned, the issue must be addressed in session. The IMT measures are aimed at assessing for RABs that may be occurring at home. A behavioral family therapist must also attend to any RABs that are mentioned or behaviorally displayed in session.

This work was influenced by Anderson, Smith, Farrell, and Riemann (2018), whose findings indicate that the enabling of carers' behaviors contributes to the maintenance of eating disorder behaviors as well as to poorer treatment outcomes. These researchers also found a correlation between carers' anxiety and carers' engagement in enabling behaviors.

Reinforcement-Impeding Behaviors

Reinforcement, of course, is defined as any consequence that increases the likelihood that a behavior will occur in the future. One of the first goals in treatment is to ensure that eating disorder behaviors are cut off from reinforcement. Think of reinforcement of maladaptive behaviors as the lifeblood of the eating disorder. Even unintentional reinforcement of eating disorder behaviors feeds the disorder. Therefore, as many RABs as possible must be decreased. In turn, they must be replaced with reinforcement-impeding behaviors.

A carer who uses strict supervision to ensure that a child does not use the bathroom immediately after a meal is engaging in a RIB. Because the child is prevented from purging—an eating disorder behavior that would be reinforced by a maladaptive reduction in negative emotions in the moment—the behavior of supervising the child after a meal impedes the reinforcement of purging. The larger picture is more complex, but this RIB, in short, decreases the likelihood that the behavior of purging will occur in the future.

Conveniently, the RIB acronym can be mapped onto the process of implementing a RIB; that is, impeding a person from receiving reinforcement from an eating disorder behavior is somewhat akin to ribbing (teasing), although the connotation here is more one of aggravation. Implementing RIBs is not pleasant for the patient and very often leads to intense negative emotions. A patient is forced to experience the negative emotion that the eating disorder behavior would have temporarily ameliorated.

When RIBs are implemented, the patient is put into a situation of having to cope with negative emotions without the eating disorder behaviors. Of course, regardless of one's theoretical orientation, confronting negative emotions is a desired treatment outcome, and engaging in maladaptive and dangerous behaviors is not. Over time, a person learns to manage these negative emotions without the use of eating disorder behaviors. In the interim, however, coping with negative emotions can be extremely difficult. Rather than adaptively confronting their fear of "fatness," for instance, many patients continue to avoid negative emotions for a time by engaging in oppositional behaviors directed at the people (carers, hospital staff, and so forth) who are implementing the treatment rules. RIBs are also useful in decreasing these types of oppositional behaviors, thereby guiding a patient away from experiential avoidance.

In short, the implementation of RIBs is of the utmost importance because RIBs cut off eating disorder behaviors from their sustaining reinforcement while creating a context for the patient to experience exposure to negative emotions. Both aspects of implementing RIBs are absolutely crucial to recovery. In one manner or another, almost all the IMT family handouts are designed to help carers implement RIBs. Some explain what to do, and others explain either why or how to implement RIBs.

Recovery-Specific Positive Attention

A behaviorist is concerned not only with blocking the reinforcement of eating disorder behaviors but also with reinforcing recovery behaviors (completing meals, tolerating negative emotions without engaging in maladaptive behaviors, and so forth). Because reinforcement increases the likelihood that a behavior will occur in the future, the idea is to reinforce adaptive behaviors so that they are more likely to occur in the future. Providing reinforcement of recovery behaviors is challenging and can be met with opposition from the patient. That said, however, reinforcement is a powerful tool. Blocking the reinforcement of maladaptive behaviors can be viewed as one-half of a behaviorist's job. Tactfully and skillfully providing reinforcement of adaptive behaviors is the other half.

The term *positive reinforcement* is commonly misused to mean "praise," and overt praise of recovery behavior can often prompt a behavioral outburst, and so a term specific to this treatment was devised for labeling the broad concept of reinforcing adaptive behaviors. In this work, we refer to any warm and compassionate verbal or nonverbal reinforcement of recovery behavior as *recovery-specific positive attention* (Rec-SPA). Here, the word "positive" is used to describe the warm and affirmative quality of the attention being provided. As already suggested, this attention does not have to be verbal; for instance, a warm smile given to a patient after they take a bite of a challenge food qualifies as Rec-SPA. Unlike such treatments as parent–child interaction therapy for children between the ages of two and seven (Bodiford-McNeil & Hembree-Kigin, 2010), in which praise is very specific ("Good job sitting in the blue chair"), reinforcement provided for recovery behavior must often be more subtle. As the eating disorder recedes, however, more overt praise ("Good job finishing your pizza") is met with less resistance—generally a good indication that the patient's self is able to receive the praise without the eating disorder's attempt to protect itself by warding off the praise. Further, carers are encouraged to express both gratitude and pride to their child in the form of earnest Rec-SPA. Rec-SPA as a concept includes not just overt praise but also warm nonverbal cues (such as smiling), affirmative nonverbal cues (such as giving a thumbs-up), and expressions of gratitude and pride. These are all examples of reinforcers that the patient's healthy self, not the eating disorder, will find reinforcing. Therefore, they serve as reinforcers of recovery.

In our experience, clinicians who are experienced with eating disorders have different concerns about the concept of providing reinforcement for recovery-oriented behaviors than do inexperienced clinicians. Experienced eating disorder clinicians can be concerned about patients who have a negative reaction to positive feedback, whereas clinicians without experience in this specialty may not even be aware that this is a typical response about which to be concerned. Further, both groups of clinicians express concern about exerting too much environmental influence over the patient's behavior with shaping techniques, without addressing the patient as an individual. Here, both concerns are addressed.

Saying "Good job for completing your meal" to a patient with a SEED does not always end with "Thank you so very much—that really means the world to me." In fact, taking so unrefined a tack as overpraising can end in a reaction of the fiery variety. Because patients report that praise causes them to feel distressed, clinicians advise people not to praise behaviors that are in line with recovery. To a behaviorist, however, tolerating distress is an essential component of treatment. By itself, the argument "I want to avoid something that challenges my eating disorder and causes me distress" is not generally accepted as being in line with treatment goals. But if a patient can tolerate no Rec-SPA whatsoever, the goal of implementing Rec-SPA is temporarily put on hold. At the same time, a behavioral technique cannot be forbidden forever just because it challenges the eating disorder. It should also be noted that specific guidelines on tactfully implementing Rec-SPA are provided in this manual. Further, a behaviorist can help a carer implement Rec-SPA by offering in-session demonstrations and providing feedback.

Of course, the ultimate goal in treatment is for recovery behaviors to occur on their own, without the need for overt reinforcement from others. External reinforcement is a means to an end. A carer can provide consistent reinforcement to a child in grade school for finishing homework, with the expectation that this reinforcement will prepare the child for a lifetime of responsibly completed assignments, and carers of patients in the early stages of eating disorder treatment can do the same thing. First, however, it is necessary to lay the foundation that completing meals and tolerating negative emotions, for instance, are desired behaviors, which will be reinforced before patients engage in these behaviors on their own. The eating disorder has its own set of desired behaviors and provides its own reinforcements for them. Carers and others who are implementing treatment rules (such as hospital staff) must create a different set of goals and rewards that are separate from the eating disorder's system.

To learn more about Rec-SPA, it is helpful to thoroughly read FAM Handout 1.27, FAM Handout 1.28, FAM Handout 1.29, FAM Handout 1.30, FAM Handout 1.31, and FAM Handout 1.32 as well as FAM Handout 2.18 and the portions of this manual that describe the administration of these handouts.

Eating Disorder–Protecting Behaviors

At any given time, a patient may use an eating disorder–protecting behavior (such as saying, "Go to hell") to reject recovery-specific positive attention (such as "Nice job finishing the sandwich") from a carer or therapist. In that moment, the patient is being driven to protect the eating disorder by deflecting the Rec-SPA. At the same time, however, there is also a recovering self who is present and who may still be getting reinforced, to some extent. Over time, patients can learn to tolerate the negative emotions that arise when warmth and affirmation are provided for engaging in recovery behaviors. Further, both RIBs and Rec-SPA can be used to help patients learn to control the impulse to engage in an eating disorder–protecting behavior.

In a sense, after the establishment of a context in which eating disorder behaviors are cut off from reinforcement, effectively providing as much Rec-SPA as possible is the overarching aim of behavioral family treatment. But when a patient is driven to protect the eating disorder, providing Rec-SPA is not so linear. The goal is to be like a skilled fighter who attempts to dodge attacks and land a punch; in this case, one dodges the eating disorder–protecting behaviors and lands a reinforcement of recovery behaviors. It is important to always be on the lookout for a dodged reinforcement in the form of an attack, sulking, aloofness, ranting, or shutting down. Once you have managed to become skilled at recognizing dodged reinforcement, the puzzle of sorting out how to regroup and land a reinforcement begins.

For instance, a carer says, "Good job completing your meal," and a patient responds with the eating disorder–protecting behavior of saying, "Because of you, I feel fat now." The skilled carer chooses to actively ignore (not attend to) the eating disorder–protecting behavior. When the eating disorder–protecting response is ignored, it is not provided with social reinforcement. Further, if the patient's verbal barb is not engaged with, the patient is not allowed the space for an emotional outburst that results in behavioral dysregulation. Instead, a carer directs their child toward the next recovery behavior of sitting and watching television after a meal until one hour has passed (that is, supervision preventing bathroom use immediately after a meal). The child gives the carer a nasty look, pauses, and then says, "Fine." After the child engages in the recovery behavior of sitting on the couch, the carer says, "OK. Thanks for sitting with me." The patient then laughs and playfully says, "I really hate you" to the carer. The unflappable carer shrugs and dispassionately says, "I know, I know" while turning on the television and pays no mind to the second verbal barb.

In this example, the carer unequivocally affirms the position that completing the meal is the desired thing to do. The carer not only skillfully dodges reinforcement of the eating disorder–protecting behavior ("Because of you, I feel fat now") with active ignoring but also does not back down from directing the child toward the next recovery behavior of sitting on the couch. Undeterred by the child's first eating disorder–protecting behavior, the carer persists in providing the clear message that sitting on the couch is the desired activity. Although the patient engages in a second eating disorder–protecting behavior by provocatively saying, "I really hate you" to the carer, the patient behaviorally complies. The carer also skillfully avoids reinforcing the eating disorder–protecting behavior while persisting in moving on to the activity of watching television with the patient as a distraction from the patient's using the bathroom.

In the context of engaging in interventions to target the eating disorder, here are some other examples of eating disorder–protecting behaviors:

- Lashing out angrily at the carer: "You are such a bad parent!"

- Knowingly attempting to induce guilt in the therapist: "You are a terrible therapist for making me feel fat."

- Unknowingly inducing guilt, such as simply crying and withdrawing after an intervention

- Focusing only on perseverative eating disorder–related topics rather than moving forward (for example, after quickly mentioning feeling proud for finishing a meal, changing the subject to focus on obsessive thoughts such as *I'm fat now*)

- Changing the subject or being evasive when reinforcement is provided

- Distracting when being provided with feedback or reinforcement (for example, looking at one's phone while verbal reinforcement is being provided)

- Ignoring the carer or therapist

Managing Behaviors in Session

During family therapy sessions, patients will engage in eating disorder behaviors, and carers will engage in RABs. Although the IMT family handouts describe much about how maladaptive child and carer behaviors should be addressed at home, a brief discussion is warranted here about the nuances of what may arise in session. In addition to being able to teach about skills, a behavior therapist must be able to demonstrate them. Being able to demonstrate these skills in the moment, as both eating disorder behaviors and RABs arise, requires both agility and the ability to integrate the concepts covered in this section of the manual. It also takes practice.

To illustrate how this balancing act may play out, let us consider the example of a patient named Sally who is hiding potato chips in her pockets during the family's third in-session snack. During this session, to help model adaptive behavior for both the patient and the two carers, the therapist decides to eat some potato chips with the family. While eating the chips, the therapist notices Sally putting chips in her pockets, but the carers do not. The therapist decides to model a directive for the carers: "Sally, please empty your pockets." The therapist also delivers a prompt: "Since some food was hidden, how will it be made up for?" When one of the carers then directs their child to take more chips from the bag to make up for the hidden chips, the therapist gives the carer who picked up on the prompt a reinforcing nod of approval. The other carer then says, "Thanks for eating more chips from the bag, Sally." After the family meal, a therapist gives each carer verbal and written feedback on how they did eating in session, in terms of RABs, RIBs, and Rec-SPA. Progress that has been made over time is discussed. Throughout the session, in short, a behavioral family therapist attempts to foster growth by balancing the use of behavioral techniques directly with the patient and with the carers.

In this example, the therapist models the behavior of eating for the patient but also emphasizes for the carers how important it is for them to do the same thing with their child. Instead of letting a RAB go by, the therapist models the RIB of directing the child to display the hidden food in her pockets. Further, instead of letting the eating disorder win by allowing the amount of hidden food to go uneaten simply because it was in the child's pocket, the therapist prompts the carers to engage in the RIB of ensuring that the patient eats an equivalent amount of food. Because one carer gives the child a directive to eat chips from the bag, to make up for the food that was hidden, the therapist provides that carer with the nonverbal reinforcement of a nod for providing the RIB of giving an appropriate directive. The other carer then provides Rec-SPA to the patient for complying with the directive of eating more chips after having hidden food. This is to be reinforced by the therapist as well. Verbal and written feedback are then provided to the carers about how they performed. In this example, modeling, reinforcement, and providing feedback are integrated throughout the snack as well as afterward, in a feedback meeting. In behavioral family therapy, a variety of behavioral strategies must be employed throughout a given session in order to shape adaptive behavior on the part of both the patient and the carers.

Conducting Behavioral Family Therapy with IMT

Now that core IMT concepts have been covered, this section of the manual focuses on the structure of IMT family therapy (that is, the use of IMT family materials to administer behavioral family therapy).

IMT Family Therapy: Stages and Phases

Stage 1

Patients start treatment in stage 1 with self-eclipsing eating disorders (SEEDs) and with carers whose authority has been undermined by the eating disorder. The overarching stage 1 goal is to get the patient out of immediate danger. In service of this larger goal, the aim is to help carers in the endeavor of decreasing RABs, increasing RIBs, and providing Rec-SPA. In short, the carers assume a position of benevolent authority in stage 1, prohibiting eating disorder behaviors from being reinforced and actively providing reinforcement for recovery.

Stage 2

Once the patient's behaviors no longer require the same degree of external reinforcement, that reinforcement is slowly withdrawn in stage 2. Through self-initiated engagement in recovery behaviors, the patient becomes able to earn freedom as rules are systematically and intentionally decreased. In other words, stage 2 is characterized mainly by a reduction in carers' involvement and by an increase in the patient's self-directed recovery. Before the responsibility of recovery is totally handed over to the patient, however, it is imperative that other goals be addressed.

Whereas stage 1 family therapy has the singular goal of removing the patient from immediate danger, stage 2 has four more goals, which are more nuanced:

1. Incrementally giving the appropriate type and amount of responsibility for recovery back to the patient by working with carers

2. Using graduated exposure to decrease the patient's anxiety about specific types of food

3. Repairing the fractured relationship between patient and carers

4. Increasing the patient's and family's awareness of future treatment goals

Stage 2, Phase 1: Handing Responsibility for Recovery Back to the Patient

In phase 1 of stage 2, we talk about *earned freedoms* because the patient who is given increased responsibility for recovery is provided with the opportunity to be in a direct fight with the eating disorder and to earn freedom from it. (As this wording suggests, the freedom that is earned is earned from the eating disorder, not from the treatment rules.) These earned freedoms, or recovery responsibilities, are given to the patient over time, depending on the patient's readiness in treatment. Earned freedoms can be responsibilities such as choosing a snack or preparing lunch. At the beginning of stage 2, carers often either want to give back too many responsibilities too quickly or are reluctant to give up any control over their child's eating and related activities. Therefore, the more specific primary goal of stage 2 is to work with the carers to incrementally give the appropriate type and amount of responsibility related to the eating disorder back to the patient, over time.

Stage 2, Phase 2: Using Exposure to Decrease Anxiety About Specific Types of Food

In stage 1 IMT family therapy, the emphasis was on eating appropriate amounts of food. Eating scary types of foods was very likely a part of that process, but the patient did not undergo systematic and graduated exposure therapy regarding specific foods (such as candy bars) or food groups (such as carbohydrates). Therefore, patients in stage 2 will almost certainly continue to fear specific foods. To address this issue, session time in stage 2 will eventually be spent on food exposures. There are specific IMT handouts that guide this process, but food exposures are essentially conducted in the same way as any other types of exposures that are used with other disorders (such as obsessive-compulsive disorder, phobias, and so forth). Food exposures conducted in family sessions have the goal of decreasing the patient's fear of specific foods, thus allowing the patient to have less fear when choosing food without carers' supervision during stage 2.

Stage 2, Phase 3: Repairing Relationships

When carers must take complete control of food, supervise every meal and snack, strictly implement rules, and, in general, be extremely involved in the patient's life, the eating disorder can strain the carer–child relationship. In short, although treatment is lifesaving and necessary, the eating disorder can negatively impact the relationship when challenged. Carers can also be left exhausted and burned out by the end of family therapy. Therefore, once the eating disorder is under control, with the patient managing earned freedoms well and food exposures coming to a close, carers are encouraged to actively improve the relationship with their child, if improvement is needed. Discussions about how the eating disorder has strained the relationship and about how things might now be different should be held in session. During these conversations, the therapist should act as arbitrator and facilitate communication by summarizing the main points of what each person is saying and reflecting their emotions. The therapist should also ask each family member about how they are appreciative of everyone's individual efforts in treatment. Along with guiding in-session repair of the relationship, the therapist encourages carers to make efforts to spend quality time with their child at home. Carers should be encouraged to engage in activities with their child (for example, going to see a movie just for fun) that have nothing to do with the eating disorder itself. The stage 2 IMT family therapy handouts help guide the carers through rebuilding the relationship with their child at home.

Stage 2, Phase 4: Increasing Awareness of Hunger and Fullness Cues

At the end of stage 2, patients and carers should be made aware of future treatment goals. Once family therapy is over, the patient will enter into individual therapy. Depending on the needs of a given patient, the goals of individual therapy may include those listed here:

- Eating regularly

- Mindfully noticing hunger and fullness cues

- Eating in accordance with hunger and fullness cues

- Decreasing body avoidance behaviors (BABs)

- Decreasing body investigating behaviors (BIBs) and/or body checking

- Tolerating negative internal experiences regarding one's body

- Increasing overall body acceptance

These various goals are to be discussed with carers present. It is also to be made clear that if there is any indication (from blood work, unintentional weight loss, and so forth) that the eating disorder behaviors have returned or have a strong likelihood of returning, family therapy may need to be reinstituted.

IMT Family Therapy for Different Diagnoses

As noted earlier, IMT family therapy material may be used with patients who have any eating disorder diagnosis, as long as it is severe enough to warrant family intervention. There are, however, distinctions between treatment for anorexia nervosa (AN) and atypical anorexia nervosa (AAN) and treatments for other eating disorders, and these distinctions warrant a brief discussion here.

For patients with AN or AAN, a specific set of treatment rules is provided. Further, for patients with this diagnosis, material should be provided to the carers in relatively the same order as suggested in the session outlines. For patients with other disorders, unlike patients entering treatment with AN or AAN, there are no specific sets of rules that must be implemented. Rules are adapted, as necessary, to each patient. As for the pacing of the material administered, even if a patient has an eating disorder diagnosis other than AN or AAN (such as bulimia nervosa, other specified feeding or eating disorder, or binge eating disorder), it is recommended that the IMT material be administered in the same order in which it is presented. With respect to timing, the target is to set up family interventions where carers take control of food, start implementing rules, and start providing Rec-SPA within about a month's time. After that, the process of refining the decrease in RABs and the increase in RIBs and Rec-SPA can happen at whatever pace is best, but carers should be introduced to the basic core concepts of treatment at the start.

Nevertheless, for bulimia nervosa, other specified feeding or eating disorder, and binge eating disorder, it is often the case that less time is required in each session to discuss family material with carers once the basics of treatment have been introduced. For instance, once the terms of family involvement are negotiated, once rules are being implemented, and once reinforcement is being provided appropriately, the family piece of treatment may be running rather smoothly for patients with bulimia nervosa, other specified feeding or eating disorder, or binge eating disorder. Therefore, intense family involvement in sessions over time may not be needed for patients with these diagnoses. If this is the case, individual time should be spent in session with the patient. Regarding family snacks, multiple family meals and snacks are held over time in this model. If this does not seem necessary for patients who do not have AN or AAN, then multiple in-session family snacks do not need to be held. Conversely, this is extremely rarely the case in the treatment of AN and AAN, and carers should be present for the majority of each session if not for the whole session.

Adapting Rules to Bulimia Nervosa, Other Specified Feeding or Eating Disorder, and Binge Eating Disorder

Because of the self-eclipsing nature of AN and AAN, patients entering treatment with this illness have a specific set of rules that must be implemented to facilitate health restoration (such as weight gain) as well as psychological health. Although, as suggested by LeGrange & Lock (2007), family treatment of bulimia nervosa can be, on the whole, much more collaborative in nature than treatment for anorexia nervosa, bulimia nervosa can also present as very self-eclipsing on occasion. If it becomes clear that a patient is not able to manage eating and bathroom responsibilities without support, it is acceptable to adapt the strictness of treatment for anorexia nervosa to bulimia nervosa as well as to any other eating disorder that may present as self-eclipsing and dangerous (that is, other specified feeding or eating disorder and, in rare cases, binge eating disorder). The BOB versions of the IMT family handouts are specifically for these disorders and are intended to be used flexibly.

For example, in FAM Handout 1.9: Ten Treatment Rules for Carers of Children with Eating Disorders (BOB Version), the rules can be as strict as necessary, and they can also be exactly the same as those listed in FAM Handout 1.8: Twelve Treatment Rules for Carers (AN Version). Nevertheless, even though the rules for BOB disorders may end up being the same as the rules for anorexia nervosa, separate handouts should still be used because the AN versions of handouts discuss issues specific to weight restoration.

Adapting Rules to Health-Restored Anorexia Nervosa or Health-Restored Atypical Anorexia Nervosa

Recently after patients with anorexia nervosa or atypical anorexia nervosa have been health-restored (designated RAN)—for instance, at higher levels of care—treatment with family interventions may be required. In these instances, it is most often the case that handouts for the BOB disorders will be most appropriate.

Family Handouts for BOB Disorders

The BOB versions of family handouts have been designed to be used in the context of family therapy alone, or in combination with individual family therapy interventions. Whether a patient receives family therapy or combined family and individual therapy depends on the level of pathology the patient is expressing (see the information on concurrent family and individual therapy in part 1 of this manual).

IMT Family Therapy Measures

In IMT family therapy, there are several versions of measures that warrant discussion here. These measures are meant not only to assess adaptive and maladaptive behaviors of the patient and carer—who report on each other as well as on themselves—but also to serve as a reminder of treatment goals. A more detailed description of the measures is provided here.

MEASURES FOR ANOREXIA NERVOSA

IMT Family Therapy, Intake: Patient Measure (AN/BOB)

IMT Family Therapy, Stage 1: Patient Measure (AN)

IMT Family Therapy, Stage 2: Patient Measure (AN)

IMT Family Therapy, Intake: Carer Measure (AN/BOB)

IMT Family Therapy, Stage 1: Carer Measure (AN)

IMT Family Therapy, Stage 2: Carer Measure (AN)

MEASURES FOR BOB DISORDERS

IMT Family Therapy, Intake: Patient Measure (AN/BOB)

IMT Family Therapy, Stage 1: Patient Measure (BOB)

IMT Family Therapy, Stage 2: Patient Measure (BOB)

IMT Family Therapy, Intake: Carer Measure (AN/BOB)

IMT Family Therapy, Stage 1: Carer Measure (BOB)

IMT Family Therapy, Stage 2: Carer Measure (BOB)

The preceding lists show IMT family therapy measures, consisting of carer and patient versions at stage 1 and stage 2 for AN and BOB disorders. The IMT family therapy intake measures are used for both AN and BOB disorders, and there is both a patient and a carer version of each intake measure. The intake measures are administered during the session prior to session 1 (that is, before the first active treatment session). Sometimes there can be several intake sessions, but the intake measures need to be administered only once.

The IMT intake measures assess both patient and carer reports of the patient's physical symptoms. Not only is it important to get thorough knowledge of the patient's medical history from the physician, it is helpful to get a sense of what medical issues the family is aware of. It is important that the patient and carers have full knowledge of medical symptoms. As the patient's health improves in treatment, it is helpful to have a baseline checklist of medical issues that can be held up for comparison. It can concretely be referred to as evidence of "improved health" after eating.

Readers versed in family-based treatment will recognize that the exclusion of the TABLE skills from the intake measures prevents contamination of the invaluable observational data that can be collected during the first session when the family eats together. In other words, if carers were told beforehand what they should do, there would be no opportunity to observe their actual problematic behaviors, and thus the measures would be tainted.

Both the intake and the weekly measures assess the disordered behavior of the patient as well as the RABs of the carer, as reported by both parties. In other words, the patient reports on their own eating disorder/body image behavior as well as on the carer's RABs. In turn, the carer reports on the patient's eating disorder/body image behavior as well as on their own RABs. Weekly measures, unlike the intake measures, assess RIBs in addition to the implementation of specific skills taught to the carers in treatment.

Because the weekly measures track the implementation of specific skills taught to the carers, the family must learn skills in order to complete the measures. After the required skills have been learned, it is recommended that carers and patients complete an IMT family measure each week. This is a helpful clinical tool and provides information about what priorities there are to discuss in session. Remember that the IMT measures are clinical tools, not exact research measures. Therefore, they are intended to provide patients and carers with clinical information and feedback about performance on each treatment goal. Each item is to be examined individually for clinical utility, not added into a scale. The measures also do not need to be precisely administered at every single session (such as before the skills are learned).

Along with patient-specific IMT treatment targets, the IMT intake measures assess for some carer-specific treatment targets (such as maladaptive strategies that carers may be using to influence their child to eat). Note that carers' adaptive strategies do not appear in the IMT intake measures. Only when the skills (that is, the TABLE skills) have been taught (after the in-session family snack) do they appear in the IMT measures. When completing the assessments, allow for time during intake to address questions about the items.

Lastly, the IMT measures are weekly reminders of the adaptive behaviors that patients as well as carers are meant to be working on in treatment. By rating their adaptive behaviors each week, patients and carers are reminded of treatment goals and expectations. More on administering the IMT family measures is explained in the detailed session outlines.

IMT Bullying Questionnaire   The IMT Bullying Questionnaire (IMT-BQ) comprehensively assesses for ways in which the patient may be the victim or perpetrator of bullying about size, shape, weight, and a number of other issues. It is available at www.imt-ed.com.

Who Is Involved in Care?

In treatment, all members of the family—carers, siblings, grandparents who live in the home, and so forth—are invited and encouraged to attend all sessions. In practice, it is usually challenging to get everyone to session, but efforts to get as many people in as possible should typically be made. This section reviews how a therapist can manage various family members coming to session.

Siblings

When present, the therapist should make an active effort to engage nonparent family members (such as siblings) in discussion. Their input is valuable. A helpful clinical technique for this circumstance is used in family-based treatment; the technique was adapted from the Milan Associates' research on family therapy (Palazzoli, Boscolo, Cecchino, & Prata, 1980) and is called *circular questioning*. This technique is used to ask one person a question about the dynamic between other members of the family. For instance, a therapist can direct the following question to the brother of a patient: "How do you think your parents are managing at home with your sister's eating disorder?" Because objective data is gathered on the IMT measures regarding the patient's report of their parents' behavior as well as parents' report of their child's behavior, less time is generally spent in sessions using IMT material on circular questioning involving the patient and carer as opposed to when other family members (siblings, grandparents, and so forth) are present.

Further, having nonparent family members present in session is helpful because their roles can be clarified. Siblings can have their questions addressed by the therapist, who can also clarify their role in treatment, with all present. Siblings can also be provided with written information on this topic, such as FAM Handout 1.14: The Sibling's Role in Treatment. Providing psychoeducation about the sibling's role in treatment with everyone present can prevent misunderstandings as well as role drift. In this context, the phrase "role drift" refers to the tendency of parentified siblings to take on the role of implementing treatment rules (preparing food, supervising meals, supervising the hour after meals, and so forth). If everyone is aware that a sibling should not, for instance, be put in the role of supervising meals, this accountability can help guard against role drift.

Patients

In the context of family therapy in which it would be optimal if carers had total control over food (as in the treatment of anorexia nervosa), there are occasions when it may be helpful for a therapist to speak one-on-one with a patient. More often than not, however, it has been our experience that this detracts from the main treatment goals of teaching carers to decrease RABs, increase RIBs, and provide Rec-SPA. Carers, patients, and therapists alike have a preconceived notion of what therapy is—namely, a patient and a therapist sitting in a room and collaboratively working toward solving a problem. Therefore, carers, patients, and therapists are all equally likely to think that treatment *should* involve one-on-one time between therapist and patient. Carers may push for it, citing such reasons as "It's important that my child like you." A patient with a SEED might provide a reason, such as "I have something really important to talk to you about," only for the therapist to realize later that this was the eating disorder's way of running out the session clock and effectively blocking interventions. A therapist who has been subjected to intense anger secondary to a patient's eating disorder might cite a reason to cut into family session time, such as "It's important to have rapport with the patient." Although rapport with an individual patient with a self-acknowledged disorder is important, what is more important in this context is saving their life by providing psychoeducation and training to the carers. Patients will express anger, even at therapists. That's part of this job! In plain language, the goal is not to get a patient to like you. In short, these examples from carers, patients, and therapists are all too familiar and reasonable-sounding, but they all detract from the main goal of family therapy, which is to train carers to fight the eating disorder. Therefore, it is important to guard against the trap of spending too much family session time meeting individually with a patient.

The situation is somewhat different, however, in the context of family therapy in which carers do not need to take complete control over food, as in the treatment of a self-acknowledged eating disorder (SAED) without serious medical complications. A therapist should first prioritize psychoeducation of family interventions and discussion of any RABs from the past week as well as how to increase RIBs and Rec-SPA. Once family objectives are met, the remaining session time should be spent working on individual goals.

Carers

In line with the idea that the main objective of family therapy is to train carers to fight against the eating disorder, if carers cannot get their child with the eating disorder to come to session, all is not lost. Unlike in therapy for self-acknowledged disorders, the patient does not necessarily have to be present for meaningful work to take place. Particularly in stage 1 of treatment, the primary objective is to teach carers how to decrease RABs at home, increase RIBs, and provide Rec-SPA. Ideally, the patient would be present for family meals, snacks, and discussions, but it has been our experience that it is not completely necessary to have the patient present for every session. If patients *do* attend sessions with carers, implementing circular questioning can be a way of increasing participation of all involved and gleaning very helpful information.

Other Carers: Multifamily Groups

Although this manual does not go into detail regarding the implementation of multifamily groups, IMT family handouts have been used in multifamily groups designed for carers only. These groups are conducted by allowing carers to support one another, and to share their experiences with implementing treatment, and in other areas. Depending on the particular group administration, these groups have been run either by providing handouts to members in à la carte fashion, with a group leader administering select handouts to group members struggling with specific issues, or by running the group in linear fashion and administering a given planned handout each week.

Dietitians and the Treatment Team

Eating disorder–trained dietitians, working at higher levels of care, are essential members of the treatment team. Our experience of having eating disorder–trained dietitians involved in behavioral family-based treatment is that they are able to provide helpful concrete behavioral plans (such as meal plans) for carers and patients to execute. In an outpatient setting, a dietitian who is eating disorder–savvy may be helpful to include in the treatment team if therapy session time seems to be taken up by meal planning. If a given patient does have a dietitian, ensure that the dietitian is not focused on the exact number of calories eaten, the nutritional breakdown of each food, or having the patient monitor food. The dietitian can, however, help the carer plan meals to ensure weight gain. Typically, a behavior therapist would help plan the specifics of a behavior plan in session. When your behavior plan is around food, however, doing all the math to ensure that the patient is meeting their estimated daily caloric intake goals can be quite time-consuming. Additionally, if the patient has food allergies, diabetes, celiac disease, or some other medical issue that limits their diet, it can be very useful to have an eating disorder–trained dietitian on the treatment team. Often, however, carers come in insisting on using a particular dietitian who is not trained in eating disorders and keeps planning skimpy meals because the patient has a "bond" with that person. This is a RAB and should be pointed out as such. If this RAB does not sharply halt at the start of treatment, work with this particular dietitian should be discontinued.

Using IMT Materials in Family Therapy

This section of the manual describes the process of using behavioral principles and IMT handouts to run family therapy sessions for adolescents who have eating disorders.

Before Reading On, Read the Handouts! Prior to reading on in this manual, it is highly recommended that the therapist read through the IMT family handouts and become familiar with the concepts presented. Because this manual discusses how to employ these handouts in session, it is important to understand their content. Because the handouts are meant to clearly illustrate treatment concepts for both family members and therapists, an explanation of the treatment concepts covered by the handouts is not redundantly provided here. This manual simply describes how a therapist may employ the handouts contextually.

Notes on All Handouts for IMT Family Therapy (Stage 1 and Stage 2)

- The *1* or the *2* at the beginning of a handout number indicates the stage of IMT family therapy in which the handout is used.

- Handouts labeled *FAM* are intended solely for carers.

- Handouts labeled *FAM/PT* are intended for patients as well as for carers.

- Handouts labeled *PT* are specifically for patients and correspond to similar handouts written solely for carers (understandably, early patients in IMT family therapy felt excluded when handouts were given only to carers). Some PT handouts and their FAM counterparts should be administered in different sessions, as described here.

- Some handouts have AN and BOB versions.

- In the material that follows, the notation (+*Patient Version*) or (+*Patient Copy*) indicates that the therapist should give the patient either the PT version of a specific handout or simply another copy of the handout given to carers.

- In the material that follows, the notation (+*School Copy*) indicates that the therapist should give a copy of the handout described to any staff member (such as a teacher, guidance counselor, school psychologist, or nurse) in the patient's school who is involved in meal support.

- In the material that follows, the notation (+*Sibling Copy*) indicates that the therapist should give a copy of the handout described to the patient's sibling(s).

Stage 1 IMT Family Therapy

After administration of the IMT patient and carer intake measures (included in the online Clinician Resources downloadable at www.newharbinger.com/42235), the following handouts are used in stage 1 of IMT family therapy:

FAM Handout 1.1: Family Therapy: Not the Typical Type of Therapy

FAM Handout 1.2: FAQs: Why Family Therapy?

FAM Handout 1.3: Five Roles and Expectations in IMT Family Treatment

FAM Handout 1.4: TABLE Skills

FAM Handout 1.5: ED WINS

FAM Handout 1.6: Self-Eclipsing Eating Disorders

FAM Handout 1.7: Reinforcement-Allowing and Reinforcement-Impeding Behaviors

FAM Handout 1.8: Twelve Treatment Rules for Carers (AN Version)

FAM Handout CM.1: Twelve Treatment Rules for Carers of Children with Anorexia*

FAM Handout 1.9: Ten Treatment Rules for Carers of Children with Eating Disorders (BOB Version)

FAM Handout CM.2: Ten Treatment Rules for Carers of Children with Eating Disorders*

FAM Handout 1.10: Following the Rules

FAM Handout 1.11: Treatment Involvement Plan (AN Version)

FAM Handout 1.12: Treatment Involvement Plan (BOB Version)

FAM Handout 1.13: Ten Treatment Rules For Schools

FAM Handout 1.14: The Sibling's Role in Treatment

FAM Handout 1.15: Ten Reasons Why Your Child Despises Supervised Eating

FAM/PT Handout 1.16: Twelve Eating Disorder and Recovery Behaviors (AN Version)

FAM/PT Handout 1.17: Ten Eating Disorder and Recovery Behaviors (BOB Version)

FAM Handout CM.3: Eating Disorder Behaviors Online*

FAM/PT Handout 1.18: Recovery-Delaying Behaviors

FAM Handout 1.19: Twelve Smart Carer Responses to Tricky Behaviors (AN Version)

FAM Handout 1.20: Ten Smart Carer Responses to Tricky Behaviors (BOB Version)

FAM Handout 1.21: What Foods Are Unhealthy in Treatment? Reexamining Food Rules

FAM Handout 1.22: The Dieting Carer

FAM/PT Handout 1.23: Stop the "Fat" Talk!

FAM Handout 1.24: Separating the Eating Disorder from the Person

FAM Handout 1.25: Presenting a United Front

FAM Handout 1.26: Three Tricky Ways Eating Disorders Disguise Themselves

FAM Handout CM.4: Be a Detective*

FAM Handout 1.27: Giving Recovery-Specific Positive Attention

FAM Handout 1.28: Giving Recovery-Specific Positive Attention (AN Version)

FAM Handout 1.29: Giving Recovery-Specific Positive Attention (BOB Version)

FAM Handout 1.30: Shaping Your Child's Behavior

FAM Handout 1.31: Seven Roadblocks to Giving Recovery-Specific Positive Attention

FAM Handout 1.32: Strict or Soft? When to Do What

FAM Handout 1.33: Are We There Yet?

FAM Handout 1.34: Keep On Trucking! The Importance of Continuing Therapy

PT Handout 1.1: Five Roles and Expectations in IMT Treatment

PT Handout 1.2: Ten Reasons Why You Might Despise Supervised Eating

PT Handout 1.3: Healthy Versus Unhealthy Foods

PT Handout 1.4: Four Roadblocks to Receiving Recovery-Specific Positive Attention

PT Handout 1.5: Are We There Yet?

* Because of their sensitive content, these four handouts are provided by the clinician (see appendix B).

In stage 1, in addition to the designated patient versions of handouts, we recommend that patients be given copies of the following handouts:

- FAM Handout 1.4

- FAM Handout 1.5

- FAM Handout 1.8 (AN Version) or FAM Handout 1.9 (BOB Version)

- FAM/PT Handout 1.16: Twelve Eating Disorder and Recovery Behaviors (AN Version) or FAM/PT Handout 1.17: Ten Eating Disorder and Recovery Behaviors (BOB Version)

- FAM/PT Handout 1.23: Stop the "Fat" Talk!

In stage 1, in addition to FAM Handout 1.13, which is intended specifically for schools, we recommend that the following handouts be given to schools that have staff members (guidance counselors, psychologists, and so forth) who are involved in the supervision of meals:

- FAM Handout 1.4

- FAM Handout 1.5

- FAM Handout 1.15

- FAM Handout 1.16 (AN Version) or FAM Handout 1.17 (BOB Version); both of these handouts include the Food and Behavior Log

- FAM/PT Handout 1.18

- FAM Handout 1.19 (AN Version) or FAM Handout 1.20 (BOB Version)

- FAM Handout CM.4

- FAM Handout 1.27, FAM Handout 1.28 (AN Version), and FAM Handout 1.29 (BOB Version)

Stage 1: Objectives

In real life, administration of the material does not always happen as planned. This manual was created *by* clinicians in the trenches *for* clinicians in the trenches, and it is understood that not every handout will be administered exactly as mapped out here. It is suggested that each clinician carefully read through this section to get a thorough understanding of how this material is meant, in its purest form, to be implemented. Because it is important to understand the context in which each IMT family handout must be administered, sessions in which family material is to be used are described here. Further, it is important to order the handouts in a particular way in treatment. Therefore, unlike the IMT group interventions, which can be administered in à la carte fashion, the administration of IMT family interventions should be linear. The implementation of interventions also depends on the readiness of the carers and the patient as well as on the achievement of goals. For instance, if a patient is not ready to start making their own dinner, the intervention of earned freedoms (gaining back control of food) will not yet occur.

Therefore, it is important for a clinician administering IMT family therapy to adhere to the order of IMT family handouts and implement interventions at appropriate times. It is less important, however, to adhere perfectly to administering every handout as suggested in the description of a specific session. For instance, the specific session (6 or 8) in which FAM Handout 1.27, FAM Handout 1.28, or FAM Handout 1.29 (dealing with recovery-specific positive attention) gets administered is less important than whether the carers have yet to develop a firm grasp of treatment rules. If the carers are still struggling with the core concepts of buying, preparing, serving, and monitoring food and require troubleshooting in session, they will not be ready to progress to learning about Rec-SPA. Therefore, we suggest progressing though the material linearly, as required, but not rigidly marching on with the agenda of the material if the concepts in the previously presented material have not been adequately mastered. It is suggested that therapists use figure 3.3.1, including the implementation of handouts, as a checklist and regard the detailed session guides as examples of how to conduct the sessions in which to meet the objectives listed in the figure.

Objectives for Intake

- ☐ Conduct appropriate medical screening prior to the intake appointment.
- ☐ Administer the IMT family intake measure to carers and patient.
- ☐ Gather adequate information on intake.
- ☐ Educate family about medical complications.
- ☐ Introduce the concept of weekly weigh-ins.
- ☐ Use the Intake Food Log to conduct baseline assessment of meals.
- ☐ Administer the following handouts for homework:
    - ☐ FAM Handout 1.1
    - ☐ FAM Handout 1.2
    - ☐ FAM Handout 1.3

Objectives for Behavioral Assessment and Sharing Initial Feedback

- ☐ Begin to administer the other IMT family measures (and continue to administer them in each session).
- ☐ Begin to weigh the patient; plot the patient's BMI (and continue to do so at each session), and share, if able.
- ☐ Have an in-session family meal (or snack) for assessment purposes and to initiate carer education.
- ☐ Review the following handouts with carers:
    - ☐ FAM Handout 1.4
    - ☐ FAM Handout 1.5
- ☐ Introduce the concept of supporting meals.

Objectives for Psychoeducation and Feedback

- ☐ Review Intake Logs for as long as necessary.
- ☐ Provide psychoeducation about SEEDs.
- ☐ Provide psychoeducation and feedback on RABs.
- ☐ Provide psychoeducation and reinforcement for RIBs.
- ☐ Introduce, as appropriate, the following handouts:
    - ☐ FAM Handout 1.6
    - ☐ FAM Handout 1.7
    - ☐ FAM Handout 1.8
    - ☐ FAM Handout 1.9
    - ☐ FAM Handout 1.10
    - ☐ FAM Handout 1.11
    - ☐ FAM Handout 1.12
    - ☐ FAM Handout 1.13
    - ☐ FAM Handout 1.14
- ☐ Introduce the following handouts:
    - ☐ FAM Handout 1.15
    - ☐ FAM/PT Handout 1.16
    - ☐ FAM/PT Handout 1.17
    - ☐ FAM/PT Handout 1.18
    - ☐ FAM Handout 1.19
    - ☐ FAM Handout 1.20

- ☐ Introduce the Food and Behavior Log (AN or BOB version) (see FAM/PT Handout 1.16 and FAM/PT Handout 1.17)
- ☐ Introduce the stage 1 IMT family measures.
- ☐ Introduce the following handouts:
    - ☐ FAM Handout 1.21
    - ☐ FAM Handout 1.22
    - ☐ FAM/PT Handout 1.23
    - ☐ FAM Handout 1.24
    - ☐ FAM Handout 1.25
- ☐ Introduce the following handouts, if needed:
    - ☐ FAM Handout 1.26
    - ☐ FAM Handout 1.27
- ☐ Ensure that "fat" talk is limited before moving on to Rec-SPA.
- ☐ Ensure that carers' own eating behaviors are in line with showing support for the patient before moving on to Rec-SPA.
- ☐ Use the following handouts to provide further psychoeducation about Rec-SPA:
    - ☐ FAM Handout 1.28
    - ☐ FAM Handout 1.29
    - ☐ FAM Handout 1.30
    - ☐ FAM Handout 1.31
    - ☐ FAM Handout 1.32

Objectives for Shaping Carers' Rec-SPA in Session

- ☐ Conduct an in-session family snack in which feedback is provided about Rec-SPA.
- ☐ If needed, conduct additional in-session family snack(s) with feedback provided about decreasing RABs, increasing RIBs, and providing Rec-SPA.

Objectives for Middle of Stage 1

- ☐ Continue troubleshooting in session.
- ☐ Introduce FAM Handout 1.33, if needed (this handout is for AN and AAN only).

Objectives for Encouragement Regarding the Transition to Stage 2

- ☐ Congratulate each member of the family for the part played.
- ☐ Encourage them to keep working together.
- ☐ Administer IMT family measures to carers and patient and compare to scores on intake.
- ☐ Introduce FAM Handout 1.34.

Figure 3.1.1. Stage 1 Objectives

A given family will present with a variety of strengths as well as obstacles to be overcome. Depending on these factors, treatment will be accelerated or decelerated. The detailed sessions described in this section of the manual represent the most accelerated version of treatment. If everything goes swimmingly, if carers are able to quickly grasp and implement interventions, and if patients comply, then interventions can be administered at the pace presented here. If obstacles are presented, however, then the pacing of treatment will be impacted. Regardless of the obstacles, there is a given set of linear objectives to be met at each stage of behavioral family therapy using IMT material (see figure 3.3.1).

Stage 1: Detailed Administration Instructions

In what follows, instead of discussing the handouts individually, as we did in parts 1 and 2 of this manual, we provide context by describing the whole session in which a particular handout is administered. After we describe each session, we list the objectives that the session should have met. As necessary, however, we do offer descriptions of how to use certain handouts differently on the basis of the patient's diagnosis.

IMT Intake Assessment

This section discusses the intake session prior to the implementation of active treatment.

Before Intake

It is imperative that carers schedule a physician's appointment prior to attending the intake session to ensure the patient is cleared for treatment at a given level of care (such as outpatient). If a patient is cleared for intake at the level of care in which you offer services, inform carers that they are to bring (or have faxed over) appropriate medical records, a growth chart, and any other relevant medical and psychiatric documentation.

It is advisable to block off a double, back-to-back session for the intake. If this is not possible, separate intake sessions should take place in the same week if a patient carries medical risk but is still appropriate for outpatient care. In other words, if the patient is cleared by a physician for outpatient care but still has significant physical issues to address with treatment (such as being underweight), the intake process should not be prolonged. Active treatment should not be delayed. If the family is having difficulty scheduling two sessions in the same week, explain the necessity of administering the treatment in a timely fashion. Request that families arrive twenty minutes early to the intake to fill out a compilation of written assessments.

Before Intake: Administration of Assessments and IMT Intake Measures

It is very much encouraged that written assessments be used in addition to clinical interviewing. It is particularly important to obtain information on the patient's history of self-harm and suicidality, cognitive impairments, and carers' resources.

We recommend administering the Eating Disorder Examination Questionnaire (EDE-Q; Fairburn & Beglin, 1994) along with other symptom inventories. Again, we recommend Allison and Baskin (2009) as a comprehensive reference for choosing additional assessments.

Regardless of the outside assessments chosen, the patient and carers must complete the IMT intake measures prior to the first family meeting (for instance, have the patient and family come thirty minutes prior to the start of session to complete paperwork and measures). The IMT intake measures were specifically created to provide the therapist with information about how the patient and family are functioning at baseline with respect to some of the behavioral treatment targets in IMT (for example, negotiating about the type of food being served) as well as physical symptoms experienced.

Before Intake: To-Dos

☐ Select and administer reliable and valid assessments.

☐ Administer the IMT intake measures to patient and carers prior to the start of session.

☐ Optional: Plan to administer the IMT Bullying Questionnaire (IMT-BQ), available at www.imt-ed.com, prior to the start of session.

Comprehensive Clinical Interview on Intake

50 minutes

In addition to gathering all the usual data about a patient's development, treatment history, medication history, history of presenting illness, current psychiatric symptoms, family psychiatric history, medical problems, and mental status, there is some particular information that must be gathered during the first clinical interview for the purposes of administering a behavioral family treatment.

With the family together, ask for information about how meals are typically conducted. Get a sense of who buys and prepares the food in the household (for example, the carer, patient, housekeeper, and so forth). Also ask what strategies the carers have already employed in attempting to feed their child (for example, purchasing the patient's old favorite foods, monitoring meals, and so forth) and the effectiveness of those strategies. Assess for the patient's reactions to carers' attempts at getting them to eat.

Comprehensive Clinical Interview: Meeting the Carers

If the patient is able to remain outside the room without risk (that is, if the patient is not a flight risk), it may be productive to meet separately with the carers. When alone with the carers, assess for how afraid they are of their child's oppositional behavior. Do they attempt to avoid the child? Are they fearful that the child will retaliate or self-harm? Has the child made threats to the carers? If they challenge the eating disorder, are they afraid their child will become sicker? Ask carers what their own eating habits are currently like. Does everyone eat together as a family? When was the last time that happened? How did that go? Further, assess the degree to which the carers perceive that the child can recover with their support. Are they hopeless about recovery? Do they have a laissez-faire attitude about recovery and assume it is a phase the child will naturally grow out of? It is also helpful to get an idea about their attitudes toward the eating disorder and their child. Are they resentful, passive, or angry about any perceived obstinacy regarding the patient "not wanting" to recover? It is also important to get a sense of who or what is viewed as the cause of the eating disorder. Do they blame themselves?

It is also going to be imperative to get a sense of the carers' current ability to be able to implement the treatment. Do they have resources? Can they take time off from work? Is there a stay-at-home carer? Is there a housekeeper or extended family member (such as a grandparent) who can help with meal preparation? Can the carers put the child's needs before their own? How willing are the carers to give up parts of their current lifestyle to implement treatment? How able are carers to implement treatment? Are there any other siblings or family members with special needs or serious medical issues?

In addition to determining level of care and a working diagnosis, in behavioral family-based treatment, an assessment of whether carer involvement is feasible should be made at intake. If carer involvement is not feasible, it may influence the determination as to whether the patient is appropriate for an outpatient level of care. In other words, a patient may have a SEED requiring outside help and may also be in a situation in which family cannot feasibly support the patient in treatment. Even if this patient were medically cleared for outpatient care, without a feasible way to involve the family, the disorder may not remit without outside help. Therefore, referral to a higher level of care may be appropriate. Again, for guidance regarding whether a given patient's carers can feasibly be involved in care, consultation with the specialist community at the Academy for Eating Disorders (AED) is recommended.

Comprehensive Clinical Interview: Meeting the Patient

Next, meet with the patient alone. As in every other type of clinical assessment, it is important to inquire about suicidal and homicidal ideation, plans, and attempts as well as about alcohol and substance use, sexual history, and risky behavior. Beyond this, if a therapist is able to productively communicate with the patient, it may be helpful to determine what they are hoping to get out of therapy, if they believe they have an eating disorder, how much they are able to articulate wanting to recover, what they currently value (such as family, thinness, creativity, and so forth), and what has gotten worse in their lives since the eating disorder started.

Comprehensive Clinical Interview: Reconvening

After meeting with the patient individually, the therapist should reconvene with all family members present and gauge everyone's individual knowledge about the dangerous nature of eating disorders. Are the carers aware of medical complications? What is the extent of the patient's denial of the eating disorder and medical risks? What is the extent of the carers' denial of the eating disorder and medical risks? From here, move into a psychoeducational discussion of the medical complications.

Explaining the Dangers of Eating Disorders

15 minutes

Regardless of the eating disorder the patient has, if it is serious enough to require behavioral family treatment, the dangers of the specific disorder must be directly explained to the carer. This must not be sugarcoated or put lightly to protect the feelings of the carer. The exact and dangerous nature of the disorder must be made clear to the carer. It is the duty of the therapist to warn the carer of exactly how much danger their child is in.

Although the reality of the disorder is quite disconcerting, therapists will only be doing the patient a disservice by shielding the carers from terribly important information. Initially, carers may be less committed to treatment because they are not fully aware of the consequences of this illness. As an educated professional, the therapist must impart critical information about the risks of anorexia nervosa during the very first meeting with the family. Further, the aim of the therapist is to appropriately raise carers' anxiety, for the purpose of mobilizing them to act.

Although it is beyond the scope of this manual to discuss the medical risks, we highly recommend reading chapter 16 in the second edition of *The Oxford Handbook of Eating Disorders* (Agras, 2010), to familiarize yourself with the medical complications of anorexia nervosa and refeeding syndrome, as well as the medical guide by the Academy for Eating Disorders (available at www.aedweb.org).

Explaining the Dangers of Anorexia Nervosa and Atypical Anorexia Nervosa

Anorexia nervosa and atypical anorexia nervosa are lethal mental illnesses. Prior to the start of treatment, a physician must assess malnourished patients for their risk of refeeding syndrome, which could be fatal. Very simply explained, when the body has been starved for a period of time as short as four to five days, and food is subsequently introduced into the system, the body can suddenly "go into shock," causing serious medical complications or death. Therefore, to ensure that the patient neither remains malnourished nor gains weight too quickly, both of which can be dangerous, the carer must rely on the judgment of medical professionals to make a decision about the appropriate level of care prior to the start of treatment.

Given the risks involved in anorexia nervosa and atypical anorexia nervosa, a therapist must be up front with carers about the potential medical consequences, including death. With the knowledge of medical consequences, carers may be more inclined to commit themselves to playing an active role in treatment. Further, in an outpatient setting, carers must take the patient to required medical appointments as often as necessary to assess for signs of medical risk, monitor vital signs, obtain lab work, set weight goals, and so forth. Note that if the carers do not take their child to the doctor as often as necessary, they will be thwarting the treatment and potentially putting their child's life at risk. Explain that, in view of the serious nature of this illness, it is imperative that medical monitoring be a part of the treatment plan and that treatment cannot proceed without this component. Especially as a patient starts to gain weight, they may look relatively healthier, but the patient may be purging, taking dangerous substances to make themselves sick, have abnormal lab work or cardiac issues, or simply have a build that is deceptively healthy-looking.

Explaining the Dangers of BOB Disorders

Eating disorders, including bulimia nervosa and other specified feeding or eating disorder, are among the mental illnesses with the highest mortality rates. Discuss the medical complications associated with purging (for example, the potential for esophageal tear and rupture, serious electrolyte imbalances, ulcers) and laxative use (for example, prolapsed rectum) as well as the risk of infertility. Do not withhold information about the dangers of these disorders for fear of "worrying" the carers. They have a right to know about the dangers of these illnesses. Carers' raised anxiety is very often a necessary component of treatment. Without this anxiety, they may not be galvanized to support the patient in family therapy. Additionally, it may be helpful to cite all the psychological impairments that come with BOB disorders, such as social withdrawal over time, decreased ability to focus on what is valued, and so forth.

Taking an Empathetic Stance

While providing information about the dangers of the eating disorder to the family, it is important to maintain an empathetic stance. Reflect to the family that this information is upsetting and that feelings of anxiety and sadness are expected at this stage. Let them know that you will help them move through treatment.

Never Making Assumptions

No one can say that someone is not medically at risk for a serious event or death just because they don't look "really sick." Never assume, on the basis of looks or self-reports alone, that a patient with a diagnosable eating disorder is physically healthy. Studies are starting to show that atypical anorexia nervosa, for instance, has significant related morbidity and mortality (Moskowitz & Weiselberg, 2017). The patient must get ongoing reports from a physician to confirm that they are receiving the appropriate level of care.

Including Physicians in the Treatment Team

If you have not worked with a patient's physician before, provide carers with a copy of the AED's *Eating Disorders: A Guide to Medical Care* to give to the pediatrician, or send it directly to the physician. It is available for free on their website (www.aedweb.org) in ten languages to date. If the patient's physician is uncomfortable with medical monitoring, suggest that they look for an adolescent medicine physician, if available. It has been our experience that physicians specializing in adolescent medicine are more likely to have familiarity with the treatment of eating disorders.

Lack of education about the medical aspects of eating disorders may be a barrier that keeps mental health professionals from feeling comfortable treating eating disorders. The good news is that the therapist is not expected to have the entire skill set of a multidisciplinary team. The therapist must work with the patient's physician, who does the job of monitoring the patient's physical health. A big part of being an eating disorder therapist is learning to rely on others on the multidisciplinary team to guide treatment. Remember, your job is to stick to what you know—the psychological and behavioral components.

Working closely with physicians has many benefits for the therapist. Rather than having to discern whether your patient is trying to "trick the scale," it is the physician's responsibility to uncover this. Physicians should be weighing patients as often as necessary in hospital gowns to ensure that the patients are not hiding any items on their body to surreptitiously increase their weight. Further, physicians can test urine for water loading (drinking a lot of fluid to artificially inflate weight) and monitor lab work for signs that the patient may be at medical risk (such as for hypophosphatemia). As a therapist, you are not equipped to monitor the medical issues that arise from eating disorder symptoms. Further, physicians can provide safe recommendations to carers regarding daily caloric intake and the extent of exercise limits. Malnourished patients may not engage in physical activity until weight restoration is achieved, because exercise is counterproductive to weight gain and potentially dangerous.

Introducing Weigh-ins and Logs

10 minutes

Along with attending regular medical appointments, it is important to adhere to several other necessary treatment components. It is imperative that weekly weights are monitored. If a patient has not seen their physician in the past week, the therapist should weigh the patient, bearing in mind that different scales may yield slightly different weights. If the patient would rather not know their weight, it is acceptable to have blind weigh-ins (where the patient is weighed backwards and then the scale is cleared) at the beginning of treatment, either at physician appointments or with you. The patient will be undergoing many types of exposures throughout the treatment as carers decrease RABs, increase RIBs, and even provide Rec-SPA. Therefore, if the exposure of telling a patient their weight is added, it may detract from more pressing exposures, such as completing meals. Once a patient is ready and able to hear their weekly weights without this usurping important family therapy session time or detracting from achieving goals related to eating, this is implemented. When a patient is ready, the patient should be told their weight, and it should be plotted and shown to the patient (as is done in extended cognitive behavioral therapy). It is not necessary to take the patient's weight during the intake assessment. Ensure, however, that you obtain weight and a growth chart from the patient's physician prior to starting the first treatment session.

In addition to weigh-ins, the family will be introduced to the idea of monitoring food intake with logs and reviewing this in sessions. Review the Intake Food Logs. Because carers are not yet monitoring all meals, they are not aware of everything the patient is eating. Explain that a good-faith effort should be made to record what their child eats (for example, "a small salad with vinegar"), without including calories, for each meal and that the log is not expected to be filled out perfectly. Explain that some data about what their child is eating as well as what meals are currently being eaten together is the type of information that is useful to you. Encourage carers to follow the specific instructions in the log. Explain that logs will be very helpful as treatment goes on as well as during the intake phase.

Homework Assignment

15 minutes

Instruct the carers to complete, as homework, the intake logs for carers. Inform them that caloric content is not to be recorded. Instead, explain that the general volume of food as well as the type of food (such as a cup of milk) are to be written in the log. Additionally, introduce carers to the idea that a core component of IMT is the administration of handouts. Explain that the handouts are not *recommended* but *required* reading. Also explain that although there will be a lot of handouts given at the beginning of treatment, the assigned reading tapers off over the first couple of months. Inform the carers that the handouts were created to make the treatment process run more smoothly and so that they can reference information discussed in session. To begin, when IMT is administered as suggested, carers should be given FAM Handout 1.1, FAM Handout 1.2, and FAM Handout 1.3.

Telling Carers to Bring a Family Meal

As is done in family-based therapy, before the end of session ask carers to bring all immediate family members (that is, siblings and others residing in the home) and a family meal to the next session for all family members to consume. Instruct the carers to bring everything that they will need (such as food, beverages, cups, plates, and utensils) to feed the entire family this meal. They should not bring food for the therapist. Although modeling behavior at later sessions will be important, during the first family meal, the therapist will be observing and then providing feedback.

If carers inquire as to why this is required, explain that although the ways in which they eat together are common knowledge for them, each family is different. You also might want to elaborate that the information that you can learn from actually watching them eat rather than just hearing their accounts will be valuable to you and the treatment.

Under no circumstances should a therapist provide a food plan or concrete suggestions about what or how much food the carers should bring to the first family meal. A major goal of the first family meal is assessment; therefore, valuable information will be missed if the therapist is overly directive. Further, a second major goal is to create an opportunity for real-time intervention to counteract unhelpful support strategies. With no prior knowledge of how meal support should be conducted, the carers are likely to engage in unhelpful habits, as defined in IMT by FAM Handout 1.5. After the observation period of the meal is over, each time carers engage in the ED WINS habits or violate a treatment rule, it becomes an opportunity to coach carers in session. The therapist also has the opportunity to model effective strategies for meal support.

Lastly, it may be helpful to inform carers that the session next week may also be an extended one. Because family meals often take up a fair bit of time, as does providing feedback, often leaving about ninety minutes for this session is practical.

Carers: To-Dos

- ☐ Set up recurring medical appointments (such as once per week or twice per month).

- ☐ Bring the AED's *Eating Disorders: A Guide to Medical Care* to the next appointment (or the therapist can send it to the physician).

- ☐ Complete the Intake Food Log for homework.

- ☐ Read FAM Handout 1.1, FAM Handout 1.2, and FAM Handout 1.3.

- ☐ Carers are to bring a family meal to the first IMT family therapy session.

- ☐ Plan for the next session to be extended (ninety minutes).

Handout Suggestions

- Because IMT involves numerous handouts, you may provide (or suggest that the family keep) binders or folders to organize the material.

- Suggest that carers make time after each session to read the assigned homework handouts.

- Carers can be given copies of the stage 1 IMT family measures in the future to keep with the handouts to track their progress in treatment.

Stage 1, Intake Session: To-Dos

90 minutes, split into two intake sessions conducted in the same week

- ☐ Administer a selection of assessments, IMT intake measures, and so forth.
- ☐ Conduct a comprehensive clinical interview.
  - ☐ Assess for all standard information:
    - ☐ History of presenting illness
    - ☐ Comorbid psychiatric diagnoses
    - ☐ Treatment and medication history
    - ☐ Patient's school and social functioning
    - ☐ Patient's medical history
    - ☐ Patient's developmental milestones
    - ☐ Traumatic events, abuse history, and loss
    - ☐ Suicidal and homicidal ideation
    - ☐ Perceptual disturbances
    - ☐ Family psychiatric history
    - ☐ Family medical history
  - ☐ Assess for potential treatment rule-outs:
    - ☐ Active suicidality or recent self-harm
    - ☐ Active substance use
    - ☐ Cognitive impairments
    - ☐ Carers' inability to put patient's health needs first
  - ☐ With the patient, assess for the self-eclipsing nature of the disorder:
    - ☐ The extent to which thinness is valued and other values are cited
    - ☐ How much the patient is able to report wanting to recover
    - ☐ Degree to which patient believes they have an eating disorder and awareness of ramifications
  - ☐ With the carers, regarding IMT family therapy specifically, assess for the following items:
    - ☐ Who buys and prepares food
    - ☐ Patient's daily food intake
    - ☐ Patient's safe/preferred foods as well as patient's feared/avoided foods
    - ☐ Strategies the carers have tried
    - ☐ Effectiveness of carers' current strategies
    - ☐ Patient's reaction to carers' attempts to control food
    - ☐ Degree to which carers are afraid of the patient's oppositional behavior

- ☐ If and how the carers avoid the patient
- ☐ The specific fears carers have about challenging the patient
- ☐ Specific threats patient has made to the carers
- ☐ Opinions about the cause of the eating disorder
- ☐ Functional impacts of the eating disorder
- ☐ Degree of perceived dangerousness of the eating disorder and knowledge of medical issues

☐ Maintain a direct and empathetic stance while providing education about medical complications.

- ☐ Inform the family about the medical risks of eating disorders and the risk for AN refeeding syndrome.
- ☐ Discuss that the physician will help guide decisions around the appropriate level of care for the patient.
- ☐ The physician will provide guidance on the patient's target weight and activity restriction.

☐ Inform the family about the need for frequent visits to the physician.

☐ Provide a copy of the AED's *Eating Disorders: A Guide to Medical Care* to give to the primary care doctor.

☐ Introduce the concept of weekly weigh-ins.

☐ Assign homework:

- ☐ Schedule a physician appointment ASAP if they have not done so already.
- ☐ Carers complete Intake Food Log.
- ☐ Carers read FAM Handout 1.1, FAM Handout 1.2, and FAM Handout 1.3 (the patient version of the latter handout, PT Handout 1.1, is given after session 1).
- ☐ Bring all immediate family members and a meal to the first session.

Stage 1, Session 1: First Family Meal

For this first therapy session, it is highly recommended to allot ninety minutes. As treatment progresses, however, family sessions should be approximately sixty minutes long. Assuming the patient has seen their physician, schedule this session as soon after completing the intake as possible. If the patient has not seen their physician, it is strongly recommended that this session be postponed until after they have done so, to be sure that they are at the appropriate level of care.

Assessment and Tracking

15 minutes

By contrast with most other treatment sessions, prior to the first session, the IMT family measures should not be administered. Because the family has not yet learned all the skills, treatment rules, and eating disorder and recovery behaviors inquired about in the IMT measures, it is not appropriate to administer them until these skill domains are addressed in session. With the exception of the IMT family measures, administer any other measures that are appropriate prior to session.

Once these are administered, the session should begin by taking a weight and briefly reviewing the Intake Food Log. Therapists should also check to ensure that carers have read the assigned handouts. For carer behaviors that were in line with treatment (completing logs, doing the reading, and so forth), verbal reinforcement should be provided.

Weight Tracking

If the patient has not been weighed by their physician that week, weigh the patient in session. Note that because the physician weighs the patient in a gown, the patient is likely to weigh several pounds more on your scale. Regardless of who obtains the weight, calculate the patient's body mass index (BMI) weekly. There are many free BMI calculators available online and in smartphone app format. Ideally, you should plot the patient's BMI using spreadsheet software. Also note that anorexia nervosa can stunt growth, and that the physician may be using the patient's projected height rather than their current height to calculate an accurate BMI. Therefore, ask the patient's physician what height is appropriate to use in the BMI calculation.

If you have weighed the patient, share the weight with the carers. Again, if the patient does not feel ready to know their weight at the beginning of treatment, take blind weights, or weigh the patient without disclosing their weight to the patient. Either way, the carers must be informed of the weight. Blind weighing is not necessarily recommended; however, it may be temporarily indicated if the patient has a strong aversion to knowing their weight or a history of falsely altering measurements (for example, by water loading or wearing weights).

Homework Review: Intake Logs and Reading

Prior to the in-session family meal, look over the Intake Food Log the carers have completed. Provide positive verbal reinforcement for the completion of the log. At this point in session, the therapist is not to provide feedback on what the patient has eaten. Instead, the therapist is to gather data. If the carers did not complete the Intake Food Log, ask carers, "What got in the way?" Attempt to problem solve in session. Also check for completion of reading FAM Handout 1.1, FAM Handout 1.2, and FAM Handout 1.3. Ask carers if they have any questions. If the carers have read the handouts, be sure to provide positive verbal feedback.

Eating in Session

50 minutes

After weights are discussed and the homework is reviewed, it is time to have the family meal. Before beginning, the therapist should ensure that FAM Handout 1.4 and FAM Handout 1.5 are printed out. Next, it is time for the family to begin eating.

Eating in Session: Carer Behavior During the Meal

The behavior therapist's main objective during the first half of the family meal is to watch the carers' adaptive and maladaptive implementation of strategies aimed at increasing the food intake of their child. Although the carers have not yet been provided with psychoeducation about what adaptive strategies may be, they still may be employed. Before the session, make a copy of the clinician's checklists for the TABLE skills and the ED WINS habits (see appendix F). If the carers happen to engage in any of the adaptive TABLE skills, use the checklist to make a tally mark in the box next to those skills. Conversely, if the carers engage in any of the ED WINS habits, use the checklist to make a tally mark in the box next to those behaviors. If there are two carers present, it is sometimes helpful to draw a lengthwise dividing line down the middle of the tally box and write each carer's initials at the top of the column thus created so that the behavior of each carer can be tracked individually.

Eating in Session: Patient Behavior During the Meal

The patient may engage in many behaviors, like taking microbites of food, restricting, attempting to hide the food, breaking the food up to create crumbs they do not intend to eat, spitting the food out, and so forth. During the first half of the meal, do not intervene. Observe the patient's behavior while taking note of the carers' behavior. About halfway through the process of quietly assessing each family member's behavior, simply start intervening and modeling adaptive support behavior for the carer. Of course, use as many of the TABLE skills to model support as is appropriate, and refrain from engaging in any of the ED WINS habits.

Providing Feedback and Psychoeducation

15 minutes

Here, we cover the provision of recovery-specific positive attention (Rec-SPA, pronounced "RECK-spa") to the patient and feedback to the family.

Providing Recovery-Specific Positive Attention to the Patient

After the family meal is over, provide a form of Rec-SPA to the patient. As described in FAM Handout 1.27, FAM Handout 1.28 (AN Version), and FAM Handout 1.29 (BOB Version), Rec-SPA is similar in nature to labeled praise, but praise is not necessarily recommended, particularly at the start of treatment. In practice, people with SEEDs seem to find praise particularly aversive this early in treatment. Therefore, rather than praise for behavior, some sort of positive attention should be given. For instance, a behavioral family therapist could provide an empathetic statement after the first family meal, followed by an affirmation and perhaps even gratitude. For instance, a therapist might say to a patient, "I can see how challenging this was for you. Because eating this meal with your family here was really important to do, thank you for pushing yourself and eating dinner in my uncomfortable office." In this example, the therapist compassionately acknowledges the patient's discomfort while inherently displaying the sentiment that emotional challenges are to be met rather than avoided, because it is important. The therapist also shows respect for the patient by expressing gratitude. Even more specifically, the therapist is subtly showing respect for the patient's ability to make adaptive choices by "deciding" to eat dinner in an uncomfortable office. Yes, the patient was likely told that they had to be there. Yet not all patients make it through the door. This patient did. That deserves recognition.

But if a patient is displaying oppositional behaviors during the family meal, perhaps showing warmth nonverbally (such as with a smile after the patient takes an appropriately sized bite) would be more appropriate. Remember that it is important to modulate your level of engagement with the patient, depending on their readiness for Rec-SPA. Because Rec-SPA is experienced as aversive (it prompts confusion and negative emotion), think of administering Rec-SPA almost as an additional exposure—it is helpful to the patient's recovery, but there is only so much that a person can take at once. Of course, Rec-SPA is more than just exposure. It is meant to reinforce the idea that eating is healthy and to shape the child's behavior away from eating disorder behavior and toward recovery behavior.

Providing Feedback

Provide behavior-specific feedback to the family from FAM Handout 1.4 and FAM Handout 1.5. By contrast with later discussions about reinforcement specifically, reviewing the TABLE skills and the ED WINS habits in the first session should be done with the patient present. Solicit the carers' thoughts about how they did with respect to using TABLE skills and engaging in ED WINS habits. Take a warm and encouraging stance when reviewing the TABLE skills. When reviewing the ED WINS habits, it is important to maintain a lack of judgment. You can empathize with the carers and reflect any anxiety or frustration they might be feeling. Normalize the experience of negative emotions during refeeding. At the same time, you must acknowledge that while it is completely understandable for them to be scared for their child's welfare and frustrated, they must also work to adaptively change their behavior in order to productively help their child. Lastly, having the patient present for this will also send the message to the patient that you want their carers to be fair to them.

Interestingly, reviewing FAM Handout 1.4 and FAM Handout 1.5 with the carers may be the patient's first positive experience with the therapist. When reviewing FAM Handout 1.4 and FAM Handout 1.5, the therapist becomes the buffer between the child and any aversive maladaptive strategies the carers may be engaging in. The therapist's good intentions can become clearer when initially instructing the carers to decrease maladaptive strategies and increase adaptive ones. Particularly because the treatment rules have not yet been introduced, the patient may get their first glimpse into the potential benefits of treatment without having intense anxiety to accompany this positive assessment. From this practice model, we view this first opportunity for the patient to view a benefit of treatment as important. We also view the building of a relationship between the patient and the therapist over time as very important. As the child sees the therapist as a positive figure or even as a role model, the dissonance created with the eating disorder is intensified. A dilemma arises within the patient: "The eating disorder is saying that weight gain is bad, but my therapist whom I trust wants to help me gain weight. Who is right?" A strong patient–therapist bond of this nature may facilitate the undermining of eating disorder beliefs.

What's Next?

After you are done reviewing FAM Handout 1.4 and FAM Handout 1.5, inform the carers that they will have several weeks to practice honing the TABLE skills and minimizing the ED WINS habits at home before a family snack will be conducted in a later session.

Encourage carers to eat as many meals and snacks as is feasible with their child during the coming week. For these meals and snacks, carers should try serving foods they judge to be appropriate. During those meals, they are to use the TABLE skills as often as possible and avoid using the ED WINS habits. Keep this short, sweet, and relatively vague (in comparison to providing lengthy, detailed, and concrete treatment rules at this stage). Carers should be reminded that this is only the first week of treatment and that they are not expected to do anything perfectly. In fact, it is expected that they will simply try this out during the week specifically so there is something to work with next session. The ball just needs to get rolling.

It is not advisable to administer either FAM Handout 1.8 (AN Version) or FAM Handout 1.9 (BOB Version), nor is it advisable to administer FAM Handout 1.10 at this point. If these handouts are administered too early in treatment, and without time to provide proper context (that is, the information that the treatment rules represent ideals), then carers may feel overwhelmed. Patients also are not yet ready to hear about treatment rules. It is often the case that both carers and patients need to be introduced to the idea of treatment rules over time. Further, after the first in-session meal, carers are often tired and have already learned quite a bit about the TABLE skills and the ED WINS habits. Therefore, it is typically advisable to wait until the following session to discuss the treatment rules.

Homework Assignment

5 minutes

At the end of (a long) session 1, carers are asked to continue completing the Intake Food Log for next session. They are also asked to review FAM Handout 1.4 and FAM Handout 1.5. The therapist should provide the carers with an extra copy of these handouts so the family can post them near the table where they eat meals together. The carers are also to use the TABLE skills during meals at home. Encourage carers to eat as many meals as they currently think is feasible with their child during the coming week. Lastly, the patient is provided with a copy of PT Handout 1.1, on roles in treatment, to read for homework.

Stage 1, Session 1: To-Dos

☐   Allot time for an extended session (90 minutes).

- ☐ Assess and plot BMI.
- ☐ Review the Intake Food Log and provide feedback.
- ☐ Conduct the family meal.
- ☐ Provide feedback and review FAM Handout 1.4 and FAM Handout 1.5.
- ☐ Assign homework:
  - ☐ Carers continue completing the Intake Food Log until next week.
  - ☐ Carers are to review FAM Handout 1.4 and FAM Handout 1.5.
  - ☐ Carers are to post FAM Handout 1.4 and FAM Handout 1.5 near where the family eats meals together.
  - ☐ Carers are to eat as many meals as is feasible with their child and use the TABLE skills.
  - ☐ Patient reads PT Handout 1.1 on roles in treatment.

Stage 1, Session 2: Psychoeducation About Supervised Eating

Here, unlike in the first active treatment session, a single session of sixty minutes is sufficient. In this session (or portion of treatment, since the first part of this session continues the work of the intake session), carers are introduced to core treatment concepts and rules.

Assessment, Tracking, and Troubleshooting

15 minutes

The IMT family measures should not yet be administered in this session. Other select measures, however, should be administered. In this session, as in all other sessions, weight should be taken, plotted, and reviewed, if appropriate. The Intake Food Log should then be reviewed in session. Because this is the first session carers are attending after (presumably) attempting to monitor food and implement TABLE skills while minimizing ED WINS habits, a thorough review of the Intake Food Log should be conducted. Take note of how many meals and snacks carers were able to supervise, what was consumed, and if it was more than was recorded in the initial Intake Food Log. If there was an increase, point out this difference to carers and provide them with verbal reinforcement. It may also be appropriate in the moment to provide the patient with Rec-SPA. It is also important to discuss what did not go well and to troubleshoot in session. Be sure that this troubleshooting does not take up the entire session. Inform the carers that there is a lot of psychoeducation on the agenda for this session. Some behavioral family therapists find it helpful to set formal agendas in family sessions.

Psychoeducation: Supervised Eating

Duration varies

Here, we discuss a crucial psychoeducation piece of stage 1 that encompasses SEEDs, RIBs, RABs, and rules as well as treatment planning, a description of treatment roles, and information about why patients may resist supervised eating.

SEEDs, RIBs, RABs, Treatment Rules, and Planning

This session should be spent largely on providing psychoeducation to the carers. Because of how extensive this topic is, the material often takes two sessions rather than one to cover. Particularly if carers are still warming up to the idea of having to take control of food away from their child, it may be wise to spend more time describing the nature of eating disorders before getting to treatment rules and planning.

SELF-ECLIPSING EATING DISORDERS

At this stage in treatment, it is important to describe the self-eclipsing nature of a given patient's eating disorder. It will likely be more palatable to describe the self-eclipsing nature of eating disorders verbally. Be sure to cover the topics presented in FAM Handout 1.6. For homework, provide carers with a copy of this handout. It is best not to provide patients with a copy of this handout, because they may find some of the content (meant to illustrate points for carers) triggering.

RIBs AND RABs

For the topic of RIBs and RABs, it is likely best to either ask to speak to the carers alone for a period of time or to very briefly discuss the overall concept in session with the patient present, but without introducing any terminology. If carers are still not on board with playing an active role in supervising meals, it is best to speak to them alone about RIBs and RABs. In general, it is best to avoid teaching patients about reinforcement in treatment. This content is for carers and therapists. If carers are alone in the session, once again, it is helpful to cover the content of these topics verbally and then assign FAM Handout 1.7 for homework.

If the patient is present in this portion of the session for any reason, it suffices to simply say that because the eating disorder is self-eclipsing, carers need to help take the power away from the eating disorder and prevent it from growing stronger. Be sure that in this scenario the carers are given FAM Handout 1.7 for homework and that private time is made in the next session to discuss it.

TREATMENT RULES (+PATIENT COPY: FAM HANDOUT 1.8 [AN VERSION] OR FAM HANDOUT 1.9 [BOB VERSION]) (+SCHOOL VERSION: FAM HANDOUT 1.13)

Hopefully by this stage, carers are on board with playing an active role in treatment, and treatment rules can be discussed. There are two sets of treatment rules, one for AN and the other for BOB disorders. If one of the BOB disorders needs as much monitoring as AN, it is best to use the BOB handouts anyway and simply write out a plan using FAM Handout 1.12 (BOB Version), which is as strict as the rules for AN. Further guidance on how to do this is provided in what follows. FAM Handout 1.8 (AN Version) and FAM Handout 1.11 (AN Version) specifically pertain to weight gain.

- *Giving a disclaimer:* Before administering the treatment rules with the whole family present, it is important to explain that it is not going to be easy to implement them right away, exactly as written. There is typically a scaling-up period in which carers must practice implementing the rules, getting comfortable with them over time, and developing a sense of mastery. The rules can be thought of as a set of ideals for how treatment should be carried out at home. Real life, however, is much messier. Carers should be encouraged to do the best they can implementing the treatment rules each week.

- *Presenting the rules:* After providing the preceding disclaimer, it is helpful to review FAM Handout 1.8 (AN Version) or FAM Handout 1.9 (BOB Version) and FAM Handout 1.10 with the entire family present; the patient, if present, also receives a copy of FAM Handout 1.8 (AN Version) or FAM Handout 1.9 (BOB Version) and FAM Handout 1.10. Answer questions in session as they arise. If carers are seeking more concrete guidance, it may also be helpful to provide them with a copy of FAM Handout CM.1 or FAM Handout CM.2, both of which are found in appendix B. If carers ever have a question about a rule, the extended version of the treatment rules can be consulted. It is not recommended that the extended version be given to everyone, since it can be overwhelming. Provide this only to carers who are particularly willing and able to participate in treatment and who also request further clarification. The extended version can also be a useful reference for the therapist. Encourage the carers to focus on FAM Handout 1.8 (AN Version) or FAM Handout 1.9 (BOB Version) and not get caught up in the details of the extended version of the treatment rules. The extended version exists for reference and to provide extra support, if needed. In short, the extended version is to be administered only when necessary.

- *Giving the patient a copy of the rules:* If the patient is presenting as compliant, if the discussion goes smoothly, and if the patient is receptive, give them a copy of FAM Handout 1.8 (AN Version) or FAM Handout 1.9 (BOB Version) and FAM Handout 1.10. Otherwise, hold off until the patient is ready to receive their copies of these handouts, because the patient's oppositional behaviors may interfere with treatment. For patients who are compliant, providing them with copies of these handouts includes them in the process. The idea here is that it lets the patient know that they are a part of this treatment process and are expected to comply with the rules. Presenting the patient with copies of these handouts may bring forth negative emotions associated with the eating disorder. From a behavioral standpoint, if the patient is compliant, confronting negative emotions about treatment rules at this stage is a healthy and necessary part of treatment. Providing copies of these handouts is also designed to foster a healthy acceptance of the treatment rules. Disempowering the eating disorder and accepting the treatment rules go hand in hand. Lastly, clearly establishing the rules sets the stage for later administration of Rec-SPA for compliance with treatment rules.

WRITING TREATMENT INVOLVEMENT PLANS

Although the patient will need to be present for a discussion of what the treatment rules will be, disruptive behaviors may spring up during implementation conversations that must be navigated. If a patient is likely to engage in recovery-delaying behavior (that is, blocking the therapist from formalizing plans to implement treatment rules in session), it may be helpful to meet with carers alone while discussing the particulars of how the treatment rules will be implemented.

FAM Handout 1.11 (AN Version) and FAM Handout 1.12 (BOB Version) present treatment involvement plan templates. Both handouts enumerate the treatment rules and include prompts that guide the therapist and the family in planning out how each of the treatment rules will be implemented. For instance, carers are to write down exactly who will supervise each meal during the coming week. In short, the object is to concretely plan in session how each of the rules will be executed.

TREATMENT RULES FOR SCHOOLS

Depending on the level of care, encourage carers to give FAM Handout 1.13 to the school, if someone will be supervising meals there. The handout includes a letter addressed to that faculty or staff member along with the treatment rules for schools. Other handouts that can be given to the school, and which include AN and BOB versions of the treatment rules, are listed in the notes on handouts at the beginning of this section of the manual.

THE SIBLING'S ROLE IN TREATMENT (+SIBLING COPY: FAM HANDOUT 1.14)

Prior to the end of session, explain to siblings with all present that their role is not to enforce the treatment rules. It is important that siblings play an age-appropriate role in treatment. Further, we recommend that siblings play a role that is in line with the natural dynamics of the family. For instance, if a patient was close with a sibling prior to the illness, perhaps rekindling a bond through after-meal activities and acting as a confidant would be best. If the siblings were not close or are far apart in age, it is not appropriate to expect that a sibling will take on this type of role. Siblings are also not to be put to work as entertainers or distractors. Clinically, we recommend that if a sibling with a bond to the patient volunteers to help engage the patient during and/or after meals and to be a confidant, they may do so for as long as they would like. It is important for siblings impacted by the eating disorder to have a voice in treatment. Siblings should be encouraged to contribute to family sessions regarding their experience. It is also important to make efforts to safeguard them against being overburdened with responsibility by presenting clear boundaries. Therefore, it is helpful to go over the specifics of FAM Handout 1.14 in session. Additionally, provide both the sibling(s) and the carers with FAM Handout 1.14 to read for homework.

SUPERVISED EATING (+PATIENT VERSION: PT HANDOUT 1.2) (+SCHOOL COPY: FAM HANDOUT 1.15)

The eating disorder's wrath may be at its height after the treatment rules are introduced. Review the list of ten reasons why people and eating disorders despise supervised eating. Typically, it may be helpful to start off by saying something empathetic to the patient. Whether the patient is expressing severe anxiety or anger, having an empathetic stance is important. You might say, "I know that the number one thing that the eating disorder wants to control is food, and that is being taken away from you. I'll bet that is really scary. Let's go over some reasons other people have given for absolutely hating supervised eating. I want you to let me know which of these you feel." Reviewing this list provides the patient an opportunity to organize their confusing emotional reactions to the treatment rules. It also provides education for the carers as to what the patient may be experiencing. It has been our experience that by demystifying the patient's emotional experience in this way, both the patient and the carer are more likely to comply with the treatment rules.

COMING BACK TO FAM HANDOUT 1.15 LATER IN TREATMENT

This handout is helpful to return to throughout the course of treatment when the patient experiences emotion dysregulation. Going through the FAM Handout 1.15 list in session and asking which of the reasons resonates with the patient is helpful in many ways. First, these reasons may help the patient articulate why it is that they do not like the supervised eating process. This will also help the family and therapist understand the reasons. Knowing the reasons the patient reports finding supervised eating aversive is helpful to the treatment of the patient in several ways. In session, when the patient is not immediately faced with eating, they may be more likely to admit how much the eating disorder is actually in play. For instance, the patient might say something like "Supervised eating is annoying and all, but I really just don't want to gain weight." In that case, the carer would be alerted to the fact that the eating disorder is in play during mealtimes when their child claims, for instance, "I just hate supervised eating because you are so annoying!"

Conversely, if a patient says something less oppositional, such as "It's just that I literally feel sick from being stuffed with food," you can validate that experience. As the therapist, you can teach the carer to validate it as well. For instance, you can say something like "I can only imagine how hard it must be to not want to eat at all and have to be stuffed to the gills instead. You've been doing a really good job pushing through this experience and working toward putting your eating disorder behind you." Then you may say to the carers, "Now that you know why it is that your child doesn't like the supervised eating experience, you can remember to appreciate their struggle, which is the A in the TABLE skills." It is important to remember that even if the reason the patient does not like supervised eating is valid, they must still engage in recovery behavior.

Homework Assignment

5 minutes

Carers are asked to continue completing the Intake Food Log and reviewing the handouts provided in session. (Once FAM Handout 1.15 has been reviewed, the stage 1 Food and Behavior Log can be completed). Carers are also charged with implementing the treatment rules as best they can at home. It might be helpful to recommend that carers keep a copy of the treatment rules on their person to prevent them from giving in to the eating disorder.

Remind siblings and carers to read FAM Handout 1.14 for homework. If the patient is open, provide them with PT Handout 1.2. Particularly if the patient is agitated, it may be helpful to hold off on giving them a copy of the treatment rules until they have come to further accept them.

Stage 1, Session 2: To-Dos

☐ Assess and plot BMI.

☐ Review the Intake Food Log and provide feedback.

☐ Verbally reinforce carers for RIBs (without discussing terminology yet).

☐ Introduce the concept of SEEDs.

☐ Introduce RABs and RIBs.

☐ Introduce the treatment rules via FAM Handout 1.8 (AN Version) or FAM Handout 1.9 (BOB Version).

☐ Possibly provide the extended version of the treatment rules, if helpful, via FAM Handout CM.1 or FAM Handout CM.2.

☐ Complete the treatment involvement plan as part of FAM Handout 1.11 (AN Version) or FAM Handout 1.12 (BOB Version).

☐ Clarify the sibling or siblings' role in treatment via FAM Handout 1.14.

☐ Introduce FAM Handout 1.15 and PT Handout 1.2.

☐ Assign homework:

    ☐ Carers continue completing the Intake Food Log until next week.

    ☐ Carers start to implement the treatment involvement plan.

    ☐ FAM Handout 1.14 is assigned reading for siblings and carers.

    ☐ Patient is to read PT Handout 1.2.

    ☐ As necessary, carers provide the school with FAM Handout 1.13 and all other appropriate handouts.

Stage 1, Session 3: Psychoeducation About Eating Disorder Behaviors

The main objective of this session or portion of treatment is to provide psychoeducation about the patient's eating disorder behaviors.

Assessment, Tracking, and Troubleshooting

20 minutes

As previously discussed, the patient's BMI should be plotted at the start of each session. Following this, each session should start with reviewing the Intake Food Log, pointing out RABs, providing verbal reinforcement for RIBs, and troubleshooting what could have gone better. Because this is the first session after the treatment rules have been introduced, carers will likely have a lot of questions. In session, address these questions, validate emotions, and normalize the experience the family members are having. It is also important, however, to balance doing all of this with introducing new core treatment concepts in session. It is all too easy to let entire sessions of troubleshooting go by without providing continued psychoeducation. Therefore, remind the family that there is important material to cover in this session that will help them implement treatment rules in the future. There will also be more time allotted in future sessions to troubleshooting issues that arise. The first handful of sessions are more focused, however, on teaching new material. It can be helpful to tell carers this so they can be aware of the pacing of treatment. Additionally, it can be particularly helpful to set agendas at the start of session. Typically, allotting about one-third of the session to troubleshooting in the beginning of treatment is recommended.

Psychoeducation: Eating Disorder Behaviors

Duration varies

The majority of this session or portion of treatment is spent reviewing FAM/PT Handout 1.16 (AN Version) or FAM/PT Handout 1.17 (BOB Version); FAM/PT Handout 1.18; FAM Handout 1.19 (AN Version) or FAM 1.20 (BOB Version); the Food and Behavior Log included in FAM/PT Handout 1.16 (AN Version) and FAM/PT Handout 1.17 (BOB Version); and the IMT family measures.

Eating Disorder and Recovery Behaviors (+Patient Copy: FAM/PT Handout 1.16 or FAM/PT Handout 1.17)

Once the troubleshooting of issues that arose at home has come to a close, introduce FAM/PT Handout 1.16 (AN Version) or FAM/PT Handout 1.17 (BOB Version). The patient as well as carers get a copy of the appropriate handout for the correct diagnosis in session.

Eating Disorder Behaviors in the Context of Treatment

In the left-hand column of the table in FAM/PT Handout 1.16 (AN Version) and FAM/PT Handout 1.17 (BOB Version) is a list of eating disorder behaviors *in the context of treatment*. In other words, these behaviors are not diagnostic criteria. One cannot recognize or diagnose an eating disorder on the basis of the behaviors listed in this table. They are what occur when a person with an eating disorder is in the type of treatment where reinforcement for maladaptive eating disorder behaviors is blocked and adaptive behavior is encouraged. In more behavioral language, this is a list of what occurs when eating disorder behaviors are being extinguished with decreased RABs and increased RIBs. In a sense, these are various forms of extinction bursts. More specifically, the eating disorder is attempting to seek reinforcement in some way, given the set of limited reinforcement options. Therefore, although these are commonly referred to as *eating disorder behaviors* for simplicity's sake, in this context they are considered *reinforcement-seeking behaviors* or, more specifically, *reinforcement-seeking eating disorder behaviors*. Remember, reinforcement can come in the form of relief from negative internal experiences, such as fear of "fatness."

Because it can be confusing for carers and therapists alike to determine whether a behavior is part of the eating disorder, each of these two handouts makes it clear that if a person with an eating disorder is in behavioral family treatment and is displaying the behaviors listed in the left-hand column of the table, those behaviors are part of the eating disorder. Therefore, efforts should be made to block reinforcement of these behaviors with decreased RABs and increased RIBs. In short, the listed behaviors must be shaped down.

EATING DISORDER THOUGHTS AND STATEMENTS IN THE CONTEXT OF TREATMENT

Each of the reinforcement-seeking eating disorder behaviors listed in the table is accompanied by sentences reflecting a type of eating disorder thought or statement. These sentences are included primarily to give carers an idea of what to listen for when their child is making either overtures or demands for reinforcement. The sentences are also included to help facilitate patients' insight into the connection between their eating disorder behaviors and thoughts.

RECOVERY BEHAVIORS IN TREATMENT

Just as reinforcement-seeking eating disorder behaviors need to be shaped down in treatment, recovery behaviors need to be shaped up. Recovery behaviors are listed in the right-hand column of the table in FAM/PT Handout 1.16 (AN Version) and FAM/PT Handout 1.17 (BOB Version). Recovery behaviors are the healthy opposite of reinforcement-seeking eating disorder behaviors. All recovery behaviors consist of taking action in line with physical and mental health (for example, eating a complete meal and tolerating associated negative emotions) while denying the eating disorder reinforcement.

In treatment, recovery behaviors can be reinforced both socially and internally (or, in behavioral language, *automatically*). For instance, a carer can provide Rec-SPA to increase the frequency of a recovery behavior over time; for example, saying "I'm proud of you for eating, Son" results in more completed meals over time. A patient can also feel positive emotions for engaging in recovery behaviors; for example, feeling proud for completing a meal also results in more completed meals over time. In general, however, it seems that the more self-eclipsing a given disorder is, the more social reinforcement is needed in treatment before a patient can access the feeling of automatic internal reinforcement.

Recovery behaviors as well as reinforcement-seeking eating disorder behaviors change over time and according to the stage of treatment. In stage 1 of IMT family therapy, recovery behaviors involve abdicating control over food, disempowering the eating disorder, and allowing carers to have control over food. In stage 2, however, recovery behaviors involve taking more initiative (with support) to confront foods that are feared. In IMT individual therapy, RAE and BAE (regular and appetitive eating) / (body acceptance and exposure) have their own versions of what recovery behaviors look like; these involve taking full initiative to confront fears and beat the eating disorder.

RECOVERY STATEMENTS IN TREATMENT

Each of the recovery behaviors in the right-hand column of the table in FAM/PT Handout 1.16 (AN Version) and FAM/PT Handout 1.17 (BOB Version) is accompanied by sentences reflecting a type of statement about the self, or a type of accepting attitude, that can facilitate recovery behaviors. These sentences are included primarily to give patients an idea of the mentality that can facilitate recovery. It is extremely difficult, of course, just to start thinking in a different way, and this is not expected of patients. In fact, it is helpful to explain to patients and carers, very clearly, that no one can just "snap to it" and have a totally non–eating disorder attitude. Only through behavior change, over time, can thoughts change. Behavior change *precedes* a change in thoughts. Therefore, at this stage, patients are to practice recovery behaviors, and the accepting attitude will come in time.

Introducing the Food and Behavior Log

5 minutes

Once FAM/PT Handout 1.16 (AN Version) or FAM/PT Handout 1.17 (BOB Version) has been introduced, it is helpful to quickly introduce the new type of food and behavior log that carers will be completing each week. Tell carers that although it may be cumbersome at first, they will get more practiced at detecting eating disorder and recovery behaviors and will be able to indicate relatively quickly which behaviors were present at each meal or snack.

EATING DISORDER BEHAVIORS ONLINE

The clinician must administer FAM Handout CM.3 directly. It is found in appendix B of this manual. This handout contains sensitive information, and so it is best to administer it in a controlled fashion to carers only. The handout was created to make carers aware of different ways the eating disorder can be maintained by technology use. For instance, adolescents now take selfies and post them online for feedback, seeking out "thinspiration" and "fitspiration," and they use weight-loss apps to count calories, monitor weight, and monitor exercise. They also engage in bullying one another online by making negative comments on body size, shape, and weight (a practice known as *meanspiration*). Children have long been considered either bullies or bullied, but in our experience it has often been true that the same patient who is bullied online also engages in bullying others online. Both bullying others and being bullied are monitored in the IMT measures, particularly as they pertain to Internet use. Technology use more broadly is also monitored, to deter body checking and other eating disorder behaviors.

RECOVERY-DELAYING BEHAVIORS (+PATIENT COPY) (+SCHOOL COPY)

Recovery-delaying behaviors are behaviors that specifically interfere with the recovery process. There are *carer-accountable* recovery-delaying behaviors and *patient-accountable* recovery-delaying behaviors. There is certainly overlap between eating disorder behaviors and recovery-delaying behaviors; however, there are undoubtedly some behaviors that directly hinder the treatment. The eating disorder can certainly be a factor in these behaviors, but if the behavior gets in the way of treatment, it is a recovery-delaying behavior. Consider, for example, the behavior of purging within one hour of taking medication. The purging is part of the eating disorder, but because the purging occurs within one hour of taking the medication, it interferes with pharmacotherapy. Therefore, this is an example of a recovery-delaying behavior. For more information, see FAM/PT Handout 1.18.

"WHAT DO I DO WHEN…?" (+SCHOOL COPY)

Especially for carers in desperate need of help in the early weeks of treatment, FAM Handout 1.19 (AN Version) or FAM Handout 1.20 (BOB Version) can be very helpful. When the carer has a question about how to respond to an eating disorder behavior, they can consult this handout as a guide. The idea is that instead of doing something like phone coaching in the moment (as in dialectical behavior therapy), the carer has this handout to consult. This handout is intended to indirectly help carers increase their sense of independence and mastery. Although they are to consult the handout in the beginning stages of treatment, the idea is that they will, over time, increasingly rely on their own experience and their own developing expertise in the supervised eating process.

Introducing the IMT Measures

15 minutes

Once all relevant handouts are reviewed, the carers and patient will be asked to complete the IMT family therapy measures. Behaviors from FAM Handout 1.4, FAM Handout 1.5, FAM/PT Handout 1.16 (AN Version), FAM/PT Handout 1.17 (BOB Version), FAM Handout CM.3, and FAM/PT 1.18 are covered in the measures. Prior to administration of the measures, state their importance in providing you with a clear picture of what to address in treatment and how both the carers and the patient are progressing through treatment. Also explain that the answers given on the IMT measures will serve as your guide in future sessions. Next, hand out the measures; however, before carers and patients complete them, go through each section and explain the objective. The groundwork laid in this session regarding the IMT measures will likely make the process of tracking progress in treatment easier over time.

To start, it is important to explain that carers and patients fill out similar measures so that information from different perspectives is gathered. Let the family know that, moving forward, you will discuss any major differences in answers on the measures in treatment. Point out to the patient that the carers will be reporting on the patient's behavior and will also have an opportunity to present their perspective on their own behaviors (that is, TABLE skills and ED WINS habits).

When introducing the stage 1 IMT family therapy measures, it will be important to explain each of the sections. Review the following information with the family.

EATING DISORDER BEHAVIOR: CARER PRESENT

The behaviors listed in this section of the measure are the same ones listed in the left-hand column of the table in FAM/PT Handout 1.16 (AN Version) and FAM/PT Handout 1.17 (BOB Version). They are listed in the measure under "carer present" because in the context of behavioral family therapy, the carer is to shape these behaviors by decreasing RABs and increasing RIBs. The primary function of most of these behaviors is conceptualized as decreasing negative internal experiences (technically speaking, *negative reinforcement*). The one exception to this is viewing pro–eating disorder content online, which is considered here to be an eating disorder–exacerbating behavior. Behaviors listed under "carer present" are in contrast to those listed under "carer unaware," which are reinforcement-seeking (that is, often relief-seeking) eating disorder behaviors that the patient engaged in that the carer was not aware of.

EATING DISORDER BEHAVIOR: CARER UNAWARE

The eating disorder behaviors the patient engages in that the carer is not aware of are listed in the next section. These behaviors are categorically very difficult for carers to prevent. Therefore, it is important for the carer to report on the expected frequency of these events, and it is important to hold the patient accountable for reporting these behaviors. In session, a therapist can cross-check the answers given by the patient and the carer and provide Rec-SPA to the patient whenever a "carer unaware" behavior is disclosed. Carers should be trained to provide Rec-SPA (rather than punishment) for the disclosure of "carer unaware" behavior.

Although the patient's eating disorder is likely too strong for the patient to curb urges to engage in these behaviors on their own, patients are at least expected to be honest in treatment. The patient's role in treatment is to honestly report on the eating disorder. Although it may be difficult at times, expectations can be put in place for the patient to be accountable for honesty. It may not always happen, but it seems fair to ask for it. Stating that the patient must be honest on the IMT measures can be framed as an important first step in taking responsibility. As in the treatment of any other type of disorder, it is imperative to meet the patient where they are.

RECOVERY-DELAYING BEHAVIORS: PATIENT IS TO REPORT

Although recovery-delaying behaviors are also very much part of the eating disorder itself, they directly interfere with the administration of treatment. Therefore, they are taken seriously. Particularly for this category of behaviors, the expectation set by the therapist is that the patient will honestly report behaviors. This may not always happen, but the expectation must always be clear. If a patient reports purging within an hour of taking prescribed medication, attempting to trick the scale, secretly not taking prescribed medications, or taking mood-altering substances, it is important to notify all relevant treatment team members (including the physician) as well as the carers. Because the eating disorder weakens a person's physical health, these behaviors could have serious consequences. Particularly because treatment team members and carers must be notified, it is particularly important to provide Rec-SPA for the disclosure of information and affirmation that disclosure was the right course of action. Carers are to be instructed to do the same. Disclosure regarding behaviors is movement forward in treatment and should be shaped with positive attention, not punishment. It is important to note that punishment would decrease the behavior of disclosure, not necessarily the destructive behaviors themselves. In the context of behavioral family therapy, the patient is usually being watched as closely as possible already. If, under these circumstances, secretive destructive behaviors occurred, the reinforcement (for example, tremendous relief) gained from engaging in these behaviors (such as purging) will usually outweigh any punishment a carer has in mind. If the aim is to decrease dangerous behaviors, and if carers are unable to do this in an outpatient setting, then higher levels of care should be considered, not punishment for disordered behavior.

BEHAVIOR OF YOUR CARER/YOUR BEHAVIOR: ED WINS HABITS

ED WINS habits are quintessentially unhelpful carer behavior. They are rated by carers and the patient. For the question about ED WINS habits, note that the patient should rate the behavior of the carer who most often supervises meals. If a patient has two carers who are about equally in charge of refeeding, you can ask the patient to give an average rating based on both carers' behavior. There is also a question in this section about whether siblings are inappropriately implementing treatment rules.

BODY COMMENTING

The "body commenting" category is meant to measure both bullying and victimization behavior, online and *in vivo*. Clinically, we have found that the same patient can both engage in bullying behavior and be victimized. Both situations can negatively impact recovery. Therefore, we maintain that it is important to assess for these factors throughout treatment. For a more complete assessment of bullying behavior, see the IMT Bullying Questionnaire (IMT-BQ), available at www.imt-ed.com.

BODY IMAGE BEHAVIOR

Although the category of behaviors labeled "body image behavior" is directly addressed in the IMT individual therapy material, it also warrants measurement and tracking here. Sometimes these behaviors decrease during behavioral family therapy. Nevertheless, we have also seen these behaviors increase, particularly with patients who have AN or AAN and are weight-restoring (we often colloquially refer to this as the "whack-a-mole" phenomenon—as eating disorder behaviors increase, body image behaviors can increase). Because it is difficult to predict what will happen in treatment, the therapist needs to monitor these behaviors. It may be advisable to target some of these behaviors in behavioral family therapy if they pose a significant psychological impairment for the person (for example, if a person spends the entire day body investigating, it may be advisable to cover mirrors until body image exposure work can be focused on in treatment).

Behavior of Your Carer: TABLE Skills

It is also important to track adaptive carer behaviors over time. Be sure to provide verbal reinforcement to carers who are improving on these measures. If patients or carers need further explanation, refer them to FAM Handout 1.4.

Recovery Behavior

Recovery behaviors, as defined by FAM/PT Handout 1.16 (AN Version) and FAM/PT Handout 1.17 (BOB Version), are listed here. Assessment and tracking of the adaptive behaviors will help in shaping them with Rec-SPA. Having them listed here is also a reminder to the family of the current behavioral goals.

Earned Freedoms

The stage 2 IMT family therapy measures have all the preceding categories of behavior plus a category called "earned freedoms." Patients are to rate their level of anxiety regarding each of the examples listed in this category. This exercise is to help the therapist get an idea of where to start building the hierarchy (that is, the "roadmap"). This is not a substitute for FAM/PT Handout 2.15: Earned Freedom Roadmap, which must be completed with the family's input.

Administration

After each section of the IMT measure has been reviewed with the carers and the patient, have them complete the assessment. Answer any questions, as needed. Once the measures are complete, provide verbal reinforcement and thank everyone for completing the extensive questions. Remind the family that information gleaned from the IMT measures is extremely important because it guides the treatment.

Homework Assignment

2 minutes

Inform carers that they are to complete the Food and Behavior Log and implement the treatment rules as best they can. Carers also review relevant IMT handouts. The patient is also to review handouts provided to them.

Stage 1, Session 3: To-Dos

60 minutes

- ☐ Assess and plot BMI.
- ☐ Review the Intake Food Log and provide feedback.
- ☐ Introduce FAM/PT Handout 1.16 (AN Version) or FAM/PT Handout 1.17 (BOB Version).
- ☐ Introduce the Food and Behavior Log.
- ☐ Provide carers a copy of FAM Handout CM.3 from appendix B of this manual.
- ☐ Introduce FAM/PT Handout 1.18, and FAM Handout 1.19 (AN Version) or FAM Handout 1.20 (BOB Version).
- ☐ Review all portions of the stage 1 IMT family therapy measures.
- ☐ Have carers and patient complete the stage 1 IMT family therapy measures.

☐ Assign homework:

    ☐ Carers complete the stage 1 Food and Behavior Log.

    ☐ Carers continue to implement treatment rules.

    ☐ Carers review handouts.

    ☐ Patients review relevant handouts.

Stage 1, Session 4: Psychoeducation About Food and "Fat"

The fourth session is focused primarily on providing the family with psychoeducation about core eating disorder treatment concepts, such as why foods that are feared must be confronted and developing respectful language regarding bodies. Psychoeducation about these core concepts lays the foundation for the introduction of Rec-SPA.

Assessment, Tracking, and Troubleshooting

20 minutes

From now until the end of stage 2 family therapy, the carers and the patient should complete an IMT family measure about five to ten minutes prior to the beginning of each session. Although having the family complete IMT measures every week is considered ideal, some therapists may prefer to administer these measures every two to four weeks. Further, as previously discussed, the patient's BMI should be plotted at the beginning of session.

After taking weights, review the IMT family measures that were completed in session. Be sure to comment on the self-report scores of the carers' implementation of the TABLE skills and ED WINS habits as well as the patient's report of their carers' behavior on these items. It is not exact, but you can crudely compare these initial scores to how the carers did at the first family meal as well as the ratings from last session. Additionally, address any other areas of concern or interest.

From there, ask to see the Food and Behavior Logs. Provide feedback on the marking of reinforcement-seeking eating disorder behaviors as well as recovery behaviors. Troubleshoot the eating disorder behaviors, provide verbal reinforcement to the carers for shaping recovery behaviors, and provide Rec-SPA to the patient for engaging in the recovery behaviors.

If carers mention that the reinforcement-seeking eating disorder behaviors and the recovery behaviors are listed both on the Food and Behavior Log and on the measures, tell them that repetition of ratings provides a helpful learning experience. (Keep in mind that the measures are clinical tools, not research instruments.)

Psychoeducation: Food and "Fat"

Duration varies

Here we discuss two handouts that address specific types of foods and dieting in treatment. More specifically, we cover why it is advisable for the patient to consume so-called junk foods in treatment, why carers on a diet can be problematic, why "fat" talk is problematic, and why separating the person from the eating disorder is important. It is important to address these concepts before moving on to the topic of the carer providing Rec-SPA. If a carer does not believe that a patient should be eating junk food, would like to diet themselves, engages in "fat" talk, and is unable to decouple the eating disorder from their child, then the patient is likely to reject Rec-SPA from that carer.

Imagine this scene: A carer calls foods that the patient has to eat "unhealthy," the carer is on a diet, the carer talks about other people being "fat," the carer currently blames their child for having an eating disorder, and the carer then says to the patient, "Good job eating all your carbs...I guess." How do you think that will go over? Not great. Rec-SPA has to be genuine. This is not labeled praise for a six-year-old. It is unlikely that the insincere nature of this carer's Rec-SPA will get past an adolescent with an eating disorder. It is already challenging for a person with an eating disorder to accept Rec-SPA. If the Rec-SPA is disingenuous, it typically gets rejected with lightning speed. Therefore, unhelpful carer behavior is addressed with FAM Handout 1.21, FAM Handout 1.22, FAM/PT Handout 1.23, and FAM Handout 1.24 prior to teaching carers about Rec-SPA.

What Foods Are Unhealthy in Treatment? (+Patient Version: PT Handout 1.3)

It is difficult for patients, carers, and practitioners alike to fully grasp the food-related paradigm shift necessary for stage 1 family treatment. Culturally, we are convinced that there are "good" and "bad" foods, and that under no circumstances should a health care professional advise the eating of so-called unhealthy foods. So often, carers come in to treatment completely confused by the fact that professionals are advising them that everything they hear about limiting carbohydrates, fat, and sugar does not apply. FAM Handout 1.21 was created to help make it clear that when a person is either medically deemed malnourished and/or is afraid of food, confronting these fears is necessary.

Similarly, a common aim in treatment for obsessive-compulsive disorder with fear of germs is to decrease hand sanitizing. People are generally advised by health care professionals to sanitize, but some people with obsessive-compulsive disorder are terrified *not* to sanitize, and so they must learn to tolerate the anxiety of having unsanitized hands. No matter what professionals say about the importance of hand sanitizing, if someone has this form of obsessive-compulsive disorder, they decrease their fear by not sanitizing. The same holds true for eating disorders. Even though it is generally advisable to cut down on fats, carbohydrates, and sugars, if a person with an eating disorder is afraid of those foods, they must eat them until they have habituated to the anxiety created by eating those foods. Furthermore, if the person is underweight, the priority is to increase caloric intake. Calorie-dense foods are often the so-called unhealthy foods. Getting their weight up is the highest-priority health goal; therefore, the healthier alternative is to eat so-called unhealthy foods during treatment until the medical risk from eating disorder behaviors decreases. Even for a person with a BOB disorder who is not malnourished, but who is physically and/or psychologically impaired by fear of foods, it is healthier to confront this fear by eating these foods than to allow the dangerous disorder to endure.

The Dieting Carer

FAM Handout 1.22 does not apply to everyone. If carers are not dieting, there is no need to administer it. Before assuming that a carer of any gender is not dieting, however, it is important to ask. If a carer is dieting or has a long history of dieting, it is important to administer this handout.

This handout addresses the sticky issue of carers who are dieting while their child is in treatment for an eating disorder. The handout explains both the pros and cons of continuing to diet. It is pointed out that while suspending one's diet during the refeeding process is often helpful, it can also sometimes result in children trying to control their carers' food intake. Generally speaking, carers are strongly advised to abandon dieting at this stage in their child's recovery. If, however, the child's eating disorder begins to develop a satisfaction about their carers "getting fat" or gaining weight in any way, this strategy must be reevaluated in therapy. Further, the exception of a carer dieting for medical reasons is covered.

If the therapist suspects that carers may be defensive about this topic, we have found it helpful to give this handout to carers matter-of-factly along with other material to minimize damage to the therapeutic rapport while also acting in the child's best interest. At the following session, the therapist should inquire about carers' reactions to the handouts they received.

If a carer does not seem sold on the merits of giving up their own self-imposed diet (not for medical reasons), it may be helpful to verbally add information regarding the coming psychoeducation about Rec-SPA. A therapist can mention to carers that although the focus has been on decreasing their RABs and increasing their RIBs in an effort to shape down eating disorder behavior, soon treatment will shift to reinforcing the recovery behaviors presented in FAM/PT Handout 1.16 (AN Version) or FAM/PT Handout 1.17 (BOB Version). In order to do this, a carer must provide a warmer type of reinforcement (colloquially and incorrectly referred to as "positive reinforcement") for recovery behaviors. This typically goes over much better, however, if a carer is not engaging in recovery behaviors themselves. It may even be worth mentioning that the patient can view this as hypocritical. Framing it as temporarily letting go of a diet because it is what is best for the child may be helpful.

Stop the "Fat" Talk (+Patient Copy: FAM/PT Handout 1.23) (+School Copy: FAM/PT Handout 1.23)

FAM/PT Handout 1.23 should be given to everyone living in the home. This handout describes how speaking negatively about one's body or eating habits impacts the person with the eating disorder. Examples of types of "fat" talk are given. Additionally, examples of acceptable comments about body size, shape, and/or weight, clothing preferences, and dietary restrictions are given.

In practice, we have noted several reactions to FAM/PT Handout 1.23. Often when this handout is presented, the patient comments that the carers' "fat" talk caused the eating disorder. Alternatively, the carer may express guilt about having caused the eating disorder with "fat" talk. (Because of this, after a discussion of this handout, FAM Handout 1.24, on externalizing the eating disorder, is administered.) Psychoeducation can also be provided in the context of this handout regarding the neurobiological and genetically influenced nature of eating disorders.

In the context of this handout, it can be helpful to discuss the cultural influences on one's thinking that prompt or affect "fat" talk. For instance, the therapist can say something in session similar to this: "Although we know that 'fat' talk can trigger eating disorder thoughts and behaviors, it is not to blame for the eating disorder. 'Fat' talk alone cannot cause a neurobiological, genetically influenced illness like an eating disorder. Most teens are exposed to 'fat' talk, yet they do not all develop eating disorders. That said, it's important to understand the influence of 'fat' talk and the culture around us. Our culture says it is OK to make fun of people who are overweight. It also says that being overweight is an epidemic that must be stopped. Our culture holds up thinness as a value. For these reasons, we typically don't stop to think too much about where our beliefs about thinness came from, or about how accurate they are, or about the consequences when we express them, which is why we'll take the time now to discuss this in session."

The last sentence in the therapist's comment prompts a functional discussion on what happens when a carer engages in "fat" talk. Imagine, for example, that the carer of the patient you are treating states that after the child's weight is restored, the carer will likely go back to commenting about the patient's consumption of high-fructose corn syrup. The carer reports that she will probably say something like "Yikes! You really shouldn't be eating things like that." At that point, you should intervene. Separate what the carer can believe for herself from how ineffective a comment like this will be in the specific context of eating disorder recovery. You might say something like this: "In the context of the eating disorder, we must develop new rules. While you are permitted to have rules like this for yourself, if you impose your rules on a child who is recovering from an eating disorder, there will be some predictable consequences. For the child, the eating disorder might be triggered. Let's take a look at how a comment like this would impact the child." From there, you can ask the patient to predict what her reactions would be. The sequence of events can be drawn out on the board and might go something like this:

1. Patient recently achieved weight restoration and is eating a cookie.

2. Carer says, "Yikes! You really shouldn't be eating things like that."

3. Patient feels hurt, misunderstood, and judged.

4. Patient thinks *I should restrict.*

5. Patient decides to stop eating the cookie and engage in compulsive exercise to make up for the calories consumed.

6. Eating disorder is triggered.

SEPARATING THE EATING DISORDER AND THE PERSON (+SCHOOL COPY: FAM HANDOUT 1.24)

It is crucial to separate the eating disorder from the child in treatment. Although the concept of externalizing the eating disorder is present in earlier handouts, it has not yet been explicitly presented. It is important to present this handout or concept if at any point in the treatment a carer expresses doubt or guilt about having caused the eating disorder. Although it is numbered FAM Handout 1.24, and although administration of this handout precedes the administration of the Rec-SPA material, the concepts in this handout (or even the handout itself) are to be discussed whenever necessary throughout treatment. It can be confusing for carers to play such an active role in recovery. They sometimes come to the conclusion that because they are part of the solution, they must have been part of the problem. Therapists should take a very compassionate approach to this topic and provide carers with information about the science on the neurobiology and genetics of eating disorders (see Hill and Dagg, 2012). Therapists can also empower carers by providing psychoeducation as well as teaching and modeling skills to help carers shape their child's eating disorder behavior.

Homework Assignment

2 minutes

Prior to the end of session, ask to meet with carers alone for two minutes. Inform carers that, as usual, they are to complete the Food and Behavior Log (all portions), continue implementing treatment rules, and read FAM Handout 1.25 and (if it applies) FAM Handout 1.26 as well as FAM Handout CM.4 for homework. Tell carers that FAM Handout CM.4 must be kept in a secure place. FAM Handout CM.4 is found in appendix B of this manual. The clinician must provide this handout to the carers. The patient is not allowed access to this handout, because it could provide maladaptive suggestions to the eating disorder. Further, the patient should be told not only to review relevant handouts but also to bring some additional reading material or schoolwork to the next session, since the therapist will spend most of that session alone with the carers.

Stage 1, Session 4: To-Dos

- ☐ Administer IMT measures five to ten minutes prior to session.
- ☐ Assess and plot BMI.
- ☐ Review the Food and Behavior Log and provide feedback.
- ☐ Review FAM Handout 1.22, FAM/PT Handout 1.23, and FAM Handout 1.24.
- ☐ Assign homework with the patient and carers present:
    - ☐ Carers complete the Food and Behavior Log.
    - ☐ Continue implementing treatment rules as planned.
    - ☐ Tell carers to read FAM Handout 1.25 and FAM Handout 1.26 for homework.
    - ☐ Provide carers with a copy of FAM Handout CM.4 from appendix B of this manual.

☐ Instruct carers to keep FAM Handout CM.4 away from the patient.

☐ Instruct carers to review handouts, as needed.

☐ Instruct patient to review relevant handouts and to bring extra reading material or schoolwork to the next session, which the therapist will spend largely with the carers alone.

Stage 1, Session 5: Recovery-Specific Positive Attention

As mentioned earlier, this session will largely be spent with the carers, without the patient present. The patient will be invited into the session to discuss answers on the IMT measure and discuss how the week went. It is important for the patient to provide their perspective. Additionally, it is important to have the opportunity for the therapist to provide Rec-SPA to the patient and model this for the carers at the start of session, even though the concept has not yet formally been taught to them. It is particularly important to provide Rec-SPA to the patient at the start of this session, if possible, so that it can be referenced later in the session as an example when teaching the carers the concept.

Assessment, Tracking, and Troubleshooting

15 minutes

About five to ten minutes prior to the start of session, the carers and patient should complete an IMT family measure (although exceptions can be made). Again, the patient's BMI should be recorded and plotted at the beginning of session. With the patient present, the Food and Behavior Log from the previous week must be reviewed along with the IMT measures. Provide feedback and troubleshoot accordingly. Be sure to provide Rec-SPA to the patient for recovery behaviors during the troubleshooting portion of the session.

Homework Review

15 minutes

Ask to speak to the carers alone to conduct homework review of FAM Handout 1.25, FAM Handout 1.26, and FAM Handout CM.4 Each of these handouts ranges from somewhat private to very private. To review these handouts, simply begin with FAM Handout 1.25 and ask what the carers thought of it. After finishing discussion of this, move to discussion of the next handout.

PRESENTING A UNITED FRONT

The issue of carers arguing about how to treat the eating disorder comes up often and frequently interferes with treatment. Whether the carers are married, divorced, or about to get a divorce, it is essential that they be strongly encouraged to work together for the health of the child. FAM Handout 1.25 is a simple reminder of this. When asking carers what they thought of this handout when reading it for homework, it may have brought to the surface various issues. Take some time in session to troubleshoot disagreements about the implementation of rules, conceptualizations of the eating disorder, and so forth.

THREE TRICKY WAYS EATING DISORDERS DISGUISE THEMSELVES (+SCHOOL COPY: FAM HANDOUT 1.26)

Carers are often duped by the eating disorder's cogent arguments about food, nutrition, and health. The concept of apparent competence, as originally introduced by dialectical behavior therapy for borderline personality disorder (Linehan, 1993), applies to eating disorders as well. As can be expected, apparent competence manifests itself differently in eating disorders and in borderline personality disorder. Therefore, we have reworked the concept of apparent competence to apply to eating disorders, and we describe three categories of manifestations based on our clinical observations.

Because it is so easy to be fooled by what the eating disorder is saying, we decided to issue a warning in the form of this handout for carers. As you can see from the handout itself, the bottom line is that no matter how skillful the eating disorder is, treatment compliance is mandatory. It is helpful to verbally reiterate this for carers.

BE A DETECTIVE

Again, the patient is not to see FAM Handout CM.4. In order to effectively curb eating disorder behaviors and increase the accuracy of information reported to the therapist, the carer must be aware of tricky behaviors the eating disorder may compel their child to engage in.

Recovery-Specific Positive Attention

Duration varies

If carers are comfortable with serving their child challenge foods (such as junk foods) in treatment, curbing their own dieting behavior, banning "fat" talk, and separating the eating disorder from the child, it is time to move on to Rec-SPA. It is also helpful if they are presenting a united front.

GIVING RECOVERY-SPECIFIC POSITIVE ATTENTION

Before providing FAM Handout 1.27 along with FAM Handout 1.28 (AN Version) or FAM Handout 1.29 (BOB Version), it may be helpful to verbally introduce carers to the topic of Rec-SPA. It might be helpful by starting out by providing a copy of FAM/PT Handout 1.16 (AN Version) or FAM/PT 1.17 (BOB Version) with the list of reinforcement-seeking behaviors in the left-hand column and recovery behaviors in the right-hand column. Point out that until now you have been focused on decreasing the eating disorder behaviors listed at the left and not increasing the behaviors listed at the right.

It may then be helpful to introduce the idea like this: "The tool used to increase recovery behaviors is a sensitive one that must be used very delicately, like a fine sculptor's blade. If used carelessly and unskillfully, one can get cut. If it is used with care and skill, however, one can help sculpt something worthwhile. This delicate and sensitive tool by which to shape recovery behavior is known as Rec-SPA. This is short for 'recovery-specific positive attention.' Basically, the idea is to show your child positive attention when they are engaging in a recovery behavior. You can't, however, just be so bold as to enthusiastically say, 'Great job!' That will backfire. You might get an explosive reaction. The positive attention must be given skillfully. There is an art to it. First, you must get good at noticing when your child is engaging in recovery behavior. Not coincidentally, you have been training for this by logging your child's recovery behavior on the Food and Behavior Logs as well as on the measures. Now that you're accustomed to noticing this behavior, it is time to practice getting the tone right when attending to it. Sometimes it is best to start off subtly, by simply smiling or giving a thumbs-up, without saying anything at all. Then it might be best to graduate to expressing gratitude for a recovery behavior, such as saying thank you. Over time, it can get more specific, such as 'Thank you for finishing your meal.' From there, you may want to start expressing pride, such as 'I'm really proud of you for finishing your meal.' Once the disorder has really receded, the coast can be clear to say something as bold as 'Really good job finishing your meal.'"

DISLIKING PRAISE

It is also helpful to discuss the patient's dislike of praise. For instance, the patient may report that they feel angry when praised now because their behavior was rarely praised in the past. If this is the case, talk to the carers about what their barriers to praise might have been in the past. Explain to them the importance of praise in general. It may also be helpful to explain to the patient that although they were not praised much in the past, the carers will start making efforts to do so now because they care. If the patient truly wants to be praised and has been feeling unloved because of a given carer's lack of warmth, it is particularly important to explain that in order for a carer to change, they must start somewhere, even if it is painful. Finding praise aversive can be framed as a kind of growing pain—you won't like the emotional pain that is triggered by praise now, but it will ultimately bring the family closer in the end and help fight the eating disorder.

Another reason patients have stated that they find praise aversive is that they so strongly believe the eating disorder thoughts—for example, that meal completion and weight gain are failures on their part. Nevertheless, the belief in eating disorder thoughts will hopefully be lessened over time, and positive attention for recovery behaviors will eventually become tolerable and likely welcomed. In short, because it is healthy to respond positively to positive attention for engaging in healthy behaviors, the agenda of expressing positive attention should continue until the aversion is overcome. Carers must be coached through the process of sticking to the plan to express gratitude and praise to overcome the aversion.

SHAPING YOUR CHILD'S BEHAVIOR

FAM Handout 1.30 is intended to lay the foundation for teaching reinforcement strategies both for decreasing eating disorder behaviors and for increasing recovery behaviors. This handout is intended to explain to carers the importance of thinking like a behaviorist. The therapist needs to convey to the carer that the biggest services they can provide for their child are to be at the ready to identify and decrease eating disorder behaviors with the implementation of rules and to identify and increase recovery behaviors with Rec-SPA. The more flexibly they can switch between enforcing rules and warmly providing praise, just as a true behaviorist would do, the more quickly the behavior will be shaped. Part of this involves having carers refrain from expressing all their emotions to their child. The time will come for expressing emotions in family therapy; however, the beginning of stage 1 is not the time. Carers are urged to seek support from a confidant or carer peer in order to get their emotional needs met.

TIP: CONNECT CARERS TO OTHER CARERS WHO HAVE COMPLETED TREATMENT

It can be wonderful for carers to connect with others who have been through similar experiences. You can do this by way of Families Empowered and Supporting Treatment of Eating Disorders (F.E.A.S.T., www.feast-ed.org). In addition, the organization Project HEAL (www.theprojecttheal.org) launched the Communities of HEALing program in 2017 to connect carers.

SEVEN ROADBLOCKS TO GIVING REC-SPA (+PATIENT VERSION: PT HANDOUT 1.4) (+SCHOOL COPY: FAM HANDOUT 1.31)

When first considering the seemingly simple act of a carer praising a child, one may not anticipate all the problems that can arise. FAM Handout 1.31 attempts to preemptively address some of these issues. Review the list with the family in session. Ask each carer individually which of the reasons apply to them. Be sure to validate any emotions expressed by carers. At the same time, urge them to engage in the behavior of providing Rec-SPA to their child to help combat the eating disorder.

As is true about the development of any other skill, the beginning of the Rec-SPA learning curve is quite steep. Although it may feel awkward at first, carers must be encouraged to push through and continue providing Rec-SPA until it becomes more natural. Over the course of two to three weeks, carers will usually remark that although it was very difficult at first, it became much easier. Additionally, carers should be encouraged to provide *genuine* Rec-SPA. This usually aids in decreasing the initial awkwardness of providing Rec-SPA.

If carers are struggling with providing Rec-SPA for a behavior as supposedly simple as eating, remind them that the issue of which behaviors are worthy of praise is always relative. A therapist might say this to a carer: "If your child did not have an eating disorder, then giving them attention for finishing dinner would be pretty strange. But if your child is terribly afraid of eating, to the point where they are literally starved, then eating is actually a very big deal. What is worthy of positive attention is always relative."

Because it is best to first discuss Rec-SPA with carers alone, tell the carers that next week their child will get a patient version of FAM Handout 1.31 that is somewhat different from the version they received and that will be discussed in session. The patient's version, PT Handout 1.4, was specifically written for the patient so that the patient will not be triggered. Carers are to keep the carer version to themselves.

Strict or Soft? (+School Copy)

FAM Handout 1.32 further explains the concept of praising recovery behavior, despite how oppositional the child may act. Explain to carers that they do not have to praise the manner in which the patient responded; for instance, you would never recommend that the carers say, "Good job finishing your meal while complaining the whole time." You do, however, want the carers to praise or show appreciation for recovery behavior while appreciating how difficult it may have been: "Thank you for eating this even though it was difficult." This is similar to the A in the TABLE skills. Even if the person is driven by the eating disorder to snap back in the moment, it is important to stand one's ground with Rec-SPA and assert that behavior in line with recovery is indeed worthy of positive attention or praise.

It is important to instruct carers that ignoring any sort of acting-out behavior is the best way to shape these types of behaviors down. Although you clearly cannot shape eating disorder behavior by ignoring it, you can shape acting-out behavior by ignoring it. Because the function of acting-out behavior is to get a rise out of the carer, the carer can decrease the behavior aimed at ruffling their feathers by simply ignoring it. It is often difficult for carers to accept that the eating disorder may drive the patient to engage in oppositional behavior and that the most effective way to manage this behavior is to ignore it and focus on increasing recovery behavior. Rather than obviously asserting authority by punishing oppositional behavior in the context of eating disorder treatment, the carer subtly asserts authority by behaving in a manner that most effectively implements the treatment rules.

Homework Assignment

5 minutes

In addition to continuing to implement treatment rules and fill out the Food and Behavior Logs, carers are to practice identifying recovery behaviors and providing Rec-SPA to their child. They also are to review the handouts. Tell the carers that next week their child will get a patient version of FAM Handout 1.31 and that it will be discussed in session.

Carers are to bring a snack to the next session for the family. The object of the next session will be to provide Rec-SPA during the snack. Prior to the end of the present session, it may be helpful for the therapist to discuss the snack with the patient and carers together. Lastly, the therapist should prepare to eat their own snack in the session with the family next week.

Stage 1, Session 5: To-Dos

60 minutes

- ☐ Administer IMT measures prior to session.
- ☐ Assess and plot BMI.
- ☐ Review the Food and Behavior Log and provide feedback.
- ☐ Review homework handouts (FAM Handout 1.26, FAM Handout 1.27, and FAM Handout CM.4) in session with carers only.
- ☐ Introduce Rec-SPA and FAM Handout 1.27, FAM Handout 1.28 (AN Version) or FAM Handout 1.29 (BOB Version), FAM Handout 1.30, FAM Handout 1.31, and FAM Handout 1.32.
- ☐ Assign homework:
  - ☐ Carers complete the Food and Behavior Log.
  - ☐ Review FAM Handout 1.32, FAM Handout 1.33, and FAM Handout 1.34 for carers.
  - ☐ Carers bring a snack for next session.
  - ☐ Therapist brings a snack for themselves for next session.

Stage 1, Session 6: First Family Snack

This session is spent on the carers conducting an in-session snack in which Rec-SPA is provided. The therapist then provides feedback on the Rec-SPA as well as any RABs or RIBs.

Assessment, Tracking, and Troubleshooting

Duration varies

About five to ten minutes prior to the start of session, the carers and the patient should complete an IMT family evaluation (although exceptions can be made). Again, the patient's BMI should be plotted at the beginning of session.

The Food and Behavior Log should be reviewed each session, and the therapist should provide feedback accordingly. Any questions about the handouts that came up during the week should be addressed and reviewed, as necessary. In this session, the therapist should also ask how providing Rec-SPA went since the last session. Troubleshooting should be conducted at the start of session. The therapist should provide feedback on Rec-SPA as well as on RABs and RIBs.

First Family Snack

30 minutes

After weight has been plotted, IMT measures have been completed and reviewed, the Food and Behavior Log has been reviewed, the Rec-SPA handouts have been reviewed, troubleshooting of Rec-SPA over the past week has been completed, and RABs as well as RIBs have been pointed out, it is time for the first in-session family snack.

Therapist Tasks

Please note that during this snack, the therapist should eat their own snack while the family eats theirs. While taking bites of their own snack, the therapist should also be tracking the carers' behavior. As in the family meal that took place during the first active treatment session, the therapist should use the clinician's checklists for the TABLE skills and the ED WINS habits (see appendix F) to make tally marks in the boxes next to the TABLE skills and ED WINS habits that the carers engage in. Pay particular attention to the A in the TABLE skills. In the box next to the A, use a tally mark to register instances when carers express appreciation for the patient's struggle as well as instances when carers provide Rec-SPA (regardless of how well it goes over with the patient). In addition to formally tracking the carers' behavior, it is important to pay attention to the patient's reactions. Note how the Rec-SPA goes.

After the Snack

Once the snack is completed, you can ask the patient how it felt to have the carers acknowledge their efforts. Work through the emotions in session. At this point, it is time to administer PT Handout 1.4. Note that there are more roadblocks listed in the carers' version of the handout, and that PT Handout 1.4 is an edited version that is given to the patient.

Homework Assignment

5 minutes

Carers are to continue all the previous running assignments (implementing rules, decreasing RABs, increasing RIBs, providing Rec-SPA, filling out logs, reviewing handouts). The patient is to review PT Handout 1.4.

Stage 1, Session 6: To-Dos

60 minutes

☐ Administer IMT measures prior to session.

☐ Assess and plot BMI.

☐ Review the Food and Behavior Log and provide feedback.

☐ Review previously administered handouts.

☐ Troubleshoot issues involving carers' provision of Rec-SPA during the past week.

☐ Conduct an in-session family snack.

☐ Therapist eats a snack and tracks TABLE skills and ED WINS habits.

☐ Patient processes Rec-SPA with family.

☐ PT Handout 1.4 is reviewed in session.

☐ Assign homework:

    ☐ Carers continue all assignments of implementing treatment rules.

Stage 1, Session 7 and Beyond: Do What Is Needed

In this series of sessions that will constitute the majority of stage 1 treatment, the main treatment goals are to continue decreasing RABs and increasing RIBs, refine provision of Rec-SPA, ensure that carers are implementing treatment rules as planned, refine the treatment plan if needed, and review previously taught psychoeducation. Because IMT is an evidence-based practice model, we encourage clinicians to incorporate any other relevant psychoeducation that is needed. *When Your Teen Has an Eating Disorder* (Muhlheim, 2018) is a great resource. Further, in 2017, one of the coauthors of this manual (Tara Deliberto) coauthored and published research indicating that presenting adult patients with scientific papers (primary literature) on eating disorders was an acceptable and effective form of psychoeducation (Belak et al., 2017). It stands to reason that carers and intellectually advanced older adolescents may benefit from similar interventions.

Assessment, Tracking, and Troubleshooting

Duration varies

As in every session, about five to ten minutes prior to the start of session, the carers and the patient should complete an IMT family evaluation (although exceptions can be made). Again, the patient's BMI should be plotted at the beginning of session.

The Food and Behavior Log should be reviewed each session, and the therapist should provide feedback accordingly. Discuss the reduction of RABs, increasing RIBs, and refining Rec-SPA. Provide relevant psychoeducation.

Continued Psychoeducation

Duration varies

Clinicians are encouraged to review previously covered IMT family handouts and to provide any other relevant psychoeducation not covered by the IMT family handouts. We encourage clinicians to draw from research and evidence-based practices. In addition, FAM Handout 1.33 (used only for AN and AAN) may be particularly relevant to this period of stage 1 family therapy.

Continued Family Snacks

Duration varies

As needed, clinicians are encouraged to conduct extra family snacks. If a given family is struggling with a particular aspect of implementing treatment rules, TABLE skills, Rec-SPA, or decreasing the ED WINS habits, it may be helpful to provide continued in-person modeling and support. The therapist is encouraged to eat with the family to model behavior and to track TABLE skills and ED WINS habits in session.

Homework Assignment

5 minutes

Carers are to continue all the previous running assignments (implementing rules, decreasing RABs, increasing RIBs, providing Rec-SPA, filling out Food and Behavior Logs, reviewing handouts).

Stage 1, Session 7 and Beyond: To-Dos

60 minutes

☐   Administer IMT measures prior to session.

- ☐ Assess and plot BMI.

- ☐ Review the Food and Behavior Log and provide feedback.

- ☐ Review previously administered handouts.

- ☐ Troubleshoot issues involving carers' provision of Rec-SPA during the past week.

- ☐ Conduct an in-session family snack.

- ☐ Therapist eats a snack and tracks TABLE skills and ED WINS habits.

- ☐ Patient processes Rec-SPA with family.

- ☐ PT Handout 1.4 is reviewed in session.

- ☐ Assign homework:
  - ☐ Carers continue all assignments of implementing treatment rules.

Stage 1, Final Session

The final session of stage 1 is spent reviewing and processing stage 1 as well as introducing stage 2. Because this is an important session, all family members who played an active role in treatment should be present. Here, we describe how patients reach the final session of stage 1 as well as how to conduct the session.

Moving Forward

Largely regardless of diagnosis, patients reach the end of stage 1 when they are ready to start taking on some responsibility for their recovery. The main distinction, of course, between AN and BOB disorders is that patients with AN must achieve health restoration first. We begin by discussing the specifics of moving a patient with AN into stage 2, and then we outline signs that a patient may or may not be ready for this transition.

Briefly, regarding patients with AN, the final session of stage 1 should be conducted once the patient's weight has been restored and their health has been stabilized. Nevertheless, the achievement of health stabilization is a necessary but not sufficient criterion for the transition from stage 1 to stage 2. Psychological factors should also be considered. These factors are the same factors that are important for the BOB disorders.

In particular, the degree to which the nature of the eating disorder is self-eclipsing versus self-acknowledged must be discerned for patients with all disorders. Anecdotally, patients who are in the process of weight restoration often report having an internal eating disorder mantra: *I'm just going to lose it all the moment I get the chance.* Therefore, it stands to reason that someone can be complying with treatment rules until the point of weight restoration and simply biding time to be given the opportunity to lose weight.

Although sometimes it is clear that a patient will engage in eating disorder behaviors if given the chance, at other times this is subtler. For instance, a patient may appear desperate to regain responsibilities and may usurp session time by begging for the opportunity to have unsupervised meals. The desperate quality of these overtures is driven by an eating disorder fear of "fatness" that currently cannot be tolerated. In other words, because "fatness" is feared, the patient begs to regain responsibility over food so that some control over this fear can be exerted. Even with the best of intentions not to engage in eating disorder behaviors, if the skill of tolerating fear of "fatness" is not yet in place and control is being sought, restoring a patient's responsibility for food places them in a very precarious position. From clinical experience, when patients who present with this desperate quality are given responsibility for food, eating disorder behaviors quickly recommence.

From this conceptualization, the active and desperate seeking of responsibility is driven by the disordered desire to decrease fear of "fatness" with compulsive behaviors. Therefore, it can be inferred that when these behaviors are present, the nature of the disorder is self-eclipsing. If a disorder is determined to be more self-eclipsing than self-acknowledged in stage 1, it is recommended that treatment goals remain the same (carers decrease RABs, increase RIBs, and provide Rec-SPA). The idea here is that the collective external messaging provided by decreasing RABs, increasing RIBs, and providing Rec-SPA becomes internalized. Over time, these internalized messages change a self-eclipsed disorder to a self-acknowledged disorder.

There are several indicators that the disorder is no longer self-eclipsing and has become self-acknowledged. Primarily, fear of "fatness" is no longer driving decision making. A working tolerance of fear of "fatness" has developed. In other words, fear of "fatness" is not completely gone, but the patient's behavior is not governed by it, and they are not currently seeking control. Instead, there is appropriate caution about taking on responsibility. If the disorder has become self-acknowledged, then the patient will articulate very appropriate worry that the eating disorder will return.

Here are some signs that a patient may be ready to make the transition from stage 1 to stage 2:

- The patient is cautious about taking over responsibility for food.

- The patient is worried that the eating disorder will come back.

- The patient reports feeling relieved that carers have responsibility for food.

- The patient views taking on responsibility for food as a challenge.

- The patient is willing to be collaborative.

- The patient is willing to go at a slow and steady pace.

Here are some signs that a patient may not be ready to make the transition from stage 1 to stage 2:

- The patient is begging for food responsibility.

- The patient is trying to convince the therapist and carers that they are ready.

- The patient makes very clever, cogent, and charming arguments for why they are ready.

- The patient seems desperate to take over responsibility for food.

- The patient usurps session time to make overtures for food responsibility.

- The patient wants to take control.

- The patient wants to take a lot of responsibility all at once.

- The patient has clearly stated the intention to engage in eating disorder behaviors the moment they regain responsibility over food, so as to lose weight and/or regulate emotions.

Assessment, Tracking, and Troubleshooting

Duration varies

As in every session, about five to ten minutes prior to the start of session, the carers and the patient should complete an IMT family evaluation (although exceptions can be made). Again, the patient's BMI should be plotted at the beginning of session.

The Food and Behavior Log should be reviewed each session, and the therapist should provide feedback accordingly. Discuss the reduction of RABs, increasing RIBs, and refining Rec-SPA. Provide relevant psychoeducation.

Stage 1 in Review

In the final session of stage 1, it is important to review treatment thus far. Time should be spent reviewing the carers' and patient's initial IMT intake measures as well as early IMT family therapy measures. Answers given on current measures should be compared with answers given on earlier measures. Carers and patients should be provided with positive feedback on the specific behaviors they were able to shape. Reflect on how far the family has come. Spend time processing the changes that have occurred since treatment began. Allow family members time and space to express their thoughts and feelings about what occurred in stage 1. Be sure to ask about both negative and positive emotional experiences. If family members feel inclined to express gratitude to one another at this time, the therapist can encourage this. For instance, carers may start by expressing gratitude to the patient's sibling for coming to session, helping with setting the table, and spending time with the family after meals. Carers may also thank the patient for complying with treatment rules and working hard to fight the eating disorder by completing meals at home. The patient may then want to express gratitude to the carers for helping them recover and to siblings for being supportive.

Before the session is over, be sure to provide a general verbal overview of stage 2 as well as a pep talk. Introduce the idea that the patient will gradually regain responsibilities related to recovery (selecting foods, preparing foods, and so forth). Explain that the process will be collaborative and that decisions will be made in session rather than at home, but do not go over the specifics yet. Providing the family with a general verbal overview at this time is recommended, to help them mentally prepare for reading the specifics outlined in the handouts. After generally reviewing stage 2, be sure to encourage family members to keep up the good work with a pep talk. The pep talk has to include the following elements:

- It has been difficult so far.

- Everyone has done well.

- It will continue to be difficult.

- Everyone must continue to play their roles.

- The eating disorder may come back.

- Everyone must be on their guard.

Here is an example of a pep talk: "For all the reasons discussed today, and more, it has been really tough for your family to band together to fight the eating disorder. It wasn't easy, and you have all done well. Now that stage 1 of treatment is coming to an end, things are getting a little better, which is great. At the same time, treatment is very far from over. Things are going to keep being difficult until this eating disorder is completely gone. Everyone must continue to play their roles and fight the eating disorder. At any moment, the eating disorder may rear its head again. The war is not over until it is over. Everyone must be on their guard. At times you may be exhausted, or it may feel OK to just relax about the treatment rules for a little bit. But if this happens prematurely, the eating disorder can come roaring back. Then again, sometimes families may be reluctant to give up control over food. Stage 2 has to be moved through slowly and methodically to help keep the eating disorder at bay while allowing the person who is struggling with it an opportunity to practice having responsibility for their own recovery. Does everyone understand? Any questions?"

Homework Assignment

5 minutes

Carers will be assigned the reading of FAM Handout 1.34 for homework. The carers are also asked to continue implementing all the rules, decreasing RABs, increasing RIBs, and providing Rec-SPA. They are also asked to continue completing the Food and Behavior Log until they are given the stage 2 family therapy measures.

Stage 1, Final Session: To-Dos

60 minutes

☐ Administer same assessments as on intake.

☐ Administer IMT measures.

☐ Assess and plot BMI.

☐ Review the Food and Behavior Log and provide feedback.

☐ Review any relevant psychoeducation.

☐ Compare answers to measures from present session with answers to measures from start of stage 1.

☐ Process stage 1.

☐ Introduce stage 2 generally.

☐ Give pep talk in preparation for stage 2.

☐ Troubleshoot and provide feedback and/or work individually with the patient.

☐ Assign homework:

   ☐ Carers complete the Food and Behavior Log.

   ☐ Carers read FAM Handout 1.34.

Stage 2 IMT Family Therapy

The following handouts, presented here according to the phases in which they are administered, are used in stage 2 of family therapy:

PHASE 1: EARNED FREEDOMS

   FAM Handout 2.1: Responsibilities in Recovery: Earned Freedoms

   FAM Handout 2.2: Earned Freedom Levels (AN Version)

   FAM Handout 2.3: Earned Freedom Levels (BOB Version)

   FAM Handout 2.4: "Forever Nevers," Even After Treatment Ends

   FAM Handout 2.5: The Ten Treatment Rules of Stage 2 for Carers (AN Version)

   FAM Handout 2.6: The Ten Treatment Rules of Stage 2 for Carers (BOB Version)

In stage 2, in addition to the designated patient versions of handouts, we recommend that patients be given copies of the following handouts:

FAM Handout 2.1: Responsibilities in Recovery: Earned Freedoms

FAM Handout 2.2: Earned Freedom Levels (AN Version)

FAM Handout 2.3: Earned Freedom Levels (BOB Version)

FAM Handout 2.4: "Forever Nevers," Even After Treatment Ends

FAM Handout 2.5: The Ten Treatment Rules of Stage 2 for Carers (AN Version)

FAM Handout 2.6: The Ten Treatment Rules of Stage 2 for Carers (BOB Version)

FAM Handout 2.14: Triggers: Look Out!

FAM/PT Handout 2.15: Earned Freedom Roadmap

FAM/PT Handout 2.16: Stage 2 Eating Disorder Behaviors and Recovery Behaviors

FAM/PT Handout 2.20: Challenge Foods

FAM Handout 2.21: Repairing the Relationship with Your Family

In stage 2, we recommend that the following handouts be given to schools that have staff members (guidance counselors, psychologists, and so forth) who are involved in the supervision of meals:

FAM Handout 2.1: Responsibilities in Recovery: Earned Freedoms

FAM Handout 2.2: Earned Freedom Levels (AN Version)

FAM Handout 2.3: Earned Freedom Levels (BOB Version)

FAM Handout 2.4: "Forever Nevers," Even After Treatment Ends

FAM Handout 2.7: The Ten Treatment Rules of Stage 2 for Schools

FAM Handout 2.10: How to Implement Earned Freedoms

FAM Handout 2.11: The Difference Between Rewards and Earned Freedoms

FAM Handout 2.17: Planning for Eating Disorder Urges in Stage 2

FAM Handout 2.18: Giving Recovery-Specific Positive Attention in Stage 2

Stage 2: Objectives

Just as in stage 1, treatment will be accelerated or decelerated depending on a given family's strengths and obstacles to be overcome. Regardless of the obstacles presented, however, there is a given set of objectives to be met. Figure 3.3.2 lists the objectives to be met throughout the course of stage 2 IMT family therapy.

PHASE 1: EARNED FREEDOMS

- Provide psychoeducation about temptation to hand responsibility back too quickly or too slowly.
- Provide general psychoeducation about earned freedoms.
- Introduce phase 1 handouts in linear fashion:
    - FAM Handout 2.1
    - FAM Handout 2.2
    - FAM Handout 2.3
    - FAM Handout 2.4
    - FAM Handout 2.5
    - FAM Handout 2.6
    - FAM Handout 2.7
    - FAM Handout 2.8
    - FAM Handout 2.9
    - FAM Handout 2.10
    - FAM Handout 2.11
    - FAM Handout 2.12
    - FAM Handout 2.13
    - FAM Handout 2.14
    - FAM/PT Handout 2.15
    - FAM/PT Handout 2.16
    - FAM Handout 2.17
    - FAM Handout 2.18
    - PT Handout 2.1
- Select and implement earned freedom(s).
- Introduce Weekly Earned Freedom Log: Start of Stage 2.
- Review earned freedom(s) and decide each week whether to retain or revoke.

PHASE 2: CHALLENGE FOODS

- Cover the concept in FAM Handout 2.19.
- Construct a fear hierarchy using FAM Handout 2.19 and FAM Handout 2.20.
- Conduct food exposures in session with family, following checklist in phase 2 portion of this section of the manual.
- Conduct a sufficient number of food exposures to foster the patient's ability to make recovery-oriented choices with given responsibility.
- Plan for challenge foods from the hierarchy to be eaten at home.
- Patient reviews PT Handout 2.2 and continues to work through obtaining all appropriate earned freedoms.

PHASE 3: REPAIRING RELATIONSHIPS

- Introduce Daily Earned Freedom Log: End of Stage 2.
- Each family member should complete FAM Handout 2.21 in session and share.
- Family members with history of highly critical remarks should complete FAM Handout 2.21 separately and rehearse responses to patient with therapist.
- Administer FAM Handout 2.22.
- Make a plan for quality time.
- Check in weekly on quality time throughout phase 3.

PHASE 4: INCREASING AWARENESS OF HUNGER AND FULLNESS CUES

- Administer FAM Handout 2.23.
- Patient reviews PT Handout 2.3 and completes Belly Signals Log.

PRETERMINATION

- Administer FAM Handout 2.24 and FAM Handout 2.25.
- Assign gratitude letter writing.

TERMINATION

- Congratulate each member of the family for the part played.
- Administer IMT family measures to carers and patient and compare to scores on intake.
- Each family member reads gratitude letters in session.

Figure 3.3.2. Stage 2 Objectives

Stage 2: Detailed Administration Instructions

Stage 2, Phase 1: Earned Freedoms

Phase 1 of the second stage of behavioral family therapy is focused on orienting the family to the patient receiving responsibilities for their own recovery. Read each session outline in phase 1 for more information.

Stage 2, Phase 1, Session 1: Earned Freedom Orientation

The first session of stage 2 sets the stage for the remainder of family treatment. All family members involved in treatment should attend this session. The importance of continued treatment and the basics of earned freedoms are discussed. Here, we outline how to conduct the initial session of the new treatment stage.

Assessment, Tracking, and Troubleshooting

Duration varies

Do the following at the start of session:

- Administer assessments prior to session.

- Regarding the IMT measures specifically, until the necessary stage 2 material is taught to the family, they cannot complete the stage 2 IMT family therapy measures. Therefore, it is recommended that the stage 1 IMT measures be administered instead.

- Plot patient's BMI.

- The Food and Behavior Log should be reviewed each session, and the therapist should provide feedback.

- Discuss the reduction of RABs, increasing RIBs, and refining Rec-SPA.

- Provide relevant psychoeducation, as needed.

Setting a Celebratory Tone

3 minutes

Officially welcome the family to stage 2 with a celebratory attitude. Congratulate them on their hard work. Make sure to review the behaviors that each family member engaged in that were particularly crucial to recovery. For instance, you may want to point out that a carer strictly adhered to the treatment rules, used frequent TABLE skills and ceased use of ED WINS habits, provided a lot of appropriate recovery-specific positive attention, and completed the handouts assigned as homework. Similarly, acknowledge the patient's specific behaviors, such as consistently finishing dinners while tolerating negative emotions.

Discussing the Need for Medical Appointments

2 minutes

On the one hand, you must set a celebratory tone in the first stage 2 session. On the other, you must stress the importance of ongoing medical appointments. After coordinating with the patient's physician, however, the patient may be cleared to visit the doctor on a less frequent schedule (for example, every two to four weeks). It is advisable to contact the patient's physician to be sure of the recommended frequency of visits.

The Importance of Continued Treatment

15 minutes

Before proceeding with stage 2, a therapist must assess the treatment burden. Carers may be feeling tired and could be at risk for dropping out of treatment. It is important to take the time to compassionately listen and discover not only how the eating disorder has been impacting the lives of family members but also how the treatment has been implemented. Here are some questions to ask:

- How long is their drive?

- How many times have they had to take off from work?

- What is the financial impact of treatment (copays, gas, missed work, food costs)?

- How often did the carers cry after having to feed their child who was pleading with them for mercy?

- How many times did they have to see their child sad because they were in pain from having a full stomach?

- How often were they afraid of an outburst at a meal?

- How much time did the treatment take away from spending time with each other or their other children?

A therapist must both assess the burden and compassionately empathize. Once the burden is fully assessed, a therapist can fully and compassionately validate family members' experiences. The therapist can then assert that treatment must continue, even in the face of the presented obstacles, because the eating disorder must be overcome. A therapist must remind the family of how dangerous eating disorders are and how quickly they can return if not addressed. At this stage, carers are often exhausted and optimistic about the patient's recovery, given past successes. They may be all too willing to hand over excessive responsibility before the patient is ready, providing ample opportunities for eating disorder behaviors to be reinforced and for the monster to come roaring back.

If you find yourself struggling to assert the need for continued treatment in the context of given obstacles, put yourself in the carers' position. If you were a carer currently tired from implementing treatment, unaware of high relapse rates, and not fully informed about what was at stake, would you or would you not want your provider to speak from experience and push you a little bit farther at this point in your child's illness? It is your obligation as the therapist to assess not only for unwittingly optimistic attitudes but also for exhaustion and to provide accurate information about the chances that the eating disorder behaviors will be reinforced. The family needs both your empathy and your firmness to stick to the plan. When you take the time to assess the toll that treatment has taken on the family and to empathize with them, it sends a very strong message about the importance of stage 2 treatment when you are still adamant about their continued treatment.

Psychoeducation (+Patient Copies: FAM Handout 2.1, FAM Handout 2.2 [AN Version] or FAM Handout 2.3 [BOB Version], FAM Handout 2.4, and FAM Handout 2.5 [AN Version] or FAM Handout 2.6 [BOB Version])

20 minutes

Although earned freedoms will not be implemented in the first session, the concept is concretely introduced here. Review FAM Handout 2.1, FAM Handout 2.2 (AN Version) or FAM Handout 2.3 (BOB Version), FAM Handout 2.4, and FAM Handout 2.5 (AN Version) or FAM Handout 2.6 (BOB Version) with the patient and family present, and provide copies of these handouts to the patient. These handouts contain the key concepts to present, and so they will not be reviewed here.

It is recommended that the pocket-size summary of the treatment rules in FAM Handout 2.5 (AN Version) or FAM Handout 2.6 (BOB Version) be implemented in session. The expanded version should be kept on hand in the event that questions arise and be administered to the family for reference. The therapist should also be familiar with the nuances of these rules. Explain to the family that no earned freedoms are being implemented yet, and that the rules are simply being explained at this point.

Homework Assignment (+Patient Version: PT Handout 2.1)

5 minutes

Carers read FAM Handout 2.9 and FAM Handout 2.10 for homework, and the patient reads PT Handout 2.1. The family is to continue implementing all stage 1 treatment rules and completing the stage 1 Food and Behavior Log.

Stage 2, Phase 1, Session 1: To-Dos

☐ Administer a selection of assessments and IMT stage 1 measures (even though it is stage 2).

☐ Assess and plot BMI.

☐ Review treatment progress and provide feedback.

☐ Set a celebratory tone toward decreased medical risk.

☐ Discuss the ongoing need for medical appointments in stage 2.

☐ Discuss the importance of continued treatment in stage 2.

  ☐ Assess the family's treatment burden.

  ☐ Empathize with family.

  ☐ Assert that continued treatment is needed.

☐ Introduce the concept of earned freedoms with FAM Handout 2.1 and FAM Handout 2.2 (AN Version) or FAM Handout 2.3 (BOB Version).

☐ Assign homework:

  ☐ Carers read FAM Handout 2.9 and FAM Handout 2.10.

  ☐ Patient reads PT Handout 2.1.

Stage 2, Phase 1, Session 2: How to Implement Earned Freedoms

The second session of stage 2 is the start of discussing how earned freedoms are implemented. All family members involved should attend this session. Here, we outline how to conduct the second session of stage 2.

Assessment, Tracking, and Troubleshooting

Duration varies

Do the following at the start of session:

• Administer relevant assessments prior to session, and a stage 1 IMT family measure (this is done until relevant stage 2 material is covered).

• Plot patient's BMI.

- The Food and Behavior Log should be reviewed each session, and the therapist should provide feedback.

- Discuss the reduction of RABs, increasing RIBs, and refining Rec-SPA.

- Briefly review FAM Handout 2.9 and FAM Handout 2.10, which were assigned as homework.

- Provide relevant psychoeducation, as needed.

Psychoeducation

25 minutes

With all family members present, administer FAM Handout 2.10 and FAM Handout 2.11. Spend the majority of this session making all the relevant earned freedom concepts clear. Before the patient tries out an earned freedom, all the information must be conveyed.

Homework Assignment

5 minutes

This week, carers are assigned the reading of FAM Handout 2.12 and FAM Handout 2.13.

Stage 2, Phase 1, Session 2: To-Dos

☐ Administer a selection of assessments and IMT stage 1 measures (even though it is stage 2).

☐ Assess and plot BMI.

☐ Review treatment progress and provide feedback.

☐ Cover FAM Handout 2.10 and FAM Handout 2.11 in session

☐ Assign homework:

    ☐ Carers read FAM Handout 2.12 and FAM Handout 2.13.

Stage 2, Phase 1, Session 3: Earned Freedom Implementation

The third session of stage 2 is the start of earned freedoms being implemented. All family members involved in treatment should attend this session. Here, we outline how to conduct the third session of stage 2.

Assessment, Tracking, and Troubleshooting

Duration varies

Do the following at the start of session:

- Administer a stage 1 IMT Family measure (this is done until relevant stage 2 material is covered).

- Plot patient's BMI.

- The Food and Behavior Log should be reviewed each session, and the therapist should provide feedback.

- Discuss the reduction of RABs, increasing RIBs, and refining Rec-SPA.

- Briefly review FAM Handout 2.12 and FAM Handout 2.13, which were assigned as homework.

- Provide relevant psychoeducation, as needed.

Psychoeducation: Implementing Earned Freedoms

This portion of the session is spent reviewing FAM Handout 2.12 and FAM Handout 2.13, on wise expectations about recovery and ways in which eating disorders may disguise themselves in stage 2.

TRIGGERS: LOOK OUT! (+PATIENT COPY: FAM HANDOUT 2.14)

10 minutes

FAM handouts administered since the beginning of stage 2 are largely about moving forward in recovery, with caution. FAM Handout 2.14, however, takes the focus squarely back to the eating disorder. Beyond warnings, it is helpful for carers to be provided with concrete information about how gaining responsibility may very well trigger eating disorder symptoms in patients. FAM Handout 2.14 helps families be prepared for eating disorder behaviors to temporarily reemerge in the context of being provided with earned freedoms. This will help guide the carers in contributing to the conversation about what earned freedom may be appropriate to implement.

EARNED FREEDOM ROADMAP (+PATIENT COPY: FAM/PT HANDOUT 2.15)

30 minutes

Use FAM/PT Handout 2.15 to help create a plan about the order in which to tackle earned freedoms in session. The process of completing FAM/PT Handout 2.15 is a collaborative one and includes the participation of the patient, carers, and therapist. To guide in constructing the hierarchy, use FAM Handout 2.2 (AN Version) or FAM Handout 2.3 (BOB Version) on levels of earned freedoms.

The therapist must take many factors into account when collaborating with the family to construct the earned freedom hierarchy. For instance, the therapist must assess for the patient's expressed fear of relapsing, the patient's eating disorder urges, the eating disorder's role in *not wanting* responsibility, and the eating disorder's role in *wanting* responsibility. Once information is gathered on these four topics, it must be integrated into an earned freedom hierarchy.

It can be puzzling and frustrating for carers when patients are suddenly fearful of the very freedoms for which they were previously desperate. It seems as if as soon as the carers finally want to hand over responsibility, the patient is resistant. It is important for the therapist to convey to the carers that the patient may not necessarily find it rewarding to be given an earned freedom. First, a patient fearful of earned freedoms may truly be terrified of relapse. Because resisting recovery is a hallmark of self-eclipsing disorders, having fear about relapse is a good sign. If the patient is simply afraid of relapsing, then the therapist and carers can work with the patient on building the confidence to implement earned freedoms. That said, the amount of confidence about recovery behaviors actually occurring because a patient shows hesitancy toward earned freedoms needs to be tempered with the presence of both fear of "fatness" and foods as well as eating disorder urges. In other words, if the patient is both afraid of not being supervised and has strong eating disorder urges, it is important to not inundate the patient with responsibility. But if the patient reports low fear of "fatness" as well as foods, denies urges, and shows hesitancy toward receiving earned freedoms, they should be encouraged to take on more responsibility.

The matter of constructing the earned freedom hierarchy is complicated further when considering other sources of fear about earning freedoms. The therapist must be acutely aware of the eating disorder's influence on either wanting too many earned freedoms or even avoiding them. If the eating disorder is still strong, it may of course want to abuse any control over food (for example, use an opportunity to restrict when a meal is not supervised). Conversely, the eating disorder may also not want to have control over food, for many reasons. For instance, the eating disorder may not want to have a choice between two snacks because it is the equivalent of admitting that the patient likes the food. The austere eating disorder considers liking food a weakness that must be repressed. Therefore, the earned freedom to choose between two snacks might be resisted because of the eating disorder. Further, even though having the carers take control of food was initially distressing in stage 1, the eating disorder may have habituated to this highly controlled form of eating by now. Somewhat ironically, the initial stage of treatment for eating disorders involves the implementation of an extreme amount of control over food. And once all the careful monitoring of food volume and weight starts to lessen, the eating disorder becomes agitated. In this case, anxiety about taking on earned freedom is not because the patient is fearful of relapse but because the rigid eating disorder now has an aversion to altering the rules around food.

When these more eating disorder–related causes of earned freedom aversion are present, it is important that the therapist address them early in treatment. If the eating disorder does not want to make a choice between two snacks, for instance, this should be one of the earlier earned freedoms selected. Although this earned freedom may be difficult for the patient, it still allows for almost complete control of food by carers. If an eating disorder urge is triggered by the selection of food, the carers already have an entire system in place to prevent the patient from acting on the urges. Therefore, choosing between two foods is an appropriate early earned freedom. Similarly, if the eating disorder wants the carers to keep complete control of food, start small with some of the level A earned freedoms listed in FAM Handout 2.2 (AN Version) or FAM Handout 2.3 (BOB Version).

If the eating disorder wants too many responsibilities back at once, resist the temptation to simply hand out an earned freedom because the patient is technically in stage 2. Other aspects of the eating disorder can be addressed. For instance, the therapist might want to start conducting exposures to specific types of food rather than implementing earned freedoms. It is important to resist the urge to implement earned freedoms in the context of the eating disorder asking for them. This is part of the reason why the therapist's role is to guide the family in the collaborative process of implementing earned freedoms. Family members, of course, may be acutely aware of the eating disorder's tricks at this point. When a family member suspects the eating disorder is in play, it should be taken seriously. Everyone's opinion is important when selecting an earned freedom. Because the family has been implementing the treatment at home, they have a lot of information on this disorder. At the same time, they may be worn down and at risk of overburdening the patient with responsibility. It is important for a therapist to keep an objective eye out for all these factors.

In short, construction of the hierarchy certainly involves some clinical art. Rank only earned freedoms that the patient is not currently implementing (patients with BOB disorders may have earned freedoms already). Regarding the selection of an earned freedom to implement given this hierarchy, we encourage families to start at the very bottom of the list. (This is unlike fear exposures, in which exposures start around a ranking of 6 to 9.)

Selecting an Earned Freedom to Implement

15 minutes

Considering that the therapist plays a collaborative role in helping the family choose an earned freedom, being able to gauge the approximate strength of a given patient's eating disorder is helpful. At times, patients are very straightforward about what they are and are not ready to handle. Conversely, other patients are either less skilled at judging their readiness or can be more reticent. Of course, there is also the ever-present possibility that the eating disorder is lurking in the shadows and influencing either the desire to obtain control of food or the desire to avoid it completely.

Estimating the Strength of an Eating Disorder: Two Suggestions

First, if the patient is arguing for a specific responsibility, put yourself in their shoes. Consider the patient's recent behavior in session or the patient's behavior at home as it has been described to you. Specifically, consider how *you* would react if you had a serious medical condition that put you at risk for relapse and were asked to eat five more bites of food when not wanting to, were asked to eat even though you were really full, couldn't use the bathroom after eating because it would set you up for relapse, or couldn't eat unless you were being supervised.

Second, assess whether the patient is feeling intense, eating disorder–related, negative emotions. Ask the patient specific questions about how they're feeling:

- On a scale of 0 to 10, how much anxiety are you experiencing right now (for example, while eating a snack)?

- On a scale of 0 to 10, how much guilt are you experiencing right now (for example, after eating a snack)?

- On a scale of 0 to 10, how much disgust are you experiencing right now (for example, while eating dinner)?

- On a scale of 0 to 10, how intensely would you experience negative emotions if we carried on with the current level of supervision (for example, supervising snacks)?

- On a scale of 0 to 10, how intensely would you experience negative emotions if you were to have less supervision for a specific food responsibility (for example, while eating a snack)?

Considering the answers to these questions may help you determine the strength of a given eating disorder. In short, if the patient reports intensely negative emotions for the first three questions and decreased emotions for the last two questions, then the eating disorder may very well be in play. Further, take note of any oppositional behavior. Does the patient appear to be overreacting to the idea of the carers retaining control? Young people have been known to be oppositional or emotional for various reasons, and so it is probably advisable to take account of the patient's general inclination toward emotionality and oppositionality. But if the patient is strongly advocating for a specific food responsibility and is emotional or volatile, it is likely that their behavior is being influenced by the eating disorder. The questions to ask the patient about their current experience of negative emotions will also give you information about how the eating disorder is potentially triggering the patient. As you will learn from the stage 2 IMT family handouts, patients practice having some food responsibilities in session (such as by making a peanut butter and jelly sandwich with the therapist). By asking for ratings of negative emotions in session, you can get an idea of the patient's emotional readiness for a given earned freedom.

Implementing an Earned Freedom

After carefully considering an earned freedom to try this week, discuss any concerns the patient or carer(s) have about implementing it. Discuss warning signs that the eating disorder might be emerging. Inform carers that they may discontinue the earned freedom if they suspect that the eating disorder is being strengthened by the new opportunity to engage in eating disorder behaviors, or if the patient loses weight for any reason. Encourage carers to rely on their judgment regarding the discontinuation of the earned freedom during the week in between sessions.

Reinforcement-Seeking Eating Disorder and Recovery Behaviors (+Patient Copy: FAM/PT Handout 2.16)

10 minutes

FAM/PT Handout 2.16 is very similar to FAM Handout 1.16 (AN Version) and FAM Handout 1.17 (BOB Version) from stage 1. Simply review some of the key differences of this particular handout, which creates a framework for stage 2. Most notably, there is an emphasis on the patient taking responsibility for their own recovery behaviors over time. This is exemplified in items such as eating challenging types of food, decreasing controlling behaviors while eating (for example, cutting food into tiny pieces), choosing not to engage in food measurement, and engaging in physical activity for fun rather than for weight loss.

Because carers are now quite practiced in knowing what and how to feed their child, it is no longer necessary for them to record food in stage 2 IMT family therapy. We do strongly suggest, however, that carers monitor the implementation of earned freedoms and the patient's behavior in stage 2. For this segment of treatment, there is a simple table called the Weekly Earned Freedom Log: Start of Stage 2. Carers are to simply write the earned freedom being implemented this week at the top of the form and record any eating disorder and recovery behaviors that arise around mealtimes (such as dinner) or activities (such as playing sports), using FAM/PT Handout 2.16 as a reference. If no eating disorder behaviors occur, carers are asked to make a dash through the "Eating Disorder Behavior" cell rather than leaving the cell blank. If an eating disorder behavior is logged, this provides useful data for the therapist about either the particular earned freedom being implemented or the pace at which new earned freedoms should possibly be set. Carers are encouraged to always write in a recovery behavior around mealtimes so that carers continue to hone the skill of always noticing the positive.

Nearer to the end of stage 2, when the patient has regained almost all appropriate responsibilities for food, the Daily Earned Freedoms Log: End of Stage 2 can be administered. This log is to be used as the directions indicate. Carers are to check off as many eating disorder behaviors and recovery behaviors as possible. In practice, using this log before a significant number of earned freedoms have been implemented can cause confusion about how many recovery behaviors the patient is supposed to be engaging in all at once. Therefore, administer this log only nearer to the end of stage 2.

Homework Assignment

5 minutes

The family is to implement an earned freedom at home, and carers are to complete the Weekly Earned Freedom Log: Start of Stage 2. Additionally, carers are to read and complete the "Discussion Points" section of FAM Handout 2.17.

Stage 2, Phase 1, Session 3: To-Dos

☐ Administer a selection of assessments and IMT stage 1 measures (even though it is stage 2).

☐ Assess and plot BMI.

☐ Review treatment progress and provide feedback.

☐ Assess and plot BMI.

☐ Review FAM Handout 2.12 and FAM Handout 2.13, which were assigned for homework.

☐ Introduce FAM Handout 2.14, FAM/PT Handout 2.15, and FAM/PT Handout 2.16 in session.

☐ Select an earned freedom.

☐ Introduce the Weekly Earned Freedom Log: Start of Stage 2.

☐ Assign homework:

    ☐ Family implements earned freedom.

    ☐ Carers complete the Weekly Earned Freedom Log: Start of Stage 2.

    ☐ Carers read FAM Handout 2.17.

Stage 2, Phase 1, Session 4: Recovery-Specific Positive Attention

The fourth session of stage 2 is focused primarily on providing Rec-SPA in the context of stage 2 by recognizing making recovery-oriented choices as well as planning for triggers.

Assessment, Tracking, and Troubleshooting

Duration varies

Do the following at the start of session:

- Administer a stage 2 IMT family measure for the first time.

- Plot patient's BMI.

- The Weekly Earned Freedom Log: Start of Stage 2 should be reviewed, and the therapist should provide feedback.

- Discuss any eating disorder behaviors that arose in the context of implementing the earned freedom.

- Decide if the earned freedom will be kept or must be revoked.

- Decide if another earned freedom should be added.

- Briefly review FAM Handout 2.17, which was assigned as homework.

- Provide relevant psychoeducation, as needed.

Discussing the Earned Freedom

15 minutes

From this session until the end of stage 2, examine the Weekly Earned Freedom Log: Start of Stage 2 and discuss both the carers' and the patient's feedback on how the earned freedom went. It may be helpful to meet with the patient individually to assess for eating disorder urges that may have arisen during the week. It is also advisable to ask how the eating disorder influenced the patient's behavior this week in the context of having an earned freedom. If after meeting with both the patient and carers it appears that the earned freedom implementation was a success, the patient may retain the earned freedom. Further, determine if the patient is ready for an additional earned freedom this week or would like to continue working on the previously selected one. If, however, the earned freedom proved to be too triggering, the earned freedom may be revoked. Note that if eating disorder behaviors significantly return or weight begins to destabilize, a return to implementing treatment rules from stage 1 can occur; either the exact rules can be implemented or a new treatment involvement plan can be derived from FAM Handout 1.11 (AN Version) or FAM Handout 1.12 (BOB Version).

Homework Review

FAM Handout 2.17 further prepares carers to cope with their child's potential eating disorder urges or behaviors that may arise from a given earned freedom and effectively act to help their child through them. Carers are instructed to examine their own emotions around their child's potential eating disorder urges or behaviors and start thinking about how they might respond in a helpful way. If carers did not complete the "Discussion Points" section of FAM Handout 2.17 for homework, have them complete this in session. Depending on family dynamics, it may be best to review this information in private with the carers. It may be helpful to role-play a scenario in which the patient (played by the therapist) discloses having eating disorder urges or behaviors to the carers and then to ask carers to respond effectively in session. Give carers feedback as to their performance, and offer suggestions. Role-play until the carer is able to generate an effective response to being told about eating disorder urges or behaviors.

Psychoeducation: Recovery-Specific Positive Attention in Stage 2

10 minutes

Introduce FAM Handout 2.18 on giving the patient recovery-specific positive attention in stage 2. As stated in the handout, the idea here is to start providing Rec-SPA for the patient choosing to engage in recovery-oriented behaviors when given the opportunity to engage in eating disorder behaviors. As in stage 1, patients may resist reinforcement. In this stage, reinforcement is resisted because recovery behavior is being chosen. As stated at the end of the handout, the same logic applies here as in stage 1—if the patient is resistant or oppositional, start small with nonverbal Rec-SPA (such as a smile and a thumbs-up).

Homework Assignment

5 minutes

Carers are to continue completing the Weekly Earned Freedom Log: Start of Stage 2. This week, there is also special attention paid to providing Rec-SPA in stage 2.

Stage 2, Phase 1, Session 4: To-Dos

- ☐ Administer a selection of assessments and IMT stage 2 measures prior to session.
- ☐ Assess and plot BMI.
- ☐ Review Weekly Earned Freedom Log: Start of Stage 2 and provide feedback.
- ☐ Select a new earned freedom, if appropriate.
- ☐ Review FAM Handout 2.17, which was assigned for homework.
- ☐ Introduce FAM Handout 2.18 in session.
- ☐ Assign homework:
  - ☐ Family implements earned freedom.
  - ☐ Carers complete the Weekly Earned Freedom Log: Start of Stage 2.
  - ☐ Review handouts as necessary.

Stage 2, Phase 1, Session 5 and Beyond

Beginning in session 5 and for the remainder of phase 1 in stage 2, administer the stage 2 IMT family measures. It is also appropriate to continue plotting the patient's BMI until the termination of treatment. Regarding homework, have the carers continue to fill out the Weekly Earned Freedom Log: Start of Stage 2. The process of discussing the previous week's earned freedom, determining the eating disorder's influence, deciding whether to retain the earned freedom, and selecting a new earned freedom should continue. Lastly, as earned freedoms get more advanced, practice the earned freedom in session, if possible. If the patient is afraid of a given earned freedom, then the practice of it in session should be conducted as an exposure—planned, using the subjective units of distress (SUD) scale throughout (SUDs ratings), and so forth. For instance, if the patient is afraid of preparing a lunch, the lunch can be made in session.

Stage 2, Phase 1, Session 5 and Beyond: To-Dos

☐ Administer a selection of assessments prior to session and stage 2 IMT measure.

☐ Assess and plot BMI.

☐ Review the Weekly Earned Freedom Log: Start of Stage 2 and provide feedback.

☐ Select a new earned freedom to implement, if appropriate (or revoke earned freedom, if appropriate).

☐ Practice earned freedoms in session, if appropriate.

☐ Review handouts.

☐ Assign homework:

    ☐ Carers complete Weekly Earned Freedom Log: Start of Stage 2.

    ☐ Implement earned freedoms.

    ☐ Review handouts as necessary.

Stage 2, Phase 2: Challenge Foods

Regardless of diagnosis, the main eating disorder behavior to target in stage 1 is food restriction (for people with AN and often for people with AAN, it is food volume that must be increased; for people with BN, it is restriction that must be decreased so that ultimately both binge eating and purging are decreased). In stage 2, however, the focus begins to shift more to targeting food avoidance. If specific categories of foods are still feared (fats, carbohydrates, and so forth) when the patient is given the responsibility to make meal and snack choices, the result may be that reinforcement-seeking eating disorder behaviors (such as selecting safe foods) rather than recovery behaviors (such as selecting scary foods) are enacted. For instance, if the patient is charged with selecting meals but is extremely fearful of fats, carbohydrates, sugars, and meat, it is unlikely that the patient will select a meal of steak, potatoes, and candied carrots. It is much more likely that the patient will be handed this earned freedom only to have it revoked, ushering in feelings of failure. Therefore, to support the patient in being handed this earned freedom, conducting relevant food exposures is sensible in safeguarding the patient.

Because food exposures are also conducted in individual therapy, the object of conducting food exposures in family therapy is not to completely extinguish fear of all foods in the hierarchy. The idea here is to shift the focus toward confronting negative emotions about food while the family is still involved so that the patient can be liberated from eating disorder–related fear and make recovery-oriented decisions when presented with the opportunity. Extinguishing fear of foods is a treatment target for individual therapy. Therefore, therapists currently administering the family therapy modality are encouraged to use their clinical judgment in conducting exposures with foods that the patient is likely to encounter often at home and is in the anxiety "sweet spot" about (that is, foods that are not too easy and not too difficult).

The Importance of Confronting Fear of Foods (+Patient Version: PT Handout 2.2)

Although distraction was a technique used to make eating more bearable in stage 1, confronting negative emotions becomes more of a target in stage 2. FAM Handout 2.19 reminds carers and patients that eating disorders are based in fear, and that fears must be confronted in therapy, despite a given food's specific nutritional value (or lack thereof).

Challenge Foods (+ Patient Copy: FAM/PT Handout 2.20)

This handout is simply a fear hierarchy of challenge foods. This should be completed in session, like any other fear hierarchy; however, in this case, the family is present. The most feared foods are to be recorded at the top of the list, and the foods should get progressively less feared as the list progresses. Refer patients to the anxiety scale at the end of the handout to help in the process of ranking challenge foods. If patients are struggling to rank foods, offer examples of foods to rank, or ask carers for examples of foods to rank (cookies, brownies, French fries, and so forth).

Notably, the level of scariness (ranking) of the foods is not static. In behavioral language, not only can exposure result in habituation to feared stimuli, but the habituation can also generalize to similar foods. In other words, as patients start to fear a particular food less, similar foods are also feared less. This changes the hierarchy. For instance, cookies may initially be ranked at 10 on the list, followed by brownies at 9. If the patient does an exposure to brownies but not to cookies, both brownies and cookies, because they are similar, could fall to 5 and 6, respectively. Therefore, relatively speaking, French fries with melted cheese would then take the top rank. As patients work through exposure exercises, the list of challenge foods will change over time. FAM/PT Handout 2.20 will need to be completed several times before the end of family therapy.

The most recently completed version of FAM/PT Handout 2.20 should be used to guide the selection of foods for in-session fear exposures in which SUDs ratings (0–10) are taken before, during, and after eating the food. Food exposures are conducted as any other exposures are conducted, the only difference being that family members are present. Therefore, the patient should typically be feeling a low level of distress (less than 4) before the session ends. The following checklist can be used in conducting a food exposure:

- ☐ Select a food that is challenging but not too distressing (ranked in the range of 6 to 9).

- ☐ Have the family bring it in.

- ☐ The therapist should eat the food as well, if possible.

- ☐ Ask the patient for a SUDs rating by saying, "On a scale of 0 to 10, how anxious do you feel, with 10 being the most anxious?"

- ☐ Everyone starts eating the food.

- ☐ Halfway through, ask for a SUDs rating: "On a scale of 0 to 10, how anxious do you feel, with 10 being the most anxious?"

- ☐ Everyone finishes eating the food.

- ☐ Once done, ask for a SUDs rating.

- ☐ Wait several minutes.

- ☐ Ask for a SUDs rating.

- ☐ If the rating is above 4, continue to wait, and then ask for another SUDs rating.

- ☐ Once a patient has a SUDs rating below 4, the exposure is complete.

- ☐ Provide Rec-SPA to the patient for choosing a challenging food and tolerating distress.

- ☐ Point out that anxiety rises and falls and is not permanent.

The list of challenge foods should also be used to guide the recommending of challenge foods to be incorporated into meals and snacks during the week. As with any fear hierarchy, the list of challenge foods can change over time. Therefore, a therapist may need to make several of these lists over the course of phase 2.

Stage 2, Phase 2: To-Dos

60 minutes

- ☐ Administer a selection of assessments and stage 2 IMT family therapy measures.

- ☐ Assess and plot BMI.

- ☐ Review the Weekly Earned Freedom Log: Start of Stage 2 and provide feedback.

- ☐ Select a new earned freedom to implement.

- ☐ Introduce FAM Handout 2.19 and FAM/PT Handout 2.20.

- ☐ In future phase 2 sessions, conduct a sufficient number of food exposures to foster the patient's ability to make recovery-oriented choices with given responsibility.

- ☐ Assign homework:

  - ☐ Carers complete Weekly Earned Freedom Log.

  - ☐ Implement earned freedoms.

  - ☐ Review handouts, as necessary.

  - ☐ Incorporate challenge foods into meals at home.

Stage 2, Phase 3: Repairing Relationships

When session time no longer has to be spent on earned freedoms, and the patient has a small number of challenge foods on the fear hierarchy above a 7, a shift into phase 3 can be made because the patient has regained most of the appropriate responsibilities and can use internal coping skills to manage fear of specific foods. The overall focus in phase 3 is on repairing the bonds among family members. As outlined in what follows, carers can also start completing the Daily Earned Freedom Log: End of Stage 2.

DAILY EARNED FREEDOM LOG: END OF STAGE 2

At the start of phase 3, patients should have most earned freedoms back. Therefore, the Daily Earned Freedom Log: Start of Stage 2 is appropriate. Carers are to quickly check off recovery behaviors and eating disorder behaviors as they arise each day.

REPAIRING THE RELATIONSHIP WITH YOUR FAMILY (+PATIENT COPY: FAM HANDOUT 2.21)

Fighting the eating disorder as a family can be a bonding experience, but it can also cause tension. This handout asks each family member to mindfully reflect on what emotions they had, both positive and negative, at the start of treatment as well as what emotions they have now. This handout also prompts family members to consider what emotions they would like to express to their family. Up to this point, carers have been instructed to "act like a behaviorist" by putting their own emotions aside and tuning in to the behavior of their child, with the goal of shaping it. Patients have been instructed to tolerate negative emotions. The emotional experience of siblings has also very likely taken a backseat. Now that the imminent danger has passed, each family member has time to reflect on their own experiences, express themselves, and ask questions.

If a carer has a history of engaging in a high frequency of critical remarks, it may be prudent to first ask carers to rehearse expressing emotions in a noncritical and nonjudgmental way to the therapist separately before coming together as a family. A therapist should coach the carer in directing negative emotions in response to eating disorder behavior at the eating disorder, not at the child. In turn, positive emotions about recovery behaviors should be directed at the child. The focus should be kept on emotional experiences and expression and away from judgment.

IMPROVING THE RELATIONSHIP WITH YOUR CHILD

As an extension of the previous conversation, FAM Handout 2.22 goes beyond repairing the relationship with the child and moves on to generally improving it. Often because carers have spent so much time implementing treatment rules with their child, the relationship has become one devoid of fun and connection. Now that carers have fewer responsibilities related to implementing rules, there is usually a drive to rush back to all the duties that have been pushed aside because of the eating disorder. This handout, however, presses carers to spend just a little more time on treatment. The thinking here is "What's a few more weeks at this point?" Because resentment can build up on both sides—patient toward carers, and carers toward patient—FAM Handout 2.22 makes a pitch for families to engage in enjoyable activities together to undo some of the tension that has accumulated. If the family has the resources, a therapist may also advise carers to take a "staycation" in which they take a few days off work to do fun things for themselves while staying at home before attempting to spend more enjoyable quality time with their children.

The end of the handout prompts carers to create a plan for quality time. This should be completed in session and followed up on in the next session and throughout phase 3 as a treatment goal. As part of homework review in all phase 3 sessions, the therapist should ask about how quality time is progressing. When the carer–child relationship has either returned to its premorbid level of functioning or improved, it is time to move to phase 4. Note that if the patient is ready to progress to learning about belly signals before the carer–child relationship has returned to baseline, phase 3 and phase 4 can sometimes overlap. For instance, the patient can start to read about individual therapy treatment goals while the family is working on quality time.

Stage 2, Phase 3: To-Dos

- ☐ Administer a selection of assessments and stage 2 IMT family therapy measures.
- ☐ Assess and plot BMI.
- ☐ Select a new earned freedom to implement.
- ☐ Introduce and review the Daily Earned Freedom Log: End of Stage 2.
- ☐ Introduce FAM Handout 2.21 and FAM Handout 2.22.
- ☐ Assign homework:
  - ☐ Carers complete Daily Earned Freedom Log: End of Stage 2.
  - ☐ Implement earned freedoms.
  - ☐ Review handouts, as necessary.
  - ☐ Spend quality time with child in recovery.

Stage 2, Phase 4: Increasing Awareness of Hunger and Fullness Cues

Toward the end of stage 2, the therapist should start introducing information about the individual therapy treatment targets into the session. This is done so that the carers have an idea of what their child will be working on in the future and will have an understanding about ways in which they can be helpful. It is also advisable to use this opportunity to talk to the carers about ways in which they actually may *not* be helpful. Introduce the carers and the patient to FAM Handout 2.23 and PT Handout 2.3, respectively.

Stage 2, Phase 4: To-Dos

60 minutes

- ☐ Administer a selection of assessments and stage 2 IMT family therapy measures.
- ☐ Assess and plot BMI.
- ☐ Review the Weekly Earned Freedom Log: End of Stage 2 and provide feedback.
- ☐ Select a new earned freedom to implement.
- ☐ Introduce FAM Handout 2.23 and PT Handout 2.3.
- ☐ Assign homework:
  - ☐ Carers complete the Weekly Earned Freedom Log: End of Stage 2.
  - ☐ Implement earned freedoms.
  - ☐ Review handouts, as necessary.

Pretermination

In order to help the family make the transition out of therapy, carers should be encouraged to remain appropriately involved and explore ways in which the carers can continue being helpful after family therapy has ended. This must be balanced with remaining vigilant for signs of the eating disorder reemerging. Carers do not need to complete any logs this week. Assign FAM Handout 2.24 and FAM Handout 2.25 for homework. Additionally, all family members should be encouraged to write a letter expressing gratitude to every other member of the family for playing a role in treatment. Although this exercise is intended for everyone, the therapist is encouraged to foster opportunities particularly for the patient to practice the expression of gratitude. Having the patient express gratitude for family members' contributions to recovery is very dissonant with the eating disorder's punitive objectives. It also is in line with showing compassion for oneself by allowing others to help when needed and acknowledging those efforts.

Pretermination: To-Dos

60 minutes

- ☐ Administer a selection of assessments and stage 2 IMT family therapy measures.
- ☐ Assess and plot BMI.
- ☐ Review the Weekly Earned Freedom Log: End of Stage 2 and provide verbal reinforcement.
- ☐ Assign homework:
  - ☐ Carers read FAM Handout 2.24 and FAM Handout 2.25 for homework.

- [ ] Patients continue to complete the Belly Signals Log.
- [ ] Family members are to prepare letters or words of gratitude for one another.

Termination

All family members should be present for the termination session. It is important to administer all relevant assessments given on intake as well as the stage 2 IMT family measures prior to session. Compare scores from this session to scores on intake, and review progress made in treatment. Also reiterate ways in which carers can be helpful to patients in individual therapy. Address any questions carers may have about the homework, or about their child making the transition to individual therapy. Be sure to acknowledge each of the roles family members played in therapy. Therapists are encouraged to introduce the topic of gratitude and to encourage family members to express thanks for their contributions. Each family member should express thanks to other family members by reading either parts or all of the letters in this session. It is particularly important for the patient to have an opportunity to express thanks to each member of the family for contributing to their recovery.

Termination: To-Dos

60 minutes

- [ ] Administer a selection of assessments and stage 2 IMT family therapy measures.
- [ ] Assess and plot BMI.
- [ ] Reiterate ways in which carers can be helpful to patients in individual therapy and address questions.

Appendixes

Appendixes

The following clinician resources are available online only at http://www.newharbinger.com/42235.

Case Conceptualization

IMT Measures

Clinician's Checklists for TABLE Skills and ED WINS Habits

Appendix A

Individual, Group, and Family IMT Handouts: A Complete List

The following handouts are available as printable PDFs for clinician users of this manual, and can be found at www .newharbinger.com/42235; see page 304 for download instructions.

Individual Therapy Module

Regular Eating (RE) and Regular and Appetitive Eating (RAE) Handouts

RAE Handout 1: Information on Eating Disorder Behaviors

RAE Handout 2: Psychological Consequences of Eating Disorder Behaviors

RAE Handout 3: Medical Consequences of Eating Disorder Behaviors

RAE Handout 4: The Road to Recovery from an Eating Disorder

RAE Handout 5: How Does Regular Eating Work?

RAE Handout 6: Five Non-RE Eating Disorder Behaviors and Five RE Recovery Behaviors

RAE Handout 7: Anxiety, Guilt, and Disgust in Recovery

RAE Handout 8: Accepting the Food You Have Eaten

RAE Handout 9: Challenges: Hard Work That Is Worth It

RAE Handout 10: Try Not to Think of a Pink Cupcake

RAE Handout 11: Distraction and Mindfulness

RAE Handout 12: Regular and Appetitive Eating

RAE Handout 13: How Does Appetitive Eating Work?

RAE Handout 14: Your Stomach Is Like a Gas Tank

RAE Handout 15: Six Non-RAE Eating Disorder Behaviors and Six RAE Recovery Behaviors

RAE Handout 16: I Can't Tell If I'm Hungry or Upset

RAE Handout 17: Food Is Everywhere, All the Time

RAE Handout 18: Why Dieting Doesn't Work

RAE Handout 19: Honoring Your Food Every Day

Body Acceptance and Exposure (BAE) Handouts

BAE Handout 1: How Does My Eating Disorder Impact Body Image?

BAE Handout 2: Body Acceptance and Exposure

BAE Handout 3: Positive Body Image and Acceptance

BAE Handout 4: Exposure: Seeing the Light

BAE Handout 5: Eleven Non-BAE Eating Disorder Behaviors and Eleven BAE Recovery Behaviors

BAE Handout 6: When Exercise Is Unhealthy

BAE Handout 7: Exercise and the Illusion of Improved Body Image

BAE Handout 8: Body Avoidance Behaviors

BAE Handout 9: NIFTY Skills for Decreasing Body Avoidance

BAE Handout 10: Body Investigating Behaviors

BAE Handout 11: ROCKS Skills for Decreasing Body Investigating

BAE Handout 12: Comparing Yourself to Others

BAE Handout 13: Real-Life and Imaginal Fears

BAE Handout 14: Getting to the Bottom of Things

BAE Handout 15: Being Compassionate Versus Hurting Yourself

BAE Handout 16: Treating Yourself with Kindness

BAE Handout 17: Body Gratitude

BAE Handout 18: Pretending It's Forever

BAE Handout 19: Imagining Recovery

BAE Handout 20: Building a Life Without the Eating Disorder

BAE Handout 21: Your Body Is Your Temple

BAE Handout 22: Feeling Connected Again

BAE Handout 23: Acknowledging the Impact on Others

BAE Handout 24: Cultivating a Daily Gratitude Practice

BAE Handout 25: Eighteen Tips for Continued Recovery

Mindfulness and Acceptance (MAC) Handouts

MAC Handout 1: The IMT Model of Eating Disorders

MAC Handout 2: Full Is Not Fat!

MAC Handout 3: Eating Disorder and Recovery Behaviors

MAC Handout 4: Coping with the Urge to Restrict (EAT MEALS Skills)

MAC Handout 5: Eating Disorder Monsters

MAC Handout 6: Lessons from Cute Stuff

MAC Handout 7: The Eating Disorder Triad

MAC Handout 8: The Eating Disorder's Anxiety

MAC Handout 9: The Eating Disorder's Disgust

MAC Handout 10: The Eating Disorder's Guilt

MAC Handout 11: The Eating Disorder's Impact on Values

MAC Handout 12: False Promises

MAC Handout 13: Noticing the Thoughts in Your Head

MAC Handout 14: Mindfulness and Leaves on a Stream

MAC Handout 15: Staying Motivated in Your Recovery (RECOVERY Skills)

MAC Handout 16: Telling Others About Your Eating Disorder

MAC Handout 17: Why You Might Despise Supervised Eating

MAC Handout 18: Coping with the Urge to Binge (NO BINGE Skills)

MAC Handout 19: Coping with the Urge to Purge (NO PURGE Skills)

Cognitive Behavioral Therapy (CBT) Handouts

CBT Handout 1: General Stressors and Eating Disorder Triggers

CBT Handout 2: Categorizing Types of Eating Disorder Thoughts

CBT Handout 3: Examining the Evidence For and Against Eating Disorder Thoughts

CBT Handout 4: Thought Record

CBT Handout 5: Weighing the Pros and Cons of Acting on Eating Disorder Urges and Impulses

CBT Handout 6: Positive Self-Talk

CBT Handout 7: Creating a Coping Card

CBT Handout 8: Active Eating Disorder Problem Solving

CBT Handout 9: Problems with Perfectionism

CBT Handout 10: Practicing Self-Care with an Eating Disorder

CBT Handout 11: Writing a Letter to Your Eating Disorder

CBT Handout 12: Relapse-Prevention Plan

CBT Handout 13: Remembering All You Have Learned

Stage 1 Family (FAM), Family/Patient (FAM/PT), and Patient (PT) Handouts

FAM Handout 1.1: Family Therapy: Not the Typical Type of Therapy

FAM Handout 1.2: FAQs: Why Family Therapy?

FAM Handout 1.3: Five Roles and Expectations in IMT Family Treatment

FAM Handout 1.4: TABLE Skills

FAM Handout 1.5: ED WINS

FAM Handout 1.6: Self-Eclipsing Eating Disorders

FAM Handout 1.7: Reinforcement-Allowing and Reinforcement-Impeding Behaviors

FAM Handout 1.8: Twelve Treatment Rules for Carers (AN Version)

FAM Handout 1.9: Ten Treatment Rules for Carers of Children with Eating Disorders (BOB Version)

FAM Handout 1.10: Following the Rules

FAM Handout 1.11: Treatment Involvement Plan (AN Version)

FAM Handout 1.12: Treatment Involvement Plan (BOB Version)

FAM Handout 1.13: Ten Treatment Rules for Schools

FAM Handout 1.14: The Sibling's Role in Treatment

FAM Handout 1.15: Ten Reasons Why Your Child Despises Supervised Eating

FAM/PT Handout 1.16: Twelve Eating Disorder and Recovery Behaviors (AN Version)

FAM/PT Handout 1.17: Ten Eating Disorder and Recovery Behaviors (BOB Version)

FAM/PT Handout 1.18: Recovery-Delaying Behaviors

FAM Handout 1.19: Twelve Smart Carer Responses to Tricky Behaviors (AN Version)

FAM Handout 1.20: Ten Smart Carer Responses to Tricky Behaviors (BOB Version)

Stage 2 Family (FAM), Family/Patient (FAM/PT), and Patient (PT) Handouts

FAM Handout 2.9: Five Roles and Expectations in Stage 2

FAM Handout 2.10: How to Implement Earned Freedoms

FAM Handout 2.11: The Difference Between Rewards and Earned Freedoms

FAM Handout 2.12: Three Wise Expectations About Recovery in Stage 2

FAM Handout 2.13: Three Tricky Ways Eating Disorders Disguise Themselves in Stage 2

FAM Handout 2.14: Triggers: Look Out!

FAM/PT Handout 2.15: Earned Freedom Roadmap

FAM/PT Handout 2.16: Stage 2 Eating Disorder Behaviors and Recovery Behaviors

FAM Handout 2.17: Planning for Eating Disorder Urges in Stage 2

FAM Handout 2.18: Giving Recovery-Specific Positive Attention in Stage 2

FAM Handout 2.19: The Importance of Confronting Fear of Foods

FAM/PT Handout 2.20: Challenge Foods

FAM Handout 2.21: Repairing the Relationship with Your Family

FAM Handout 2.22: Improving the Relationship with Your Child

FAM Handout 2.23: Belly Signals

FAM Handout 2.24: Stick With It!

FAM Handout 2.25: Supporting Your Child in the Future

PT Handout 2.1: Five Roles and Expectations in Stage 2

PT Handout 2.2: The Importance of Confronting Fear of Foods

PT Handout 2.3: Belly Signals

Appendix B

Clinician-Provided IMT Family Handouts

Because of their sensitive content, the following four handouts are provided by the clinician. They are available as printable PDFs for clinician use at www.newharbinger.com/42235; see page 304 for download instructions. Also available (from www.imt-ed.com, although not in this manual) is the IMT Bullying Questionnaire (IMT-BQ), which comprehensively assesses for ways in which the patient may be the victim or perpetrator of bullying about size, shape, weight, and a number of other issues.

FAM Handout CM.1: Twelve Treatment Rules for Carers of Children with Anorexia Nervosa

1. Carers choose the food.

   - You must select the type and amount of food for your child to eat. Your child currently has an eating disorder that is affecting their physical as well as their mental health. Therefore, your child is not able to make decisions about food at this time. If your child attempts to negotiate the type or quantity of food to be eaten, ignore this behavior, and strictly enforce the treatment rules.

2. Serve only full-fat and full-calorie foods.

   - No diet foods, fat-free foods, or reduced-calorie foods are allowed. What the eating disorder perceives as "unhealthy" food is now actually medicine for your child. To help meet nutritional goals, your child needs to eat calorie-dense foods like bagels, pizza, and so forth.

   - Many carers have found it helpful to think about what their child liked to eat before the eating disorder took over. Instead of basing food selections on what the eating disorder is claiming to want now, you must serve foods your child used to enjoy before the eating disorder started. If they used to like fried food, serve fried foods, even if doing so causes your child to become anxious or act out.

   - Water is not allowed during the weight-stabilization process. Only beverages with calories are permitted.

3. Portion sizes must be sufficient to meet treatment goals.

   - You must aid in restoring your child's health by providing adequately portioned meals and snacks that promote weight gain.

   - Your child will very likely protest the amount of food to be eaten or will want to stop eating before the meal is completed. It is important to continue serving adequate portion sizes for weight gain, despite these eating disorder behaviors. The fact that treatment is difficult and unpleasant does not mean that it should be avoided. Eating enough food for weight gain is exactly what your child needs.

4. Carers prepare the food.

   - Under no circumstance may your child weigh, measure, or prepare food. They may not help you make the meal or make suggestions regarding measurements of food. Your child is prohibited from knowing what is in the food. Your child should not be in the kitchen when you are preparing food, nor should they go grocery shopping.

   - Your child is not permitted to know how much food they are being given. Do not measure out exact portion sizes. You should largely estimate what you think is an appropriate amount to feed your child.

   - At the beginning of treatment, eating in restaurants is not recommended. Eating should take place only at home or in the treatment program.

5. Three meals and two snacks must be served every day.

   - No matter what the circumstances may be, your child must eat three meals and two snacks per day. Your child has a serious medical and psychological condition for which food is the medicine. Oversleeping, taking naps, having social obligations, and so forth, are not reasons to skip eating or to eat less than necessary.

6. All meals and snacks are supervised.

  - To ensure that all meals and snacks are being fully consumed, your child must be supervised during meals and snacks, preferably by a primary carer involved in attending therapy sessions. If this is not possible, you must arrange for an adult at school (such as a nurse or a guidance counselor) or a trusted adult family member to supervise your child's meals. This person should be educated about the meal supervision process. Talk to your therapist about this.

  - If you did not see your child eat, act as if your child didn't eat. For instance, if they report having eaten a snack but another adult involved in meal supervision did not see them eat it, they must eat another snack.

  - You must watch your child throughout the entire meal or snack to ensure that it's finished.

  - Watch for attempts to hide food.

  - Use FAM Handout 1.4: TABLE Skills and FAM Handout 1.5: ED WINS to help guide you during meal and snack supervision.

  - Siblings and peers are not allowed to supervise meals. Siblings and friends can voluntarily provide support, distraction, and relief. They are never saddled with responsibility for meal or snack supervision.

7. All meals and snacks must be completed.

  - At the very beginning of treatment, 100 percent completion of meals and snacks may not be possible. This is OK. Patients can work up to 100 percent completion.

  - To prevent the eating disorder from winning, the goal is 100 percent completion of all meals and snacks. When the eating disorder gets away with not finishing food, the desire to restrict will grow stronger, as will the belief that doing so is possible. Therefore, 100 percent completion is essential.

  - Even if your child becomes extremely sad, angry, or anxious, you must insist that the meal or snack be completed.

8. If rule 7 is broken, portion sizes must be increased at the next meal or snack.

  - If a meal or snack cannot be completed for some reason, the very next meal or snack portion must be proportionately increased. This prevents the eating disorder from winning. It also lets your child know that there is no getting out of finishing meals and snacks.

  - An Ensure or a Mighty Shake may be given in substitution for a meal or snack.

  - The eating disorder may be able to win a battle, but you cannot let it win the war.

9. Activity and exercise must be limited according to physician's recommendations.

  - During the weight-stabilization process, activity and exercise must be limited. Ask your child's physician about exercise and activity limits. The more calories your child burns, the more food you must feed them.

10. Technology must be monitored for online eating disorder behavior.

  - Although it may not be possible to fully prevent a child from viewing pro–eating disorder content or using nutrition and/or weight-loss apps, you must make a good-faith reasonable effort to limit this behavior by using parental control settings, password changes, and parental supervision of technology.

  - If your child views any pro–eating disorder content, it must be reported to the therapist.

11. All prescribed medications must be taken as directed.

   · If your child has been prescribed medications, you must ensure that they are taken as directed.

   · Skipping doses, cutting doses in half, and so forth, are prohibited.

12. One hour must pass after eating before your child uses the restroom.

   · To prevent eating disorder behaviors, your child may not go to the restroom in the hour after a meal or snack. Restrooms are used prior to a meal or snack. If it's an emergency, your child must either sing, count, or speak to you loudly the entire time while in the bathroom to ensure that no purging is occurring. Alternatively, you can require that they not turn on the faucet or flush the toilet unless you are present.

   · Even if your child has never purged before, it is recommended that this rule be enforced because purging can emerge in the context of treatment.

FAM Handout CM.2: Ten Treatment Rules for Carers of Children with Eating Disorders

Please read the following general treatment rules for carers of children with eating disorders such as bulimia nervosa, binge eating disorder, and eating disorder not otherwise specified. After you review this handout, treatment ground rules will be determined in session and written down for your reference.

1. Carers play an active role in meal and snack planning, preparation, and/or supervision.

    · Your child's therapist will help your family determine the appropriate degree of parental involvement in meal planning, preparation, and/or supervision.

    · These treatment recommendations will be made on the basis of your input, the specifics of your child's disorder (diagnosis, severity of symptoms, and so forth), and the therapist's professional experience and education.

    · Recommendations regarding the degree of parental involvement will naturally change and progress over time. In the beginning of treatment, it is normal to make several edits to the exact plan before settling into a groove. When the eating disorder starts to remit, it is also natural that the degree of parental involvement will be scaled back. If eating disorder symptoms increase, parental involvement will increase.

    · In determining the degree and nature of parental involvement in treatment, negotiations or deals are not to be made with the eating disorder. For instance, it is not permitted that your child's eating disorder will express itself via a tantrum, with the aim of preventing family involvement in treatment and, for example, agreeing to parental involvement only on Mondays.

    · It is permitted for your child's expressed degree of readiness for a given intervention to be taken into account. For instance, it is in line with the aim of treatment to tell the patient that because the eating disorder is severe, parental involvement must occur every day, but that because they expressed that they are extremely afraid of pizza, pizza will not be served until they say they are ready. In this way, the carer is put in the healthy position of consistent caregiver and rule enforcer while the child's concerns about being overwhelmed with anxiety are being addressed.

2. Food selection must be less and less avoidant of challenge (feared) foods.

    · On the basis of your child's input as well as your own, the therapist will make recommendations about which foods and beverages to start cutting out of your child's diet and which to start adding.

    · At the end of treatment, your child should not be eating any diet foods, fat-free foods, reduced-calorie foods, or diet beverages.

    · At the beginning of the process of devising a plan for foods that will be reincorporated into the child's diet, many carers have found it helpful to think about what their child liked to eat before the eating disorder took over.

3. Portion sizes must be adequate and nonrestrictive.

    · When preparing or serving meals, you must aid in restoring your child's psychological and physical health by providing adequately portioned meals and snacks. This helps decrease the eating disorder behavior of restriction.

- Your child will very likely protest the amount of food to be eaten or will want to stop eating before the meal is completed. It is important to continue serving adequate portion sizes for weight gain, despite these eating disorder behaviors. The fact that treatment is difficult and unpleasant does not mean that it should be avoided. Eating enough food for weight gain is exactly what your child needs.

4. Carers prepare the food as often as necessary.

   - With input from your family, the therapist will make treatment recommendations about your involvement with food preparation, such as how often to prepare the food and the extent to which your child will participate.

5. Meals and snacks are eaten with support as often as necessary.

   - With input from your family, the therapist will make treatment recommendations about your involvement in supervising meals and snacks. Supervising meals typically involves eating with your child, monitoring their food intake, and ensuring that eating disorder behaviors do not occur after the meal.

   - Only if deemed necessary, an adult at school (such as a nurse or a guidance counselor) or a trusted adult family member may need to supervise meals and snacks while your child is at school.

   - Use FAM Handout 1.4: TABLE Skills and FAM Handout 1.5: ED WINS to help guide you during meal and snack supervision.

   - In many cases, it is advisable to watch for attempts to hide food.

   - Siblings and peers are not allowed to supervise meals. Siblings and friends can voluntarily provide support, distraction, and relief. They are never saddled with responsibility for meal or snack supervision.

6. The therapist will make recommendations for managing restriction.

   - Taking into account input from your family and the severity of the eating disorder, the therapist will make recommendations for what to do if a meal or snack is restricted or skipped.

7. Exercise must be limited according to the treatment team's recommendations.

   - During the physical and psychological recovery from an eating disorder, exercise must be limited.

   - If the eating disorder is impacting your child physically, your child's physician will set limits on both exercise and activity.

   - If the eating disorder is not significantly impacting your child's physical health, your child is still being impacted psychologically. The therapist will make recommendations regarding the amount of exercise that is psychologically healthy for your child to be engaging in at the current time.

   - At the core of eating disorders is a fear of "fatness." The disorder causes people to avoid this fear instead of facing it head-on. One of the ways people avoid this fear is through exercise. Therefore, for a time during the recovery process, exercise is limited for psychological as well as physical reasons. This helps patients face their fears and move toward recovery. Once symptoms (fear of "fatness," eating disorder behaviors, and so forth) are significantly diminished, the therapist will make recommendations to start reintroducing exercise.

   - Recovery from an eating disorder has more long-term health benefits than any exercise could have during this limited period. Eating disorders can be or can develop into life-threatening conditions and are not to be underestimated.

8. Technology must be monitored for online eating disorder behavior.

   - Although it may not be possible to fully prevent a child from viewing pro–eating disorder content or using nutrition and/or weight-loss apps, you must make a good-faith reasonable effort to limit this behavior by using parental control settings, password changes, and parental supervision of technology.

   - If your child views any pro–eating disorder content, it must be reported to the therapist.

9. All prescribed medications must be taken as directed.

   - If your child has been prescribed medications, you must ensure that they are taken as directed.

   - Skipping doses, cutting doses in half, and so forth, are prohibited.

10. One hour must pass after eating before your child uses the restroom.

   - To prevent eating disorder behaviors, your child may not go to the restroom in the hour after a meal or snack. Restrooms are used prior to a meal or snack. If it's an emergency, your child must either sing, count, or speak to you loudly the entire time while in the bathroom to ensure that no purging is occurring. Alternatively, you can require that they not turn on the faucet or flush the toilet unless you are present.

   - Even if your child has never purged before, it is recommended that this rule be enforced because purging can emerge in the context of treatment.

FAM Handout CM.3: Eating Disorder Behaviors Online

Technology and Eating Disorders

As technology and social media have advanced, eating disorder behavior has taken on new forms. People with eating disorders can now take pictures of their bodies and post them online. Once posted, these pictures are open for public comment. Whether the comments are positive or negative, they are problematic.

If someone has been engaging in severe caloric restriction and intolerance behaviors (purging, taking laxatives, obsessively exercising, and so forth), takes a picture of their body, and posts it online, positive comments can seem to justify and reinforce all the person's unhealthy behaviors. Further, some people with eating disorders specifically post pictures to inspire others to lose weight or exercise or seek motivation to lose weight or exercise. They may also view other online content for inspiration or motivation to engage in eating disorder behaviors. This is called *thinspiration* or *fitspiration* (*thinspo* or *fitspo* for short). Thinspiration gets its name because it is intended to inspire or motivate people to restrict food intake, avoid certain foods, lose weight, and/or become more "fit." People with eating disorders typically seek out thinspiration and fitspiration on pro-anorexia (pro-ana) or pro-bulimia (pro-mia) websites, in online forums, or on Twitter and Instagram.

Another eating disorder behavior that has emerged in the context of social media is that people with eating disorders post pictures of themselves (selfies) specifically to solicit shaming remarks. This is called *meanspiration*, or *meanspo*. Further, some people with eating disorders provide meanspo to others, writing shaming remarks on others' posted photos. Others engage in unsolicited body shaming by writing bullying remarks on others' photos. These types of behaviors are very damaging for the person with the eating disorder to be engaging in. Therefore, it is crucial to assess for these types of behaviors and address them in treatment.

Selfies and Body Checking

It seems that many teenagers these days consider taking selfies a hobby, but people with eating disorders take selfies to check, measure, and examine their bodies or post about their bodies on social media. As a method of body checking, taking selfies is psychologically very unhealthy. Carers should regularly monitor their child's phone to check for body pictures. If found, there are several consequences. Because the eating disorder drove your child to do this, your child should not be punished for taking selfies of body parts, but the body checking pictures must be deleted by the carer, and the frequency of monitoring should increase. This behavior must also be reported to your therapist as well as on the IMT measures.

Apps for Weight Loss, Counting Calories, and Exercising

Use of weight-loss apps, calorie-counting apps, and exercise-related apps is also extremely common. During treatment, use of these apps is prohibited.

A Healthy Alternative

Instead of seeking out thinspiration or fitspiration, an alternative behavior is to visit prorecovery sites such as Mirror Mirror (https://www.mirror-mirror.org) and Project HEAL (www.theprojectheal.org).

Appropriately Limit Access to Websites and Social Media

During treatment, we recommend implementing age-appropriate limits on social media and apps to decrease body checking behavior with pictures and to decrease the behavior of seeking out or participating in thinspiration, fitspiration, meanspiration, and online body shaming. Because the teenager has had many food freedoms taken away, it would hurt your relationship with your teenager to take away any more freedoms than necessary. If you are having difficulty deciding what reasonable limits on social media would be, ask your therapist about this. Options can include using parental controls, using kid-friendly browsers like Kiddle or KidSplorer, changing browser settings, changing passwords, and checking browser and download histories.

FAM Handout CM.4: Be a Detective

Carers need to be aware of eating disorder tricks and signs in order to effectively monitor their child and battle the eating disorder. You have to be a detective!

Behavior to Look Out For

- Altering weight on the scale by putting on heavy jewelry or having extra weight (for example, batteries) in pockets

- Purging in the shower, garbage, plastic bags, or buckets

- Hiding or storing vomit

- Hiding food in socks, in pockets, under a table or chair, in a backpack or purse, or by feeding the dog

- Drinking water to feel full or to superficially increase weight during weigh-ins

- Increasing sodium intake to retain water

- Visiting pro-anorexia (pro-ana) or pro-bulimia (pro-mia) websites and blogs
  - Using thinspiration (thinspo) or fitspiration (fitspo)
  - Engaging in meanspiration (meanspo)
  - Collecting pictures representing their ideal body
  - Joining online groups for people with eating disorders
  - Seeking out diet-focused content

- Using "marker" clothes (such as an old pair of skinny jeans) to compare one's body against

- Chewing gum to hide breath odor or to keep full

- Chewing and spitting out food

- Complaining of feeling too sick or full to eat

- Using laxatives, diuretics, diet pills, and/or caffeine

- Going on liquid cleanses or fasts

Signs of Purging

- Eating "marker" foods (nuts, carrots, Doritos, and so forth) at the beginning of a meal (after the meal, the presence of these foods in vomit will signal to your child that they've purged everything they ate)

- Disappearing after meals

- Drinking milk to reduce burning in throat after vomiting

- Red, puffy eyes

- Puffy cheeks

- Toilet or shower/sink drains clogged by vomit

- Vomit-soiled toilet, shower, or sink

- Have your child sing "Row, Row, Row Your Boat" or count while going to the bathroom within one hour after eating. This will ensure that the child is not vomiting in secret, because they will be singing or counting the whole time.

- Do not allow your child to turn on the faucet or flush the toilet unless you are present.

Exercise

- Take your child's pulse to assess for compulsive exercising and compare to their resting heart rate.

- Notice if your child is shaking their legs and/or moving around, and ask them to stop.

- If your child is not fully sitting in their seat, ask them to sit down.

Appendix C

IMT Logs: A Complete List

The following logs are available as printable PDFs for clinician users of this manual, and can be found at www.new harbinger.com/42235; see page 304 for download instructions.

Regular Eating Log (in RAE Handout 6)

Regular and Appetitive Eating Log (in RAE Handout 15)

Belly Signals Log (in RAE Handout 15)

NIFTY Skills Log for Body Avoidance Behaviors (in BAE Handout 9)

ROCKS Skills Log for Body Investigating Behaviors (in BAE Handout 11)

Intake Food Log

Food and Behavior Log (AN Version) (in FAM/PT Handout 1.16)

Food and Behavior Log (BOB Version) (in FAM/PT Handout 1.17)

Weekly Earned Freedom Log: Start of Stage 2 (in FAM/PT Handout 2.16)

Daily Earned Freedom Log: End of Stage 2 (in FAM/PT Handout 2.16)

Bibliography

Agras, W. S. (2010). *The Oxford handbook of eating disorders* (2nd ed.). New York, NY: Oxford University Press.

Allen, H. N., & Craighead, L. W. (1999). Appetite monitoring in the treatment of binge eating disorder. *Behavior Therapy, 30,* 253–272.

Allison, D., & Baskin, M. (2009). *Handbook of assessment methods for eating behaviors and weight-related problems* (2nd ed.). Thousand Oaks, CA: SAGE.

American Psychiatric Association (2000). *Diagnostic and statistical manual of mental disorders* (4th ed., text revision). Washington, DC: Author.

American Psychiatric Association (2013). *Diagnostic and statistical manual of mental disorders* (5th ed.). Washington, DC: Author.

Anderson, L., Murray, S, & Kaye, W. (2017). *Clinical handbook of complex and atypical eating disorders.* New York, NY: Oxford University Press.

Anderson, L., Smith, K., Farrell, N. & Riemann, B. (2018, November). *The relationship between family accommodation and enabling behaviors and eating disorder treatment outcomes.* Paper presented at 52nd Annual Meeting of the Association for Behavioral and Cognitive Therapies. Washington, DC.

Antony, M., & Swinson, R. (1998). *When perfect isn't good enough: Strategies for coping with perfectionism.* Oakland, CA: New Harbinger.

Arcelus, J., Mitchell, A., Wales, J., & Nielsen, S. (2011). Mortality rating in patients with anorexia nervosa and other eating disorders. *Archives of General Psychiatry, 68,* 724–731.

Bach, P., & Moran, D. (2008). *ACT in practice: Case conceptualization in Acceptance and Commitment Therapy.* Oakland, CA: New Harbinger.

Bacon, L. (2008). *Health at every size: The surprising truth about your weight* (2nd ed.). Dallas, TX: BenBella Books.

Barnes, R. D., & Tantleff-Dunn, S. (2010). Food for thought: Examining the relationship between food thought suppression and weight-related concerns. *Eating Behaviors, 11,* 175–179.

Beck, J. (2011). *Cognitive behavioral therapy: Basics and beyond* (2nd ed.). New York, NY: Guilford Press.

Becker, A., Franko, D. Speck, A., & Herzog, D. (2003). Ethnicity and differential access to care for eating disorder symptoms. *International Journal of Eating Disorders, 33,* 205–212.

Becker, C., Zayfert, C., & Anderson, E. (2004). A survey of psychologists' attitudes towards and utilization of exposure therapy for PTSD. *Behaviour Research and Therapy, 42,* 277–92.

Belak, L., Deliberto, T, Shear, M., Kerrigan, S., & Attia, E. (2017). Inviting eating disorder patients to discuss the academic literature: A model program for psychoeducation. *Journal of Eating Disorders, 5,* 49.

Bermudez, O., Devlin, M., Dooley-Hash, S., Guarda, A., Katzman, D., Madden, S., ... Waterhous, T. (2016). *Eating disorders: A guide to medical care* (3rd ed.). Reston, VA: Academy for Eatbing Disorders.

Bodiford-McNeil, C., & Hembree-Kigin, T. (2010). *Parent-child interaction therapy* (2nd ed.). New York, NY: Springer.

Bourne E., & McKay, M. (1998). *Overcoming specific phobia—therapist protocol: A hierarchy and exposure-based protocol for the treatment of all specific phobias.* Oakland, CA: New Harbinger.

Brewerton, T. (2007). Eating disorders, trauma, and comorbidity: Focus on PTSD. *Eating Disorders, 15,* 284–304.

Bulik, C., Sullivan, P., Weltzin, T., & Kaye, W. (1995). Temperament in eating disorders. *International Journal of Eating Disorders, 17,* 251–261.

Burns, D. (2008). *Feeling good: The new mood therapy.* New York, NY: HarperCollins.

Cachelin, F., Rebeck, R., Veisel, C., & Streigel-Moore, R. (2001). Barriers to treatment for eating disorders among ethnically diverse women. *International Journal of Eating Disorders, 30,* 269–278.

Cash, T. (2008). *The body image workbook: An eight-step program for learning to like your looks.* Oakland, CA: New Harbinger.

Clausen, L., Rosenvinge, J., Friborg, O., & Rokkedal, K. (2010). Validating the Eating Disorder Inventory-3 (EDI-3): A comparison between 561 female eating disorder patients and 878 females from the general population. *Journal of Psychopathology and Behavioral Assessment, 33,* 101–111.

Cohen, J., Mannarino, A, & Debliner, E. (2012). *Trauma-focused CBT for children and adolescents: Treatment applications.* New York, NY: Guilford Press.

Costin, C., & Schubert Grabb, G. (2012). *8 keys to recovery from an eating disorder.* New York, NY: Norton.

Crago, M., Shisslak, C., & Estes, L. (1996). Eating disturbances among American minority groups: A review. *International Journal of Eating Disorders, 19,* 239–248.

Craighead, L.W. (2006). *The appetite awareness workbook: How to listen to your body and overcome bingeing, overeating, and obsession with food.* Oakland, CA: New Harbinger.

Crow, S., Peterson, C., Swanson, S., Raymond, N., Specker, S., Eckert, E., & Mitchell, J. E. (2009). Increased mortality in bulimia nervosa and other eating disorders. *American Journal of Psychiatry, 166,* 1342–1346.

Deliberto, T. & D. Hirsch. (2019). *Client resources for treating eating disorders in adolescents.* Oakland, CA: New Harbinger.

Deliberto, T., Jacobs, S., Novak, S., Grabicki, S., Sanderson, W., & Hildebrandt, T. (2013, April). Thought suppression of food mediations: The relationship between fear of weight gain and binge eating. Poster presented at the International Conference on Eating Disorders, Montreal, Canada.

Deliberto, T., Jacobs, S., Novak, S., McVey-Noble, M., Sanderson, W., & Hildebrandt, W. (2014, March). Thought suppression as a predictor of binge and intuitive eating. Poster presented at International Conference on Eating Disorders, New York, NY.

Deliberto, T., Jacobs, S., Sanderson, W., & Hildebrandt, T. (2013, April). The Eating Beliefs and Behaviors Questionnaire (EBBQ): A new measure of eating disorder treatment targets. Poster presented at International Conference on Eating Disorders. Montreal, Canada.

Deliberto, T., Jacobs, S., Sanderson, W., & Hildebrandt, W. (2014, March). The Eating Beliefs and Behaviors Questionnaire (EBBQ): A measure of intuitive eating. Poster presented at International Conference on Eating Disorders. New York, NY.

Deliberto, T. L., Reinharth, J., & Sanderson, W. (2012, November). A preliminary study of disordered eating beliefs and behaviors able to be directly targeted with cognitive behavioral interventions. Poster presented at 45th Annual Convention of the Association for Behavioral and Cognitive Therapies, National Harbor, MD.

Fairburn, C. (2008). *Cognitive behavior therapy and eating disorders.* New York, NY: Guilford Press.

Fairburn, C. (2013). *Overcoming Binge Eating* (2nd ed.). New York, NY: Guilford Press.

Fairburn, C., & Beglin, S. (1994). Eating Disorder Examination Questionnaire (EDE-Q 6.0). In C. Fairburn (Ed.), *Cognitive behavior therapy and eating disorders* (pp. 309–314). New York, NY: Guilford Press.

Foa, E. B., & Rothbaum, B. O. (1998). *Treating the trauma of rape: Cognitive-behavioral therapy for PTSD.* New York, NY: Guilford Press.

Foa, E. B., Hembree, E. A., & Rothbaum, B. O. (2007). *Prolonged exposure therapy for PTSD: Emotional processing of traumatic experiences—therapist guide.* New York, NY: Oxford University Press.

Foa, E. B., Yadin, E., & Lichner, T. (2012). *Exposure and response (ritual) prevention for obsessive-compulsive disorder: Therapist guide* (2nd ed.). New York, NY: Oxford University Press.

Franklin, J., Schiele, B., Brozek, J., & Keys, A. (1948). Observations on human behavior in experimental semistarvation and rehabilitation. *Journal of Clinical Psychology, 4,* 28–45.

Frieling, H., Römer, K. D., Scholz, S., Mittelbach, F., Wilhelm, J., De Zwaan, M., … & Bleich, S. (2010). Epigenetic dysregulation of dopaminergic genes in eating disorders. *International Journal of Eating Disorders, 43,* 577–583.

Garfinkel, P. E., & Newman, A. (2001). The eating attitudes test: Twenty-five years later. *Eating and Weight Disorders, 6,* 1–21.

Garner, D. (2004). *Eating Disorder Inventory-3: Professional manual.* Lutz, FL: Psychological Assessment Resources.

Garner, D. M., Vitousek, K. M., & Pike, K. M. (1997). Cognitive-behavioral therapy for anorexia nervosa. In D. M. Garner & P. E. Garfinkel (Eds.), *Handbook of treatment for eating disorders* (2nd ed.) (pp. 94–144). New York, NY: Guilford Press.

Gilbert, P. (2009). *The compassionate mind: A new approach to life's challenges.* Oakland, CA: New Harbinger.

Gleaves, D., Eberenz, K., & May, M. (1998). Scope and significance of posttraumatic symptomatology among women hospitalized for an eating disorder. *International Journal of Eating Disorders, 24,* 147–156.

Gordon, K., Brattole, M., Wingate, L., & Joiner, T. (2006). The impact of client race on clinician detection of eating disorders. *Behavioral Therapy, 37,* 319–325.

Goss, K. (2010). *The compassionate-mind guide to ending overeating.* Oakland, CA: New Harbinger.

Grilo, C., White, M., Gueorguieva, R., Wilson, T., & Masheb, G. (2013). Predictive significance of the overvaluation of shape/weight in obese patients with binge eating disorder: Findings from a randomized controlled trial with 12-month follow-up. *Psychological Medicine, 43,* 1335–1344.

Gutiérrez, F., Vall, G., Peri, J., Baillés, E., Ferraz, L., Garriz, M., et al. (2012). Personality disorder features through the life course. *Journal of Personality Disorders, 26,* 763–774.

Harned, M., Korslund, K., & Linehan, M. (2014). A pilot randomized controlled trial of Dialectical Behavior Therapy with and without the Dialectical Behavior Therapy Prolonged Exposure protocol for suicidal and self-injuring women with borderline personality disorder and PTSD. *Behaviour Research and Therapy, 55,* 7–17.

Hay, P., Touyz, S., Arcelus, J., Pike, K., Attia, E., Crosby, R., Madden, S., … Meyer, C. (2018). A randomized controlled trial of the compuLsive Exercise Activity theraPy (LEAP): A new approach to compulsive exercise in anorexia nervosa. *International Journal of Eating Disorders, 51,* 999–1004.

Hayes, S. (1991). A relational control theory of stimulus equivalence. In L. J. Hayes & P. N. Chase (Eds.), *Dialogues on verbal behavior* (pp. 19–30). Oakland, CA: Context Press.

Hayes, S. (2005). *Get out of your mind and into your life: The new acceptance and commitment therapy.* Oakland, CA: New Harbinger.

Hildebrandt, T., Loeb, K., Troupe, S., & Delinsky, S. (2012). Adjunctive mirror exposure for eating disorders: A randomized controlled pilot study. *Behaviour Research and Therapy, 50,* 797–804.

Hill, L., & Dagg, D. (2012). *Family eating disorder manual: Guiding families through the maze of eating disorders.* Columbus, OH: Center for Balanced Living.

Keel, P., Brown, T., Holm-Denoma J., & Bodell, L. (2011). Comparison of DSM-IV versus proposed DSM-5 diagnostic criteria for eating disorders: Reduction of eating disorder not otherwise specified and validity. *International Journal of Eating Disorders, 44,* 553–560.

Klump, K. L., Kaye, W. H., & Strober, M. (2001). The evolving genetic foundations of eating disorders. *Psychiatric Clinics of North America, 24,* 215–225.

Koenig, K. (2005). *The rules of "normal" eating.* Carlsbad, CA: Gurze Books.

Koenig, K. (2007). *The food and feelings workbook: A full course meal on emotional health.* Carlsbad, CA: Gurze Books.

Krüger, A. Kleindienst, N. Priebe, K., Dyer, A., Steil, R., Schmahl, C., Bohus, M. (2014). Non-suicidal self-injury during an exposure-based treatment in patients with posttraumatic stress disorder and borderline features. *Behaviour Research and Therapy, 61,* 136–141.

Lavender, J. M., Jardin, B. F., & Andersen, D. A. (2009). Bulimic symptoms in undergraduate men and women: Contributions of mindfulness and thought suppression. *Eating Behaviors, 10,* 228–231.

Leahy, R. (2017). *Cognitive therapy techniques: A practitioner's guide* (2nd ed.). New York, NY: Guilford Press.

LeGrange, D., & Lock, J. (2007). *Treating bulimia in adolescents: A family-based approach.* New York, NY: Guilford Press.

Levinson, C., Rapp, J., & Riley, E. N. (2014). Addressing the fear of fat: Extending imaginal exposure therapy for anxiety disorders to anorexia nervosa. *Eating and Weight Disorders, 19,* 521–524.

Levinson, C. A., & Byrne, M. (2015). The fear of food measure: A novel measure for use in exposure therapy for eating disorders. *International Journal of Eating Disorders, 48,* 271–283.

Levinson, C. A., Rodebaugh, T. L., Fewell, L., Kass, A., Riley, E. N., Stark, L., … & Lenze, E. J. (2015). A pilot randomized control trial of D-cycloserine facilitation of exposure therapy in patients with anorexia nervosa. *Journal of Clinical Psychiatry, 76,* 787–793.

Linehan, M. M. (1993). *Cognitive-behavioral treatment of borderline personality disorder.* New York, NY: Guilford Press.

Linehan, M. M. (2014a). *DBT skills training handouts and worksheets* (2nd ed.). New York, NY: Guilford Press.

Linehan, M. M. (2014b). *DBT skills training manual* (2nd ed.). New York, NY: Guilford Press.

Lock, J., & LeGrange, D. (2005). *Help your teenager beat an eating disorder.* New York, NY: Guilford Press.

Lock, J., LeGrange, D., Agras, W. S., & Dare, C. (2001). *Treatment manual for anorexia nervosa: A family-based approach.* New York, NY: Guilford Press.

Lock, J., LeGrange, D., Agras, W. S., Moye., W., Bryson, S., & Jo, B. (2010). Randomized clinical trial comparing family-based treatment with adolescent-focused individual therapy for adolescents with anorexia nervosa. *Archives of General Psychiatry, 67,* 1025–1032.

Lock, J., LeGrange, D., & Russell, G. (2013). *Treatment manual for anorexia nervosa: A family-based approach* (2nd ed.). New York, NY: Guilford Press.

Luoma, J., Hayes, S., & Walser, R. (2007). *Learning ACT: An acceptance and commitment therapy skills-training manual for therapists.* Oakland, CA: New Harbinger.

Martina Petronella Laurenssen, E., Hutsebaut, J., Jerta Feenstra, D., Van Busschbach, J., & Luyten, P. (2013). Diagnosis of personality disorders in adolescents: A study among psychologists. *Child and Adolescent Psychiatry and Mental Health, 7,* 3.

Mazzeo, S. E., & Bulik, C. M. (2009). Environmental and genetic risk factors for eating disorders: What the clinician needs to know. *Child and Adolescent Psychiatric Clinics of North America, 18,* 67–82.

Miller, K. (2013). Endocrine effects of anorexia nervosa. *Endocrinology and Metabolism Clinics of North America, 42,* 515–528.

Moskowitz, L., & Weiselberg, E. (2017) Anorexia nervosa/atypical anorexia nervosa. *Current Problems in Pediatric and Adolescent Health Care, 47,* 70–84.

Muhlheim, L. (2018). *When your teen has an eating disorder: Practical strategies to help your teen recover from anorexia, bulimia, and binge eating.* Oakland, CA: New Harbinger.

Nadeau, P. (2009). Treating bulimia in adolescents: A family-based approach. *Journal of the Canadian Academy of Child and Adolescent Psychiatry, 18,* 67–68.

Neff, K. (2011). *Self-compassion: The proven power of being kind to yourself.* New York, NY: HarperCollins.

Palazzoli, S., Boscolo, L., Cecchino, G., & Prata, G. (1980). Hypothesizing—circularity—neutrality: Three guidelines for the conductor of the session. *Family Process, 19,* 3–12.

Pike, K. M., Devlin, M. J., & Loeb, K. L. (2004). Cognitive-behavioral therapy in the treatment of anorexia nervosa, bulimia nervosa, and binge eating disorder. In J. K. Thompson (Ed.), *Handbook of eating disorders and obesity* (pp. 130–162). New York, NY: Wiley.

Pike, K. M., Walsh, B. T., Vitousek, K., Wilson, G. T., and Bauer, J. (2003). Cognitive behavior therapy in the posthospitalization treatment of anorexia nervosa. *American Journal of Psychiatry, 160,* 2046–2049.

Polivy, J. (1996). Psychological consequences of food restriction. *Journal of the American Dietetic Association, 96,* 589–592.

Polivy, J. (1998). Behavioral inhibition: Where are we and where should we be heading? *Psychologic Inquiry, 9,* 237–240.

Polivy, J., & Herman, C. P. (1985). Dieting and binging: A causal analysis. *American Psychology, 40,* 193–201.

Polivy, J., & Herman, C. P. (2002). If at first you don't succeed: False hopes of self-change. *American Psychologist, 57,* 677–687.

Polivy, J., Coleman, J., & Herman, P. C. (2005). The effect of deprivation on food cravings and eating behavior in restrained and unrestrained eaters. *International Journal of Eating Disorders, 38,* 301–309.

Richards, P., Crowton, S., Berrett, M., Smith, M., & Passmore, K. (2017). Can patients with eating disorders learn to eat intuitively? A 2-year pilot study. *Eating Disorders, 25,* 99–113.

Sala, M., Reyes-Rodriguez, M., Bulik, C., & Bardone-Cone, A. (2013). Race, ethnicity, and eating disorder recognition by peers. *Eating Disorders, 21,* 423–436.

Sandoz, E., Wilson, K., & Dufrene, T. (2011). *The mindfulness and acceptance workbook for bulimia: A guide to breaking free from bulimia using acceptance and commitment therapy.* Oakland, CA: New Harbinger.

Schaefer, L., Burke, N., & Thompson, J. K. (2018). Thin-ideal internalization: How much is too much? *Eating and Weight Disorders.* doi: 10.1007/s40519–018–0498-x.

Smith, T., & Hawks, S. (2006). Intuitive eating, diet composition, and the meaning of food in healthy weight promotion. *American Journal of Health Education, 37,* 130–136.

Steinglass, J., Albano, A., Simpson, H., Carpenter, K., Schebendach, J., & Attia, E. (2012). Fear of food as a treatment target: Exposure and response prevention for anorexia nervosa in an open series. *International Journal of Eating Disorders, 45,* 615–621.

Stice, E., & Presnell, K. (2007). *The body project: Promoting body acceptance and preventing eating disorders facilitator guide.* New York, NY: Guilford Press.

Testa, R. J., Coolhart, D., and Peta, J. (2015). *The gender quest workbook: A guide for teens and young adults exploring gender identity.* Oakland, CA: New Harbinger.

Tirch, D., Silberstein, L., & Kolts, R. (2016). *Buddhist psychology and cognitive-behavioral therapy: A clinician's guide.* New York, NY: Guilford Press.

Törneke, N. (2010). *Learning RFT: An introduction to relational frame theory and its clinical application.* Oakland, CA: New Harbinger.

Tribole, E., & Resch, E. (2012). *Intuitive eating: A revolutionary program that works* (2nd ed.) New York, NY: St. Martin's Press.

Tylka, T., & Wilcox, J. (2006). Are intuitive eating and eating disorder symptomatology opposite poles of the same construct? *Journal of Counseling Psychology, 53,* 474–485.

W., Bill. (2014). *Alcoholics Anonymous: The original text of the life-changing landmark.* New York, NY: Tarcher.

Wegner, D. M., & Zanakos, S. (1994). Chronic thought suppression. *Journal of Personality, 62,* 615–640.

Wegner, D. M., Schneider, D. J., Carter, S. R., & White, T. L. (1987). Paradoxical effects of thought suppression. *Journal of Personality and Social Psychology, 53,* 5–13.

Yager, J., Devlin, M., Halmi, K., Herzog, D., Mitchell, J. E. III, Powers, P., & Zerbe, K. J. (2010). *Practice guideline for the treatment of patients with eating disorders* (3rd ed.). Washington, DC: American Psychiatric Association. https://psychiatryonline.org/pb/assets/raw/sitewide/practice_guidelines/guidelines/eatingdisorders.pdf.

Zakzanis, K., Campbell, Z., & Polsinelli, A. (2010). Quantitative evidence for distinct cognitive impairment in anorexia nervosa and bulimia nervosa. *Journal of Neuropsychology, 4,* 89–106.

About the Authors

Tara L. Deliberto, PhD, is an assistant professor at Weill Cornell Medicine, the medical college of Cornell University. Deliberto opened and directed New York–Presbyterian Hospital's Eating Disorders Partial Hospitalization Program, where she now trains doctoral students in the treatment of eating disorders. Through Weill Cornell Medicine, she maintains a private Integrative Modalities Therapy (IMT) practice in New York, NY. Deliberto also maintains a leadership position at the Academy for Eating Disorders, as well as an editorial position at *Eating Disorders: The Journal of Treatment and Prevention*.

Dina Hirsch, PhD, is senior psychologist at Northwell Health, and associate professor of psychiatry at Zucker School of Medicine at Hofstra University. She maintains a private practice in Long Island, NY, where she specializes in evidence-based treatment of eating disorders.

Index

E

earned freedoms, 199, 233, 252–259; discussing the results of, 260; hierarchy of, 256–257; implementation of, 254–259; logs for monitoring, 259; orientation to, 252–254

EAT MEALS skills, 132–134

"Eat Whenever/Whatever You Want" exercises, 98

eating: intuitive, 52, 59; supervised, 157–160, 223–227. See also regular and appetitive eating

Eating Attitudes Test-26 (EAT-26), 12, 60

Eating Beliefs and Behaviors Questionnaire (EBBQ), 71

eating disorder–exacerbating behaviors (EDEBs), 43, 204, 231

eating disorder–protecting behaviors, 42–43, 117–118, 127, 138, 149, 195–196

eating disorder–related morality, 144–145

Eating Disorder and Recovery Behaviors handout, 130–131

Eating Disorder Examination Questionnaire (EDE-Q), 12, 60, 122, 212

Eating Disorder Monsters handout, 134–136

eating disorder not otherwise specified (EDNOS), 14

Eating Disorder Triad handout, 138–141

Eating Disorders: A Guide to Medical Care, 215

eating disorders, 3; biological factors in, 41; comorbid personality disorders and, 26–28; core concepts in treating, 30–48; dangerous behaviors related to, 30; diagnosis and mortality rates of, 13–15; disguises used by, 238–239; estimating the strength of, 257–258; etiology and onset of, 41–42; explaining the dangers of, 214; exposures in treating, 53; functional conceptualization of, 32–42; importance of medical clearance for, 28–29; power dynamics of, 186–192; protecting and exacerbating behaviors in, 42–43; psychoeducation on behaviors of, 227–234; race, ethnicity, gender and, 11; self-eclipsing, 44, 45–46, 184–186; separating the person from, 237; sequence of behaviors in, 86; telling others about, 156–157; triggers for, 165–166

Eating Disorder's Anxiety handout, 141–142

Eating Disorder's Disgust handout, 142–143

Eating Disorder's Guilt handout, 144–146

Eating Disorder's Impact on Values handout, 146–148

ED WINS habits, 221, 222, 232, 243

ego-dystonic disorders, 46, 97

ego-syntonic disorders, 4, 44–46, 97

Eighteen Tips for Continued Recovery handout, 112

Eleven Non-BAE Eating Disorder Behaviors and Eleven BAE Recovery Behaviors handout, 101

emotions: alexithymia of, 90; dysregulation of, 226; labeling of, 97; linked, 34, 36–37, 40–41; negative, 38, 39, 68, 139; positive, 68, 141; regulation of, 14

empathetic stance, 215

empowerment: of the child, 188; of the therapist, 188–190

environmental factors, 41–42

ethnicity/race considerations, 11

etiology of eating disorders, 41–42

evidence-based practice approach, 1, 52, 59, 244

exacerbating behaviors, 43, 204, 231

Examining the Evidence for and Against Eating Disorder Thoughts handout, 167–168

Exercise and the Illusion of Improved Body Image handout, 101

exercise, handouts on, 101

exposure: criteria for administering, 74, 75; eating disorder treatment and, 53; to ED triggers, 165–166; food-related, 92–93, 199, 263; imaginal, 56

Exposure: Seeing the Light handout, 101

external reinforcement, 31

externalizing the eating disorder, 87, 237

F

F.E.A.S.T. community, 240

False Promises handout, 148–150

family: meals and snacks with, 217, 220–221; repairing relationships with, 264–265

family therapy, 184–267; administration instructions, 212–219, 252; anorexia nervosa and, 4, 20–21, 200; challenge foods in, 262–264; for different diagnoses, 200–201; eating disorder–protecting behaviors and, 195–196; family meals/snacks in, 219–223, 242–243, 244; IMT materials used in, 7, 206–267; individual therapy with, 62, 78–80, 204; intake session in, 212–219; managing behaviors in sessions of, 196–197; measures used in, 201–203; objectives of, 10–11, 209–212, 250–251; people involved in process of, 203–205; power dynamics of eating disorders and, 186–192; pretermination and termination of, 266–267; psychoeducation in, 223–238, 244, 253–254, 261; Rec-SPA in, 194–195, 221, 238–242, 260–261; reinforcement dynamics and, 192–195; repairing relationships in, 264–265; self-eclipsing eating disorders and, 184–186; stages and phases in, 198–200

"fat" talk, 236–237

"fatness": fear of, 37, 55–57, 60, 245–246; psychoeducation on food and, 234–237; stopping talk about, 236–237

intake assessment, 212–219

Intake Food Logs, 216

Integrative Modalities Therapy (IMT), 1; components of, 6–7; development of, 3–6; flexible use of, 19–20; handouts used in, 3, 13; higher levels of care for, 19, 20; implementation of, 16–30; intake assessment, 212–219; measures used in, 12, 71–73, 231; medical clearance and management for, 28–29; outpatient settings for, 16–18, 19; overview of modalities in, 7–11; rationale for terminology of, 15–16

internal experiences: avoidance of, 83; eating disorder sequence of, 126–127; fostering tolerance of, 53–54, 55

internal reinforcement, 31, 40

intolerance behaviors, 39, 85; avoiding specific examples of, 121; binge eating disorder and, 13, 17; compensatory behaviors and, 13, 85; redirecting in group therapy sessions, 116–117

intuitive eating, 52, 59

ironic processing, 38, 83, 94

J

Jacobs, Stephanie, 71

judgments about food, 37

K

kindness, 109

L

lab work, 30

learned associations, 34

Leaves on a Stream exercise, 152

Lessons from Cute Stuff handout, 136–138

letter writing: to all eating disorders, 149; to your eating disorder, 179–180

linked emotions: description of, 34, 36–37; therapy for, 40–41

M

Maudsley treatment, 4

meals, family, 217, 220–221

meanspiration, 43, 70, 230

measures used in IMT, 12, 71–73, 201–203, 231

medical appointments, 215, 252

Medical Care Standards Guide of the Academy for Eating Disorders, 13, 28

Medical Consequences of Eating Disorder Behaviors handout, 87–88

medical issues: "facts" and emotions about, 57; medical clearance and management, 28–29

mindfulness: body gratitude exercise, 109; developing a daily practice of, 153; distraction and, 94–95; in eating disorder group setting, 118–119, 164–165; take-home points about, 152

mindfulness and acceptance (MAC) group, 10, 22

mindfulness and acceptance (MAC) handouts, 124–163

Mindfulness and Leaves on a Stream handout, 152–153

Minnesota Starvation Experiment, 9, 98

mirror exposure therapy, 106

modeling: confidence in patients, 48; fearlessness of "fatness," 57

morality, 144–146

mortality rate: of anorexia nervosa, 15; of atypical anorexia nervosa, 14; of bulimia nervosa, 14; of other specified feeding or eating disorder, 14

motivation in recovery, 153–156

multifamily groups, 205

N

nausea vs. disgust, 143

negative emotions, 38, 39, 68, 139

negative reinforcement, 31, 231

NIFTY skills, 102

NO BINGE skills, 161–162

NO PURGE skills, 163

nonadaptive behaviors, 69–70

Noticing the Thoughts in Your Head handout, 150–152

O

objective binge, 84

obsession, food, 38, 98

OSFEDx disorders, 16

other specified feeding or eating disorder (OSFED): diagnosis of, 14; family involvement for, 78–79, 200; higher levels of care for, 19; medical management of, 29; outpatient treatment of, 17; RAE used for, 59–60; rules adapted to, 201

out-in-the-open eating, 161

outpatient settings: AN and AAN treatment in, 20–26, 61, 64; IMT implementations in, 16–18, 19; necessary interventions in, 80–81

P

patients: clinical assessment of, 214; fragilizing, 187–188; recovery conceptualized by, 47

perceptual distortions, 39, 43–44

perfectionism, problems with, 175–177

personality disorders, 26–28; barriers to diagnosing in youth, 26–27; treating comorbid eating disorders and, 27–28

physical health improvements, 69

physician involvement, 215–216

positive body assessments, 104

Positive Body Image and Acceptance handout, 100

positive emotions, 68, 141

positive reinforcement, 31, 194

Positive Self-Talk handout, 171–173

power dynamics of eating disorders, 186–192; carers taking power in, 187; empowerment of the child in, 188; influencing shifts in, 190; life cycle of power in, 186–187; power struggles in, 190–192; therapist empowerment in, 188–190

Practicing Self-Care with an Eating Disorder handout, 177–179

praise: patient's disliking of, 240; Rec-SPA and, 194, 221

Pretending It's Forever handout, 110–111

pretermination phase of therapy, 266–267

prevention, relapse, 180–181

problem solving, active ED, 174–175

Problems with Perfectionism handout, 175–177

Project HEAL, 240

promises: false, 148–149; recovery, 131

protecting behaviors, 42–43, 117–118, 127, 138, 149, 195–196

psychoeducation: on earned freedoms, 253–254, 255, 256–257; on eating disorder behaviors, 227–234; on food and "fat," 234–238; of Rec-SPA, 261; on supervised eating, 223–227

Psychological Consequences of Eating Disorder Behaviors handout, 87

purging: coping with the urge for, 162–163; emotion regulation through, 14

Q

quality time with children, 265

R

race/ethnicity considerations, 11

RAE. See regular and appetitive eating

RAN distinction, 16, 63

Ran, Romi, 9

Real-Life and Imaginal Fears handout, 104–108

real-life body fears: body exposure plan, 105–106; fear hierarchy example, 105

recovery: behaviors for, 130–131, 136, 228, 229, 233; building a bridge to, 161; conceptualizing, 46–48; morals related to, 145–146; reinforcing, 67, 68, 136; statements for, 229; staying motivated in, 153–156

RECOVERY skills, 154–155

recovery-delaying behaviors, 230, 232

recovery-specific positive attention (Rec-SPA), 67, 194–195, 221, 238–242, 260–261

redirection in group therapy, 117

refeeding syndrome, 30, 214

Regular and Appetitive Eating Log, 96

Regular and Appetitive Eating Measure, 72

regular and appetitive eating (RAE), 5, 8–9, 51–52; adult patients and, 52; BAE administered with, 58; criteria for administering, 73–74; handouts for, 82–99; health-restored AN and, 63–64; necessary interventions for, 81; objectives of, 8, 75–76; therapy populations and, 51–52; treatment drift in, 65–66. See also body acceptance and exposure

Regular Eating Log, 89–90

Regular Eating Measure, 71

reinforcement, 31, 192–195; of adaptive behaviors, 67–69, 116–117; of collective eating disorder behaviors, 40; of perceptual disturbances, 43–44; of positive emotion ratings, 141

reinforcement-allowing behaviors (RABs), 189, 192–193, 224

reinforcement-inhibiting behaviors (RIBs), 189, 193–194, 224

reinforcement-seeking behaviors, 228, 258

Relapse Prevention Plan handout, 180–181

relational frame theory, 44

relationships, repairing, 199, 264–265

Remembering All You Have Learned handout, 181–182

research, areas of encouraged, 12

restriction of food: avoidance and, 37, 65, 83; binge eating disorder and, 38; coping with urge for, 132–134

Road to Recovery from an Eating Disorder handout, 88

ROCKS skills, 103–104

role drift, 203

rolling admissions, 114, 122

rules: group therapy, 120–121; treatment, 224–225

Accessing the Client and Clinician Resources for Treating Eating Disorders in Adolescents

The Integrated Modalities Therapy program outlined in this volume, *Treating Eating Disorders in Adolescents: Evidence-Based Interventions for Anorexia, Bulimia, and Binge Eating*, uses a wealth of client handouts for individual, group, and family interventions. These integral client resources, plus essential clinician resources, are available for free for clinician users of this manual:

1. Client Resources Part 1 Section 1: Individual Therapy Modality, Regular Eating (RE) and Regular and Appetitive Eating (RAE) Handouts (19 handouts)

2. Client Resources Part 1 Section 2: Individual Therapy Modality, Body Acceptance and Exposure (BAE) Handouts (25 handouts)

3. Client Resources Part 2 Section 1: Group Therapy Modality, Mindfulness and Acceptance (MAC) Handouts (19 handouts)

4. Client Resources Part 2 Section 2: Group Therapy Modality, Cognitive Behavioral Therapy (CBT) Handouts (13 handouts)

5. Client Resources Part 3 Section 1: Family Therapy Modality, Stage 1 Family (FAM), Family/Patient (FAM/PT), and Patient (PT) Handouts (39 handouts)

6. Client Resources Part 3 Section 2: Family Therapy Modality, Stage 2 Family (FAM), Family/Patient (FAM/PT), and Patient (PT) Handouts (30 handouts)

7. Clinician Resources:

   - Case Conceptualization form

   - IMT Measures forms

   - Clinician's Checklists for TABLE Skills and ED Wins Habits

   - Clinician-Provided IMT Family Handouts (this is the same content as Appendix B of this volume, in printable PDF format)

Download Instructions

1. At www.newharbinger.com/42235, either sign in to your existing newharbinger.com account, or create an account. You will land on the book's accessory page; click on the link for each of the seven PDFs to download files.

2. Save the PDFs to your hard drive, opening them any time you want to search for a handout or print out all or part of the PDF files.

3. If you have any difficulty accessing or downloading the Client and Clinician Resources, visit newharbinger. com/accessories, or call our customer service line at 800-748-6273.

Complete Client Resources for Clients and Carers

For those who do not have a copy of this manual, the complete Client Resources (parts 1, 2, and 3), in PDF format, are available for separate purchase at www.newharbinger.com/44451. This collection of the complete, printable IMT handouts is offered at a moderate cost to give clinicians a convenient way to provide clients and carers with all the materials they'll need throughout the course of treatment, and to foster wider use of these interventions within the therapeutic community.

MORE BOOKS *from*
NEW HARBINGER PUBLICATIONS

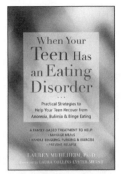

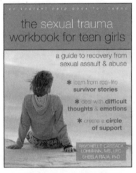
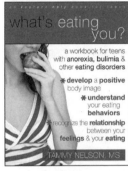